# ACCA

## Applied Skills

# Audit and Assurance (AA)

## Workbook

For exams in September 2023, December 2023, March 2024 and June 2024

Fourth edition 2023

ISBN: 9781 0355 0042 0

Previous ISBN: 9781 5097 4408 4

ISBN (for internal use only): 9781 0355 0131 1

e-ISBN: 9781 0355 0095 6

**British Library Cataloguing-in-Publication Data**

A catalogue record for this book is available from the British Library

**Published by**

BPP Learning Media Ltd

BPP House, Aldine Place

142–144 Uxbridge Road

London W12 8AA

learningmedia.bpp.com

Printed in the United Kingdom

> Your learning materials, published by BPP Learning Media Ltd, are printed on paper obtained from traceable sustainable sources.

Contains public sector information licensed under the Open Government Licence v3.0

We are grateful to the Association of Chartered Certified Accountants for permission to reproduce past examination questions and extracts from the syllabus. The suggested solutions in the further question practice bank have been prepared by BPP Learning Media Ltd, except where otherwise stated.

BPP Learning Media is grateful to the IASB for permission to reproduce extracts from IFRS® Standards, IAS® Standards, SIC and IFRIC. This publication contains copyright © material and trademarks of the IFRS Foundation®. All rights reserved. Used under license from the IFRS Foundation®. Reproduction and use rights are strictly limited. For more information about the IFRS Foundation and rights to use its material please visit www.IFRS.org.

**A note about copyright**

# Contents

**Introduction**

Helping you to pass                                                          iv

Introduction to the Essential reading                                        vi

Introduction to Audit and Assurance (AA)                                     viii

Essential skills areas to be successful in Audit and Assurance (AA)          xv

1   The concept of audit and other assurance engagements                     1

2   Statutory audit and regulation                                           17

3   Corporate governance                                                     31

4   Internal audit                                                           47

Skills checkpoint 1                                                          67

5   Professional ethics and quality management procedures                    69

6   Risk assessment                                                          103

Skills checkpoint 2                                                          135

7   Audit planning and documentation                                         145

8   Introduction to audit evidence                                           157

9   Internal control                                                         173

10  Tests of controls                                                        193

Skills checkpoint 3                                                          235

11  Audit sampling and automated tools and techniques                        243

12  Non-current assets                                                       263

13  Inventory                                                                285

14  Receivables                                                              309

15  Bank and cash                                                            329

16  Payables and accruals                                                    341

17  Non-current liabilities, capital and directors' emoluments               359

Skills checkpoint 4                                                          375

18  Not-for-profit organisations                                             381

19  Audit review and finalisation                                            395

20  Reports                                                                  413

Skills checkpoint 5                                                          437

Index                                                                        445

Bibliography                                                                 449

# Helping you to pass

## BPP Learning Media – ACCA Approved Content Provider

As an ACCA Approved Content Provider, BPP Learning Media gives you the opportunity to use study materials reviewed by the ACCA examining team. By incorporating the examining team's comments and suggestions regarding the depth and breadth of syllabus coverage, the BPP Learning Media Workbook provides excellent, ACCA-approved support for your studies.

These materials are reviewed by the ACCA examining team. The objective of the review is to ensure that the material properly covers the syllabus and study guide outcomes, used by the examining team in setting the exams, in the appropriate breadth and depth. The review does not ensure that every eventuality, combination or application of examinable topics is addressed by the ACCA Approved Content. Nor does the review comprise a detailed technical check of the content as the Approved Content Provider has its own quality assurance processes in place in this respect.

BPP Learning Media do everything possible to ensure the material is accurate and up to date when sending to print. In the event that any errors are found after the print date, they are uploaded to the following website: www.bpp.com/learningmedia/Errata.

## The PER alert

Before you can qualify as an ACCA member, you not only have to pass all your exams but also fulfil a three-year practical experience requirement (PER). To help you to recognise areas of the syllabus that you might be able to apply in the workplace to achieve different performance objectives, we have introduced the 'PER alert' feature (see the next section). You will find this feature throughout the Workbook to remind you that what you are learning to pass your ACCA exams is equally useful to the fulfilment of the PER requirement. Your achievement of the PER should be recorded in your online My Experience record.

# Chapter features

Studying can be a daunting prospect, particularly when you have lots of other commitments. This Workbook is full of useful features, explained in the key below, designed to help you to get the most out of your studies and maximise your chances of exam success.

### Key term

Central concepts are highlighted and clearly defined in the Key terms feature. Key terms are also listed in bold in the Index, for quick and easy reference.

### Formula to learn

This boxed feature will highlight important formula which you need to learn for your exam.

### PER alert

This feature identifies when something you are reading will also be useful for your PER requirement (see 'The PER alert' section above for more details).

### Exam focus point

This feature provides tips about how a specific topic may be examined.

### Example

These will give examples to help demonstrate the concepts you are reading about.

### Exercise

Exercises suggest tasks which can be done to further your understanding.

### Activity

Activities give you essential practice of techniques covered in the chapter.

### Essential reading

Links to the Essential reading are given throughout the chapter. The Essential reading is included in the free eBook, accessed via the Exam Success Site (see inside cover for details on how to access this).

Figure 1.1: Key to icons

At the end of each chapter you will find a Knowledge diagnostic, which is a summary of the main learning points from the chapter to allow you to check you have understood the key concepts. You will also find a Further study guidance which contains suggestions for ways in which you can continue your learning and enhance your understanding. This can include: recommendations for question practice from the Further question practice and solutions, to test your understanding of the topics in the Chapter; suggestions for further reading which can be done, such as technical articles and ideas for your own research. The Chapter summary provides more detailed revision of the topics covered and is intended to assist you as you prepare for your revision phase.

# Introduction to the Essential reading

The electronic version of the Workbook contains additional content, selected to enhance your studies. Consisting of revision materials and further explanations of complex areas including illustrations and activities, as well as practice questions and solutions and background reading, it is designed to aid your understanding of key topics which are covered in the main printed chapters of the Workbook.

A summary of the content of the Essential reading is given below.

|   | Chapter | Summary of Essential reading content |
|---|---------|--------------------------------------|
| 1 | The concept of audit and other assurance engagements | • Accountability, stewardship and agency |
| 2 | Statutory audit and regulation | • Small company audit exemption<br>• Regulation of auditors |
| 3 | Corporate governance | • Additional guidance to support corporate governance principles<br>• Audit committees |
| 4 | Internal audit | • Nature and purpose of internal audit assignments |
| 5 | Professional ethics and quality management procedures | • Engagement letters |
| 6 | Risk assessment | • Materiality<br>• Performance materiality<br>• Gaining an understanding of the entity and its environment<br>• Fraud, laws and regulations |
| 7 | Audit planning and documentation | • Impact of interim work on the final audit<br>• Examples of working papers |
| 8 | Introduction to audit evidence | • Audit procedures to obtain audit evidence |
| 9 | Internal control | • Components of an internal control system<br>• Recording accounting and control systems |
| 10 | Test of controls | • Internal auditor's reports |
| 11 | Audit sampling and automated tools and techniques | • Audit sampling<br>• Automated tools and techniques<br>• Audit data analytics |
| 12 | Non-current assets | • Assertions<br>• Use of a management's expert<br>• Auditing accounting estimates |
| 13 | Inventory | • Assertions<br>• The physical inventory count<br>• Valuation of inventory |

| | Chapter | Summary of Essential reading content |
|---|---|---|
| | | • Using the work of internal audit |
| 14 | Receivables | • Assertions |
| | | • External confirmations |
| | | • Other audit procedures for receivables |
| 15 | Bank and cash | • Bank confirmation letter |
| | | • Cash counts |
| 16 | Payables and accruals | • Assertions |
| | | • Supplier statements |
| | | • Other audit procedures for payables, accruals, purchases and expenses |
| | | • Audit considerations relating to an entity using a service organisation |
| 17 | Non-current liabilities, capital and directors' emoluments | • Non-current liabilities |
| | | • Provisions and contingencies |
| | | • Share capital, distributions and reserves |
| | | • Directors' emoluments |
| 18 | Not-for-profit organisations | • Accounting for not-for-profit organisations |
| | | • Planning the audit |
| | | • Audit evidence |
| | | • Assumed knowledge from Financial Accounting |
| 19 | Audit review and finalisation | • Subsequent events |
| | | • Going concern |
| | | • Written representations |
| | | • Overall review of financial statements |
| 20 | Reports | • ISA 700 (Revised) *Forming an Opinion and Reporting on financial Statements* |
| | | • ISA 701 *Communicating Key audit Matters in the Independent Auditor's Report* |
| | | • ISA 705 (Revised) *Modifications to the Opinion in the Independent Auditor's Report* |
| | | • ISA 706 (Revised) *Emphasis of Matter Paragraphs and Other Matter Paragraphs* |
| | | • The auditor's report as a means of communication |

# Introduction to Audit and Assurance (AA)

## Overall aim of the syllabus

This exam requires students to develop knowledge and understanding of the process of carrying out the assurance engagement and its application in the context of the professional regulatory framework.

## Brought forward knowledge

The Audit and Assurance syllabus assumes prior knowledge and understanding of the accounting topics in Financial Accounting (with the exception of group financial statements). A summary of such knowledge is included in the Essential reading relating to Chapter 18.

## The syllabus

The broad syllabus headings are:

| A | Audit framework and regulation |
|---|---|
| B | Planning and risk assessment |
| C | Internal control |
| D | Audit evidence |
| E | Review and reporting |
| F | Employability and technology skills |

## Main capabilities

On successful completion of this exam, you should be able to:

| A | Explain the concept of audit and assurance and the functions of audit, corporate governance, including ethics and professional conduct. |
|---|---|
| B | Demonstrate how the auditor obtains and accepts audit engagements, obtains an understanding of the entity and its environment, assesses the risk of material misstatement (whether arising from fraud or other irregularities) and plans an audit of financial statements. |
| C | Describe and evaluate internal controls, techniques and audit tests, including IT systems to identify and communicate control risks and their potential consequences, making appropriate recommendations. Describe the scope, role and function of internal audit. |
| D | Identify and describe the work and evidence obtained by the auditor and others required to meet the objectives of audit engagements and the application of the International Standards on Auditing (ISAs). |
| E | Explain how consideration of subsequent events and the going concern principle can inform the conclusions from audit work and are reflected in different types of auditor's report, written representations and the final review and report. |
| F | Demonstrate employability and technology skills. |

## Links to other exams

This diagram shows where direct (solid line arrows) and indirect (dashed line arrows) links exist between this exam and others that may precede or follow it.

Although ACCA's diagram shows Financial Reporting feeding into Audit and Assurance, the accounting knowledge assumed in the Audit and Assurance exam will only be that covered within Financial Accounting.

## Achieving ACCA's Study Guide Outcomes

This BPP Workbook covers all the Audit and Assurance syllabus learning outcomes. The tables below show in which chapter(s) each area of the syllabus is covered.

| A | Audit framework and regulation | |
|---|---|---|
| A1 | The concept of audit and other assurance engagements | Chapter 1 |
| A2 | External audits | Chapter 2 |
| A3 | Corporate governance | Chapter 3 |
| A4 | Professional ethics and the ACCA's Code of Ethics and Conduct | Chapter 5 |

| B | Planning and risk assessment | |
|---|---|---|
| B1 | Obtaining, accepting and continuing audit engagements | Chapter 6 |
| B2 | Objective and general principles | Chapter 6 |
| B3 | Assessing audit risks | Chapter 6 |
| B4 | Understanding the entity, its environment and the applicable financial reporting framework | Chapter 6 |
| B5 | Fraud, laws and regulations | Chapter 6 |
| B6 | Audit planning and documentation | Chapter 7 |

| C | Internal control | |
|---|---|---|
| C1 | Systems of internal control | **Chapter 9** |
| C2 | The use and evaluation of systems of internal control by auditors | **Chapter 9** |
| C3 | Tests of controls | **Chapter 10** |
| C4 | Communication on internal control | **Chapter 10** |
| C5 | Internal audit and governance and the differences between external and internal audit | **Chapter 4** |
| C6 | The scope of the internal audit function, outsourcing and internal audit assignments | **Chapter 4** |

| D | Audit evidence | |
|---|---|---|
| D1 | Assertions and audit evidence | **Chapter 8** |
| D2 | Audit procedures | **Chapter 11** |
| D3 | Audit sampling and other means of testing | **Chapter 11** |
| D4 | The audit of specific items | **Chapters 12 – 17** |
| D5 | Automated tools and techniques | **Chapter 11** |
| D6 | The work of others | **Chapter 12** |
| D7 | Not-for-profit organisations | **Chapter 18** |

| E | Review and reporting | |
|---|---|---|
| E1 | Subsequent events | **Chapter 19** |
| E2 | Going concern | **Chapter 19** |
| E3 | Written representations | **Chapter 19** |
| E4 | Audit finalisation and the final review | **Chapter 19** |
| E5 | The Independent Auditor's Report | **Chapter 20** |

| F | Employability and technology skills | |
|---|---|---|
| F1 | Use computer technology to efficiently access and manipulate relevant information | |
| F2 | Work on relevant response options, using available functions and technology as would be required in the workplace | |
| F3 | Navigate windows and computer screens to create and amend responses to exam requirements, using the appropriate tools | |
| F4 | Present data and information effectively, using the appropriate tools | |

The complete syllabus and study guide can be found by visiting the exam resource finder on the ACCA website: www.accaglobal.com/gb/en.html.

# The exam

## Computer-based exams

Applied Skills exams are all computer-based exams (CBE).

## Approach to examining the syllabus

The Audit and Assurance syllabus is assessed by a three-hour exam. The pass mark is **50%**. All questions in the exam are **compulsory**.

The exam will have a duration of 3 hours.

| Format of the exam | | Marks |
|---|---|---|
| Section A | Section A questions will be selected from the entire syllabus. This section comprises three 10 mark case-based questions. Each case has five objective test questions worth 2 marks each. | 30 |
| Section B | Section B of the exam comprises one 30 mark question and two 20 mark questions. This section will predominantly examine one or more aspects of audit and assurance from planning and risk assessment, internal control or audit evidence, although topics from other syllabus areas may also be included. | 70 |
| | | 100 |

### Remote invigilated exams

In certain geographical areas it may be possible for you to take your exam remotely. This option, which is subject to strict conditions, can offer increased flexibility and convenience under certain circumstances. Further guidance, including the detailed requirements and conditions for taking the exam by this method, is contained on ACCA's website at https://www.accaglobal.com/an/en/student/exam-entry-and-administration/about-our-exams/remote-exams/remote-session-exams.html.

The table below provides details of when each element of the syllabus has been examined in the most recent sittings.

| Chapter | | Mar/Jun 2022 | Sep/Dec 2021 | Mar/Jun 2021 | Sep/Dec 2020 | Mar/Jul 2020 | Sep/Dec 2019 | Mar/Jun 2019 | Sep/Dec 2018 | Mar/Jun 2018 | Sep/Dec 2017 |
|---|---|---|---|---|---|---|---|---|---|---|---|
| | **Audit framework and regulation** | | | | | | | | | | |
| 1 | The concept of audit and other assurance engagements | | | | | | | | | | |
| 2 | External audits | | | | | | | | | | |
| 3 | Corporate governance | | | | | | | B Q16d | | | |
| 5 | Professional ethics and ACCA's Code of Ethics and | | B Q16c | B Q17a | B Q16d | B Q16a, b | | | | | B Q16a |

| Chapter | | Mar/Jun 2022 | Sep/Dec 2021 | Mar/Jun 2021 | Sep/Dec 2020 | Mar/Jul 2020 | Sep/Dec 2019 | Mar/Jun 2019 | Sep/Dec 2018 | Mar/Jun 2018 | Sep/Dec 2017 |
|---|---|---|---|---|---|---|---|---|---|---|---|
| | Conduct | | | | | | | | | | |
| | **Planning and risk assessment** | | Q B16a | | Q B16a | | | | | | |
| 6 | Obtaining and accepting audit engagements | B Q16a | | | | | | | | | |
| 6 | Objective and general principles | | | B Q17c | | | | | | | |
| 6 | Assessing audit risks | | | B Q17b | B Q16b | B Q16c | B Q16b, c | B Q17 | B Q16c | B Q17b | B Q17c |
| 6 | Understanding the entity and its environment | B Q16b | | | | | | | B Q16a, b | | |
| 6 | Fraud, laws and regulations | | B Q16b | | | B Q18c | B Q16a | | | B Q17a | |
| 7 | Audit planning and documentation | | | | | | | | | | B Q17a, b |
| | **Internal control** | | | | | | | | | | |
| 9 | Systems of internal control | | | B Q16c | | | | B Q16a | | B Q16a | B Q16b |
| 9 | The use and evaluation of systems of internal control by auditors | B Q17a, c | B Q17b | B Q16a | B Q17a | | | | | | |
| 10 | Tests of controls | B Q17b | | B Q16b | B Q17 | B Q17 | B Q17 | B Q16b | B Q17b | B Q16a, b | B Q16c |
| 10 | Communication on internal control | | | | | | | | B Q17a | | |
| 4 | Internal audit and governance and the differences between external and internal audit | | | | | | | | | | |
| 4 | The scope of the internal audit function, outsourcing and internal audit assignments | | | | | | | | | B Q16c | |
| | **Audit evidence** | | | | | | | | | | |

| Chapter | | Mar/Jun 2022 | Sep/Dec 2021 | Mar/Jun 2021 | Sep/Dec 2020 | Mar/Jul 2020 | Sep/Dec 2019 | Mar/Jun 2019 | Sep/Dec 2018 | Mar/Jun 2018 | Sep/Dec 2017 |
|---|---|---|---|---|---|---|---|---|---|---|---|
| 8 | Financial statement assertions and audit evidence | | | | | | | | | | |
| 11 | Audit procedures | | | | | | | | | | |
| 11 | Audit sampling and other means of testing | | | | | | | | | | |
| 12–17 | The audit of specific items | B Q16d, B Q18a, b, c | B Q16d, B Q18a, b, c | B Q16d, B Q18a, b, c | B Q16c, B Q18a, b, c | B Q16d, B Q18a, b | B Q16d, e, B Q18a, b | B Q16c, B Q18a, b, c | B Q16d, e, B Q18a, b | B Q16d, B Q18a, b, c | B Q16d, B Q18a, b, c |
| 11 | Computer-assisted audit techniques | | | | | | | | | | |
| 12 | The work of others | | | | | | | | | | |
| 18 | Not-for-profit organisations | | | | | | | | | | |
| | **Review and reporting** | | | | | | | | | | |
| 19 | Subsequent events | | | | | | | B Q18d | | | |
| 19 | Going concern | | | | | | B Q18c, d | | B Q18c | | |
| 19 | Written representations | | | | | | | | | | |
| 19 | Audit finalisation and the final review | | | | | | | | | | |
| 20 | Auditor's reports | B Q18d | B Q18d | B Q18d | B Q18d | B Q18d | | | B Q18d | B Q18d | B Q18d |

Since December 2016, the ACCA have released a 'hybrid' exam every two sittings which shows only questions set in Section B of the exam.

### Interchangeable Terminology

The Financial Accounting syllabus has changed to reflect **computerised systems**. The impact on Audit and Assurance is that some terminology may be used interchangeably within learning materials and exams. At the time of writing this Workbook it had not been released, but the ACCA will be publishing a technical article covering the changes. The following terminology will be used interchangeably:

- Cashbook and bank ledger accounts
- Sales day book and detailed sales listing

- The trade receivables control account and trade receivables account
- The receivables ledger and list of individual customers
- Purchases day book and detailed purchases listing
- The payables ledger control account and trade payables account
- The purchase ledger and list of individual suppliers.

# Essential skills areas to be successful in Audit and Assurance (AA)

We think there are three areas you should develop in order to achieve exam success in AA:

(a) Knowledge application

(b) Specific AA skills

(c) Exam success skills

These are shown in the diagram below.

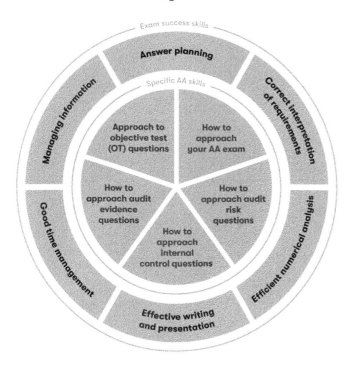

## Specific AA skills

These are the skills specific to AA that we think you need to develop in order to pass the exam.

In this Workbook, there are five **Skills Checkpoints** which define each skill and show how it is applied in answering a question. A brief summary of each skill is given below.

### Skill 1: How to approach your AA exam

Passing AA is much more about exam technique than detailed knowledge. Therefore, it is important that you plan your approach to the exam, and practise this approach, before you sit your exam.

A step-by-step technique for ensuring that you have a planned approach to your AA exam is outlined below:

**Step 1** Attempt Section A first. Read the requirements to each of the OT questions before reading the OT case scenario.

Do not rush through this section of the exam.

**Step 2** Then attempt Section B. Read all requirements in detail and use the scenario fully.

Skills checkpoint 1 covers this technique in detail through application to an exam-standard question.

### Skill 2: How to approach audit risk questions

In the exam, it is highly likely that you will need to attempt a scenario-based question on audit risk.

**Step 1** Allow some of your allotted time to read the requirement and the scenario. Don't rush into starting to write your answer.

Start by analysing the requirements so that you know what you are looking for when you read the scenario.

**Step 2** Re-read the scenario and set out an answer plan using the risks you identify as you read through.

Work through each paragraph of the scenario identifying specific audit risks. Remember you have a highlighter tool available in the assessment platform and a scratch pad tool is available too for you to make notes as you read through the scenario. Each risk is worth one mark and the auditor's response is also worth one mark, so you would need five properly explained risks and responses to gain ten marks.

**Step 3** Where there are more than the required number of audit risks, choose those that you can best explain.

Use your headings to write your answer, describe the audit risk in detail explaining the potential impact on the financial statements. Also remember to explain the practical steps the auditor would take and the work they would do.

A blank table will be provided for audit risk and response questions. One column will be for risks and one column for responses. Start each risk or response in a new cell of the table provided in the appropriate column. Enter the related risks and responses on the same row.

Skills checkpoint 2 covers this technique in detail through application to an exam-standard question.

## Skill 3: How to approach internal control questions

Similarly, to Skill 2, it is likely that you will need to attempt a scenario-based question on internal controls in your exam.

There are several types of questions which may be tested:

- Identify and explain control deficiencies and make recommendations to address each deficiency;
- Explain direct controls and describe tests of control to ensure the controls are operating effectively; and
- Control deficiencies, recommendations and tests of control.

We will consider how you should approach such questions using the example of the first type of question although the same approach should be applied to all three types.

A step-by-step technique for attempting deficiencies questions is outlined below.

**Step 1** Allow some of your allotted time to read the requirement and the scenario. Don't rush into starting to write your answer.

Start by analysing the requirements so that you know what you are looking for when you read the scenario.

**Step 2** Re-read the scenario and set out an answer plan using the points you identify as you read through.

Work through each paragraph of the scenario identifying specific points to make, for example deficiencies. Each deficiency is worth one mark and the recommendation is also worth one mark, hence why you would need six properly explained deficiencies and recommendations to gain 12 marks.

**Step 3** Often there are more than the required number of deficiencies in a scenario, therefore choose the ones for which you can provide a recommended control.

A blank table will be provided for deficiency and recommendation questions. One column will be for deficiencies and one column for recommendations. Start each point in a new cell of the table provided in the appropriate column. Enter the related deficiencies and recommendations on the same row. Explain the deficiency in terms of its impact on the entity. Also remember to explain the recommendation, what internal control should be implemented and by whom.

Skills checkpoint 3 covers this technique in detail through application to an exam-standard question.

## Skill 4: How to approach audit evidence questions

These questions can appear in both sections of the exam. It is very important that you discern exactly what the requirement is asking for and that you use any scenario provided in the exam.

A step-by-step technique for approaching audit evidence questions is outlined below.

**Step 1**  Identify exactly what you are being asked for in the requirement: audit procedures, tests of controls or substantive procedures.

Also identify whether the requirement is testing audit procedures that relate to a particular assertion.

**Step 2**  Now that you have understood what the requirement demands you are much better placed to answer it. Consider the following:

- Is there a scenario you should use?
- Can you remember the accounting treatment for the item? Would that give you a starting point?
- What audit procedures have you learnt/used at work?
- Can you use the mnemonic AEIOU to help you to generate audit procedures?

**Step 3**  Enter your audit procedure using the 'verb-document-reason' approach.

- What do you want to be done (eg recalculate, agree, vouch)?
- To which document (eg invoice, physical asset, board minutes)?
- Why (eg to ensure that receivables are recoverable (valuation))? You might choose to link this to an assertion.

Start each audit procedure on a new line.

Skills checkpoint 4 covers this technique in detail through application to an exam-standard question.

## Skill 5: Approach to objective test (OT) questions

Section A comprises 30% of the exam and consists of three OT case questions. Candidates can be tempted to rush through this section in order to make up time for Section B however this is a risky approach because there are a lot of marks you could lose.

A step-by-step technique for approaching OT questions is outlined below:

**Step 1**  **Answer the questions you know first.**

If you're having difficulty answering a question, move on and come back to tackle it once you've answered all the questions you know. It is often quicker to answer discursive style OT questions first, leaving more time for calculations. The AA exam doesn't have many calculations but you may be asked to calculate financial statement ratios.

**Step 2**  **Answer all questions.**

There is no penalty for an incorrect answer in ACCA exams, there is nothing to be gained by leaving an OT question unanswered. If you are stuck on a question, as a last resort, it is worth selecting the option you consider most likely to be correct, and moving on. Make a note of the question, so if you have time after you have answered the rest of the questions, you can revisit it.

**Step 3**  **Read the requirement first!**

The requirement will be stated in bold text in the exam. Identify what you are being asked to do, any technical knowledge required and **what type of OT question** you are dealing with. Look for key words in the requirement such as "which TWO of the following," or "which of the following is NOT".

Skills checkpoint 5 covers this technique in detail through application to an exam-standard question.

## Exam success skills

Passing the AA exam requires more than applying syllabus knowledge and demonstrating the specific AA skills; it also requires the development of excellent exam technique through question practice.

We consider the following six skills to be vital for exam success. The Skills Checkpoints show how each of these skills can be applied specifically to the AA exam.

### Exam success skill 1

#### Managing information

Questions in the exam will present you with a lot of information. The skill is how you handle this information to make the best use of your time. The key is determining how you will approach the exam and then actively reading the questions.

#### Advice on developing managing information

#### Approach

The exam is three hours long. There is no designated 'reading' time at the start of the exam, however, one approach that can work well is to start the exam by spending 10-15 minutes carefully reading through all of the questions to familiarise yourself with the exam.

Once you feel familiar with the exam, consider the order in which you will attempt the questions; always attempt them in your order of preference. For example, you may want to leave to last the question you consider to be the most difficult.

If you do take this approach, remember to adjust the time available for each question appropriately – see Exam success skill 6: Good time management.

If you find that this approach doesn't work for you, don't worry – you can develop your own technique.

#### Active reading

You must take an active approach to reading each question. In Section B questions in particular, focus on the requirement first, taking note of key verbs such as 'prepare', 'comment', 'explain', 'discuss', to ensure you answer the question properly. Then read the rest of the question, making notes of any relevant technical information you think you will need.

### Exam success skill 2

#### Correct interpretation of the requirements

The active verb used often dictates the approach that written answers should take (eg 'explain', 'discuss', 'evaluate'). It is important you identify and use the verb to define your approach. The **correct interpretation of the requirements** skill means correctly producing only what is being asked for by a requirement. Anything not required will not earn marks.

#### Advice on developing correct interpretation of the requirements

This skill can be developed by analysing question requirements and applying this process:

Step 1    **Read the requirement**

Firstly, read the requirement a couple of times slowly and carefully and highlight the active verbs. Use the active verbs to define what you plan to do. Make sure you identify any sub-requirements.

Step 2    **Read the rest of the question**

By reading the requirement first, you will have an idea of what you are looking out for as you read through the case overview and exhibits. This is a great time saver and means you don't end up having to read the whole question in full twice. You should do this in an active way – see Exam success skill 1: Managing Information.

**Step 3** **Read the requirement again**

Read the requirement again to remind yourself of the exact wording before starting your written answer. This will capture any misinterpretation of the requirements or any missed requirements entirely. This should become a habit in your approach and, with repeated practice, you will find the focus, relevance and depth of your answer plan will improve.

## Exam success skill 3

### Answer planning: Priorities, structure and logic

This skill requires the planning of the key aspects of an answer which accurately and completely responds to the requirement.

### Advice on developing answer planning: priorities, structure and logic

Everyone will have a preferred style for an answer plan. You can use the scratch pad tool provided in the assessment to make notes on. Choose the approach that you feel most comfortable with, or, if you are not sure, try out different approaches for different questions until you have found your preferred style.

## Exam success skill 4

### Efficient numerical analysis

This skill aims to maximise the marks awarded by making clear to the marker the process of arriving at your answer. This is achieved by laying out an answer such that, even if you make a few errors, you can still get some credit for your calculations. It is vital that you do not lose marks purely because the marker cannot follow what you have done.

### Advice on developing efficient numerical analysis

There are not many marks available for numbers in the AA exam, however you may need to calculate ratios such as the receivables collection period.

This skill can be developed by applying the following process:

**Step 1** **Use the provided template/standard formula where relevant**

If answers can be laid out in a standard formula then always plan to do so. This will help the marker to understand your working and allocate the marks easily. It will also help you to work through the figures in a methodical and time-efficient way. For questions asking you calculate ratios, you are likely to be given a table with the names of the ratios you are being asked to calculate in one column and a space to enter the answer in the other column. The requirement will tell you whether or not formulae are required.

**Step 2** **Show your workings**

Keep your workings as clear and simple as possible and ensure they are cross-referenced to the main part of your answer. Where it helps, provide brief narrative explanations to help the marker understand the steps in the calculation. This means that if a mistake is made you should not lose any subsequent marks for follow-on calculations.

**Step 3** **Keep moving!**

It is important to remember that, in an exam situation, it is difficult to get every number 100% correct. The key is therefore ensuring you do not spend too long on any single calculation. If you are struggling with a solution then make a sensible assumption, state it and move on.

## Exam success skill 5

### Effective writing and presentation

Written answers should be presented so that the marker can clearly see the points you are making, presented in the format specified in the question. The skill is to provide efficient written answers with sufficient breadth of points that answer the question, in the right depth, in the time available.

### Advice on developing effective writing and presentation

**Step 1    Use headings**

Using the headings and sub-headings from your answer plan will give your answer structure, order and logic. This will ensure your answer links back to the requirement and is clearly signposted, making it easier for the marker to understand the different points you are making. Making your headings bold will also help the marker.

**Step 2    Write your answer in short, but full, sentences**

Use short, punchy sentences with the aim that every sentence should say something different and generate marks. Use full sentences, ensuring your style is professional.

**Step 3    Do your calculations first and explanation second**

Questions sometimes ask for an explanation with suitable calculations, such as materiality. The best approach is to prepare the calculation first then add the explanation. Performing the calculation first should enable you to explain what you have done.

## Exam success skill 6

### Good time management

This skill means planning your time across all the requirements so that all tasks have been attempted at the end of the three hours available and actively checking on time during your exam. This is so that you can flex your approach and prioritise requirements which, in your judgment, will generate the maximum marks in the available time remaining.

### Advice on developing Good time management

The exam is 3 hours long, which translates to 1.8 minutes per mark. Therefore a 20-mark requirement should be allocated a maximum of 36 minutes to complete your answer before you move on to the next task. At the beginning of a question, work out the amount of time you should be spending on each requirement and note the finishing time for that question. If you take the approach of spending 10-15 minutes reading and planning at the start of the exam, adjust the time allocated to each question accordingly.

### Keep an eye on the clock

Aim to attempt all requirements, but be ready to be ruthless and move on if your answer is not going as planned. The challenge for many is sticking to planned timings. Be aware this is difficult to achieve in the early stages of your studies and be ready to let this skill develop over time.

If you find yourself running short on time and know that a full answer is not possible in the time you have, consider recreating your plan in overview form and then add key terms and details as time allows. Remember, some marks may be available, for example, simply stating a conclusion which you don't have time to justify in full.

## Question practice

Question practice is a core part of learning new topic areas. When you practice questions, you should focus on improving the Exam success skills – personal to your needs – by obtaining feedback or through a process of self-assessment.

Sitting this exam as a computer-based exam and practicing as many exam-style questions as possible in the ACCA CBE practice platform will be the key to passing this exam. You should attempt questions under timed conditions and ensure you produce full answers to the discussion parts as well as doing the calculations. Also ensure that you attempt all mock exams under exam conditions.

ACCA have launched a free on-demand resource designed to mirror the live exam experience helping you to become more familiar with the exam format. You can access the platform via the Study Support Resources section of the ACCA website navigating to the CBE question practice section and logging in with your my ACCA credentials.

# 1 The concept of audit and other assurance engagements

## Learning objectives

On completion of this chapter, you should be able to:

| Syllabus learning outcomes | Syllabus reference no. |
| --- | --- |
| Identify and describe the objective and general principles of external audit engagements | A1 (a) |
| Explain the nature and development of audit and other assurance engagements | A1 (b) |
| Discuss the concepts of accountability, stewardship and agency | A1 (c) |
| Define and provide the objectives of an assurance engagement | A1 (d) |
| Explain the five elements of an assurance engagement | A1 (e) |
| Describe the types of assurance engagement | A1 (f) |
| Explain the level of assurance provided by an external audit and other review engagements and the concept of true and fair presentation | A1 (g) |
| Describe the limitations of external audits | A2 (e) |

## Business and exam context

Assurance is another word for "comfort". This chapter aims to help you understand more about what assurance is, why we need it, and the different levels of assurance that can be given.

The external audit is an example of an assurance engagement because, by providing an opinion on the financial statements, the external auditor is providing assurance to the entity's shareholders as to whether or not the financial statements are 'reliable'. Other key assurance services in the syllabus include review engagements and internal audit assignments.

We will also see that there are essentially two levels of assurance: reasonable assurance and limited assurance.

# Chapter overview

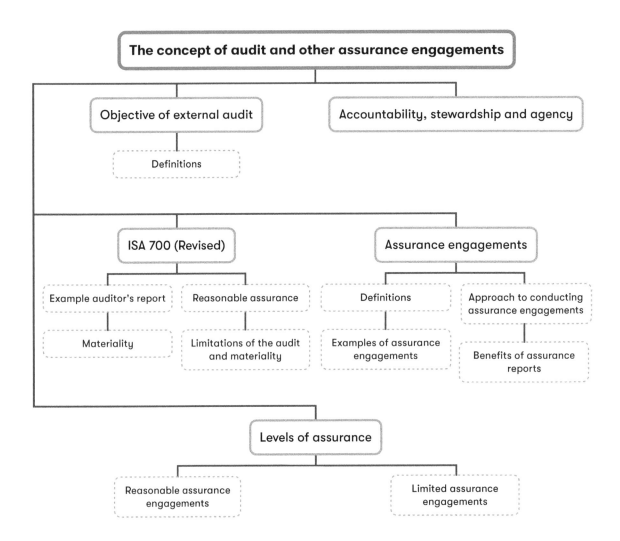

The concept of audit and other assurance engagements

- Objective of external audit
  - Definitions
- Accountability, stewardship and agency

- ISA 700 (Revised)
  - Example auditor's report
    - Materiality
  - Reasonable assurance
    - Limitations of the audit and materiality
- Assurance engagements
  - Definitions
    - Examples of assurance engagements
  - Approach to conducting assurance engagements
    - Benefits of assurance reports

- Levels of assurance
  - Reasonable assurance engagements
  - Limited assurance engagements

 BPP

# 1 Objective of external audit

## 1.1 Definitions

ISA 200 *Overall Objectives of the Independent Auditor and the Conduct of an Audit in Accordance with International Standards on Auditing (ISAs)* has the following definitions:

**The objective of an audit:** of financial statements is to enable the auditor to express an opinion on whether the financial statements are prepared, in all material respects, in accordance with an applicable financial reporting framework. (ISA 200: para. 3)

**The objectives of an auditor:** are to obtain reasonable assurance about whether the financial statements as a whole are free from material misstatement, whether due to fraud or error, in order to enable them to express an opinion on whether the financial statements are prepared, in all material respects, in accordance with an applicable financial reporting framework. (ISA 200: para. 11)

# 2 Accountability, stewardship and agency

An audit provides assurance to the shareholders and other stakeholders of a company on the financial statements because it is independent and impartial.

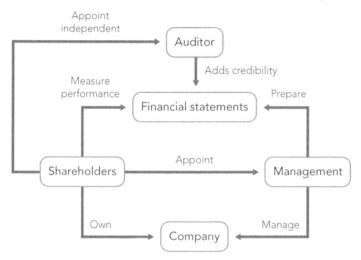

In a company the management act as agents for the body of shareholders (the principals). They are accountable to the shareholders for their stewardship of the entity's assets which are placed under their control.

They achieve this by preparing financial statements which are presented to the shareholders.

Most incorporated entities are legally required to have their financial statements audited, although many smaller entities are exempt from the requirement.

Auditors must be independent of the entity they are auditing, and seek to provide an opinion to the shareholders as to whether the financial statements are 'presented fairly', or give a true and fair view.

**True:** Information is factual and conforms with reality. In addition, the information conforms with required standards and law. The financial statements have been correctly extracted from the books and records.

**Fair:** Information is free from discrimination and bias and in compliance with expected standards and rules. The accounts should reflect the commercial substance of the company's underlying transactions.

**Present fairly:** The financial statements show a true and fair view. They are factual and free from bias.

The auditor's opinion enhances the credibility of the financial statements by providing reasonable assurance that the financial statements are free from material misstatement.

Reasonable assurance is a high level of assurance.

The auditor can also be seen as an agent of the body of shareholders as they report to and are appointed by them.

## Essential reading

See Chapter 1 of the Essential reading for more information on accountability, stewardship and agency.

The Essential reading is available as an Appendix of the digital edition of the Workbook.

# 3 ISA 700 (Revised) *Forming an Opinion and Reporting on Financial Statements*

At the end of the audit process the auditors should be in a position to express their opinion to the shareholders as to whether the financial statements have been prepared, in all material respects, in accordance with the applicable financial reporting framework.

The opinion is expressed in the auditor's report. If the auditors are satisfied that the financial statements are presented fairly, they will issue a report which gives an unmodified opinion.

## 3.1 Example auditor's report – unmodified opinion (listed entity)

**INDEPENDENT AUDITOR'S REPORT**

To the Shareholders of ABC Company [or Other Appropriate Addressee]

**Report on the Audit of the Financial Statements**

**Opinion**

We have audited the financial statements of ABC Company (the Company), which comprise of the statement of financial position as at 31 December 20X1, and the statement of comprehensive income, statement of changes in equity and statement of cash flows for the year then ended, and notes to the financial statements, including a summary of significant accounting policies.

In our opinion, the accompanying financial statements present fairly, in all material respects, (or *give a true and fair view of*) the financial position of the Company as at 31 December 20X1, and (of) its financial performance and its cash flows for the year then ended in accordance with International Financial Reporting Standards (IFRSs).

**Basis for Opinion**

We conducted our audit in accordance with International Standards on Auditing (ISAs). Our responsibilities under those standards are further described in the *Auditor's Responsibilities for the Audit of the Financial Statements* section of our report. We are independent of the Company in accordance with the International Ethics Standards Board for Accountants' *Code of Ethics for Professional Accountants* (IESBA Code) together with the ethical requirements that are relevant to our audit of the financial statements in [jurisdiction], and we have fulfilled our other ethical responsibilities in accordance with these requirements and the IESBA Code. We believe that the audit evidence we have obtained is sufficient and appropriate to provide a basis for our opinion.

**Key Audit Matters**

Key audit matters are those matters that, in our professional judgment, were of most significance in our audit of the financial statements of the current period. These matters were addressed in the context of our audit of the financial statements as a whole, and in forming our opinion thereon, and we do not provide a separate opinion on these matters.

[Description of each key audit matter in accordance with ISA 701.]

**Responsibilities of Management and Those Charged with Governance for the Financial Statements**

Management is responsible for the preparation and fair presentation of the financial statements in accordance with IFRSs and for such internal control as management determines is necessary to enable the preparation of financial statements that are free from material misstatement, whether due to fraud or error.

In preparing the financial statements, management is responsible for assessing the Company's ability to continue as a going concern, disclosing, as applicable, matters related to going concern and using the going concern basis of accounting unless management either intends to liquidate the Company or to cease operations, or has no realistic alternative but to do so.

Those charged with governance are responsible for overseeing the Company's financial reporting process.

**Auditor's Responsibilities for the Audit of the Financial Statements**

Our objectives are to obtain reasonable assurance about whether the financial statements as a whole are free from material misstatement, whether due to fraud or error, and to issue an auditor's report that includes our opinion. Reasonable assurance is a high level of assurance, but is not a guarantee that an audit conducted in accordance with ISAs will always detect a material misstatement when it exists. Misstatements can arise from fraud or error and are considered material if, individually or in the aggregate, they could reasonably be expected to influence the economic decisions of users taken on the basis of these financial statements.

As part of an audit in accordance with ISAs, we exercise professional judgment and maintain professional scepticism throughout the audit. We also:

- Identify and assess the risks of material misstatement of the financial statements, whether due to fraud or error, design and perform audit procedures responsive to those risks, and obtain audit evidence that is sufficient and appropriate to provide a basis for our opinion. The risk of not detecting a material misstatement resulting from fraud is higher than for one resulting from error, as fraud may involve collusion, forgery, intentional omissions, misrepresentations, or the override of internal control.

- Obtain an understanding of internal control relevant to the audit in order to design audit procedures that are appropriate in the circumstances, but not for the purpose of expressing an opinion on the effectiveness of the Company's internal control.

- Evaluate the appropriateness of accounting policies used and the reasonableness of accounting estimates and related disclosures made by management.

- Conclude on the appropriateness of management's use of the going concern basis of accounting and, based on the audit evidence obtained, whether a material uncertainty exists related to events or conditions that may cast significant doubt on the Company's ability to continue as a going concern. If we conclude that a material uncertainty exists, we are required to draw attention in our auditor's report to the related disclosures in the financial statements or, if such disclosures are inadequate, to modify our opinion. Our conclusions are based on the audit evidence obtained up to the date of our auditor's report. However, future events or conditions may cause the Company to cease to continue as a going concern.

- Evaluate the overall presentation, structure and content of the financial statements, including the disclosures, and whether the financial statements represent the underlying transactions and events in a manner that achieves fair presentation.

We communicate with those charged with governance regarding, among other matters, the planned scope and timing of the audit and significant audit findings, including any significant deficiencies in internal control that we identify during our audit.

We also provide those charged with governance with a statement that we have complied with relevant ethical requirements regarding independence, and to communicate with them all relationships and other matters that may reasonably be thought to bear on our independence, and where applicable, related safeguards.

From the matters communicated with those charged with governance, we determine those matters that were of most significance in the audit of the financial statements of the current period and are therefore the key audit matters. We describe these matters in our auditor's report unless law or regulation precludes public disclosure about the matter or when, in extremely rare circumstances, we determine that a matter should not be communicated in our report because the adverse consequences of doing so would reasonably be expected to outweigh the public interest benefits of such communication.

The engagement partner on the audit resulting in this independent auditor's report is [name].

[Signature in the name of the audit firm, the personal name of the auditor, or both, as appropriate for the particular jurisdiction]

[Auditor Address]

[Date]

## 3.2 Materiality

Materiality is covered in detail in Chapter 6; however, for now you should note its definition:

KEY
TERM

> **Materiality:** is an expression of the relative significance or importance of a particular matter in the context of the financial statements as a whole. A matter is **material** if its omission or misstatement would **reasonably be expected to influence the economic decisions** of users taken on the basis of the financial statements. Materiality depends on the size of the item or error judged in the particular circumstances of its omission or misstatement. (ISA 200: para. 6)

## 3.3 Reasonable assurance

No auditor can give a 100% guarantee that the financial statements are free from material misstatement but 'reasonable assurance' is the highest level of assurance that can be given.

Reasonable assurance is not absolute assurance because there are inherent limitations of an audit which result in the auditor forming an opinion on evidence that is persuasive rather than conclusive.

## 3.4 Limitations of the audit and materiality

The assurance given by auditors is limited by the fact that auditors use judgement in deciding what audit procedures to use and what conclusions to draw, and also by the limitations of every audit.

 BPP

These are illustrated in the following diagram:

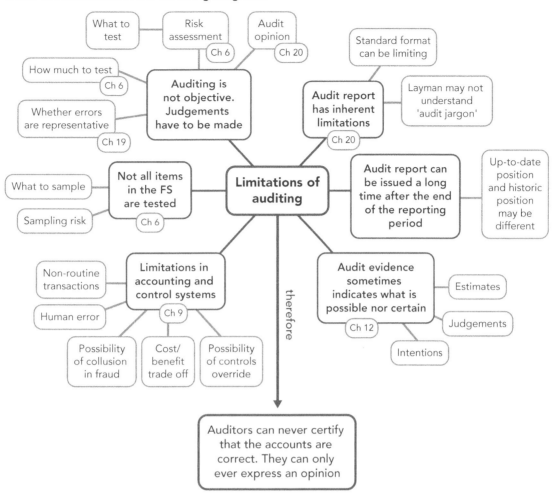

# 4 Assurance engagements

## 4.1 Definitions

KEY
TERM

**Assurance engagement:** is one in which: a **practitioner** aims to obtain sufficient appropriate evidence in order to express a conclusion designed to enhance the degree of confidence of the **intended users** other than the **responsible party** about the outcome of the measurement or evaluation of an underlying **subject matter** against **criteria**. (IFAC, 2016(e))

**Practitioner:** 'the individual conducting the engagement (usually the engagement partner or other members of the engagement team, or as applicable, the firm'. (ISAE 3000 (Revised): para. 12r)

**Intended users:** 'the individual(s) or organisation(s), or group(s) thereof that the practitioner expects will use the assurance report'. (ISAE 3000 (Revised): para. 12m)

**Responsible party:** 'the party responsible for the underlying subject matter'. (ISAE 3000 (Revised): para. 12v)

## 4.2 Elements of an assurance engagement

There are **five elements** to an assurance engagement. These are illustrated by the diagram below:

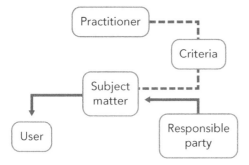

The five elements can be remembered using the mnemonic **CREST**:

| | |
|---|---|
| **C** | **Criteria:**<br>The subject matter is evaluated or measured against criteria in order to reach an opinion. |
| **R** | **Report:**<br>A written report containing the practitioner's opinion is issued to the intended user, in the form appropriate to a reasonable assurance engagement or a limited assurance engagement. |
| **E** | **Evidence:**<br>Sufficient appropriate evidence needs to be gathered to support the required level of assurance. |
| **S** | **Subject matter:**<br>The data to be evaluated that has been prepared by the responsible party. It can take many forms, including financial performance (eg historical financial information), non-financial performance (eg key performance indicators), processes (eg internal controls) and behaviour (eg compliance with laws and regulations). |
| **T** | **Three party relationship:**<br>The three parties are the intended user, the responsible party and the practitioner. |

Assurance describes the process whereby one party is trying to provide a level of comfort to another party about a subject matter.

Many assurance engagements are undertaken voluntarily; however, some, such as the statutory audit, happen as a result of a requirement imposed on the entity by another party (for example, legislation, a regulator or a bank). (IFAC, 2017)

### Activity 1: Assurance and assurance reports

What other examples of assurance and assurance reports exist?

Consider the following scenarios:

**Required**

1   You are currently thinking of buying a house built in 1900. What assurance report could you obtain and who might provide this?

2   You work for a local council which is just about to issue a $10,000 grant to an organisation which runs sports activity courses for children with special needs. What assurance report could you obtain and who might provide this?

Solution

---

## 4.3 Examples of assurance engagements

These include:

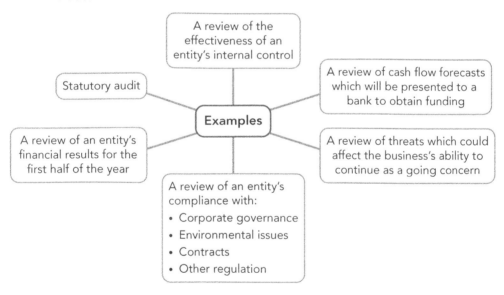

- A review of the effectiveness of an entity's internal control
- A review of cash flow forecasts which will be presented to a bank to obtain funding
- Statutory audit
- Examples
- A review of threats which could affect the business's ability to continue as a going concern
- A review of an entity's financial results for the first half of the year
- A review of an entity's compliance with:
  - Corporate governance
  - Environmental issues
  - Contracts
  - Other regulation

## 4.4 Approach to conducting assurance engagements

Assurance engagements should be performed according to the following process:

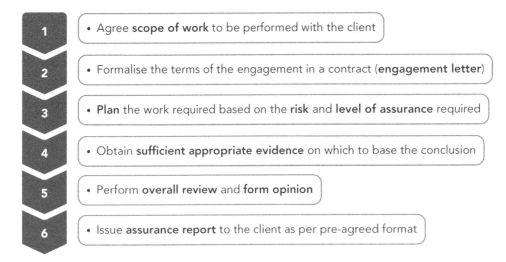

1. • Agree **scope of work** to be performed with the client
2. • Formalise the terms of the engagement in a contract (**engagement letter**)
3. • **Plan** the work required based on the **risk** and **level of assurance** required
4. • Obtain **sufficient appropriate evidence** on which to base the conclusion
5. • Perform **overall review** and **form opinion**
6. • Issue **assurance report** to the client as per pre-agreed format

## 4.5 Benefits of assurance reports

An assurance report provides the following benefits to the users of information:

- Provides an **independent opinion** from an external source that **enhances the credibility** of the information.
- Reduces **management bias**.
- Any non-standard or modified opinion draws attention to risk.
- Relevance of information is improved because of the expertise and knowledge of the assurance firm.

# 5 Levels of assurance

ISAE 3000 (Revised) *Assurance Engagements Other than Audits or Reviews of Historical Financial Information* distinguishes between two forms of assurance engagements:

- **Reasonable assurance** engagements
- **Limited assurance** engagements

The two types and levels of assurance are discussed below.

## 5.1 Reasonable assurance engagements

A **reasonable assurance** engagement provides a **high, but not absolute** level of assurance.

In order to give reasonable assurance, a significant amount of testing and evaluation is required to support the practitioner's conclusion.

The external audit is therefore a key example of a reasonable assurance engagement.

The conclusion formed in any report relating to a reasonable assurance engagement would usually be expressed in a **positive form**, for example:

'In our opinion internal control is effective, in all material respects, based on XYZ criteria.'

## 5.2 Limited assurance engagements

**Limited assurance** is a lower level of assurance. The nature, timing and extent of the procedures carried out by the practitioner in a limited assurance engagement would be limited compared with what is required in a reasonable assurance engagement. Nevertheless, the procedures performed should be planned to obtain a level of assurance which is meaningful, in the practitioner's professional judgement.

 **BPP**

For a limited assurance engagement, the conclusion conveys whether, based on the procedures performed and evidence obtained, a matter(s) has come to the practitioner's attention to cause the practitioner to believe the subject matter information is materially misstated. (ISAE 3000 (Revised): para. 12ib)

This would usually be expressed in a **negative form of words**, for example:

'Based on our work described in this report, nothing has come to our attention that causes us to believe that internal control is not effective, in all material respects, based on XYZ criteria.'

## 5.3 Summary

| Type of engagement | Evidence – gathering procedures | Assurance report |
|---|---|---|
| Reasonable assurance eg statutory audit | Sufficient appropriate evidence is obtained by: <br><br>• Obtaining an understanding of the entity <br>• Assessing risk <br>• Responding to risk <br>• Performing further procedures (sampling) to draw a conclusion | Positive |
| Limited assurance eg review of cash flow forecasts | The evidence gathered is limited, involving techniques such as enquiry and analytical procedures | Negative |

# Chapter summary

## The concept of audit and other assurance engagements

### Objective of external audit

**Definitions**
- Objective of an audit
- Objectives of an auditor

### Accountability, stewardship and agency

- Management act as agents for the shareholders
- Management are accountable to the shareholders for their stewardship of the entity's assets
- Management prepare financial statements for the shareholders

### ISA 700 (Revised)

**Example auditor's report**
- Will be covered in detail in Chapter 20
- Shows:
  – Audit opinion
  – Reasonable assurance
  – Responsibilities of management and the external auditor

**Materiality**

A matter is material if its omission/misstatement would reasonably be expected to influence the economic decisions of users taken on the basis of the financial statements

**Reasonable assurance**

High level but not absolute

**Limitations of the audit and materiality**

Can only ever express an opinion due to:
- Limitations in accounting and control systems
- Use of sampling
- Use of judgement
- Evidence is persuasive rather than conclusive

### Assurance engagements

**Definitions**
- Practitioner expresses an opinion on information prepared by a responsible party to an intended user
- Five elements (CREST):
  – Criteria
  – Report
  – Evidence
  – Subject matter
  – Three party relationship

**Examples of assurance engagements**
- Statutory audit
- Internal controls review
- Cash flow forecast review
- Going concern review
- Compliance review
- Review of interim financial statements

**Approach to conducting assurance engagements**
- Scope of work
- Engagement letter
- Plan work
- Obtain sufficient appropriate evidence
- Overall review and form opinion
- Issue assurance report

**Benefits of assurance reports**
- Independent opinion enhances credibility of information
- Reduces management bias
- Non-standard opinion identifies risk
- Improved relevance due to expertise of practitioner

### Levels of assurance

**Reasonable assurance engagements**
- High level of assurance, not absolute
- Positive form of opinion
- Example: Statutory audit

**Limited assurance engagements**
- Lower level of assurance
- Negative form of opinion
- Example: Review engagements

 BPP

# Knowledge diagnostic

### 1. Objective of an external audit

The objective of an **external audit** is for the auditor to provide an independent opinion on the financial statements as to whether they are free from material misstatement, whether due to fraud or error, and whether they are prepared, in all material respects, in accordance with an applicable financial reporting framework.

### 2. Stewardship

Management/those charged with governance act as agents for the body of shareholders and are accountable to them for their stewardship of the entity's assets.

### 3. The auditor's report

The auditor's report follows a standard format in order for users to be able to clearly see the opinion given, basis of work done and the respective responsibilities of management and the external auditor. The auditor's report will be covered in detail in chapter 20.

### 4. The external audit

The external audit is only one example of an assurance engagement. The audit provides reasonable assurance which is a high level of assurance (although not absolute).

### 5. Elements of an assurance engagement

There are five elements to an assurance engagement, remember these using the mnemonic CREST.

### 6. Levels of assurance

An assurance engagement can provide one of two levels of assurance: reasonable assurance which is usually reported in terms of positive form of opinion and limited assurance which is usually reported in terms of negative form of opinion.

# Further study guidance

## Question practice

Now try the following from the Further question practice bank (available in the digital edition of the workbook):

- Section A Q16 and Q17
- Section B Q58 Audit and assurance engagements

## Further reading

This is very much an introductory chapter and so there are no technical articles or study support videos on the ACCA website for this area. However the start of the course is a great time to understand the approach you'll need to take to the Audit and Assurance exam and so you should read the following exam technique articles:

Exam technique article:

- Read the mind of the marker (https://www.accaglobal.com/content/dam/ACCA_Global/Students/resourceFinder/Read-the-mind-of-AA-marker-DEC2020.pdf)
- Examiner approach (https://www.accaglobal.com/uk/en/student/exam-support-resources/fundamentals-exams-study-resources/f8/technical-articles/approach-sept16.html)

## Own research

Have you or a friend/family member ever bought a flat or house and had a survey performed? This is a type of assurance report! Have a look at the report and see if you can identify the five elements of an assurance engagement and judge the level of assurance provided and whether the opinion is in a positive or negative form.

# Activity answers

## Activity 1: Assurance and assurance reports

### 1 Assurance report when buying a house

Here you would want some comfort as to whether or not the house you plan to buy is structurally sound, whether the roof is in good condition, whether there is any damp and so on. Most house buyers would have a survey carried out by a building surveyor prior to completing a purchase. This survey is carried out by an independent party who is professionally qualified and would give you confidence/comfort that there are no major issues with the property you plan to purchase.

**Tutorial note.** The Audit and Assurance (AA) assessment is a computer-based exam (CBE). Throughout this workbook we will present some answers in a format similar to the one you are likely to see when you use the word processor within the ACCA assessment platform. It is important you get as familiar as you can with the CBE environment before you take the real exam. The CBE Practice Platform provided by the ACCA is a free on-demand resource where you can do this and access past exam content. You can access it on the ACCA website in the study resources area. Just because we show answers in the style of the CBE environment, it doesn't mean all activities are exam standard, especially in the early chapters when the workbook aims to build up your AA knowledge. The aim is to get you used to seeing answers in the CBE style as early as possible and to remind you to try the CBE environment for yourself when you can.

### 2 Assurance report relating to a grant

Here the council body will be concerned that the money they have given is used for the designated purpose. They will need assurance that the money has been spent on sports equipment, sports hall premises, staff and so forth rather than on items which are not related to this cause. The council could require the organisation to provide them with a report stating that the money was spent in accordance with the stipulations of the grant. This report would need to be produced by an independent body, perhaps an accountant.

**Tutorial note.** You can see that above the area you will be given to type in during the CBE you have access to tools you would have in a normal word processor. This includes formatting tools to embolden or underline words, bullet points and alignment buttons. We will see in later chapters you are sometimes given template tables ready for you to type into depending on the type of question.

# 2

# Statutory audit and regulation

## Learning objectives

On completion of this chapter, you should be able to:

| Syllabus learning outcomes | Syllabus reference no. |
| --- | --- |
| Describe the regulatory environment within which external audits take place | A2 (a) |
| Discuss the reasons and mechanisms for the regulation of auditors | A2 (b) |
| Explain the statutory regulations governing the appointment, rights, removal and resignation of auditors | A2 (c) |
| Explain the regulations governing the rights and duties of auditors | A2 (d) |
| Explain the development and status of International Standards on Auditing (ISAs) | A2 (f) |
| Explain the relationship between International Standards on Auditing and national standards | A2 (g) |

## Business and exam context

This chapter covers the regulatory framework within which the external auditor operates and how the auditing profession is regulated. It is important that you understand the rights and duties the auditor has and also the specific processes that must be followed when auditors are appointed, removed and resign.

There are several bodies which govern auditing and financial reporting and it is essential that you understand the role of the International Auditing and Assurance Standards Board and how International Standards on Auditing are set.

# Chapter overview

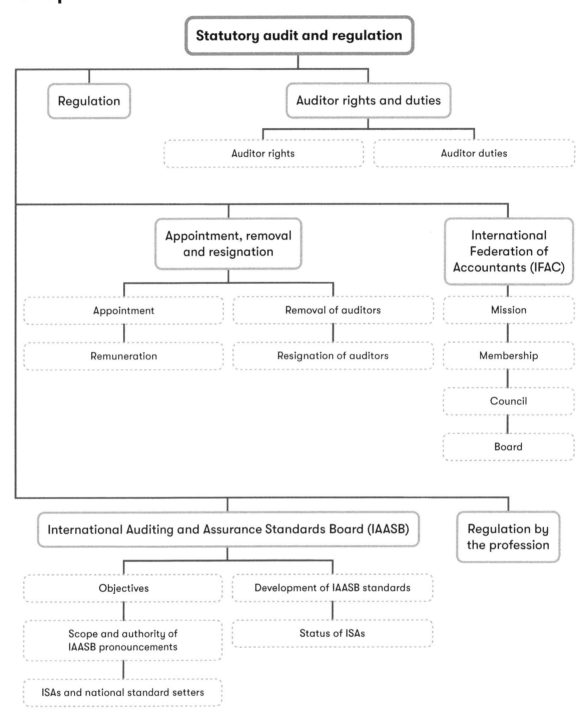

# 1 Regulation

The audit is primarily a statutory concept which means that an audit is required by statute (law) and the majority of companies are required by national law to have an audit.

A key exception to this requirement is that given to small companies. Many European Commission (EC) countries have a small company exemption from audit that is based on the turnover (revenue) and total assets at the year-end.

## Essential reading

See Chapter 2 of the Essential reading for more information on smaller companies and the advantages and disadvantages of retaining the audit of smaller companies.

The Essential reading is available as an Appendix of the digital edition of the Workbook.

### Exam focus point

Note that, unless otherwise stated, companies in the AA exam will require an audit.

The auditing profession is subject to **regulation** from a range of sources:

## Essential reading

See Chapter 2 of the Essential reading for more information on the regulation of auditors.

The Essential reading is available as an Appendix of the digital edition of the Workbook.

# 2 Auditor rights and duties

The rights and duties of auditors are often set out in law, to ensure that the auditors have sufficient power to carry out an effective audit.

Here we look at the rights and duties of auditors in the **UK as an example** where the relevant legislation is the **Companies Act 2006**.

Note that the rights and duties of auditors may be different in other jurisdictions.

## 2.1 Auditor rights

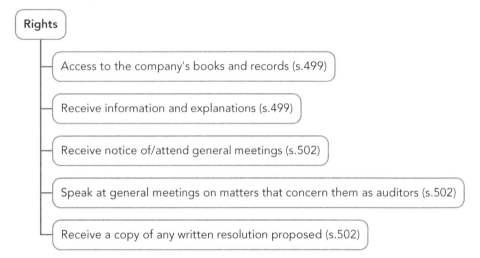

**Rights**

- Access to the company's books and records (s.499)
- Receive information and explanations (s.499)
- Receive notice of/attend general meetings (s.502)
- Speak at general meetings on matters that concern them as auditors (s.502)
- Receive a copy of any written resolution proposed (s.502)

## 2.2 Auditor duties

**Duties**

- Report opinion on:
- Whether financial statements are fairly presented (s.495)

**Duties**

- **Report opinion on additional statutory requirements:**
- Adhere to local law (s.495)
- Maintain adequate records and returns (s.498)
- Ensure financial statements agree to records (s.498)
- Ensure consistency of other information (s.496)
- Ensure disclosure of directors' benefits (s.498)

The Companies Act 2006 (s.501) makes it an offence for a company's officer knowingly or recklessly to make a statement in any form to an auditor which is misleading, false or deceptive.

# 3 Appointment, removal and resignation

Chapter 1 identified the importance of the auditor being **independent** and their role as an **agent of the shareholders**.

In most jurisdictions this is established in the law relating to appointment, removal and resignation of auditors.

## 3.1 Appointment

The auditors should be appointed by and therefore answerable to the **shareholders**.

The table below shows the ideal position using the UK as an example.

| Auditor appointment (UK, Companies Act 2006: s.489-490) | |
|---|---|
| **Directors** | Can appoint auditor: <br><br> (a) Before company's **first period for appointing auditors** <br><br> (b) Following a period during which the company **did not have an** auditor (as exempt), at any time before the next |

 BPP

| Auditor appointment (UK, Companies Act 2006: s.489-490) | |
|---|---|
|  | period for appointing auditors<br><br>(c)  To fill a **casual vacancy** |
| Members (shareholders) | Can appoint auditor by ordinary resolution:<br><br>(a)  During a **period for appointing auditors**<br><br>(b)  If company **should have** appointed auditor during a period for appointing auditors **butfailed to do so**<br><br>(c)  If directors **fail to do so** |
| Secretary of State | Can appoint auditors if **no auditors** are **appointed** per above |

An auditor must be appointed for each financial year unless the directors reasonably resolve otherwise on the grounds that audited financial statements are unlikely to be required.

## 3.2 Remuneration

The remuneration of the auditors, which will include auditors' expenses, will be fixed by **whoever made the appointment**.

In many countries the auditor's remuneration must be disclosed in the annual financial statements of the company. (Companies Act 2006: s.492)

## 3.3 Removal of auditors

| Removal of auditors (UK, Companies Act 2006: s.510–513) | |
|---|---|
| 1 Notice of removal | **Either special notice** (28 days) with copy sent to auditor<br><br>**Or** if elective resolution in place, **written resolution** to terminate auditors' appointment<br><br>Directors must convene a meeting within a reasonable period of time. |
| 2 Representations | **Auditors** can make **representations** on why they ought to stay in office. They may require company to state in notice that representations have been made and send copy to members. |
| 3 If resolution passed | (a)  Company must **notify** regulatory authority<br><br>(b)  Auditors must **deposit statementof circumstances** at company's registered office **within 14 days** of ceasing to hold office. Statement must be sent to regulatory authority, eg ACCA. |
| 4 Auditor rights | Can **receive notice** of and **speak** at:<br><br>(a)  A general meeting at which their term of office would have expired<br><br>(b)  A general meeting where casual vacancy caused by their removal is to be filled |

## 3.4 Resignation of auditors

| Resignation of Auditors (UK, Companies Act 2006: s.516-518) | |
|---|---|
| 1 Resignation procedures | Auditors deposit **written notice** together with **statement of circumstances** relevant to members/creditors or statement that no such circumstances exist.<br><br>A statement of circumstances must always be submitted for a quoted company/public interest entity, even if the auditor considers that there are no circumstances that should be brought to the attention of members or creditors.<br><br>Certain exemptions apply for non-public interest entities. |
| 2 Notice of resignation | Sent by **company** to regulatory authority. |
| 3 Statement of circumstances | Sent by:<br><br>(a)  Auditors to regulatory authority<br><br>(b)  Company to everyone entitled to receive a copy of accounts |
| 4 Convening of general meeting | **Auditors** can **require directors** to call an **extraordinary general meeting** to discuss circumstances of resignation.<br><br>Directors must send out notice for meeting within **21 days** of having received requisition by auditors. |
| 5 Statement prior to general meeting | **Auditors** may require company to circulate (different) **statement of circumstances** to everyone entitled to notice of meeting. |
| 6 Other rights of auditors | Can **receive all notices** that relate to:<br><br>(a)  A general meeting at which their term of office would have expired<br><br>(b)  A general meeting where casual vacancy caused by their resignation is to be filled<br><br>Can **speak** at these meetings on **any matter** which **concerns them as auditors**. |

# 4 International Federation of Accountants (IFAC)

IFAC was set up in 1977 and is based in New York. It is a non-profit, non-governmental and non-political international organisation of accountancy bodies. The ACCA is a member of IFAC.

*Role*

Not-for-profit organisation

(1) Elects members of Board
(2) Determines financial contributions

Supervises IFAC's work programme

Carries out IFAC's work programme

(1) Set high-quality auditing (ISAs) and assurance (ISAEs) standards
(2) Facilitates convergence of international and national standards
(3) Strengthen public confidence in profession

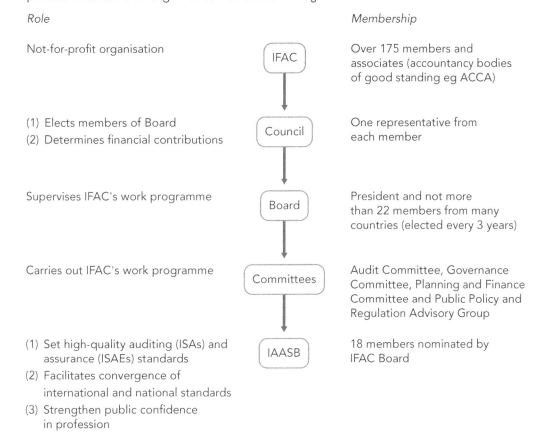

*Membership*

Over 175 members and associates (accountancy bodies of good standing eg ACCA)

One representative from each member

President and not more than 22 members from many countries (elected every 3 years)

Audit Committee, Governance Committee, Planning and Finance Committee and Public Policy and Regulation Advisory Group

18 members nominated by IFAC Board

## 4.1 Mission

IFAC's mission is 'to serve the public interest, strengthen the global accountancy profession and contribute to the development of strong international economies by establishing and promoting adherence to high-quality professional standards, furthering the international convergence of such standards, and speaking out on public interest issues where the profession's expertise is most relevant.' (IFAC, 2017)

## 4.2 Membership

Any accountancy body may join IFAC if it is recognised by law or general consensus within its own country as a substantial national organisation of good standing within the accountancy profession.

Members of IFAC automatically become members of the International Accounting Standards Committee Foundation, which is an independent not-for-profit, private sector organisation which sets international financial reporting standards through its standard-setting body, the International Accounting Standards Board.

## 4.3 Council

This consists of one representative from each member body of IFAC. It elects the members of the Board and establishes the basis of financial contributions by members.

## 4.4 Board

The Board consists of the President and not more than 22 members elected by the Council for 3-year terms. Elections to the Board are held annually so that one-third of the Board retires each year.

The role of the Board is to supervise the general IFAC work programme.

The work programme itself is implemented by smaller working groups or the following standing technical committees:

- International Auditing and Assurance Standards Board
- Compliance Committee
- Education Committee
- Ethics Committee
- Financial and Management Accounting Committee
- Public Sector Committee
- Transnational Auditors Committee (executive arm of the Forum of Firms)

# 5 International Auditing and Assurance Standards Board (IAASB)

The IAASB was established to develop and issue standards and statements on auditing, assurance and related services on behalf of the IFAC Board.

The 18 members of the IAASB are nominated by the IFAC Board based on names put forward by the member bodies and Forum of Firms.

## 5.1 Objectives

The objective of the IAASB, on behalf of the IFAC Board, is to serve the public interest by setting high-quality auditing and assurance standards and by facilitating the convergence of international and national standards, thereby enhancing the quality and uniformity of practice throughout the world and strengthening public confidence in the global auditing and assurance profession. The IAASB achieves this objective by:

(a) Establishing high-quality auditing standards and guidance for financial statement audits that are generally accepted and recognised by investors, auditors, governments, banking regulators, securities regulators and other key stakeholders across the world

(b) Establishing high-quality standards and guidance for other types of assurance services on both financial and non-financial matters

(c) Establishing high-quality standards and guidance for other related services

(d) Establishing high-quality standards for quality management covering the scope of services addressed by the IAASB

(e) Publishing other pronouncements on auditing and assurance matters, thereby advancing public understanding of the roles and responsibility of professional auditors and assurance service providers

## 5.2 The scope and authority of IAASB pronouncements

The IAASB's pronouncements govern assurance and related services that are conducted in accordance with international standards. They do not override the local laws or regulations.

The pronouncements of the IAASB examinable fall into two categories:

- International Standards on Auditing (ISAs)
- International Standards on Assurance Engagements (ISAEs)

The IAASB's standards contain basic principles and essential procedures together with related guidance in the form of explanatory and other material. The basic principles and essential procedures are to be understood and applied in the context of the explanatory and other material that provide guidance for their application. It is therefore necessary to consider the whole text of a standard to understand and apply the basic principles and essential procedures.

In exceptional circumstances, a professional accountant may judge it necessary to depart from a requirement of a standard to achieve more effectively the objective of the engagement. When such a situation arises, the professional accountant should be prepared to justify the departure.

## 5.3 ISAs and national standard setters

Many national standard setters are moving towards the adoption of ISAs in place of their previous local auditing standards, with a large number of countries having adopted or incorporated ISAs into their national auditing standards or using ISAs as a basis for preparing national auditing standards.

```
┌──────────┐  ◄───────────────────  ┌─────────────────────────────────────┐
│  IAASB   │   Two-way communication │ Liaison group of national standard  │
│          │  ───────────────────►   │ setters eg UK Financial Reporting   │
└──────────┘                         │ Council (FRC)                       │
                                     └─────────────────────────────────────┘
```

Annual meetings with liaison group to:

- Share knowledge on international and national developments affecting the priority of topics on future standard-setting agendas
- Bring the strengths of the IAASB and national auditing standard setters to bear on standards at an early stage in their development
- Achieve close co-operation and strengthened communication eg by closer collaboration on projects and minimising duplication
- Achieve wider involvement by national auditing standard setters in IAASB task forces or to advance research agendas

Standard setters who:

- Are significantly active in the development of national auditing standards
- Have adopted or plan to adopt ISAs, or are demonstrably committed towards the achievement of convergence of international and national standards
- Are sufficiently resourced to participate actively in collaborative efforts
- Represent the world's largest economies

## 5.4 The development of IAASB standards

The development of IAASB standards adheres to the following process:

> **Research and consultation**
> A project task force is established to develop a draft standard or practice statement.

⬇

> **Transparent debate**
> A proposed standard is discussed at a meeting, open to the public.

⬇

> **Exposure for public comment**
> Exposure drafts are put on the IAASB's website and widely distributed for comment for a minimum of 120 days.

⬇

> **Consideration of comments**
> Any comments as a result of the exposure draft are considered at an open meeting of the IAASB, and it is revised as necessary.

⬇

> **Affirmative approval**
> Approval is made by the affirmative vote of at least $\frac{2}{3}$ of IAASB members.

## 5.5 Status of ISAs

As statutory audit is governed by local legislation, the status of ISAs will vary between countries:

- National standards may continue to exist but aligned with the principles of ISAs.
- The ISAs could be adopted without any additional guidance relating to national circumstances (eg South Africa).
- The ISAs could be adopted but with additional specific guidance added (eg ISAs (UK)).

# 6 Regulation by the profession

Bodies such as ACCA play a part in the regulation of the profession as follows:

| Education and training of auditors | As a member of IFAC, ACCA must comply with IFAC's international standards and guidelines on: <br><br>• Pre-qualification education and training <br>• Continuing professional education |
|---|---|
| Implementation and enforcement of ethical requirements | IFAC member bodies such as ACCA must prepare ethical requirements based on IFAC's International Code of Ethics for Professional Accountants. <br><br>Member bodies must provide high standards of professional conduct and ensure that ethical requirements are observed. <br><br>Disciplinary action should normally be taken in the following instances: <br><br>• Failure to observe the required standard of professional care, skills or competence; <br>• Non-compliance with the rules of ethics; or <br>• Discreditable or dishonourable conduct. <br>The power for disciplinary action may be provided by legislation or by the constitution of the professional body. |

# Chapter summary

**Statutory audit and regulation**

## Regulation

- National legislation
- National regulation and standard setting
- International standard setting
- Professional bodies

## Auditor rights and duties

### Auditor rights

- Access to books and records
- Right to information and explanations
- General meetings:
  - Receive notice/attend
  - Speak
  - Receive copy of written resolution proposed

### Auditor duties

Report opinion on:
- Whether fs are fairly presented
- Additional statutory requirements:
- Adhere to local law
- Adequate records/returns
- Fs agree to records
- Consistency of other information
- Disclosure of directors' benefits

## Appointment, removal and resignation

### Appointment

- Appoint annually
- Usually by shareholder (ordinary resolution)
- Directors may appoint:
  - First auditor
  - To fill a casual vacancy
  - Appointed by Secretary of State if not appointed by shareholders or directors

### Remuneration

Fixed by whoever appointed the auditors

### Removal of auditors

- Notice of removal
- Representations
- Statement of circumstances
- Auditor rights

### Resignation of auditors

- Notice of resignation
- Statement of circumstances
- Convene general meeting
- Statement prior to general meeting
- Other rights of auditors

## International Federation of Accountants (IFAC)

### Mission

- Strengthen global accountancy profession
- High quality professional standards

### Membership

Accountancy bodies, eg ACCA

### Council

One representative from each member body

### Board

- Members elected for three-year terms
- Supervise IFAC work programme

## International Auditing and Assurance Standards Board (IAASB)

### Objectives
Set high quality auditing and assurance standards

### Scope and authority of IAASB pronouncements
- Do not override local laws/regulations
- Structure:
  - Basic principles and essential procedures
  - Explanatory material

### ISAs and national standard setters
Process of convergence with many national standard setters adopting ISAs

### Development of IAASB standards
- Research and consultation
- Transparent debate
- Exposure for public comment
- Consideration of comments
- Affirmative approval (2/3 of IAASB members)

### Status of ISAs
- Varies between countries
- National standards exist, aligned with principles of ISAs
- ISAs adopted, no additional guidance
- ISAs adopted, with specific guidance added

## Regulation by the profession
- Education and training
- Implementation and enforcement of ethical requirements

# Knowledge diagnostic

### 1. Sources of regulation

The regulation of auditors comes from a range of sources.

### 2. Auditors' rights and duties

Auditors' **rights and duties** are usually governed by **national legislation**, for example the Companies Act 2006 in the UK.

### 3. Auditors' rights

Auditors' rights exist in order for them to be able to gather all of the evidence required so that they can perform an effective audit.

### 4. Appointment of auditors by shareholders

Auditors will usually be **appointed** at a company's general meeting by the **shareholders**. This requires an ordinary resolution (>50% votes).

### 5. Appointment of auditors by other parties

Where the shareholders fail to appoint an auditor, the auditor may be appointed by the directors or the Secretary of State (if the directors fail to appoint).

### 6. Remuneration

The auditor's remuneration will be set by those who appointed them.

### 7. Removal of auditors

Auditors must receive **special notice** (28 days) of any intention to **remove** them from office. They are entitled to make representations to defend themselves.

### 8. Statement of circumstances

In the event of the auditors being **removed** from office, they must deposit a **statement of circumstances** at the company's registered office.

### 9. Resignation of auditors

When an auditor **resigns**, they must submit written notice plus a **statement of circumstances**. They can ask the directors to convene an extraordinary general meeting if warranted by the circumstances.

### 10. IFAC

**IFAC** is an international organisation of accountancy bodes. Its mission is to establish and promote adherence to **high-quality professional standards**.

### 11. IAASB

**IAASB pronouncements** (ISAs and ISAEs) **do not overrule** local laws or regulations but where they form part of the regulatory framework (e.g. in the UK) they are mandatory.

### 12. Regulation by the profession

**Professional bodies**, such as ACCA, establish regulations relating to **education and training** and **ethics**.

# Further study guidance

## Question practice

Now try the following from the Further question practice bank (available in the digital edition of the workbook):

- Section A Q18 and Q19
- Section B Q59 Standards

## Further reading

There are no technical articles or study support videos on the ACCA website for this area. However, this is a great time to look at the essential skills for AA including the steps to success and how to tackle the exam. There are a range of resources on the ACCA's Introduction to Audit and Assurance page.

ACCA's Introduction to Audit and Assurance page:

- Introduction to Audit and Assurance (https://www.accaglobal.com/gb/en/student/exam-support-resources/fundamentals-exams-study-resources/f8/session-cbe-introduction.html)

## Own research

Choose a country which is not the UK and research the rights and duties of auditors in that jurisdiction. Think about how and why they may be different from those stipulated in the Companies Act 2006.

# 3

# Corporate governance

## Learning objectives

On completion of this chapter, you should be able to:

| Syllabus learning outcomes | Syllabus reference no. |
| --- | --- |
| Discuss the objectives, relevance and importance of corporate governance. | A3 (a) |
| Discuss the provisions of international codes of corporate governance (such as the Organisation for Economic Co-operation and Development (OECD)) that are most relevant to auditors. | A3 (b) |
| Describe good corporate governance requirements relating to directors' responsibilities (eg for risk management and internal control) and the reporting responsibilities of auditors. | A3 (c) |
| Evaluate corporate governance deficiencies and provide recommendations to allow compliance with international codes of corporate governance. | A3 (d) |
| Analyse the structure and roles of audit committees and discuss their benefits and limitations. | A3 (e) |
| Explain the importance of internal control and risk management. | A3 (f) |

## Business and Exam context

The concept of corporate governance was introduced in Chapter 1. In this chapter, we will look at the codes of practice that have been put in place to ensure that companies are well managed and controlled. The UK Corporate Governance Code is an internationally recognised code which we will use as an example of a code of best practice. The audit carried out by the external auditors is a very important part of corporate governance, as it is an independent check on what the directors are reporting to the shareholders.

We will also see the important role played by the audit committee, a sub-committee of the board of directors. Its role is to oversee a company's risk assessment procedures and its financial statements and monitor the internal audit function and the independence of the external auditor. External auditors liaise with the audit committee over the audit, and internal auditors will report their findings about internal control effectiveness to it.

# Chapter overview

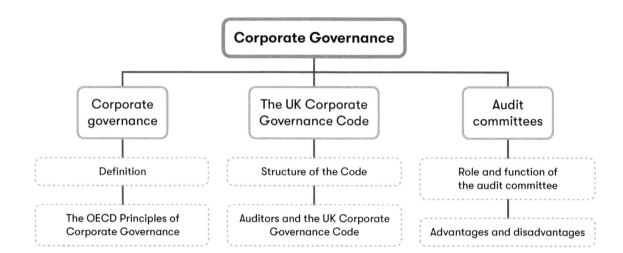

# 1 Corporate governance

## 1.1 Definition

> **Corporate governance:** the internal systems or means by which companies are **directed** and **controlled**.

It describes the framework of rules and practices by which a board of directors ensures accountability, fairness, and transparency in a company's relationship with each of its stakeholders.

In recent decades, there have been several reviews performed in many different countries in order to try to establish a set of principles for corporate governance.

> **PER alert**
>
> One of the PER performance objectives (PO4) requires you to demonstrate that you contribute to effective governance in your area. You evaluate, monitor and implement risk management procedures, complying with the spirit and the letter of policies, laws and regulations. Reviewing this chapter should help you achieve that objective.

## 1.2 The OECD Principles of Corporate Governance

The OECD has developed its own Principles of Corporate Governance.

These Principles provide best practice recommendations on corporate governance and are used worldwide as a benchmark for establishing guidelines on this area.

The Principles address the following six areas:

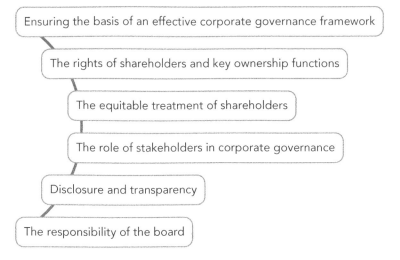

Ensuring the basis of an effective corporate governance framework

The rights of shareholders and key ownership functions

The equitable treatment of shareholders

The role of stakeholders in corporate governance

Disclosure and transparency

The responsibility of the board

The OECD document provides detailed recommendations expanding on each of the principles. In reality, each country can then develop its own corporate governance code for companies to follow.

# 2 The UK Corporate Governance Code

## 2.1 Structure of the Code

In the UK, the UK Corporate Governance Code gives guidance to companies as to how they should be directed and controlled.

 **BPP**

The UK Corporate Governance Code was revised by the Financial Reporting Council (FRC) in July 2018 and offers guidance under the following headings:

The Code applies to **listed companies** and is part of the UK Stock Exchange listing rules.

Listed companies **must** include a corporate governance report in their annual report. The report should describe how the company applies the principles in the Code and should include a statement as to whether or not the company complies with the provisions of the Code.

Where the company does not comply with certain provisions of the Code, the corporate governance report should provide an explanation for the non-compliance. This is known as the '**comply or explain**' basis.

The UK Corporate Governance Code is an example of how the OECD Principles can be implemented and the requirements listed companies must adhere to in order to satisfy the UK Stock Exchange listing rules.

The broad principles of the Code are as follows:

| Principles of the UK Corporate Governance Code (for listed UK companies) |
|---|
| **Board Leadership and Company Purpose** |
| Principle A |
| A successful company is led by an effective and entrepreneurial board, whose role is to promote the long-term sustainable success of the company, generating value for shareholders and contributing to wider society. |
| Principle B |
| The board should establish the company's purpose, values and strategy, and satisfy itself that these and its culture are aligned. All directors must act with integrity, lead by example and promote the desired culture. |
| Principle C |
| The board should ensure that the necessary resources are in place for the company to meet its |

objectives and measure performance against them. The board should also establish a framework of prudent and effective controls, which enable risk to be assessed and managed.

Principle D

In order for the company to meet its responsibilities to shareholders and stakeholders, the board should ensure effective engagement with, and encourage participation from, these parties.

Principle E

The board should ensure that workforce policies and practices are consistent with the company's values and support its long-term sustainable success. The workforce should be able to raise any matters of concern.

(FRC UK Corporate Governance Code: Section 1)

### Division of Responsibilities

Principle F

The chair leads the board and is responsible for its overall effectiveness in directing the company. They should demonstrate objective judgement throughout their tenure and promote a culture of openness and debate. In addition, the chair facilitates constructive board relations and the effective contribution of all non-executive directors, and ensures that directors receive accurate, timely and clear information.

Principle G

The board should include an appropriate combination of executive and non-executive (and, in particular, independent non-executive) directors, such that no one individual or small group of individuals dominates the board's decision-making. There should be a clear division of responsibilities between the leadership of the board and the executive leadership of the company's business.

Principle H

Non-executive directors should have sufficient time to meet their board responsibilities. They should provide constructive challenge, strategic guidance, offer specialist advice and hold management to account.

Principle I

The board, supported by the company secretary, should ensure that it has the policies, processes, information, time and resources it needs in order to function effectively and efficiently.

(FRC UK Corporate Governance Code: Section 2)

### Composition, Succession and Evaluation

Principle J

Appointments to the board should be subject to a formal, rigorous and transparent procedure, and an effective succession plan should be maintained for board and senior management. Both appointments and succession plans should be based on merit and objective criteria and, within this context, should promote diversity of gender, social and ethnic backgrounds, cognitive and personal strengths.

Principle K

The board and its committees should have a combination of skills, experience and knowledge. Consideration should be given to the length of service of the board as a whole and membership regularly refreshed.

Principle L

Annual evaluation of the board should consider its composition, diversity and how effectively members work together to achieve objectives. Individual evaluation should demonstrate whether each director continues to contribute effectively.

(FRC UK Corporate Governance Code: Section 3)

**Audit, Risk and Internal Control**

Principle M

The board should establish formal and transparent policies and procedures to ensure the independence and effectiveness of internal and external audit functions and satisfy itself on the integrity of financial and narrative statements.

Principle N

The board should present a fair, balanced and understandable assessment of the company's position and prospects.

Principle O

The board should establish procedures to manage risk, oversee the internal control framework, and determine the nature and extent of the principal risks the company is willing to take in order to achieve its long-term strategic objectives.

(FRC UK Corporate Governance Code: Section 4)

**Remuneration**

Principle P

Remuneration policies and practices should be designed to support strategy and promote long-term sustainable success. Executive remuneration should be aligned to company purpose and values, and be clearly linked to the successful delivery of the company's long-term strategy.

Principle Q

A formal and transparent procedure for developing policy on executive remuneration and determining director and senior management remuneration should be established. No director should be involved in deciding their own remuneration outcome.

Principle R

Directors should exercise independent judgement and discretion when authorising remuneration outcomes, taking account of company and individual performance, and wider circumstances.

(FRC UK Corporate Governance Code: Section 5)

## Essential reading

See Chapter 3 of the Essential reading which sets out the broad principles of the UK Corporate Governance Code.

The Essential reading is available as an Appendix of the digital edition of the Workbook.

## Activity 1: Reviewing corporate governance

### Introduction and client background

Dress You Like Co is a clothing manufacturer, based in the UK, which has been trading for over ten years. It operates from two sites, a factory where clothes are made and a head office where the administration is carried out. Completed inventory orders are despatched from both the factory and the head office.

In an effort to reduce costs, Dress You Like Co now imports its material from one sole supplier based overseas.

Dress You Like Co sells its finished products to small independent retailers and also one major supermarket chain. The supermarket chain often requires additional deliveries without much prior notice and so Dress You Like Co has to maintain a high level of inventory should this occur. Credit terms are normally 30 days, but the supermarket is given 60-day credit terms.

Dress You Like Co is not a listed company but its directors believe that the company's annual report should provide as much information as possible to shareholders. Consequently, they have voluntarily included a corporate governance report each year in their annual report.

As the audit senior, you have been asked to review Dress You Like Co's corporate governance report for the **year ended 30 September 20X5**. Your firm did **not** complete the audit for the year in question and your audit manager has given you a series of questions to answer in order to get a better understanding as to how the company is directed and controlled.

Review the corporate governance report extract below and answer the questions which follow;

**Dress You Like Co Corporate Governance Report extract for the year ended 30 September 20X5**

As a clothing manufacturer, Dress You Like Co operates within a particularly challenging sector. I believe that in order to conquer modern economic challenges, we must continue to act responsibly in all of our business decisions and monitor our performance closely. Strong leadership (governance) and tight control are fundamental to the success of our business.

### Board leadership and company purpose

As Chair of the board of directors, my role is to lead the board and make sure that each of our directors is fulfilling their role effectively. I will ensure that the board is unified, ably supported by our non-executive directors and offers a greater service to the company as a board than its members could individually.

On 1 January 20X5, I appointed Mary Batter to take over from me as Chief Executive Officer. Relinquishing this position has meant that I could concentrate solely on my role as Chair rather than dividing my time between the two roles.

As Chief Executive Officer, Mary and her team will seek to develop the company's strategy and steer the company through the years ahead.

### Composition, succession and evaluation

During the year an independent consultant conducted a board evaluation. This included individual interviews with each director to gather their opinions on issues ranging from how effective the current board is and risk management to how we can better conduct our relationships with shareholders. To be consistent with best practice, this evaluation will now become an annual occurrence.

As mentioned above Mary Batter joined us this year. She was appointed on the recommendation of the Nomination Committee and completed a tailored induction process.

All directors are offered training throughout the year and are subject to annual re-election.

### Audit, risk and internal control

The board is responsible for risk management and for maintaining a system of internal controls. The risks affecting the company are widespread; however, key risks are firstly the ability to predict customer demand in terms of tastes and fashions and secondly security of inventory. We have an internal audit department which we outsource to an independent firm.

The audit committee reviews the effectiveness of the board's risk management procedures.

| Our board | |
| --- | --- |
| Gary Lewis (Chair) | Chair of Nomination Committee |
| Mary Batter (CEO) | Member of Nomination Committee |
| Katie Escombe (Chief Finance Officer) | Executive Director |
| Bob Part (Non-executive Director) | Chair of the Audit Committee<br>Member of the Remuneration and Nomination Committees |
| Adam Knight (Non-executive Director) | Chair of the Remuneration Committee<br>Member of the Audit and Nomination Committees |

| Our board | |
|---|---|
| Jeremy Flage (Non-executive Director) | Member of the Audit, Remuneration and Nomination Committees |

1. Why should the role of the Chair and the Chief Executive Officer ideally be carried out by two different people?

2. How does Dress You Like Co ensure that board members are properly equipped to do their job?

3. Why do you think the directors are re-elected each year?

4. How is the responsibility for risk management shared in Dress You Like Co?

5. Why does the company have both executive and non-executive directors?

6. Which sub-committees do the non-executive directors form and what are their roles?

**Solution**

## 2.2 Auditors and the UK Corporate Governance Code

In the UK, auditors are required to review whether listed companies have complied with specific provisions in the Code. They must then report this to shareholders in the auditor's report.

There are nine specific provisions auditors must review and report on.

The following is an example of the type of work programme the auditor may use to determine whether the specific provisions have been complied with:

|  | Provision | Yes ✓ | No ✓ |
|---|---|---|---|
| (a) | Is the directors' responsibility for preparing the annual report and accounts explained in the report? | | |
| (b) | Have the directors reviewed and reported on the effectiveness of the risk management and internal control systems | | |
| (c) | Has the board established an audit committee of at least three non-executive directors (or at least two non-executive directors for smaller companies)? | | |
| (d) | Does the audit committee have written terms of reference? | | |
| (e) | Are the terms of reference for the audit committee available/ described in the annual report? | | |
| (f) | Does the audit committee arrange methods for staff to report impropriety in financial reporting? | | |
| (g) | Does the audit committee monitor and review the effectiveness of the internal audit activities? | | |
| (h) | Does the audit committee have primary responsibility for the appointment of the external auditors? | | |
| (i) | Are there procedures in place to ensure that auditor independence is maintained where the external auditor provides non-audit services? | | |

# 3 Audit committees

**KEY TERM**

**Audit committee:** a sub-committee of the board of directors, usually containing a number of independent non-executive directors.

## 3.1 Role and function of the audit committee

The role and function of the audit committee should be set out in written terms of reference.

The diagram below summarises the responsibilities of the audit committee:

## Essential reading

See Chapter 3 of the Essential reading which sets out the detailed provisions relating to the audit committee and internal control effectiveness in the UK Corporate Governance Code.

The Essential reading is available as an Appendix of the digital edition of the Workbook.

## 3.2 Advantages and disadvantages of audit committees

| Advantages | Disadvantages |
| --- | --- |
| **Increased confidence** in the credibility and objectivity of financial reports. | There may be **difficulty selecting** sufficient non-executive directors with the necessary competence in auditing matters for the committee to be really effective. |
| Allows **executive** directors to **devote their attention to management** as the audit committee can specialise in the problems of financial reporting | The establishment of such a **formalised reporting procedure** may **dissuade** the **auditors** from raising matters of judgement and limit them to reporting only on matters of fact. |
| Provides an **impartial body** for the internal auditors to report which increases their independence | **Costs** may be increased. |
| Provides an **independent point of reference** for the external auditors | |

# Chapter summary

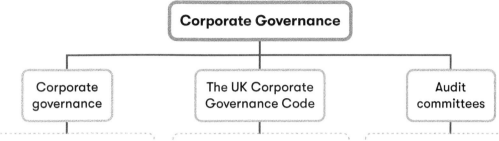

**Corporate Governance**

---

**Corporate governance**

**Definition**

The internal systems by which companies are directed and controlled

**The OECD Principles of Corporate Governance**

- Ensuring the basis of an effective corporate governance framework
- The rights of shareholders and key ownership functions
- The equitable treatment of shareholders
- The role of stakeholders in corporate governance
- Disclosure and transparency
- The responsibility of the board

---

**The UK Corporate Governance Code**

**Structure of the Code**

- UK listed companies
- Board leadership and company purpose:
  - Directors to act with integrity
- Division of responsibilities:
  - Separate Chair and CEO
  - Balanced number of executive – and NEDs
- Composition, succession and evaluation:
  - Rigorous appointment process
  - Annual board evaluation
- Audit, risk and internal control:
  - Board to monitor integrity of financial statements
  - Board to manage risk and oversee internal control framework
- Remuneration:
  - Align to company purpose/values
  - No director to set their own remuneration

**Auditors and the UK Corporate Governance Code**

Auditors must review whether management have complied with specific provisions in the Code

---

**Audit committees**

**Role and function of the audit committee**

- A sub-committee of the board which has at least three independent NEDs including one with recent, relevant financial expertise
- Role:
  - Monitor the integrity of the fs
  - Review company's internal control and risk management systems
  - Monitor and review effectiveness of internal audit
  - Monitor arrangements safeguarding the privacy of whistle blowers
- Re external auditor:
  - Make recommendations re appointment/removal
  - Approve remuneration
  - Monitor independence and objectivity
  - Implement policy on supply of non-audit services

**Advantages and disadvantages**

- Advantages:
  - Increases confidence in financial reports
  - Frees up management time
  - Impartial body for internal auditors
  - Independent point of reference for external auditors
- Disadvantages:
  - Difficulty selecting independent NEDs
  - May dissuade auditors from raising matters of judgement
  - Cost

---

# Knowledge diagnostic

### 1. Corporate governance

Corporate governance is the system by which companies are **directed and controlled**. Good corporate governance is especially important where the owners of a company are not involved in the day-to-day running of the company.

### 2. OECD Principles of Corporate Governance

The **OECD** has developed **Principles of Corporate Governance** as a reference point for national policy makers. These set out the rights of shareholders, the importance of disclosure and transparency and the responsibility of the board of directors.

### 3. UK Corporate Governance Code

The **UK Corporate Governance Code** issued by the Financial Reporting Council requires **listed** companies to include a corporate governance report in the annual report detailing how the company has been directed and controlled in terms of board leadership and company purpose, division of responsibilities, composition, succession and evaluation, audit, risk and internal control and remuneration.

### 4. Comply or explain approach

A company must explain any non-compliance with the specific provisions of the Code in their annual report.

### 5. Audit committee

All listed companies must have an audit committee which should be made up of at least three non-executive directors. Some of the main roles of the audit committee are to **monitor the integrity of the financial statements and the auditor's independence** and also **to review the company's internal controls and risk management systems.**

# Further study guidance

## Question practice

Now try the following from the Further question practice bank (available in the digital edition of the workbook):

- Section A Q1 to Q5 ABC Co
- Section B Q60 Corporate Governance

## Further reading

There are no technical articles on the ACCA website written by members of the AA examining team and other tutors which are relevant to some of the topics covered in this chapter that you should read. However, later on in Chapters 9 and 10, you will find several articles relating to internal control which are linked to this chapter.

## Own research

Identify a UK listed company which interests you and download the company's annual report from their website. Read through the disclosures relating to corporate governance and the audit committee and see if you can identify the principles of the UK Corporate Governance Code.

# Activity answers

### Activity 1: Reviewing corporate governance

1  **Chair and Chief Executive**

The Chair's role is to run/direct the board of directors so that its members can undertake their roles effectively. These duties include ensuring that the board is appropriately balanced (in terms of the numbers of executive and non-executive directors) and that each director is aware of their responsibilities and is equipped to fulfil them.

The Chief Executive Officer's role is to decide on the company's strategy and put procedures in place to achieve these.

These are very different roles and so should ideally be undertaken by two separate people.

Also separating the roles will not allow one person to have too much power.

2  **Board evaluation**

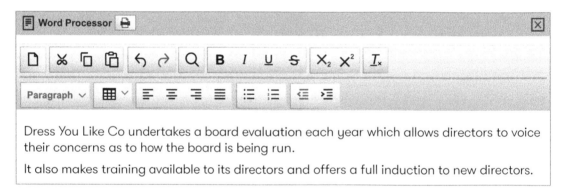

Dress You Like Co undertakes a board evaluation each year which allows directors to voice their concerns as to how the board is being run.

It also makes training available to its directors and offers a full induction to new directors.

3  **Re-election**

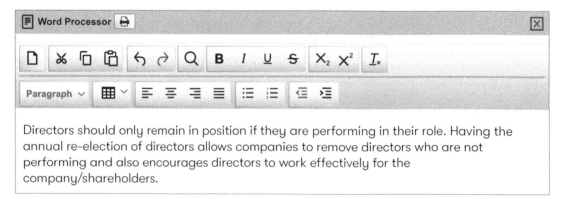

Directors should only remain in position if they are performing in their role. Having the annual re-election of directors allows companies to remove directors who are not performing and also encourages directors to work effectively for the company/shareholders.

4  **Risk management responsibility**

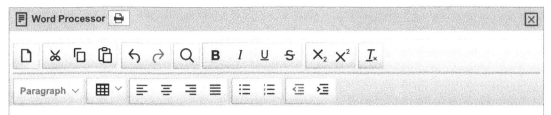

**Board of directors:**

The responsibility for risk management lies with the board of directors. It is the directors' responsibility to assess the risks that the business is exposed to. All businesses are exposed to general risks; however, there are additional, specific risks relevant to each business. Dress You Like Co is a clothing manufacturer and so there are lots of risks inherent in the business – two of these are mentioned in the scenario: changing fashion trends and the security of inventory.

Once the board has identified the key risks to which the business is exposed, it must then implement a system of internal controls (or procedures) to prevent and/or detect these risks occurring.

Internal controls could range from performing continual market research into consumer fashion tastes to installing security cameras in the factory to deter theft of inventory.

The existence of an internal audit function is often cited as a positive form of risk management and internal control.

**Audit committee:**

As well as giving the board of directors the responsibility for risk management, corporate governance principles require a company to establish an audit committee. This should comprise at least three non-executive directors (two non-executive directors for a small company).

The audit committee has a responsibility to review the company's risk management and internal control systems and should include at least one non-executive director with financial knowledge.

The audit committee must also review the effectiveness of the internal audit department where one exists. If there is no internal audit department, then the audit committee should consider annually whether or not there is a need for one.

5   **Executive and non-executive directors**

Executive directors are responsible for the day -to -day running of the company and perform operational and strategic business functions such as entering into contracts, safeguarding company assets and managing people.

Non-executive directors are not involved in the day to day running of the business. Instead they should use their experience and expertise to provide independent advice and objectivity to the board as a whole. They also perform a supervisory role and will review and monitor the executive directors to ensure that they are fulfilling their duties and running the company in the best interests of the shareholders.

In order to improve their independence, non-executive directors should not be reliant on the company for their main source of income. They often work part -time for the company and can have a specialist role within the organisation.

All directors, executive and non-executive, are required to attend as many board meetings as they reasonably can.

Also, there is no legal distinction between executive and non-executive directors; – each has the same responsibilities and rights under law.

Dress You Like Co has three executive and three non-executive directors which makes the board very well balanced.

6 **Non-executive directors and sub-committees**

As well as forming part of the board of directors as a whole, the non-executive directors also sit on the audit committee, remuneration committee and nomination committee. These are sub-committees of the board of directors.

The audit committee is responsible, amongst other things, for reviewing the effectiveness of the board's risk management processes.

The remuneration committee is responsible for making sure that the company offers a performance-related remuneration package which is sufficient to attract and retain quality directors (but not excessive).

The nomination committee is responsible for identifying and approving the appointment of new directors to the board, for example Mary Batter, the new Chief Executive Officer.

Non-executive directors have a very important role to play in each of these sub-committees and their independence and objectivity can improve the quality and relevance of the decisions taken.

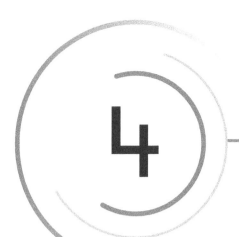

# 4     Internal audit

## Learning objectives

On completion of this chapter, you should be able to:

| Syllabus learning outcomes | Syllabus reference no. |
| --- | --- |
| Discuss the factors to be taken into account when assessing the need for internal audit. | C5 (a) |
| Discuss the elements of best practice in the structure and operations of internal audit. | C5 (b) |
| Compare and contrast the role of external and internal audit. | C5 (c) |
| Discuss the scope of internal audit and the limitations of the internal audit function. | C6 (a) |
| Explain outsourcing and the associated advantages and disadvantages of outsourcing the internal audit function. | C6 (b) |
| Discuss the nature and purpose of internal audit assignments including value for money, IT, financial, regulatory compliance, fraud investigations and customer experience. | C6 (c) |
| Discuss the nature and purpose of operational internal audit assignments. | C6 (d) |
| Discuss the responsibilities of internal and external auditors for the prevention and detection of fraud and error. | B5 (b) |
| Discuss the extent to which external auditors are able to rely on the work of experts, including the work of internal audit. | D6 (b) |

## Business and Exam context

The internal audit function (or department) is a function established by management and those charged with governance of an entity to assist in corporate governance by assessing internal controls and helping in risk management. It can be a department of employees or can be outsourced to expert service providers.

Internal auditing is different from external auditing, although the techniques used by each are very similar. While the techniques used may be similar, the focus and reasons behind the audit are different.

We will consider what the internal audit function is, what they do, and the key differences between the internal and external auditors. It is very important to know these differences as the roles are distinct and you may see questions on their roles and the differences between them in the exam.

The role of the internal auditor is far more varied than that of the external auditor and we will see the various assurance assignments that may be undertaken by internal auditors.

# Chapter overview

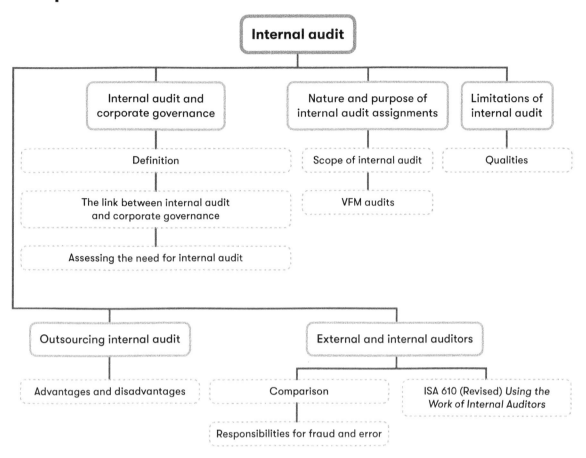

# 1 Internal audit and corporate governance

## 1.1 Definition

In the previous chapter, we saw that corporate governance relates to the internal systems or means by which companies are **directed** and **controlled**.

The UK Corporate Governance Code includes a section on **audit, risk and internal control** and this introduces the requirement for the board to "establish procedures to manage risk, oversee the internal control framework, and determine the nature and extent of the principal risks the company is willing to take in order to achieve its long-term strategic objectives" (FRC *UK Corporate Governance Code:* Principle O).

One way in which this requirement can be satisfied is for the board to create an internal audit function to assess and monitor internal control policies and procedures.

> **Internal audit function:** A function of an entity that performs assurance and consulting activities designed to evaluate and improve the effectiveness of the entity's governance, risk management and internal control processes. (IFAC, 2016(b))

## 1.2 The link between internal audit and corporate governance

There is a relationship between the board, the audit committee and corporate governance as follows:

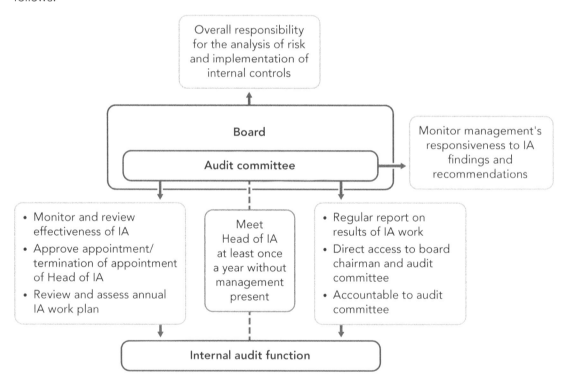

## 1.3 Assessing the need for internal audit

The UK Corporate Governance Code does not require all listed companies to have an internal audit function, although many listed companies do have one.

In the UK, where a listed entity does not have an internal audit function, the Code requires the board to review whether or not the company would benefit from having an internal audit function **on an annual basis**.

Note that many entities which are not listed also have internal audit functions as this helps the board discharge their corporate governance responsibilities.

When considering the need for an internal audit function, the board should consider:

- The cost of setting up an internal audit department versus the predicted benefit
- Predicted savings in external fees where work carried out by consultants will be carried out by the new internal audit department
- The complexity and scale of the organisation's activities and the systems supporting those activities
- Management's perceived need for assessing risk and internal control
- The pressure from external stakeholders to establish an internal audit department
- Whether it is more cost effective or desirable to outsource the work

# 2 Nature and purpose of internal audit assignments

As we have seen, the role of the internal audit function is to provide independent assurance that a company's risk management, governance and internal control processes are operating effectively.

To do this, they will examine and evaluate the quality of risk management, governance and internal control processes across all parts of a company and report this directly and independently to the audit committee.

Unlike external auditors, the internal audit function looks beyond the financial statements and considers wider issues such as the company's reputation, compliance with laws and regulations, growth, its impact on the environment and employee satisfaction levels.

This is because the key to a company's success is often managing such risks effectively.

## 2.1 Scope of internal audit

### PER alert

Being able to explain the overall role and process of internal audit, review and control is identified in the performance objectives booklet as being part of the key knowledge and understanding required for Performance Objective 20 (PO 20). This section will help you to gain that knowledge and understanding, and ultimately help you to achieve PO 20.

There are many types of work that the internal auditor performs. Those listed in the syllabus are:

The assignments internal auditors will carry out will depend on the particular circumstances of the company involved and its objectives.

A brief summary of the examples of internal audit assignments is:

- **IT audits**: Internal auditors may be asked to look specifically at controls over the accounting system, or, instead, over other computer systems that supply data to the accounting system. For example, a travel company's reservation system will usually link to the accounting system and is an important element in determining when the revenue on a flight or holiday is recorded. Or for companies with retail stores, assignments may include reviewing controls over computer systems linking tills to head office.

- **Financial audits and operational audits**: This may include testing controls operating centrally (at head office) or at branches. One example is the testing of controls over inventory counting or cash counting. This would include observation of controls in operation at warehouses or retail stores during attendance at counts.
- **Compliance audits**: Internal auditors may assist with or review compliance with laws and regulations. For example, if a company has an overseas branch, the internal audit department may review compliance with laws/regulations specific to that country (such as filing adequate financial or non-financial returns).
- **Fraud investigations**: Fraud can range from theft of assets to fraudulent financial reporting. Internal audit may be asked to investigate specific instances of suspected fraud or, more generally, to review and test controls to prevent or detect fraud.
- **Customer experience audits**: Internal auditors may be asked to assess the level of customer service. They could do this by phoning in or visiting stores/outlets and pretending to be customers. Alternatively they could review and analyse the results of customer surveys.

Value for money audits are covered in detail below.

### Exam focus point

If you are asked to suggest assignments that the internal audit function could be asked to perform, you must give specific and feasible assignments applicable to that particular company rather than just listing the general categories of assignments. Read the description of the company in the scenario carefully.

### Essential reading

See Chapter 4 of the Essential reading which provides information on the other examples of internal audit work listed in the syllabus.

The Essential reading is available as an Appendix of the digital edition of the Workbook.

## 2.2 Value for money audits

Value for money (VFM) audits may be performed by the internal audit function and try to determine whether the optimal combination of goods/services have been obtained for the lowest level of resources.

VFM audits tend to focus on three areas: economy, efficiency and effectiveness. These are commonly known as 'the three Es':

| **E**conomy | Buying the resources needed at the cheapest cost |
| --- | --- |
| **E**fficiency | Using the resources purchased as wisely as possible |
| **E**ffectiveness | Doing the right things and meeting the organisation's objectives |

Management will need to set objectives for each of the three areas, the objectives will detail the goals/aims they hope to achieve in terms of the company's economic purchase of resources, efficient use of resources and the effectiveness of achieving the company's objectives.

Once the objectives have been set, they will then need to put controls in place to ensure each objective is met.

### Activity 1: VFM objectives and controls

Dress You Like Co is a clothing manufacturer, based in the UK, which has been trading for over ten years. It operates from two sites; a factory where the clothes are made and a head office where the administration is carried out. Completed inventory orders are despatched from both the factory and the head office.

In an effort to reduce costs, Dress You Like Co now imports its material from one sole supplier based overseas.

Dress You Like Co sells its finished products to small independent retailers and also one major supermarket chain. The supermarket chain often requires additional deliveries without much prior notice and so Dress You Like Co has to maintain a high level of inventory should this occur. Credit terms are normally 30 days, but the supermarket is given 60-day credit terms.

**Required**

Suggest TWO objectives Dress You Like Co may set in each of the areas of economy, efficiency and effectiveness and describe the controls you would expect to be put in place to ensure they are achieved.

| | Objective | Control |
|---|---|---|
| Economy | | |
| Efficiency | | |
| Effectiveness | | |

**Solution**

Audits which are concerned **solely** with 'economy' objective are often termed **'best value' audits**.

# 3 Limitations of internal audit

## 3.1 Qualities

If the internal audit function is to be **effective**, then both they and their work need to possess certain qualities.

These qualities include **independence, objectivity** and **due skill and care**:

| Qualities | Description |
|---|---|
| Independence | • Internal auditors should be **independent of the activities they audit**. For example, internal auditors should **not** generally be involved in designing, installing and operating systems. Rather their role is to review the effectiveness of them. |
| | • Internal audit departments should be granted sufficient **status** to achieve independence from the various company functions. |
| | • Internal auditor's reports should be considered appropriately by directors and recommendations acted upon. Internal auditors must have a **reporting line** that is independent of the function they are auditing – highest level of management/audit committee. |
| Objectivity | Objectivity is all about maintaining an independent mental attitude. When they conduct their work, the internal auditors should consider the facts in front of them **without having any pre-conceived ideas**. |
| Due skill and care | • Need for internal auditors to have wide-ranging skills (accounting, auditing, business and management skills) |
| | • Need for a multi-disciplinary internal audit team |
| | • Need for ongoing training |
| | • Adherence to internal audit quality management manuals/procedures |
| | • Work should be planned, documented, supervised and reviewed |

Note that internal auditors are not normally subject to any regulatory authority.

# 4 Outsourcing internal audit

The internal audit function either can be provided internally by employees of the company or may be outsourced externally, for example to an accountancy or consultancy firm.

### Activity 2: Advantages and disadvantages of outsourcing

Explain FOUR advantages and disadvantages to a company of outsourcing the internal audit function.

| Advantages | Disadvantages |
|---|---|
| | |
| | |
| | |
| | |

**Solution**

Note that where the internal audit function is outsourced to the company's external auditor, there may be a **self-review threat** to the auditor's independence (Chapter 5).

# 5 External and internal auditors

## 5.1 Comparison

> **External auditor:**
> Statutory duty to give an **opinion** as to whether the financial statements 'present fairly' the activities of the business. Conducted in accordance with **ISAs**.

> **Internal auditor:**
> **Assist the board** in achieving its corporate objectives

### Activity 3: External and internal auditors

Abbie Jones has recently signed a training contract with Check & Co, a firm of Chartered Certified Accountants, and is working in the firm's audit department. She has been reviewing some of the firm's client audit files in an attempt to gain a better understanding of what an audit is. She has noticed that some clients seem to have an internal audit function whilst others do not.

Abbie is a little confused as to the difference between her role as an external auditor and the role of the internal audit function.

**Required**

You are an audit senior in Check & Co and have been asked to complete the following table for Abbie which distinguishes between the key elements of the roles of the external and internal auditor.

| | External auditor | Internal auditor |
|---|---|---|
| Objectives | | |
| Reports to | | |
| Status | | |
| Qualification | | |

Solution

---

## 5.2 Responsibilities for fraud and error (ISA 240)

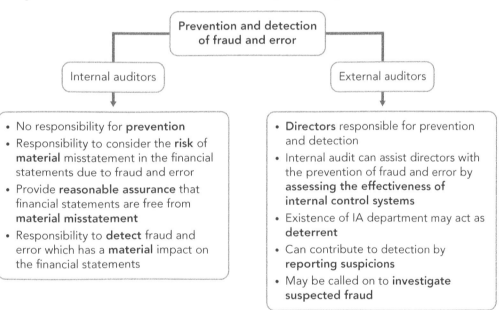

Prevention and detection of fraud and error

**Internal auditors**

- No responsibility for **prevention**
- Responsibility to consider the **risk** of **material** misstatement in the financial statements due to fraud and error
- Provide **reasonable assurance** that financial statements are free from **material misstatement**
- Responsibility to **detect** fraud and error which has a **material** impact on the financial statements

**External auditors**

- **Directors** responsible for prevention and detection
- Internal audit can assist directors with the prevention of fraud and error by **assessing the effectiveness of internal control systems**
- Existence of IA department may act as **deterrent**
- Can contribute to detection by **reporting suspicions**
- May be called on to **investigate suspected fraud**

## 5.3 ISA 610 (Revised) *Using the work of internal auditors*

### 5.3.1 Relying on the work of the internal auditor

It is possible that the objectives of some of the work performed by the internal audit department may overlap with those of the external auditor. In these cases, it **may** be possible for the external auditor to rely on the work of the internal auditor.

*ISA 610 (Revised) Using the Work of Internal Auditors* provides guidance for the external auditor when the external auditor expects to use the work of the internal audit function to modify the nature or timing, or reduce the extent, of audit procedures to be performed directly by the external auditor.

 **BPP**

The objectives of the auditor are:

(a) To determine whether the work of the internal audit function or direct assistance from internal auditors can be used and, if so, in which areas and to what extent

(b) If using the work of the internal audit function, to determine whether that work is appropriate for the purposes of the audit

(c) If using internal auditors to provide direct assistance, to appropriately direct, supervise and review their work. (ISA 610 (Revised): para. 13)

An effective internal audit function may reduce, modify or alter the timing of external audit procedures, but it can **never** eliminate them entirely. Even where the internal audit function is deemed ineffective, it may still be useful to be aware of the conclusions formed. The effectiveness of internal audit will have a great impact on how the external auditors assess the whole control system and the assessment of audit risk.

The external auditor will need to determine whether the work of the internal audit function can be used for the audit and, if so, establish the **nature and extent** of work that can be used.

The following criteria must first be considered by the external auditors when determining **whether the work of the internal audit function can be used**. (ISA 610 (Revised): para. 15)

| Criteria | Considerations |
|---|---|
| The extent to which its **objectivity** is supported by its organisational status, relevant policies and procedures | Consider the **status** of the internal audit function, to whom it **reports**, any **conflicting responsibilities**, any **constraints or restrictions**, whether those charged with governance oversee **employment decisions** regarding internal auditors, whether management acts on **recommendations** made, whether internal auditors are members of professional bodies and obligated to comply with their requirements for objectivity. (ISA 610 (Revised): paras. A5–A7) |
| The level of **competence** of the function | Consider whether the internal audit function is **adequately resourced**, whether internal auditors are **members of relevant professional bodies**, have **adequate technical training and proficiency**, whether there are **established policies for hiring and training**, whether internal auditors possess the **required knowledge** of financial reporting/the applicable financial reporting framework (ISA 610 (Revised): para. A8) |
| Whether the internal audit function applies a **systematic and disciplined approach** (including quality management) | Consider whether internal audit activities include a systematic and disciplined approach to **planning, supervising, reviewing and documenting** assignments, whether the function has **appropriate quality management procedures**, the **existence of audit manuals, work programmes** and **internal audit documentation**. (ISA 610 (Revised): para. A11) |

These can be remembered using the mnemonic 'SODIT':

- Scope of work
- Organisational status
- Due skill and care
- Independent
- Technical competence

When determining the **areas and the extent** to which the work of the internal audit function can be used,

the auditor must consider:

- Th**e nature and scope** of specific work performed or to be performed
- **The relevanc**e of that work to the audit strategy and audit plan·
- **The degree of judgemen**t involved in evaluation of audit evidence gathered by internal auditors

(ISA 610 (Revised): para. 17)

The external auditor is responsible for the audit opinion and must make all significant judgements in the audit. Therefore, the external auditor must plan to use the work of the internal audit function less (and therefore perform more of the work directly) in any areas which might involve significant judgements being made.

These will be areas where:

(a) More judgement is needed in planning/performing procedures and evaluating evidence

(b) The risk of material misstatement is high, including where risks are assessed as significant

(c) The internal audit function's organisational status and relevant policies/procedures are not as robust in supporting the internal audit function's objectivity

(d) The internal audit function is less competent

(ISA 610 (Revised): para. 18)

The external auditor must also take a 'step back' and consider whether the planned extent of internal auditors' involvement will still result in the external auditor being involved enough, in light of the fact that the external auditor is solely responsible for the audit opinion.

### 5.3.2 Direct assistance

It is also possible that the external auditors may use the internal auditors to provide **direct assistance** to them.

Direct assistance refers to the use of the internal auditors to perform audit procedures under the direction, supervision and review of the external auditor. (ISA 610 (revised): para. 14(b))

When deciding whether the internal auditors should provide direct assistance the external auditor should consider:

(a) The amount of **judgement** involved in planning and performing the relevant audit procedures, and in evaluating the audit evidence gathered

(b) The assessed **risk of material misstatement**

(c) The existence and significance of threats to the **objectivity** and the level of **competence** of the internal auditors. (ISA 610 (revised): para. 29)

Where the external auditors have used direct assistance from the internal auditors they should document:

(a) The evaluation of the existence and significance of threats to the objectivity of the internal auditors, and the level of competence of the internal auditors used

(b) The basis for the decision regarding the nature and extent of the work performed by the internal auditors

(c) Who reviewed the work performed and the date and extent of the review

ISA 610 ((Revised): para. 30) **prohibits** the use of internal auditors to provide direct assistance to perform procedures that:

(a)   Involve making **significant judgements** in the audit

(b)   Relate to **higher assessed risks of material misstatement** where more than a limited degree of **judgement** is required: for example, in assessing the valuation of accounts receivable, internal auditors may be assigned to check the accuracy of receivables ageing, but they must not be involved in evaluating the adequacy of the provision for irrecoverable receivables

(c)   Relate to work with which the **internal auditors have been involved**

(d)   Relate to **decisions** the external auditor makes **regarding the internal audit function** and the use of its work or direct assistance

The sole responsibility for the audit opinion rests with the external auditors (ISA 610 (Revised): para. 32). The external auditor must therefore evaluate whether the combination of using the internal auditors to provide direct assistance, **and** the use of the work of the internal audit function, will allow the external auditor to be sufficiently involved in the audit to express an audit opinion.

## Essential reading

See Chapter 13 of the Essential reading which illustrates how the work of an internal auditor may be used when auditing inventory.

The Essential reading is available as an Appendix of the digital edition of the Workbook.

# Chapter summary

## Internal audit

### Internal audit and corporate governance

**Definition**

A function that performs assurance and consulting activities designed to evaluate and improve the effectiveness of the entity's corporate governance, risk management and internal control processes

**The link between internal audit and corporate governance**

- Board
- Audit committee
- Internal audit function

**Assessing the need for internal audit**

- Factors that suggest increased risks or issue with internal controls
- Perceived need
- Stakeholder pressure
- Cost

### Nature and purpose of internal audit assignments

**Scope of internal audit**

- Value for money audits
- IT audits
- Financial audits
- Compliance audits
- Fraud investigations
- Customer experience audits
- Operational audits

**VFM audits**

- Economy
- Efficiency
- Effectiveness

### Limitations of internal audit

**Qualities**

- Independence
- Objectivity
- Due skill and care

### Outsourcing internal audit

**Advantages and disadvantages**

- Advantages:
  - Gain expertise without permanent cost/time commitment
  - Increased independence
  - No requirement to train
  - Can buy in ad hoc services
- Disadvantages:
  - Impact on staff morale if redundancies made
  - Increased time requirement on other staff
  - May lack specific company knowledge
  - Requirement to allow access to data
  - Cost

### External and internal auditors

**Comparison**

- External auditors: Audit opinion, statutory requirement, external to client and qualified
- Internal auditors: Assist the board, regular and ad hoc assignments

**Responsibilities for fraud and error**

- External auditors:
  - No responsibility for prevention
  - Responsible for detecting fraud that has a material impact on fs
- Internal auditors:
  - Directors responsible for prevention and detection
  - Existence of IA may act as a deterrent
  - Assess effectiveness of internal controls
  - Fraud investigations

**ISA 610 (Revised) *Using the Work of Internal Auditors***

- External auditors may be able to rely on work of internal auditor:
  - Scope of work
  - Organisational status
  - Due skill and care
  - Independent
  - Technical competence
- Direct assistance: Where external auditor requests than internal auditor performs specific procedures under their direction, supervision and review
- Consider:
  - Judgement
  - Risk of material misstatement
  - Objectivity and competence of IA
  - Auditor's opinion = external auditor's responsibility

# Knowledge diagnostic

### 1. Internal audit

Having an internal audit function is one way in which the board of directors can **demonstrate good corporate governance**. The internal audit function should report regularly to the audit committee and the audit committee should review and assess the internal audit function's work plan.

### 2. Value for money (VFM) audits

The role of the internal audit function is extremely wide and varied. **VFM audits** assess whether the business has obtained the best goods/services for the lowest level of resources. They focus on **economy**, **efficiency** and **effectiveness**.

### 3. Other internal audit assignments

Other internal audit function assignments include **IT audits, financial audits, audits to verify regulatory compliance, fraud investigations, customer experience audits** and **operational audits**.

### 4. Effective internal audit

For the work of the internal audit function to be effective, internal auditors must be **independent** and **objective** and carry out their work with **due skill and care**.

### 5. Outsourcing

An entity may **outsource** its internal audit function to accountancy or consultancy firms.

### 6. Roles of external and internal auditors

The role of the **external auditor** is clearly defined in **statute**; the role of the **internal audit function** is decided by the **management** of a specific company.

# Further study guidance

## Question practice

Now try the following from the Further question practice bank [available in the digital edition of the Workbook]:

- Section A Q20, Q21, Q24 and Q44
- Section B Q57 Objectives, characteristics and responsibilities
- Section B Q63 ZX

## Further reading

There are technical articles on the ACCA website written by members of the AA examining team and other tutors which are relevant to some of the topics covered in this chapter that you should read:

Technical articles:

- Using the work of internal auditors (https://www.accaglobal.com/gb/en/student/exam-support-resources/fundamentals-exams-study-resources/f8/technical-articles/internal-auditors.html)

## Own research

If you are working, does your company have an internal audit function? If so, find out a bit more about the types of assignments they undertake. Do you think the internal audit function helps the board run your company more effectively?

# Activity answers

### Activity 1: VFM objectives and controls

| Objective | Control |
|---|---|
| **Economy** | |
| To ensure that material is purchased at the best possible price for the quality required | The prices from the overseas supplier should be checked regularly against those offered by other suppliers. Where alternative suppliers offer better value for money, these suppliers should be used or prices renegotiated with the overseas supplier.<br><br>A list of preferred suppliers, who have been vetted for price and quality, should be established and orders only placed with these suppliers.<br><br>Establish a tender process whereby suppliers are invited to quote for the supply of materials. This may take place on a season by season or six-monthly basis. |
| To ensure that transportation and delivery costs are minimised whilst ensuring goods are received on a timely basis | Identify a list of companies which import goods from the same overseas location and invite them to tender for the delivery contract.<br><br>Regularly review the price paid under the tender to ensure it is competitive against other companies. |
| To ensure that the accommodation costs of the factory and head office are minimised | If premises are owned establish an ongoing schedule of maintenance for the property to avoid unexpected repair costs.<br><br>Establish a capital expenditure budget to ensure monies are not wasted continually repairing machines which should be replaced. |
| **Efficiency** | |
| To ensure that the clothes manufacturing process is as efficient as possible and minimises waste | The factory machines should be serviced according to a rolling schedule of maintenance in order for them to work efficiently. |
| To ensure that machine down time due to changing the machine set up for different clothing items is minimised | Orders for different clothing items should be collated and scheduled into a weekly plan of work in order to minimise the requirement to set up machines to manufacture different clothing items. |
| **Effectiveness** | |
| To ensure that all additional deliveries ordered by the supermarket are completed within the required timescales | A record should be maintained of the principal inventory lines ordered by the supermarket and a buffer of inventory for these items maintained. The level of this buffer should be reviewed on a fortnightly/monthly basis. |
| To minimise the level of inventory which becomes obsolete/un-saleable due to changing seasons/fashions | A fortnightly/monthly count of inventory held should be conducted and compared to the schedule of work planned for the next fortnight/month to ensure that only sufficient quantities of inventory are manufactured to supply orders and maintain the required buffer. |

 BPP

| Objective | Control |
|---|---|
| To monitor the company's cash flow to ensure that the company does not suffer from short-term cash flow problems given the 60-day terms given to the supermarket | Monthly cash flow forecasts should be produced by management to monitor when cash is due to be received from all customers and when cash needs to be paid out to suppliers and employees.<br><br>Establish an overdraft facility with the company's bank to cover short-term deficits in cash flow.<br><br>Implement strong credit control procedures whereby customers are contacted as soon as their account becomes overdue. Send regular customer statements to all customers and letters to those with overdue accounts. |

Note. Only **two** points were required under each heading.

### Activity 2: Advantages and disadvantages of outsourcing

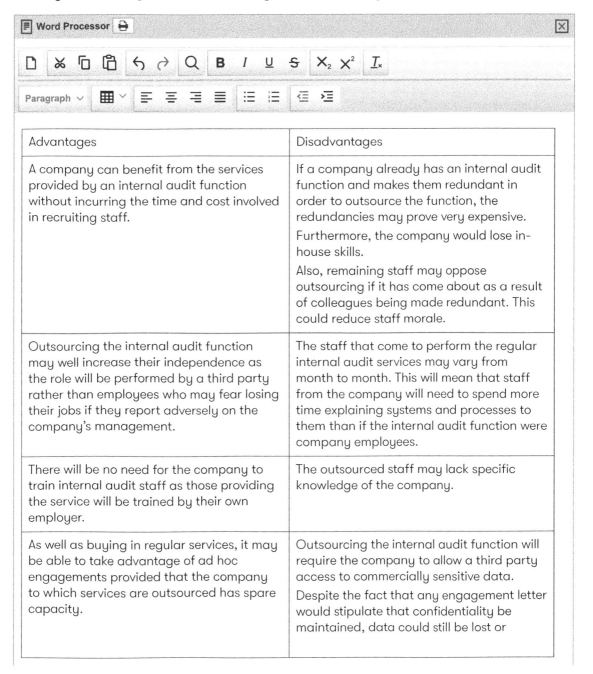

| Advantages | Disadvantages |
|---|---|
| A company can benefit from the services provided by an internal audit function without incurring the time and cost involved in recruiting staff. | If a company already has an internal audit function and makes them redundant in order to outsource the function, the redundancies may prove very expensive.<br><br>Furthermore, the company would lose in-house skills.<br><br>Also, remaining staff may oppose outsourcing if it has come about as a result of colleagues being made redundant. This could reduce staff morale. |
| Outsourcing the internal audit function may well increase their independence as the role will be performed by a third party rather than employees who may fear losing their jobs if they report adversely on the company's management. | The staff that come to perform the regular internal audit services may vary from month to month. This will mean that staff from the company will need to spend more time explaining systems and processes to them than if the internal audit function were company employees. |
| There will be no need for the company to train internal audit staff as those providing the service will be trained by their own employer. | The outsourced staff may lack specific knowledge of the company. |
| As well as buying in regular services, it may be able to take advantage of ad hoc engagements provided that the company to which services are outsourced has spare capacity. | Outsourcing the internal audit function will require the company to allow a third party access to commercially sensitive data.<br><br>Despite the fact that any engagement letter would stipulate that confidentiality be maintained, data could still be lost or |

| Advantages | Disadvantages |
|---|---|
|  | disclosed. |
| Internal auditors supplied by a bespoke outsourcing company are likely to possess relevant accounting and auditing skills which will increase the reliability of the internal auditors' work. | The cost of outsourcing the internal audit function may well increase over time and become more expensive than employing your own staff. |

**Tutorial note.** In the Audit and Assurance CBE environment, when you come across a requirement that lends itself to a tabular answer you will usually find that a template table is provided for you in the word processor area with appropriate headers (advantages and disadvantages in this case). You just need to fill in the table putting the relevant answers in the relevant column. We have shown the answer above in a format similar to that you will see on the ACCA CBE Platform.

Note. Only **four** advantages and disadvantages were required.

## Activity 3: External and internal auditors

| | **External auditor** | **Internal auditor** |
|---|---|---|
| **Objectives** | Give an opinion as to whether:<br><br>• The financial statements 'present fairly' the activities of the business; and<br><br>• Proper accounting records have been kept. | Varied and wide ranging<br><br>Determined by management/board but may include:<br><br>• Review of accounting/internal control systems<br><br>• Examination of financial/operating information<br><br>• Value for money (VFM) reviews<br><br>• Review of implementation of corporate policies, laws and regulations<br><br>• Special investigations, eg suspected fraud<br><br>• Procurement, marketing, treasury and HR reviews |
| **Reports to** | Shareholders of the company | Board of directors/audit committee |
| **Status** | Independent of/external to company they are auditing | Company employee/outsourced to a third party |
| **Qualification** | Audit partner will be qualified and hold a practising certificate as a registered auditor<br><br>Not all team members will be qualified | No formal qualifications required |

# Skills checkpoint 1

## How to approach your AA exam

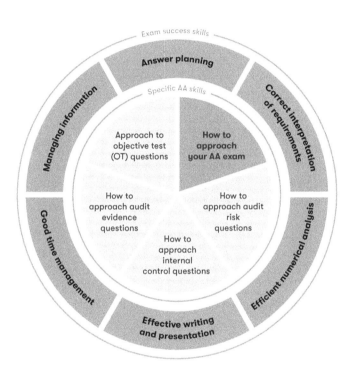

## Introduction

You can answer your AA exam in whatever order you prefer. It is important that you adopt a strategy that works best for you. We would suggest that you decide on your preferred approach and practice it by doing a timed mock exam before your real exam. Remember your AA exam will be structured as follows:

**Section A** – Three **OT case questions** worth 10 marks each. Each case question will consist of five individual OT questions worth two marks each. All syllabus areas can be tested in Section A, however each individual case does however tend to focus on a particular syllabus area, for example: corporate governance and internal audit, audit finalisation and the auditor's report, audit risk, audit evidence or internal control.

**Section B** – Section B will contain one, 30-mark question and two, 20-mark questions which will be **scenario based**. Section B questions will mainly focus on the following syllabus areas, but some marks can be drawn from any other area of the syllabus:

*   Planning and risk assessment (syllabus area B)
*   Internal control (syllabus area C)
*   Audit evidence (syllabus area D)

This Skills Checkpoint will provide you with one suggested approach for tackling your AA exam. Good luck!

# Skills Checkpoint 1: How to approach your AA exam

## AA Skill: How to approach your AA exam

We would suggest the following approach for tackling your AA exam. It is important that you adopt an approach that works best for you and practice it by completing several mock exams to time prior to your real exam.

### Complete section A first - allocated time 54 minutes

- You will have 18 mins of exam time to allocate to each of the three OT case questions in Section A. Tackle any easier OT questions first. Do not leave any questions unanswered. Even if you are unsure, make a reasoned guess. Skills Checkpoint 5 covers how to approach OT questions in more detail.

- Each individual case tends to focus on a specific syllabus area. Start with the OT case question you feel most confident with.

- The majority of the questions will be discursive; some will be knowledge based whilst others will require application to the scenario.

- If you do not feel that you need the full 54 minutes to complete Section A, you can carry this time forward to your Section B questions which tend to be more time pressured. With practice, it may be possible for you to complete Section A approximately five minutes quicker than the allocated time of 54 minutes.

### Finally, complete section B – allocated time 126 minutes

- Section B will contain one, 30-mark question and two, 20-mark questions which will be scenario based. Allocate 54 minutes to the 30-mark question and 36 minutes to each of the 20-mark questions (remembering to split your time between each of the sub requirements) but you may have a few minutes of extra time if you have completed Section A of the exam in less than the allotted time.

- Skills Checkpoints 2, 3 and 4 look specifically at the techniques you should use for audit risk, internal control and audit evidence questions. Whilst these areas may not comprise an entire question, they will usually be worth a good proportion of marks and so you should make sure you are confident using the techniques covered in these skills checkpoints

**Set some time aside to practice this approach through the completion of at least two mock exams to time.**

# 5

# Professional ethics and quality management procedures

## Learning objectives

On completion of this chapter, you should be able to:

| Syllabus learning outcomes | Syllabus reference no. |
|---|---|
| Define and apply the fundamental principles of professional ethics of integrity, objectivity, professional competence and due care, confidentiality and professional behaviour. | A4 (a) |
| Define and apply the conceptual framework, including the threats to the fundamental principles of self-interest, self-review, advocacy, familiarity and intimidation. | A4 (b) |
| Discuss the safeguards to offset the threats to the fundamental principles. | A4 (c) |
| Describe the auditor's responsibility with regard to auditor independence, conflicts of interest and confidentiality. | A4 (d) |
| Discuss the requirements of professional ethics and ISAs in relation to the acceptance/ continuance of audit engagements. | B1 (a) |
| Explain the preconditions for an audit. | B1 (b) |
| Explain the process by which an auditor obtains an audit engagement. | B1 (c) |
| Discuss the importance and purpose of engagement letters and their contents. | B1 (d) |
| Explain the overall objectives and importance of quality management procedures in conducting an audit. | B1 (e) |
| Explain the quality management procedures that should be in place over engagement resources, engagement performance, monitoring and remediation and compliance with ethical requirements. | B1 (f) |
| Evaluate quality management deficiencies and provide recommendations to allow compliance with quality management requirements. | B1 (g) |

# Business and Exam context

This chapter focuses on the ethical and professional behaviour that is expected of you as an assurance provider. It is an important syllabus area which you need to be comfortable with, as ethical matters could arise in every type of exam question. You must be able to apply the ACCA's guidance on ethical matters to any given situation, but remember that common sense is usually a good guide. This guidance comes from the ACCA's *Code of Ethics and Conduct*, which incorporates the IESBA *International Code of Ethics for Professional Accountants*.

We need ethics in our role as auditors because stakeholders place reliance on the work that we do and we are in a position of trust, so we want to make sure that we are, amongst other things, honest and objective; and that we don't do anything which could abuse this trust.

It is also necessary that we are independent of the company that we are auditing, as we seek to give confidence to users of the financial statements that we review. The key with independence is that not only is it necessary to be independent of mind, but also independent in appearance – that is, we are perceived to be truly independent by the people around us.

We need to fully understand the specific threats or actions in relation to the ethical principles that are expected of us, and any safeguards that we can put in place to prevent these threats from becoming serious issues. We will consider the various situations that may impair our ability to remain objective or independent, as well as look at the appropriate course of action to respond to those situations.

This chapter also considers confidentiality, one of the ethical principles, in more detail. We have access to a company's sensitive information, and are required to keep that information confidential. Generally speaking, we should always maintain confidentiality. However, sometimes, we are put in a position where we may have to disclose information, for example for legal reasons, so we will also consider situations where disclosure is allowed.

The final part of this chapter covers the business and ethical considerations about how auditors obtain work and the factors they need to think about before accepting an audit engagement. These factors include issues such as their assessment of management's integrity, and whether they have enough time and staff to take on the audit work.

# Chapter overview

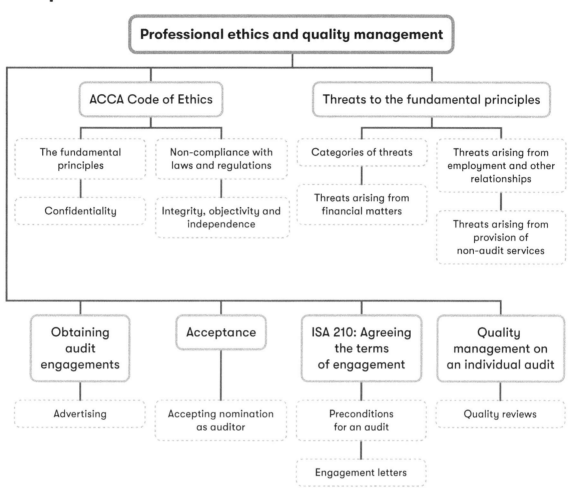

# 1 ACCA Code of Ethics and Conduct

The ACCA *Code of Ethics and Conduct* (the Code) is found in the ACCA Rulebook. The ACCA have adopted the Code of Ethics for Professional Accountants, which is issued by the International Ethics Standards Board for Accountants (IESBA).

The Code applies to all members, affiliates and students of the ACCA. These individuals are referred to in the Code as 'professional accountants'. (ACCA Code: para.7)

> ## PER alert
>
> One of the PER performance objectives is to demonstrate the application of professional ethics, values and judgements (objective 1). Applying the knowledge you gain from this chapter will help you to achieve that objective.

## 1.1 The fundamental principles

The Code sets out five fundamental principles that professional accountants should comply with:

These are explained below:

| Fundamental principle | Definition |
|---|---|
| Integrity | To be straightforward and honest in all professional and business relationships. (ACCA Code: s.110.1 A1(a)) |
| Objectivity | Not to compromise professional or business judgements because of bias, conflict of interest or undue influence of others. (ACCA Code: s.110.1 A1(b)) |
| Professional competence and due care | To attain and maintain professional knowledge and skill at the level required to ensure that a client or employing organisation receives competent professional service, based on current technical and professional standards and relevant legislation. To act diligently and in accordance with applicable technical and professional standards. (ACCA Code: s.110.1 A1(c)) |
| Confidentiality | To respect the confidentiality of information acquired as a result of professional and |

| Fundamental principle | Definition |
|---|---|
| | business relationships.<br>(ACCA Code: s.110.1 A1(d)) |
| Professional behaviour | To comply with relevant laws and regulations and avoid any conduct that the professional accountant knows, or should know, might discredit the profession.<br>(ACCA Code: s.110.1 A1(e)) |

## 1.2 Confidentiality

Members acquiring information in the course of their professional work **should not disclose** any such information to third parties **without first obtaining permission** from their clients.

Likewise, students and affiliates must treat any information given by members in the strictest confidence.

There are, however, certain circumstances where members **may disclose information to third parties without first obtaining permission** (ACCA Code: s.114.1 A1).

**Obligatory disclosure (disclosure required by law)**

- Production of documents or other evidence in the course of **legal proceedings**
- Disclosure to public authorities of **infringements of law** (eg terrorism, money laundering)

**Voluntary disclosure (professional duty/right to disclose)**

- To comply with the quality review of ACCA or another professional body
- To respond to an inquiry/ investigation by ACCA/other professional or regulatory body
- To **protect the interests of a professional accountant** in legal proceedings
- To comply with technical/ professional standards
- Where disclosure is in the **public interest**

## 1.3 Non-compliance with laws and regulations ('NOCLAR')

ISA 250 (Revised) *Consideration of Laws and Regulations in an Audit of Financial Statements* provides guidance for auditors in the area of suspected or identified instances of non-compliance with laws and regulations.

**Non-compliance with laws and regulations (NOCLAR):** acts of omission or commission, intentional or unintentional, committed by the entity, or by those charged with governance, by management or by other individuals working for or under the direction of the entity, which are contrary to the prevailing laws or regulations. Non-compliance does not include personal misconduct unrelated to the business activities of the entity. (ISA 250 (Revised): para. 12)

The **objectives** of the auditor when responding to NOCLAR are:

(a) To comply with the fundamental principles of integrity and professional behaviour;

(b) By alerting management or, where appropriate, those charged with governance of the client, to seek to:

    (i) Enable them to rectify, remediate or mitigate the consequences of the identified or suspected non-compliance; or

    (ii) Deter the commission of the non-compliance where it has not yet occurred; and

(c) To take such further action as appropriate in the public interest.    (ACCA Code: s.260.4)

Examples of laws and regulations covered by the Code include the following:

(a) Fraud, corruption and bribery

(b) Money laundering, terrorist financing and proceeds of crime

(c) Securities markets and trading

(d) Banking and other financial products and services

(e) Data protection

(f) Tax and pension liabilities and payments

(g) Environmental protection

(h) Public health and safety                                    (ACCA Code: s.260.5 A2)

**Procedures** suggested for the auditor when considering NOCLAR are to:

(a) Obtain an understanding of the NOCLAR matter.

(b) Discuss with an appropriate level of management (at least one above those parties involved or potentially involved).

(c) Advise the client to rectify the consequences, deter any future instances or disclose to whoever is considered in a position to need to know.

(d) Consider the client's response and whether it indicates any concerns over their integrity.

(e) Consider whether disclosure to an appropriate authority should be made (if applicable laws and regulations allow) or if withdrawal from the engagement may be necessary.

(f) Document all decisions, discussions and judgements.        (ACCA Code: s.260.12–260.27)

## 1.4 Integrity, objectivity and independence

Professional accountants who provide assurance services are required to be **independent** of the assurance client.

Independence has two aspects to it:

(a) Independence of mind; and

(b) Independence in appearance.

Much of the guidance in relation to ethical guidance applies to all company audits. However, there are sometimes **additional requirements** relating purely to **public interest entities**.

Public interest entities are defined as:

(a) All listed entities

(b) Entities that are of significant public interest because of their business, size or number of employees or because they have a wide range of stakeholders.

Examples include banks, insurance companies and pension firms.

# 2 Threats to the fundamental principles

## 2.1 Categories of threats

There are many circumstances, relationships and situations that could threaten the professional accountant's ability to satisfy the fundamental principles.

These threats fall into one or more of the following five categories:

These are explained below:

| Threat | Description |
|---|---|
| Self-interest threat | The risk that a financial or other interest in a client will inappropriately influence the professional accountant's judgement or behaviour.<br><br>For example, owning shares in an audit client or receiving gifts from an audit client. |
| Self-review threat | This arises where a professional accountant from the audit firm performs work for the client and this work must later be reviewed by the same person, or another professional accountant from the same firm, in order to arrive at a judgement on the subject matter. |
| Advocacy threat | The risk that a professional accountant promotes a client's position to the point that the professional accountant's objectivity is compromised.<br><br>For example, acting as an advocate on behalf of an assurance client in litigation or disputes, or promoting shares in a listed audit client. |
| Familiarity threat | The risk that due to a long or close relationship with a client, the professional accountant could be too sympathetic to their interests or too accepting of their work.<br><br>For example, if a firm has audited the same client for several years they may not question the information presented by the client as closely as in the initial years. |
| Intimidation threat | The risk that the professional accountant is deterred from acting objectively because of actual or perceived pressures, including attempts to exercise undue influence over the professional accountant.<br><br>For example, being pressured to reduce inappropriately the extent of work performed in order to reduce the fees charged. |

Where the above threats exist, appropriate **safeguards** must be put in place to eliminate or reduce them to an acceptable level.

 Activity 1: Explaining ethical threats

You are an audit manager of Check and Co. The following situations have arisen with different audit clients of your firm.

(1) In an initial meeting with the finance director of Weadon Co, an audit client, you learn that the entire audit team will be invited to the company's annual summer social event, a weekend at an exclusive spa hotel.

(2) Mr Walker has been the engagement partner for a client, Stewards Co, for nine years. He has excellent knowledge of the client and knows all of the directors of Stewards Co very well. Stewards Co is considered to be a public interest entity.

**Required**

Explain the ethical threats which may affect the independence of Check and Co in respect of each of the client audits. For each threat, explain how it may be reduced.

| Threat | Safeguards |
| --- | --- |
|  |  |

**Solution**

---

## Activity 2: Threats and safeguards

The following scenario relates to questions 1–3.

You are an audit manager of Check and Co, which has annual revenue in the region of $2,400,000. You have recently been assigned the audit of Emerald Co (Emerald), a public interest entity.

Mrs Sayer, a partner in Check and Co, is the Audit Engagement Partner for Emerald. Her daughter, Holly, joined Emerald six months ago and is working as an assistant to the receivables ledger clerk whilst she studies for her first set of accountancy exams.

Mrs Sayer has informed you that Emerald is one of your firm's most important clients as it generates fees of approximately $480,000 for Check and Co. Unfortunately, Emerald has fallen behind on its payments to Check and Co and overdue fees have built up, including the invoices issued during the last six months.

In an initial meeting with the Finance Director of Emerald, you learn that due to time pressure and staff shortages in the accounts department, the finance director has requested assistance from your firm with year-end procedures, including the preparation of the annual financial statements for the company.

1   From a review of the information above, your audit assistant has highlighted some of the potential risks to independence in respect of the audit of Emerald.

   (1)   Audit engagement partner's daughter works for Emerald.

   (2)   Audit fee is significant to Check and Co.

   (3)   Overdue fees exist.

   (4)   Firm has been asked to help provide accountancy services.

**Required**

For each of the above risks, place a tick in the box which correctly identifies the appropriate threat to independence. You may tick more than one box for each threat.

|  | Intimidation | Self-interest | Self-review |
|---|---|---|---|
| Risk (1) |  |  |  |
| Risk (2) |  |  |  |
| Risk (3) |  |  |  |
| Risk (4) |  |  |  |

2   In relation to the audit fee being significant to Check and Co:

**Required**

Which of the following safeguards should be implemented in order to comply with ACCA's Code of Ethics and Conduct?

O   Use one team to conduct the year-end audit and a separate team to perform any non-audit work.

O   Appoint a second partner from Check and Co to perform an independent partner review on the audit of Emerald that should focus on areas of judgement and estimates.

O   Discuss the situation with Emerald's audit committee and consider resigning from some services.

O   Rotate the audit engagement partner every seven years.

3   In relation to Check and Co providing accountancy services to Emerald:

**Required**

Which of the following safeguards should be implemented in order to comply with ACCA's Code of Ethics and Conduct?

O   The directors of Emerald must provide all source data and approve all journal entries.

O   Use one team to conduct the year-end audit and a separate team to provide accountancy services.

O   Appoint a second partner from Check and Co to perform an independent partner review on the audit of Emerald, which should focus on areas of judgement and estimates.

O　Check and Co should decline the offer to prepare the financial statements.

Solution

_____

## 2.2　Threats arising from financial matters

### 2.2.1　Financial interests

| Threats | Safeguards |
| --- | --- |
| Financial interests might create a **self-interest threat.** (ACCA Code: s.510.2) | |
| Examples include ownership of shares in a client by:<br><br>• The firm<br><br>• An audit team member<br><br>• An immediate family member of the audit team member<br>A self-interest threat arises as the firm, audit team member (or their immediate family) would benefit personally if the client's financial statements exceed market expectations. | • Disposal of shares (only option if firm holds shares)<br><br>• Remove individual from audit team<br><br>• Inform audit committee<br><br>• Review by an appropriate reviewer (eg an independent partner) |

### 2.2.2　Loans and guarantees

| Threats | Safeguards |
| --- | --- |
| Loans and guarantees might create a **self-interest threat**. (ACCA Code: s.511.2) | |
| Loans/guarantees with an audit client that is a bank (ACCA Code: s.R511.5):<br><br>• Loans or guarantees to the firm<br>　- No threat if immaterial to audit client or firm and on normal terms<br>　- If material to audit client or firm, apply safeguards<br>• Loans to an audit team member or their immediate family<br>　- Not a threat to independence if on normal commercial terms | Review of work performed by professional accountant from outside the firm |

| Threats | Safeguards |
|---|---|
| | |
| Loans/guarantees with an audit client that is not a bank (ACCA Code: s.R511.4):<br><br>• Loans or guarantees to/from the firm, audit team member or their immediate family | **No safeguard** can reduce the threat unless the loan is immaterial to client and firm/team member. |

### 2.2.3 Fees

| Threats | Safeguards |
|---|---|
| Fees might create a **self-interest or intimidation threat.** *(ACCA Code: s.410.2)* | |
| (i) *Relative size*<br>When the total fees generated from an audit client represent a large proportion of the total fees of that firm, the dependence on that client and concern about losing the client create a **self-interest or intimidation threat.** (ACCA Code: s.410.3 A1) | • Increase audit firm's client base to reduce dependence on the client<br>• Discuss with audit committee<br>• Resign from some services<br>• External quality review<br>• Consult ACCA or another professional accountant on any key audit areas requiring judgement |
| If the audit client is a **public interest entity,** then there are additional ethical requirements.<br>If the total fees from the client represent **more than 15%** of the total fees received by the firm for **two consecutive years,** then there is likely to be undue dependence on the client and the firm should put safeguards in place. (ACCA Code: s.R410.4) | • Disclose to those charged with governance<br>• Pre-issuance review on second year's financial statements prior to the auditor's opinion being issued<br>• Post-issuance review on second year's financial statements after the auditor's opinion has been issued |
| (ii) *Overdue fees*<br>When a significant part of fees is not paid before the audit report for the following year is issued, this might create a **self-interest threat.** (ACCA Code: s. 410.7 A1)<br>The firm may issue a favourable opinion rather than possibly lose the amounts owed. | • Obtain partial payment of overdue fees<br>• Discuss with audit committee<br>• Consider resignation if overdue fees not paid |
| (iii) *Contingent fees*<br>These are fees calculated on a predetermined basis relating to the outcome of a transaction or the result of the services performed. (ACCA Code: s.410.9 A1)<br>This creates a **self-interest threat.** | • No safeguards acceptable – contingent fees are **not allowed** for audit services, however contingent fees may be permitted for non-assurance work provided that adequate safeguards are implemented |

### 2.2.4 Gifts and hospitality

| Threat | Safeguards |
|---|---|
| Accepting gifts and hospitality from an audit client might create a **self-interest, familiarity or intimidation threat.** (ACCA Code: s.420.2) | |

| Threat | Safeguards |
|---|---|
| Acceptance of gifts from a client may create a self-interest threat because the firm/individual may feel obliged to give a favourable opinion. Acceptance of gifts may also be perceived as a bribe.<br><br>Hospitality from clients may give rise to a familiarity threat. | • Gifts and hospitality should not be accepted unless the value is **trivial** and **inconsequential**. |

## 2.3 Threats arising from employment and other relationships

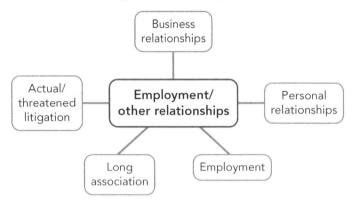

### 2.3.1 Business relationships

| Threats | Safeguards |
|---|---|
| A close business relationship with an audit client or its management might create a **self-interest or intimidation threat**. (*ACCA Code: s.520.2*) | |
| Examples include:<br><br>• Holding an interest in a joint venture with a client<br><br>• Arrangements to combine one or more services or products of the firm with one or more services or products of the client and to market the package with reference to both parties<br><br>• Distribution of a client's products/services | • Disposal of firm's interests unless clearly **insignificant**<br><br>• Removal of any individual audit team member who has an interest from the audit team |

### 2.3.2 Personal relationships

| Threats | Safeguards |
|---|---|
| Family or personal relationships with client personnel might create a **self-interest, familiarity or intimidation threat**. (ACCA Code: s.521.2) | |
| (i) *Immediate family of an audit team member*<br>**Immediate family** is defined as a **spouse (or equivalent) or dependent**.<br>A self-interest, familiarity or intimidation threat is created when an immediate family member of an audit team member is an employee is a **position to exert significant** | • Restructure the audit team's responsibilities so that the audit team member does not deal with matters that are within the responsibility of the immediate family member.<br><br>• Note that this is required where any member of the individual's **immediate** |

| Threats | Safeguards |
|---|---|
| **influence over the client's financial position, financial performance or cash flows.** (ACCA Code: s.521.4 A1)<br><br>The level of the threat depends on:<br><br>• The position held by the immediate family member<br>• The role of the audit team member | family:<br><br>– Is a director/officer of the audit client<br><br>– Is an employee in a position to exert significant influence over the preparation of the client's accounting records or the financial statements on which the firm will express an opinion; or<br><br>– Was in such a position during any period covered by the engagement or the financial statements (ACCA Code: s.R521.5) |
| (ii) Close family<br>**Close family** is defined as a **parent, child or sibling who is not an immediate family member**.<br>A self-interest, familiarity or intimidation threat is created when a close family member of an audit team member is:<br><br>• A director/officer of the audit client<br>• An employee in a position to exert significant influence over the preparation of the client's accounting records or the financial statements on which the firm will express an opinion (ACCA Code: s.521.6 A1)<br>Note 'other close relationships of an audit team member' are addressed in the same way as close family relationships. | • Restructure the audit team's responsibilities so that the audit team member does not deal with matters that are within the responsibility of the close family member.<br><br>• Remove the individual from the audit team |
| (iii) Relationships of partners and employees of the firm<br>Partners and employees of the firm shall consult in accordance with firm policies and procedures if they are aware of a personal or family relationship between:<br><br>• A partner or employee of the firm who is **not** an audit team member **and**<br>• A director/officer of the audit client and an employee of the audit client in a position to exert significant influence over the preparation of the client's accounting records or the financial statements on which the firm will express an opinion | • Structure the partner's/employee's responsibilities to reduce potential influence over the audit engagement<br><br>• Review of audit work by an appropriate reviewer |

### 2.3.3 Employment

| Threats | Safeguards |
|---|---|
| Where a partner or employee of the firm leaves to join an audit client, this might create | • Consider modification of audit plan |

**BPP**

| Threats | Safeguards |
|---|---|
| a **self-interest, familiarity or intimidation threat**. (ACCA Code: s.524.2) | • Change members of audit team<br><br>• Review by an appropriate reviewer<br><br>• Quality review<br><br>• For **public interest entities**, if an individual who was a **key audit partner** joins an audit client as a **director/officer** or an employee able to **exert significant influence** over the preparation of the client's accounting records or the financial statements on which the firm will express an opinion, **independence is compromised** unless, subsequent to the individual ceasing to be a key audit partner:<br><br>  - The audit client has issued audited financial statements covering a period of **not less than 12 months**; and<br><br>  - The individual was not an audit team member with respect to the audit of those financial statements (ACCA Code: s.R524.6) |
| Where a director/officer or employee of the audit client leaves the audit client to join the firm, a **self-interest, self-review or familiarity threat** might be created. (ACCA Code: s.522.2) | • Individual should not be assigned to the audit team if the work they performed whilst employed by the client is to be evaluated in the current period as part of the current audit engagement. |

### 2.3.4 Long association

| Threats | Safeguards | |
|---|---|---|
| When an individual is involved on an audit engagement over a long period of time, **familiarity** and **self-interest threats** might be created. (ACCA Code: s.540.2) | • Independent partner review<br>• Independent quality review<br>• Rotate senior staff | |
| For **public interest entities**, the Code sets outs a compulsory cooling-off period (ACCA Code: s.R540.11-13). These are as follows: | **Rotate after** | **Cooling-off period** |
| Engagement partner | Seven years | Five years |
| Individual responsible for the engagement quality review | Seven years | Three years |
| Key audit partner | Seven years | Two years |

A key audit partner is an audit partner on the engagement team who is responsible for key decision or judgements on significant matter with respect to the audit of the financial statements on which the firm will express an opinion other than as the engagement partner or the individual responsible for the engagement quality review.

### 2.3.5 Actual and threatened litigation

| Threat | Safeguards |
|---|---|
| When litigation with an audit client occurs, or appears likely, **self-interest and intimidation threats** are created. (ACCA Code: s.430.2) | • Disclose to the audit committee<br><br>• Removal of individual involved in litigation from the assurance team<br>• Refuse to perform the assurance engagement |

## 2.4 Threats arising from provision of non-assurance services

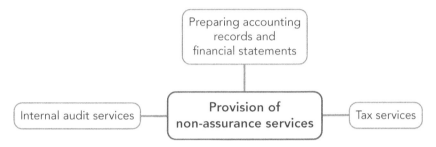

### 2.4.1 Preparing accounting records and financial statements

| Threats | Safeguards |
|---|---|
| Providing accounting and bookkeeping services to an audit client might create a **self-review threat**. *(ACCA Code: s.601.4A1)*<br>This is because it is unlikely that the firm will criticise its own work and decisions. | If the client is **not** a public interest entity:<br>• Accounting services should not be performed by audit team staff<br>• Client must provide all source data<br>• Client must approve all journal entries<br>• Discuss non-audit services with audit committee<br>If the client is a **public interest entity**:<br>• The provision of accounting or bookkeeping services is **not permitted** |

### 2.4.2 Tax services

| Threats | Safeguards |
|---|---|
| Providing tax services to an audit client might create **self-review or advocacy threats**. (ACCA Code: s.604.1) The Code divides taxation services into four categories: ||
| **Tax return preparation** (ACCA Code: s.604.5 A1) | • **Does not usually create a threat.**<br>• Tax returns are usually based on historical information and principally involve analysis and presentation of such historical information under existing tax law, including precedents and established practice.<br>• Management must take responsibility for the tax returns. |

| Threats | Safeguards |
|---|---|
| **Tax calculations for the purpose of preparing accounting entries** (ACCA Code: s. 604.8 A1)<br><br>Preparing such calculations that will be subsequently audited by the firm creates a **self-review** threat. A factor in evaluating the level of the threat is whether the calculations will have a **material effect** on the financial statements. | • Calculations must **not** be performed by a member of the audit team.<br><br>• Independent review of audit work should be conducted by a reviewer who was not involved in providing the service.<br>For **public interest entities** (ACCA Code: s. R604.10)<br><br>• Tax calculations may **not** be performed. |
| **Tax planning and other tax advisory services** (ACCA Code: s.604.12 A1)<br><br>May create a **self-review** or **advocacy** threat | • Services must **not** be performed by a member of the audit team.<br><br>• Independent review of audit work to be conducted by a reviewer who was not involved in providing the service.<br><br>• Obtain pre-clearance from the tax authorities.<br>Such services may **not** be provided where the effectiveness of the tax advice depends on a particular **accounting treatment** or **presentation** in the financial statements and the audit team has **reasonable doubt** as to the appropriateness of the related accounting treatment or presentation and the outcome/consequence of the tax advice will have a material effect on the financial statements being audited. |
| **Assistance in the resolution of tax disputes** (ACCA Code: s.604.21 A1)<br><br>May create a **self-review** or **advocacy** threat | • Assistance services must **not** be provided by a member of the audit team.<br><br>• Independent review of audit work to be conducted by a reviewer who was not involved in providing the assistance.<br>Such services may **not** be provided if they involve the **firm acting as an advocate** for the audit client before a public tribunal or court in the resolution of a tax matter and the amounts involved are **material** to the financial statements being audited. |

### 2.4.3 Internal audit services

| Threat | Safeguards |
|---|---|
| Providing internal audit services to an audit client might create a **self-review** threat if the audit team plan to rely on the work of the internal audit department. (ACCA Code: s.605.1, 605.4 A3) | • Stipulate that it is the client's responsibility to establish, maintain and monitor a system of internal controls and that client management remain responsible for evaluating and acting on internal control findings and for reporting significant findings to those charged with governance.<br><br>• Independent partner review to ensure appropriate reliance is placed on internal audit and that its work is rigorously audited. |

| Threat | Safeguards |
|---|---|
| | For **public interest entities**:<br>Internal audit services must **not** be provided **if** they relate to:<br><br>• A **significant part** of the **internal controls over financial reporting**:<br><br>• Financial accounting systems that generate information that is, individually or in the aggregate, material to the client's accounting records or financial statements on which the firm will express an opinion; or<br><br>• Amounts or disclosures that are, individually or in the aggregate, **material** to the financial statements on which the firm will express an opinion. |
| A threat to objectivity from assuming management responsibility may arise if the firm makes decisions on behalf of the client when providing internal audit services. (ACCA Code: s.R600.7) | • Client is reminded that it must evaluate and determine which recommendations of the firm should be implemented. |

### 2.4.4 Recruiting services

Providing recruiting services to an audit client might create a **self-interest, familiarity or intimidation threat**. (ACCA Code: s.609.1)

Audit firms must not make management decisions for the client. Providing the following services does not usually create a threat if personnel of the firm does not assume a management responsibility.

• Reviewing the professional qualifications of a number of applicants and providing advice on their suitability for the position
• Interviewing candidates and advising on a candidate's competence for financial accounting, administrative or control positions.

Audit firms should **not** provide a recruiting service to an audit client if the service relates to:
• Searching for, or seeking out, candidates; or
• Undertaking reference checks of prospective candidates.

With respect to the following positions:
• Director/officer of the entity; or
• A member of senior management in a position to exert significant influence over the preparation of the client's accounting records or the financial statements on which the firm will express an opinion. (ACCA Code: s.R609.7)

## 2.5 Conflicts of interest

A professional accountant must take reasonable steps to identify circumstances that could pose a conflict of interest.

A conflict of interest creates threats to compliance with the principle of **objectivity** and might create threats to compliance with the other fundamental principles. Such threats might be created when:

• A professional accountant provides a professional service related to a particular matter for **two or more clients whose interests with respect to that matter are in conflict**; or

- The **interests of a professional accountant** with respect to a particular matter and the **interests of the client** for whom the accountant provides a professional service related to that matter **are in conflict**. (ACCA Code: s.310.2)

Before accepting a new client, or where there is a change in a client's circumstances, audit firms must take reasonable steps to ascertain whether there is a conflict of interest or if there is likely to be one in the future. (ACCA Code: s.R310.5, R310.6)

### 2.5.1 Conflicts between a professional accountants' and clients' interests

A professional accountant in public practice **shall not accept or continue an engagement** in which there is, or is likely to be, a significant conflict of interest between the professional accountant and the client. (ACCA Code: s.310.14)

This might arise if the professional accountant competes directly with a client or has a joint venture or similar with a company that is in competition with the client and may threaten the professional accountant's objectivity.

Any form of financial gain which accrues, or is likely to accrue, to a professional accountant in public practice as a result of an engagement, or as a result of using information known to them about a client, will always amount to a significant conflict of interest between the professional accountant and the client, unless the financial gain is disclosed to the client in writing or advance agreement is obtained from the client. (ACCA Code: s.310.16, 310.17)

### 2.5.2 Conflicts between the interests of different clients

This situation arises when different clients are in **direct competition** with each other and where the auditor has access to information that is particularly sensitive.

An audit firm may have two or more clients whose interests may be in conflict, provided that the work the audit firm undertakes is not, itself, likely to be the subject of dispute between those clients. (ACCA Code: s. 310.23)

Where the acceptance or continuance of an engagement would, even with safeguards, materially prejudice the interests of any client, the appointment shall not be accepted or continued. (ACCA Code: s. 310.25)

Such prejudice might arise due to:

- The leakage of information from one client to another
- The audit firm being forced into a position where it has to choose between the interests of different clients (ACCA Code: s. 310.26)

### 2.5.3 Safeguards

Safeguards that may reduce threats to the fundamental principles due to conflicts of interest include:

- **Notify** all known relevant parties and **obtain their consent**
- Use of **separate engagement letters**
- Procedures to **prevent access to information** (eg separate teams, confidential and secure data access and filing and password protection)
- Clear **guidelines** for members of each engagement team on the issues of security and confidentiality
- Use of **confidentiality agreements** signed by employees and partners of the firm
- **Regular review** of the application of safeguards by an independent partner/other senior individual
- Advise one or more **clients to seek additional independent advice**

# 3 Obtaining audit engagements

## 3.1 Advertising

Subject to the rules that follow, members may seek publicity for their services and achievements and may advertise their services and products in any way they think fit.

Members may inform the public of the services they are capable of providing by means of advertising or other forms of promotion, subject to the general requirement that the medium should not reflect adversely on the member, ACCA or the accountancy profession.

Advertisements and promotional material prepared or produced by members or firms should not (either in content or presentation):

(a) Bring ACCA into disrepute or bring discredit to the member, firm or the accountancy profession

(b) Discredit the services offered by others, whether by claiming superiority for the member's or firm's own services, or otherwise

(c) Be misleading, either directly or by implication

(d) Fall short of the requirements of the UK Advertising Standards Authority's Code of Advertising and Sales Promotion, notably as to legality, decency, clarity, honesty, and truthfulness

An advertisement should be clearly distinguishable as such.

Care should be taken to ensure that any reference to fees does not mislead the reader as to the precise range of services and time commitment that the reference is intended to cover.

Any promotional activities should not amount to harassment of prospective clients.

Commissions, fees or rewards in return for the introduction of a client are permitted, provided appropriate safeguards are put in place, such as disclosure to the client.

# 4 Acceptance

New auditors should ensure that they have been appointed in a proper and legal manner.

## 4.1 Accepting nomination as auditor

Before accepting nomination as auditor, the auditor must:

| Acceptance procedures | |
|---|---|
| Ensure **professionally qualified** to act | Consider whether disqualified on legal or ethical grounds |
| Ensure **existing resources adequate** | Consider available time, staff and technical expertise |
| **Obtain references** | Make independent enquiries if directors not personally known |
| **Communicate with present auditors** | Enquire whether there are reasons/ circumstances behind the change which the new auditors ought to know, also courtesy |

The new auditors should communicate with the present auditors to determine whether there are any professional reasons as to why they should not accept appointment as auditors.

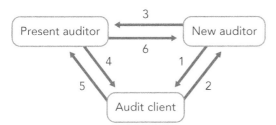

If at any point in the above process, the audit client refuses permission to correspond, then the new auditor should not accept appointment as auditor.

After accepting nomination, the new (incoming) auditor should:

(a) Ensure outgoing auditor's removal/resignation properly conducted in accordance with national regulations

(b) Ensure new appointment properly conducted – obtain a copy of the resolution passed

(c) Agree the terms of the engagement

### 4.2 Client screening

As well as contacting the previous auditors, many firms, particularly larger ones, carry out **stringent checks** on potential client companies and their management. Factors to be considered are detailed below.

#### 4.2.1 Management integrity

The integrity of those managing a company will be of great importance, particularly if the company is controlled by one or a few dominant personalities

#### 4.2.2 Risk

Potential audit clients will be classified as high or low risk, depending on the characteristics of the company:

| Low risk | High risk |
|---|---|
| Good long-term prospects | Poor recent or forecast performance |
| Well-financed | Likely lack of finance |
| Strong internal controls | Significant control deficiencies |
| Conservative, prudent accounting policies | Evidence of questionable integrity, doubtful accounting policies |
| Competent, honest management | Lack of finance director |
| Few usual transactions | Significant related party or unexplained transactions |

Where the risk level of a company's audit is determined as anything other than low, the specific risks should be identified and documented. It might be necessary to assign specialists in response to these risks, particularly industry specialists, as independent reviewers.

#### 4.2.3 Engagement economics

The expected fees from a new client should reflect the **level of risk** expected. They should also offer the same sort of return expected of clients of this nature and reflect the overall financial strategy of the audit firm. Occasionally, an audit firm will want to accept a new client to gain entry into the client's particular industry, or to establish better contacts within that industry. These factors will contribute to a total expected economic return.

#### 4.2.4 Relationship with client

The audit firm will generally want the relationship with a client to be **long term**. This is not only to enjoy receiving fees year after year, but also to allow the audit work to be enhanced by better knowledge of the client, thereby offering a better service.

#### 4.2.5 Ability to perform work

The audit firm must have the **resources** to perform the work properly, as well as any **specialist knowledge** or **skills**. The impact on existing engagements must be estimated, in terms of staff time and the timing of the audit.

## 5 ISA 210: *Agreeing the terms of audit engagements*

The objective of the auditor is to accept or continue an audit engagement only when the basis upon which it is performed has been agreed, through:

- Establishing certain preconditions for an audit are present; and
- Confirming that there is a common understanding between the auditor and management of the terms of the engagement. (ISA 210: para. 3)

## 5.1 Preconditions for an audit

The **preconditions** for an audit are as follows:

(a) The use by management of an acceptable financial reporting framework in the preparation of financial statements

(b) Obtain management's agreement (written representation) that it acknowledges and understands its responsibilities for:

    (i) Preparing the financial statements

    (ii) Establishing internal control to ensure the financial statements are free of material misstatement

    (iii) Providing the auditor with access to all records and documents and staff (ISA 210: para. 6)

If the preconditions are **not present,** the auditor **shall not accept** the proposed engagement. (ISA 210: para. 8)

## 5.2 Engagement letters

> **Engagement letters:** are the written terms of an engagement in the form of a letter.

### 5.2.1 Purpose and content of engagement letters

The auditor shall agree the terms of the engagement with management or those charged with governance as appropriate. (ISA 210: para. 9)

This should be done **before** the audit engagement to avoid misunderstandings regarding the audit. (ISA 210: para. A23)

The agreed terms of the audit engagement shall be recorded in an **audit engagement letter** or other suitable form of written agreement and **must** include the following:

- The **objective and scope** of the audit
- The **auditor's responsibilities**
- **Management's responsibilities**
- Identification of the **applicable financial reporting framework** for the preparation of the financial statements
- Reference to the **expected form and content of any reports** to be issued by the auditor
- A statement that there may be circumstances in which a report may differ from its expected form and content (ISA 210: para. 10)

The audit engagement letter **may** also make reference to the following (ISA 210: para. A24):

- Elaboration of the scope of the audit, including reference to legislation, regulations, ISAs, ethical and other pronouncements of professional bodies to which the auditor adheres
- The form of any other communication of results of the audit engagement
- The requirement for the auditor to communicate key audit matters in the auditor's report in accordance with ISA 701
- The fact that due to the inherent limitations of an audit and those of internal control, there is an unavoidable risk that some material misstatements may not be detected, even though the audit is properly planned and performed in accordance with ISAs
- Arrangements regarding planning and performance, including the composition of the engagement team
- The expectation that management will provide written representations

- The expectation that management will provide access to all information of which management is aware that is relevant to the preparation of the financial statements, including an expectation that management will provide access to information relevant to disclosures
- Agreement of management to provide draft financial statements and other information in time to allow auditor to complete the audit in accordance with proposed timetable
- Agreement of management to inform auditor of facts that may affect the financial statements, of which management may become aware from the date of the auditor's report to the date of issue of the financial statements
- Fees and billing arrangements
- Request for management to acknowledge receipt of the letter and agree to the terms outlined in it
- Involvement of other auditors and experts
- Involvement of internal auditors and other staff
- Arrangements to be made with predecessor auditor
- Any restriction of auditor's liability
- Reference to any further agreements between auditor and entity
- Any obligations to provide audit working papers to other parties

### 5.2.2 Reissuing engagement letters

On recurring audits, the auditor shall assess whether circumstances require the terms of the audit engagement to be revised and whether there is a need to remind the entity of the existing terms of the audit engagement. (ISA 210: para. 13)

Examples include:
- Any indication that the entity **misunderstands** the objectives and scope of the audit
- Any **revised or special terms** of the audit engagement
- A recent **change of senior management**
- A **significant change in ownership**
- A significant change in **nature or size** of the entity's business
- A change in **legal or regulatory requirements**
- A change in the **financial reporting framework**
- A change in **other reporting requirements** (ISA 210: para. A30)

## Essential reading

See Chapter 5 of the Essential reading for an example of an engagement letter.

The Essential reading is available as an Appendix of the digital edition of the Workbook.

## 5.3 Quality management at a firm level

The fact that auditors follow international auditing standards provides a general quality management framework within which audits should be conducted. In addition to this, they must follow the IAASB's suite of quality management standards, including ISQM 1 *Quality Management for Firms that Perform Audits or Reviews of Financial Statements, or Other Assurance or Related Services Engagements*.

Quality management at a firm level encompasses the following areas:
- The firm's risk assessment process
- Governance and leadership
- Relevant ethical requirements
- Acceptance and continuance of client relationships and specific engagements
- Engagement performance
- Resources

- Information and communication
- The monitoring and remediation process (ISQM 1: para. 6)

> ### Exam focus point
>
> ISQM 1 is not an examinable document for your *Audit and Assurance* exam, but it is a reliable source of information for you to draw upon in relation to the syllabus learning objectives in this area (quality management).

### 5.3.1 Engagement performance

The firm should take steps to ensure that engagements are performed correctly - that is, in accordance with standards and guidance *(ISQM 1: para. 31)*.

Firms often produce a manual of standard engagement procedures to give to all staff so that they know the standards they are working towards.

Good engagement performance involves:
- Direction
- Supervision
- Review
- Consultation
- Resolution of disputes

Where there are differences of opinion on an engagement team, a report should not be issued until the dispute has been resolved. This may involve the intervention of a quality reviewer.

KEY
TERM

> **Peer review:** A review of the audit file carried out by another partner in the assurance firm.
>
> **Hot review/ Pre-issuance review:** A peer review carried out **before** the auditor's report is signed. This is also known as an engagement quality review (EQR).
>
> **Cold review/ Post-issuance review:** A peer review carried out **after** the auditor's report is signed.

### 5.3.2 Monitoring

The monitoring of the firm's quality management system and procedures involves:
- **Ongoing evaluation**: Considering whether the firm has kept up to date with regulatory requirements
- **Periodic inspection**: Inspecting the audit engagements of each engagement partner over an inspection cycle

Those monitoring the system are required to evaluate the effect of any **deficiencies** found. Such deficiencies may be one-offs or systematic/repetitive deficiencies. This latter group will require **corrective action** such as:
- Remedial action with an individual
- Communication of findings with the training department
- Changes in the quality management policies and procedures
- Disciplinary action

# 6 Quality management of an individual audit

The quality management of individual audits is governed by ISA 220 (Revised) *Quality Management for an Audit of Financial Statements*.

Auditors must implement quality management procedures for each individual audit engagement so that they have reasonable assurance that:

(a) The auditor has fulfilled the auditor's responsibilities, and has conducted the audit, in accordance with professional standards and applicable legal and regulatory requirements; and

(b) The auditor's report issued is appropriate in the circumstances. *(ISA 220: para. 11)*

The **engagement partner** has overall responsibility for managing and achieving quality within an audit engagement. In order to achieve this, an engagement must manage quality in each of the following areas:

- Leadership responsibilities for managing and achieving quality on audits
- Relevant ethical requirements, including those related to independence
- Acceptance and continuance of client relationships and audit engagements
- Engagement resources
- Engagement performance
- Monitoring and remediation
- Taking overall responsibility for managing and achieving quality
- Documentation

## 6.1 Relevant ethical requirements

The engagement partner is responsible for ensuring ethical compliance. This includes identifying and addressing threats, evaluating any breaches and ensuring that engagement personnel take appropriate action (ISA 220: paras. 17-21).

## 6.2 Acceptance and continuance of client relationships and audit engagements

Again, the engagement partner is responsible for acceptance / continuance procedures in line with ISQM 1 (ISA 220: para. 22). If the engagement is ethically unacceptable then it is the **partner's responsibility to decline** it.

## 6.3 Engagement resources

The engagement partner must ensure that sufficient and appropriate resources are made available to the engagement team including human, technological, and intellectual resources.

## 6.4 Engagement performance

The engagement partner is responsible for the **direction** and **supervision** of the member of the engagement team and the **review** of their work (ISA 220: para. 29).

Direction, supervision and review is **shared** between more and less senior personnel, who should recognise the variations across different engagements. This process should also consider whether sufficient appropriate audit evidence has been obtained, and whether it supports both the conclusions reached and the various elements of the auditor's report that are to be communicated in advance.

The engagement partner is required to **stand back** and ensure their involvement in the engagement is sufficient to satisfy the requirement for taking overall responsibility.

The partner must ensure that direction, supervision and review is planned and performed in line with the firm's policies and with ISAs, and that it is responsive to the particular engagement in question (ISA 220: para. 30).

The partner is also responsible for making sure there is appropriate **consultation** on the audit - both within the audit team and outside it, where required (ISA 220: para. 35). If there are **differences of opinion**, then the partner is responsible for **resolving** them, using the firm's policies and procedures (ISA 220: paras. 37-38).

### 6.4.1 Direction

The partner is required by other auditing standards to hold a meeting with the audit team to discuss the audit, in particular the risks associated with the audit.

ISA 220 (para. A85) states that direction includes 'informing members of the engagement team of their responsibilities, such as:

- Contributing to engagement quality through their personal conduct, communication and actions
- Professional scepticism: maintaining a questioning mind
- Fulfilling relevant ethical requirements
- The responsibilities of respective engagement team members to perform audit procedures and of more experienced engagement team members to direct, supervise and review the work of less experienced engagement team members
- Understanding the objectives of the work to be performed
- Addressing threats to the achievement of quality, for example budget/resource constraints should not result in the failure to perform planned audit procedures

### 6.4.2 Supervision

The audit is supervised overall by the engagement partner, but more practical supervision is given within the audit team by senior staff to more junior staff, as is also the case with review. It includes:

- Tracking the progress of the audit engagement
- Considering the capabilities and competence of individual members of the team, and whether they have sufficient time and understanding to carry out their work
- Addressing significant issues arising during the audit engagement and modifying the planned approach appropriately
- Identifying matters for consultation or consideration by more experienced engagement team members during the audit engagement.

### 6.4.3 Review

Review includes consideration of whether:

- The work has been performed in accordance with professional standards and applicable legal and regulatory requirements
- Significant matters have been raised for further consideration
- Appropriate consultations have taken place and the resulting conclusions have been documented and implemented
- There is a need to revise the nature, timing and extent of work performed
- The work performed supports the conclusions reached and is appropriately documented
- The evidence obtained is sufficient and appropriate to provide a basis for the auditor's opinion
- The objectives of the audit procedures have been achieved

## 6.5 Engagement quality reviews

Engagement quality reviews are required for audits of listed entities and any other engagements where the audit firm has determined a quality review is required.

The engagement partner should:

(a) **Appoint** an engagement quality reviewer (where needed)

(b) **Cooperate** with the reviewer, and inform the team that they should cooperate with them too

(c) **Discuss** significant matters and judgements with the reviewer

(d) Only **date the auditor's report after the review** (ISA 220: para. 36)

## Activity 3: Quality management deficiencies

Your firm, PQ & Co is the auditor of Limitless Co, a listed UK company. You are not involved in the audit, but you have been assigned as a mentor for an audit trainee who recently started at the firm and has been working on the audit of Limitless Co. The trainee has sent you the following email:

**From:** A Trainee

**To:** A Manager

**Subject:** Limitless Co – issues

Good morning

I recently returned from my visit to the Limitless Head office where I have been working on the current year audit. I was watching an online tutorial as part of my studies about quality management a few weeks ago and after working on the Limitless audit I am not sure if our firm is reaching the quality management standards expected of a firm like ours.

The team of five trainees was meant to be under the supervision of a senior. However, that senior had been granted leave by the audit manager for the first week. The audit manager sent us an email saying we should follow last year's file until the senior returns.

When the senior returned, I asked if we would be given some background about Limitless because we didn't have a planning meeting. Unfortunately, I was told that this was not needed because it was virtually the same as the last client we worked on together.

Each trainee was given parts of the electronic audit file to complete. The company is struggling with cash flow and I was asked to review forecasts and conclude on the going concern status. I did my best but there were so many variables I just decided to go with the finance director's assumptions in the end. I was hoping the engagement partner would review my working paper on this, but it looks like nobody has reviewed it.

I was thinking about raising some of these points with the audit partner who has been working on the job the last couple of years, but I haven't had a chance yet. Apparently, no other partners have been involved or had anything to do with the client or the audit files.

I am also a bit worried because the partner questioned the amount of time I am taking on some of the work in an email after reviewing my timesheets. The email said the budget is very tight and we need to keep to it as a priority, but I don't think I can work any more quickly than I am and still get enough evidence to conclude on the work.

Maybe we can have a meeting about all this when we are both available?

**Required**

Describe THREE quality management deficiencies at PQ & Co based on the scenario and provide THREE recommendations to address those deficiencies.

| Quality management deficiency | Recommendation |
|---|---|
|  |  |

| Quality management deficiency | Recommendation |
| --- | --- |
| | |

# Chapter summary

**Professional ethics and quality management**

## ACCA Code of Ethics

### The fundamental principles
- Integrity
- Objectivity
- Professional competence and due care
- Confidentiality
- Professional behaviour

### Confidentiality
- Do not disclose without permission
- Unless:
- Required by law:
  – Legal proceedings
  – Infringements of law (money laundering, terrorism)
- Professional duty/ right:
  – Comply with quality reviews
  – Respond to inquiry/investigation
  – Protect interests of professional accountant in legal proceedings
  – Comply with technical/profession al standards

### Non-compliance with laws and regulations
- Acts of omission/ commission, intentional or unintentional, which are contrary to the prevailing laws or regulations
- Examples:
  – Fraud
  – Money laundering
  – Banking
  – Data protection
  – Tax and pensions
  – Public health and safety

### Integrity, objectivity and independence
- Independence of mind
- Independence in appearance
- Public interest entity:
  – All listed entities
  – Entities of significant public interest, eg banks, insurance companies and pension firms

## Threats to the fundamental principles

### Categories of threats
- Self-interest
- Self-review
- Advocacy
- Familiarity
- Intimidation
- Employ safeguards

### Threats arising from financial matters
- Financial interests
- Loans and guarantees
- Fees
- Gifts and hospitality

### Threats arising from employment and other relationships
- Business relationships
- Personal relationships
- Employment
- Long association
- Actual/threatened litigation

### Threats arising from provision of non-audit services
- Preparing accounting records and financial statements
- Tax services
- Internal audit services

```
                    ┌──────────────┬──────────────────┬──────────────────┐
```

**Obtaining audit engagements**

**Acceptance**

**ISA 210: Agreeing the terms of engagement**

**Quality management on an individual audit**

**Advertising**
- Adhere to guidelines
- Not reflect adversely on the profession
- Be distinguishable as an advertisement

**Accepting nomination as auditor**
- Before acceptance:
  – Professionally qualified
  – Adequate resources
  – Obtain references
  – Communicate with present auditors
- After acceptance:
  – Ensure outgoing auditor properly removed/resigned
  – Ensure new appointment properly made
  – Engagement letter

**Preconditions for an audit**
- Management using acceptable FR framework to prepare fs
- Obtain management's agreement re responsibility for:
  – Preparing fs
  – Establishing internal control to ensure fs are free from material misstatement
  – Provide auditor with access to records, documents and staff

**Engagement letters**
- Written contract
- Key contents

**Quality reviews**
- Evaluate:
  – Significant judgements made by engagement team
  – Conclusions reached (opinion/report)

# Knowledge diagnostic

### 1. ACCA Code of Ethics and Conduct

The ACCA Code of Ethics and Conduct applies to members, affiliates and students of the ACCA and details the fundamental principles of **integrity, objectivity, professional competence and due care, confidentiality** and **professional behaviour.**

### 2. Confidentiality

The auditor must not disclose confidential information obtained in their professional work without prior consent, unless there is an obligation to do so by law or a professional duty/right to disclose.

### 3. Threats to the fundamental principles

There are many circumstances that can lead to threats to the fundamental principles. These circumstances will fall into one or more of the five categories of: **self-interest, self-review, advocacy, familiarity and intimidation.**

### 4. Safeguards

Where threats exist, safeguards should be put in place to eliminate or reduce the threat.

### 5. Principles vs rules based

The ACCA Code adopts a principles-based, rather than rules-based, approach, but also gives many examples of specific situations where independence can be threatened and the relevant safeguards that may mitigate these.

### 6. Advertising

An audit firm **may** advertise to obtain new work; however any advertisements must comply with advertising standards and must not discredit others.

### 7. Accepting new clients

Before accepting nomination as auditor, the audit firm must ensure that it is properly qualified to act and that it has communicated with the outgoing auditor.

### 8. Preconditions for an audit

The auditor must also establish that the preconditions for an audit are present and confirm acceptance of the appointment in an engagement letter. You will not need to reproduce an **engagement letter** but must be familiar with its contents.

### 9. Quality management

Quality management is extremely important for the credibility of the auditing profession.

### 10. Ultimate responsibility

The audit engagement partner is ultimately responsible for ensuring that an audit has been carried out in accordance with the firm's quality management procedures.

 BPP

# Further study guidance

## Question practice

Now try the following from the Further question practice bank [available in the digital edition of the workbook]:

- Section A Q22 & Q23
- Section B Q61 Independence
- Section B Q62 Confidentiality and independence

## Further reading

There are technical articles and study support videos on the ACCA website written/recorded by members of the AA examining team and other tutors which are relevant to some of the topics covered in this chapter that you should read:

Technical articles:

- Laws and regulations (https://www.accaglobal.com/uk/en/student/exam-support-resources/fundamentals-exams-study-resources/f8/technical-articles/laws-and-regulations.html)

## Own research

Consider the ethical safeguards that exist to protect you in your workplace. Would you know the procedures you should follow if you felt pressured to manipulate information (financial or otherwise)?

# Activity answers

## Activity 1: Explaining ethical threats

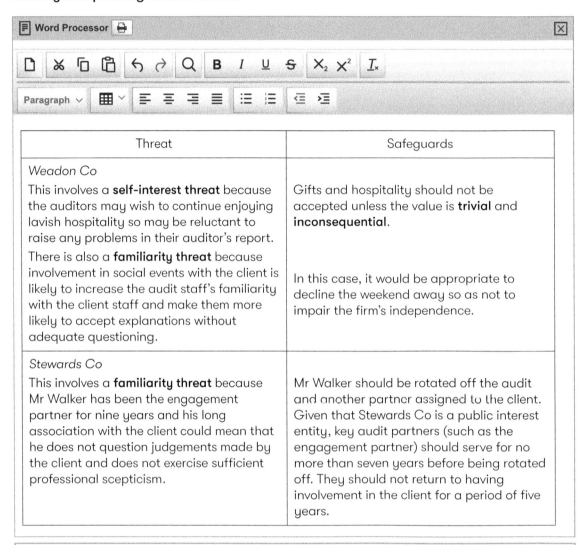

| Threat | Safeguards |
|---|---|
| *Weadon Co*<br><br>This involves a **self-interest threat** because the auditors may wish to continue enjoying lavish hospitality so may be reluctant to raise any problems in their auditor's report.<br><br>There is also a **familiarity threat** because involvement in social events with the client is likely to increase the audit staff's familiarity with the client staff and make them more likely to accept explanations without adequate questioning. | Gifts and hospitality should not be accepted unless the value is **trivial** and **inconsequential**.<br><br><br>In this case, it would be appropriate to decline the weekend away so as not to impair the firm's independence. |
| *Stewards Co*<br><br>This involves a **familiarity threat** because Mr Walker has been the engagement partner for nine years and his long association with the client could mean that he does not question judgements made by the client and does not exercise sufficient professional scepticism. | Mr Walker should be rotated off the audit and another partner assigned to the client. Given that Stewards Co is a public interest entity, key audit partners (such as the engagement partner) should serve for no more than seven years before being rotated off. They should not return to having involvement in the client for a period of five years. |

**Tutorial note.** In the CBE, a Section B question asking for threats and safeguards is likely to have a table similar to the one above in the word processor ready for you to enter your answer.

## Activity 2: Threats and safeguards

1

|  | Intimidation | Self-interest | Self-review |
|---|---|---|---|
| Risk (1) |  | X |  |
| Risk (2) |  | X |  |
| Risk (3) | X | X |  |
| Risk (4) |  |  | X |

2   The correct answer is: Discuss the situation with Emerald's audit committee and consider resigning from some services.

3　The correct answer is: Check and Co should decline the offer to prepare the financial statements.

## Activity 3: Quality management deficiencies

| Quality management deficiency | Recommendation |
| --- | --- |
| There is a lack of supervision at audits due to it being possible to grant an audit senior annual leave without assigning a replacement. The engagement partner must ensure that sufficient and appropriate resources are made available to the engagement team including human resources. | Annual leave policy should take account of the fact the firm needs to ensure adequate supervision is given within the audit team by senior staff to more junior staff. Annual leave policy should be such that it cannot be granted during an audit without assigning the responsibility of supervision to another senior unless the manager/partner are on site in their absence. |
| There was no planning meeting. The partner is required by auditing standards to hold a meeting with the audit team to discuss the audit. There has been no opportunity to inform members of the engagement team of their responsibilities, including contributing to engagement quality via their conduct and applying professional scepticism. | Planning meetings should be compulsory under the firm's quality management procedures and members of the engagement team should be made aware of their responsibilities for audit quality at that meeting. |
| The allocation of roles on the audit has been poor with a complex going concern review given to a trainee. Furthermore, there has been no review of the work in this area. Under ISA 220 (Revised) the audit partner should review documentation relating to significant matters and judgements. Clearly a going concern review where there is potentially a doubt over the going concern status is one of those matters. | Quality management procedures should make it clear the engagement partner must take responsibility for the direction and supervision of the members of the engagement team and the review of their work. The firm should carry out periodic reviews of completed files to detect any issues in this area and action should be taken to ensure these issues do not re-occur following the review. At the planning stage, work should be assigned to audit team members such that the audit engagement partner has sufficient confidence each team member is experienced enough to undertake the roles allocated to them. |
| No other partners have been involved but Limitless Co is a listed client. An engagement quality review is required for audits of listed clients. | An engagement quality reviewer should be assigned for the current and future audits of Limitless. This could be another partner in the firm, or an external reviewer appointed by the firm. |
| Instead of addressing the threat to quality of a budget constraint, the partner has | The firm's quality manual should set out that audit quality should not be |

| Quality management deficiency | Recommendation |
|---|---|
| increased the threat by stressing the need to keep within budget. This may lead to work being carried out more quickly and being incomplete, and ultimately there is a risk there will not be sufficient and appropriate evidence to support the audit opinion. | compromised by budgetary constraints and that the engagement partner is responsible for ensuring this. Where engagement partners do not comply, remedial action should be taken. |

**Tutorial note.** Only three quality management deficiencies and three related recommendations were needed.

# Risk assessment

## Learning objectives

On completion of this chapter, you should be able to:

| Syllabus learning outcomes | Syllabus reference no. |
| --- | --- |
| Identify the overall objectives of the auditor and the need to conduct an audit in accordance with ISAs. | B2 (a) |
| Explain the need to plan and perform audit engagements with an attitude of professional scepticism, and to exercise professional judgement. | B2 (b) |
| Explain the components of audit risk. | B3 (a) |
| Describe the audit risks in the financial statements and explain the auditor's response to each risk. | B3 (b) |
| Define and explain the concepts of materiality and performance materiality. | B3 (c) |
| Explain and calculate materiality levels from financial information. | B3 (d) |
| Explain how auditors obtain an initial understanding of the entity, its environment and the applicable financial reporting framework. | B4 (a) |
| Describe and explain the nature, and purpose of, analytical procedures in planning. | B4 (b) |
| Compute and interpret key ratios used in analytical procedures. | B4 (c) |
| Discuss the effect of fraud and misstatements on the audit strategy and extent of audit work. | B5 (a) |
| Explain the auditor's responsibility to consider laws and regulations. | B5 (c) |

# Business and Exam context

Auditors must ensure that they plan their audits in order to identify audit risk. The first step in planning is making sure that you understand the entity you are auditing. There is a phrase which says "you can't audit what you don't understand" and this is very true. Auditors must understand the products and services their client supplies and the markets in which it operates as well as key personnel.

If auditors know what they expect, their client's financial statements to look like it is much easier to recognise when they do not look like that and therefore spot audit risks. For example, if the auditor knows that a client has expanded during the year and financed this expansion by taking out a long-term loan then the auditor would expect to see a non-current liability in the statement of financial position. If this is not included, this indicates that there may be an error in the financial statements.

Audit risk is the risk that the auditor gives the wrong opinion on the financial statements, for example they say the financial statements are true and fair when they are not! Auditors adopt a risk-based approach to auditing, in other words, they decide on what level of overall audit risk they are willing to accept and then ensure that they perform enough audit testing to ensure that this level is met. If they get their assessment wrong at the planning stage, it could mean that the audit is not carried out correctly.

Another planning consideration is materiality, which assesses how important the auditors think something is in relation to the financial statements that they are auditing. Auditors will focus on the areas that are material, so it is very important that they set materiality at an appropriate level.

# Chapter overview

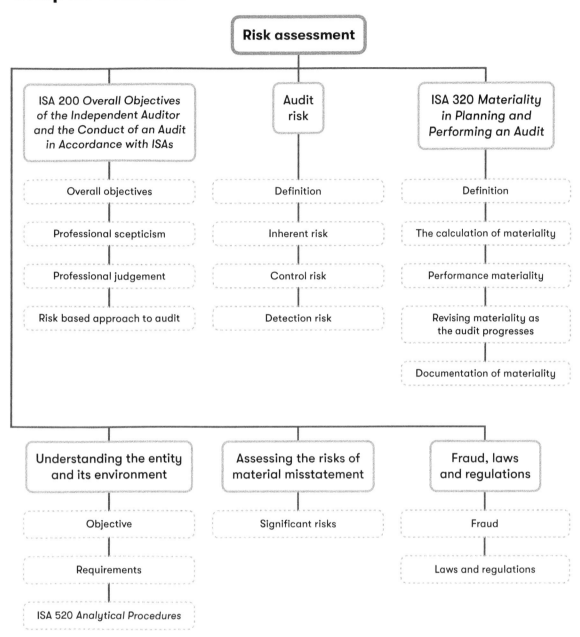

# 1 ISA 200 *Overall Objectives of the Independent Auditor and the Conduct of an Audit in Accordance with International Standards on Auditing*

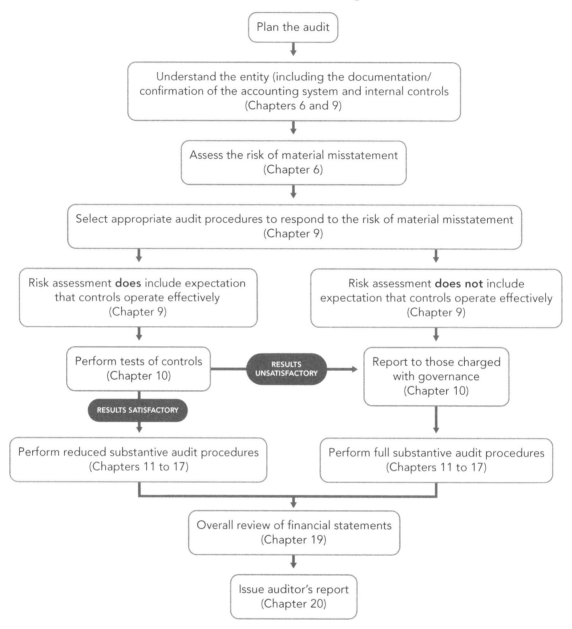

## 1.1 Overall objectives

When conducting an audit of financial statements, the overall objectives of the auditor are:

To obtain **reasonable assurance** about whether the financial statements as a whole are **free from material misstatement**, whether due to fraud or error, thereby enabling the auditor to **express an opinion** on whether the financial statements are prepared, in all material respects, in accordance with an applicable financial reporting framework; and to report on the financial statements, and communicate as required by the ISAs, in accordance with the auditor's findings. (ISA 200: para. 11)

In order to do this, the auditor should plan and perform the audit with professional scepticism and apply professional judgement.

## 1.2 Professional scepticism

> **Professional scepticism:** "an attitude that includes a questioning mind, being alert to conditions which may indicate possible misstatement due to error or fraud, and a critical assessment of audit evidence" (ISA 200: para. 13(l)).

Auditors must plan and perform an audit with an attitude of **professional scepticism** recognising that circumstances may exist that cause the financial statements to be materially misstated (ISA 200: para. 15).

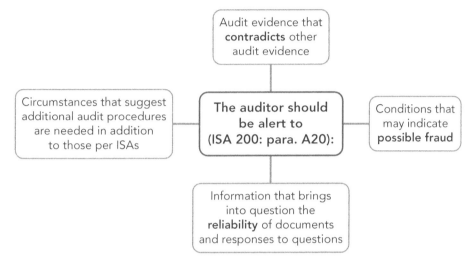

## 1.3 Professional judgement

> **Professional judgement:** "application of relevant training, knowledge and experience in making informed decisions about the courses of action that are appropriate in the circumstances of the audit engagement" (ISA 200: para. 13(m)).

ISA 200 also requires the auditor to exercise professional judgement in planning and performing an audit of financial statements (ISA 200: para. 16). Professional judgement is required in the following areas:

- Determining the level of audit risk and setting materiality
- Determining the nature, timing and extent of audit procedures to be performed
- Evaluating whether sufficient appropriate audit evidence has been obtained
- Evaluating management's judgements in applying the applicable financial reporting framework
- Drawing conclusions based on the audit evidence obtained (ISA 200: para. A23)

## 1.4 Risk-based approach to audit

The ISAs require auditors to adopt a risk-based approach to auditing. This means the auditor must:

- Analyse the risk in the client's business, transactions and systems that could lead to material misstatement in the financial statements
- Direct audit testing to risky areas

# 2 Audit risk

## 2.1 Definition

In order to obtain **reasonable assurance** that the financial statements are free from material misstatement, the auditor shall obtain **sufficient appropriate** audit evidence to reduce audit risk to an acceptably low level and thereby enable the auditor to draw reasonable conclusions on which to base the auditor's opinion (ISA 200: para. 11).

> **Audit risk:** the risk that the auditor expresses an **inappropriate audit opinion** when the financial statements are materially misstated (ISA 200: para. 13(c)). **Audit risk** is the risk that the auditor expresses an **inappropriate audit opinion** when the financial statements are materially misstated' (ISA 200: para. 13(c)).

Audit risk has **two** major components:

(a) One is **dependent on the entity** and is the risk of material misstatement arising in the financial statements (**inherent risk** and **control risk**)

(b) The other is **dependent on the auditor** and is the risk that the auditor will not detect material misstatements in the financial statements (**detection risk**)

Audit risk can be represented by the **audit risk model**:

## 2.2 Inherent risk

> **Inherent risk:** the **susceptibility** of an assertion about a class of transaction, account balance or disclosure to a **misstatement** that could be material either individually or when aggregated with other misstatements, **before consideration of any related internal controls**
>
> (ISA 200: para. 13(nii)).

Inherent risk is affected by the **nature of the entity**. For example:

- The industry in which the audit client operates
- Any regulations it is subject to
- Whether its financial statements:
    - Include complex calculations
    - Are subject to complex accounting standards
    - Include amounts derived from accounting estimates rather than routine, factual data

## 2.3 Control risk

> **Control risk:** the **risk that a material misstatement** that could occur in an assertion about a class of transaction, account balance or disclosure and that could be material, individually or when aggregated with other misstatements, **will not be prevented or detected and corrected** on a timely basis by the entity's **internal control**. (ISA 200: para. 13 (nii))

Some control risk will always exist because of the inherent limitations of internal control, for example human error. The inherent limitations of internal control are covered in Chapter 9.

## 2.4 Detection risk

> **Detection risk:** the risk that the **procedures performed by the auditor** to reduce audit risk to an acceptably low level **will not detect a misstatement** that exists and that could be material, either individually or when aggregated with other misstatements (ISA 200: para. 13(e)).

Detection risk is sub-divided into two components: sampling risk and non-sampling risk.

**Sampling risk** relates to the fact that the auditor does not, and cannot, examine all available evidence and only performs audit procedures on a sample of items. There is, therefore, always a risk that the conclusion the auditor draws based on the sample they have tested is not appropriate for the population as a whole. Sampling risk is covered in more detail in Chapter 11.

**Non-sampling risk** however describes the risk that the auditor's procedures do not detect material misstatement due to factors other than the sample tested.

Factors which increase non-sampling risk include:

- Auditor's lack of experience
- Time pressure
- Financial constraints
- Poor planning
- New client
- Lack of industry knowledge

> **Exam focus point**
>
> Whilst you must be able to describe the audit risk model and each component of audit risk, most exam questions on audit risk are scenario based. Here it is not essential to differentiate between inherent, control and detection risk but rather apply your knowledge to describe the audit risk that exists in the scenario.

# 3 ISA 320 *Materiality in Planning and Performing an Audit*

## 3.1 Definition

> **Material:** Information is **material** if its omission or misstatement could reasonably be expected to influence the economic decisions of users taken on the basis of the financial statements.

There are two aspects of materiality:

The materiality level set by the auditor will always be a matter of **judgement** and will depend on the level of audit risk. The higher the anticipated level of audit risk, the lower the value at which materiality will be set.

The materiality level set has a critical impact on several key areas:

- The **nature, timing and extent of audit procedures** performed. The lower the level at which materiality is set, the more work will need to be performed to ensure the overall audit engagement risk is kept at an acceptably low level.
- Whether to use sampling techniques
- The evaluation of the effect of misstatements in terms of:
  - Whether to **seek adjustments** to the financial statements; or
  - The degree of any auditor's report **modification.**

Materiality is also central to the assessment of individual audit risks - when assessing risks, the auditor bears in mind not just the misstatements that could arise, but whether these misstatements would be material. In this way, the auditor is able to direct their work to those areas that matter the most for the audit as a whole.

## 3.2 The calculation of materiality

During audit planning, the auditor establishes materiality for the **financial statements as a whole** by exercising judgment.

The following **benchmarks and percentages** may be appropriate in the calculation of materiality for the financial statements as a whole:

### Formula to learn

| Value | Percentage (%) |
|-------|----------------|
| Revenue | 1/2 to 1 |
| Total assets | 1 to 2 |
| Profit before tax | 5 to 10 |

The figure chosen will depend on the confidence the auditor has in the client's figures, the uses the financial statements will be put to and any other factors affecting the auditor's judgment.

Once the materiality level for the financial statements as a whole has been set, it is important to consider what would happen if this materiality level was applied directly to, for example, different account balances (such as receivables and inventory). It could be that a number of balances (or elements making up those balances) are untested or dismissed on the grounds that they are immaterial. However, a number of errors or misstatements could exist in those untested balances, and these could aggregate to a material misstatement.

For this reason, the auditor is required to set **performance materiality** levels which are **lower than the materiality for the financial statements as a whole**. This means a lower threshold is applied during testing. The risk of misstatements which could add up to a material misstatement is therefore reduced.

### Essential reading

See Chapter 6 of the Essential reading for more information on determining materiality.

The Essential reading is available as an Appendix of the digital edition of the Workbook.

## 3.3 Performance materiality

KEY
TERM

**Performance materiality:** "the amount or amounts set by the auditor at **less than materiality for the financial statements as a whole** to reduce to an appropriately low level the probability that the aggregate of uncorrected and undetected misstatements exceeds materiality for the financial statements as a whole".

It also refers to "the amount or amounts set by the auditor at less than the materiality level or levels for particular classes of transactions, account balances or disclosures" (ISA 320: para. 9).

Determining performance materiality involves the auditor's professional judgment. It is affected by their understanding of the entity and the results of risk assessment procedures. It can be qualitative and quantitative.

For example, if there are particular account balances that could reasonably be expected to significantly influence the decisions of users (for example, revenue for the year) then the auditors may decide to use performance materiality when performing their audit procedures.

### Essential reading

See Chapter 6 of the Essential reading for more information on determining performance materiality.

The Essential reading is available as an Appendix of the digital edition of the Workbook.

## 3.4 Revising materiality as the audit progresses

Materiality may need to be revised due to events that occur during the audit, **new information**, or a **change in the auditor's understanding** of the entity and its operations as a result of performing further audit procedures.

In evaluating whether the financial statements give a true and fair view, the auditor should assess the materiality of the aggregate of uncorrected misstatements. This is normally documented on a schedule of unadjusted differences.

### 3.4.1 Documentation of materiality

ISA 320 (para. 14) requires the following to be documented:

- Materiality for the financial statements as a whole
- Materiality level or levels for particular classes of transactions, account balances or disclosures if applicable
- Performance materiality
- Any revision of the above as the audit progressed

# 4 Risk assessment, and understanding the entity and its environment

### PER alert

Objective 19 of the PER performance objectives is to prepare for and collect evidence for audit. An important aspect of preparing for an audit is understanding the nature of the client's organisation. The knowledge you gain in this section will assist you in demonstrating the achievement of this element of PO 19 in practice.

## 4.1 Objective

ISA 315 *Identifying and Assessing the Risks of Material Misstatement* was revised by the IAASB in 2019, and it is on this version of ISA 315 that you may be examined for your Audit & Assurance exam. The 2019 revisions of the ISA were far-reaching, and focused mainly on strengthening requirements in relation to the auditor's assessment of the risks of material misstatement. This is a key part of the Audit & Assurance exam.

It states that the objective of the auditor here is to:

Identify and assess the risks of material misstatement, whether due to fraud or error, at the financial statement and assertion levels thereby providing a basis for designing and implementing responses to the assessed risks of material misstatement (ISA 315: para. 11).

The auditor first identifies the risks and then assesses their severity. This will then allow them to design responses to the risks in accordance with ISA 330 *The Auditor's Responses to Assessed Risks*. The auditor must understand the entity in order to perform an adequate risk assessment.

ISA 315 considers the risk assessment itself to be part of the audit evidence (ISA 315: para. *13*). Risk assessment procedures have to include:

- Inquiries of management;
- Analytical procedures; and
- Observation and inspection (*ISA 315: para. 14*)

The auditor may use information from last year's audit, but this must be evaluated to consider whether it remains relevant and appropriate this year (ISA 315: para. 16).

The auditor may also seek to use **automated tools and techniques** as part of the risk assessment. ISA 315 gives the following examples of this.

- Remote observation tools (eg drones) could be used when inspecting certain assets
- Auditors can obtain digital downloads of accounting records and use data analytics techniques (ranging from spreadsheets to more complex systems) to perform analysis that assists in the prioritisation of significant risks of material misstatement
- The analysis of accounting records could include journals to identify those posted outside of normal working hours or by staff who do not normally post such items
- Entire populations of transactions could be analysed to identify situations that could indicate a higher position on the spectrum of inherent risk (eg account balances that are zero at the reporting date but which have seen significant transactions and journal entries during the period, suggesting possible manipulation)
- To assist the auditor, key messages from data analytics procedures are often presented using a dashboard (sometimes referred to as data visualisation) which highlights significant matters for the auditor's attention

(ISA 315: paras. A31, A35, A137, A161 and A203)

As the ISA points out, the auditor must perform their risk assessment **in a way that is not biased toward obtaining corroborative evidence, or excluding contradictory evidence** (ISA 315: para. 13). Thus the auditor must exercise professional scepticism, and be open to evidence that may undermine the narrative that management gives them.

> ### Exam focus point
>
> Questions in the *Audit & Assurance* exam may ask you to identify 'audit risks' and explain the 'auditor's response' to those risks. This reflects the way the ISAs encourage real-life auditors to think, and is something that you should get used to doing.

ISA 315 distinguishes two main types of risk: risks at the **financial statement level**, and at **the assertion level**.

Risks at the financial statement level are pervasive to the financial statements and may affect any assertion - for example, the effects of a poor management attitude to internal control could be felt in any area of the financial statements.

Risks at the assertion level are more specific and will take the form of specific issues - for example, a company which keeps inventory in multiple locations will be subject to the inherent risk that not all inventory will be counted, and may also be subject to a control risk in relation to the entity's system for counting that inventory.

In order to assess these risks, the auditor must obtain an understanding of three things:

- The entity and its environment
- The applicable financial reporting framework (this is IFRS for the *AA* exam)
- The entity's system of internal control

## 4.2 Understanding the entity and its environment

As part of understanding the entity and its environment, the auditor must understand the following (ISA 315: paras. 19-20).

- The entity's **organisational structure**, ownership and governance, and its **business model**, including the extent to which the business model integrates the use of IT
- Industry, regulatory and other external factors
- The **measures** used, internally and externally, to assess the entity's **financial performance**
- IFRS and the entity's **accounting policies**
- How the **inherent risk factors** affect the susceptibility of assertions to misstatement

The following diagram gives summarises the factors the auditor should consider when obtaining an understanding of the entity and its environment.

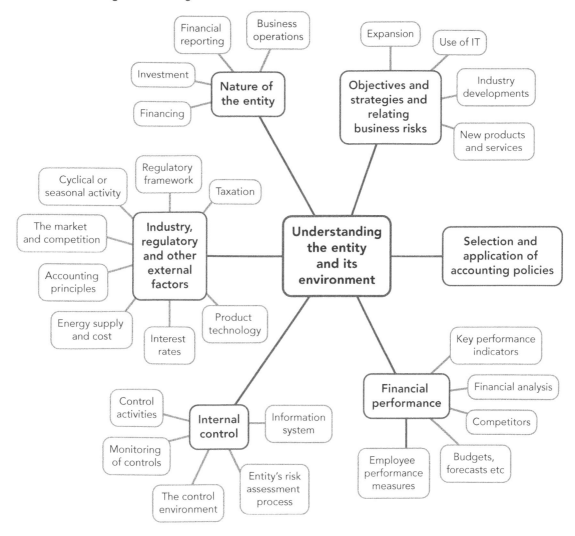

As mentioned above, ISA 315 requires auditors to perform procedures to obtain this understanding.

## Essential reading

See Chapter 6 of the Essential reading for information on enquiry and observation and inspection, which should be used to obtain an understanding of the entity.

The Essential reading is available as an Appendix of the digital edition of the Workbook.

## 4.3 Understanding the entity's system of internal control

The auditor must understand the entity's system of internal control. This has five elements:

(a) Control environment

(b) The entity's risk assessment process

(c)  The entity's process to monitor internal control

(d)  The information system and communication

(e)  Control activities

These elements are covered in detail in Chapter 9 of this Workbook.

The auditor must understand the entity's **risk assessment process** relevant to the preparation of the financial statements, ie its process for (ISA 315: para. 22):

- **Identifying business risks** (which are relevant to financial reporting objectives)
- Assessing the significance of risks
- Addressing risks

The auditor then evaluates whether the risk assessment process is appropriate for an entity of its nature complexity.

ISA 315 gives auditors five inherent risk factors (ISA 315: para. A7):

- Complexity;
- Subjectivity;
- Change;
- Uncertainty; or
- Susceptibility to misstatement due to **management bias** or other **fraud** risk factors insofar as they affect inherent risk.

The final risk factor here (management bias or fraud) was a new inclusion in the 2019 revision of the ISA, and can be understood as an attempt to respond to criticisms of auditors in this area.

## Exam focus point

**Fraud** is a hot topic in the profession at the moment, and is therefore examinable. It is important that you understand the auditor's responsibilities in relation to it (covered in detail later in this Chapter), and are able to identify when fraud might be taking place.

The auditor must understand the entity's process to **monitor internal control**:

- **How** the entity monitors the effectiveness of controls, and how it remedies any deficiencies identified
- The **sources of information** used to monitor controls

The auditor then evaluates whether this monitoring process is appropriate for an entity of its nature and complexity (ISA 315: para. 24).

## Activity 1: Audit risks and auditor's response

### Introduction and client background

You are an audit senior in Check and Co and you are commencing the planning of the audit of Dress You Like Co for the year ending 30 September 20X6. This audit was won by your firm in January 20X6.

Dress You Like Co is a clothing manufacturer, based in the UK, which has been trading for over 10 years. It operates from two sites: a factory where the clothes are made and a head office where the administration is carried out. Completed inventory orders are despatched from both the factory and the head office and errors can sometimes occur concerning the transfer of inventory between sites.

In an effort to reduce costs, Dress You Like Co now imports its material from one sole supplier based overseas. Any delays in supply are likely to have a significant impact on Dress You Like Co's relationships with its customers and could lead to the loss of contracts. Unfortunately, some delays have been experienced with the new supplier and it has been difficult to find alternative suppliers at short notice.

Dress You Like Co sells its finished products to small independent retailers and also one major supermarket chain. The supermarket chain often requires additional deliveries without much prior notice, so Dress You Like Co has to maintain a high level of inventory should this occur. Credit terms are normally 30 days, but the supermarket is given 60-day credit terms. Dress You Like Co's cash flow and working capital have deteriorated during the year.

### Personnel

Also, as part of the cost-cutting exercise mentioned above, Dress You Like Co froze the finance director's salary this year despite giving other directors a 5% salary increase. This decision was made based on the fact that the finance role was no more demanding than in previous years. The finance director was not happy about this decision and left the company in March 20X6. He is now suing the company for constructive dismissal; the company is not proposing to make any provision or disclosure of this as it does not believe the ongoing claim has any merit. The finance director has not yet been replaced and his work is being done by his assistant on top of her existing workload.

Dress You Like Co had previously outsourced their internal audit department but cancelled this contract in May 20X6 in a further effort to cut costs. The internal audit department used to perform monthly bank and supplier statement reconciliations and a monthly check on the controls over inventory despatch at each location.

### Required

Describe SIX audit risks and explain the auditor's response to each risk in planning the audit of Dress You Like Co.

| Audit risk | Auditor's response |
|---|---|
|  |  |
|  |  |
|  |  |
|  |  |

| Audit risk | Auditor's response |
|------------|--------------------|
|            |                    |
|            |                    |
|            |                    |

Solution

## 4.4 ISA 520 *Analytical Procedures*

Analytical procedures mean the analysis of relationships to identify inconsistencies and unexpected relationships.

The auditor should apply analytical procedures as risk assessment procedures and in the overall review at the end of the audit.

They can also be used as a source of substantive audit evidence when their use is more effective or efficient than tests of details in reducing detection risk for specific financial statement assertions.

Analytical procedures include the following types of comparisons:

(a) Prior periods

(b) Budgets and forecasts

(c) Industry information

(d) Predictive estimates ie expectations

(e) Relationships between elements of financial information, ie ratio analysis

(f) Relationships between financial and non-financial information, eg payroll costs to the number of employees

The auditor must apply analytical procedures as risk assessment procedures to obtain an understanding of the entity and its environment.

Application of analytical procedures may indicate aspects of the entity of which the auditor was unaware and will assist in assessing the risks of material misstatement in order to determine the nature, timing and extent of further audit procedures.

Common ratios for use in analytical procedures include:

| Ratio | Calculation |
| --- | --- |
| **Profitability ratios** | |
| Return on capital employed (ROCE) | $$\frac{\text{Profit before interest and tax (PBIT)}}{\text{Share capital + reserves + Non-current liabilities}}$$ |
| Net profit margin | $$\frac{\text{PBIT}}{\text{Revenue}}$$ |
| Asset turnover | $$\frac{\text{Revenue}}{\text{Share capital + reserves + Non-current liabilities}}$$ |
| Gross profit margin | $$\frac{\text{Gross profit}}{\text{Revenue}}$$ |
| **Liquidity ratios** | |
| Current ratio | $$\frac{\text{Current Assets}}{\text{Current Liabilities}}$$ |
| Quick ratio (acid test) | $$\frac{\text{Current Assets - Inventories}}{\text{Current Liabilities}}$$ |
| Inventory holding period | $$\frac{\text{Inventories}}{\text{Cost of sales}} \times 365 \text{ days}$$ |
| Receivables collection period | $$\frac{\text{Trade receivables}}{\text{Credit sales}} \times 365 \text{ days}$$ |
| Payables payment period | $$\frac{\text{Trade payables}}{\text{Credit purchases}} \times 365 \text{ days}$$ |

| Ratio | Calculation |
|---|---|
| **Gearing** | |
| Debt/equity | $\dfrac{\text{Interest bearing debt}}{\text{Share capital and reserves}}$ |
| Interest cover | $\dfrac{\text{PBIT}}{\text{Finance costs}}$ |

## Activity 2: Ratios and risk

You have also been provided with the following draft accounts of Dress You Like Co for the year ended 30 September 20X6:

**EXTRACTS FROM THE DRAFT STATEMENT OF FINANCIAL POSITION AS ON 30 SEPTEMBER 20X6**

| | Draft 20X6 $'000 | Actual 20X5 $'000 |
|---|---|---|
| Inventory: Finished goods | 13,800 | 4,900 |
| Receivables: Trade (supermarket) | 11,800 | 8,300 |
| Trade (other) | 700 | 600 |
| Bank: | 0 | 200 |
| Payables: Trade | 2,060 | 1,470 |
| Other | 500 | 450 |
| Bank overdraft: | 750 | 0 |

**EXTRACTS FROM THE DRAFT STATEMENT OF PROFIT OR LOSS FOR THE YEAR ENDED 30 SEPTEMBER 20X6**

| | Draft 20X6 $'000 | Actual 20X5 $'000 |
|---|---|---|
| Revenue (supermarket) | 53,500 | 49,000 |
| Revenue (other) | 8,200 | 6,700 |
| Cost of sales (supermarket) | (51,895) | (45,080) |
| Cost of sales (other) | (7,380) | (5,900) |
| Gross profit | 2,425 | 4,720 |
| Other expenses | (1,400) | (2,450) |
| Profit before taxation | 1,025 | 2,270 |

**Required**

1  Calculate THREE ratios for BOTH years, which would assist the audit senior in planning the audit.

2   Using the ratios calculated, describe the MAIN audit risk and explain the auditor's response to this risk in the planning of Dress You Like Co.

**Solution**

---

# 5   Assessing the risks of material misstatement

Once the auditor has obtained an understanding of the entity and its environment, they shall **assess the risks of material misstatement in the financial statements** and identify significant risks.

## 5.1   Significant risks

> **Significant risk:** An identified risk of material misstatement:
>
> - For which the assessment of inherent risk is close to the upper end of the **spectrum of inherent risk** due to the degree to which inherent risk factors affect the combination of the likelihood of a misstatement occurring and the magnitude of the potential misstatement should that misstatement occur; or
>
> - That is to be treated as a significant risk in accordance with the requirements of other ISAs.
>
> (ISA 315: para. 12l)

The auditor will begin simply by identifying risks, but will then need to consider how severe each risk is in terms of the 'spectrum of inherent risk'. Significant risks are essentially the most severe risks.

Routine, non-complex transactions are **less** likely to give rise to significant risks as client staff are likely to be more used to processing these transactions and such transactions are likely to be subject to robust internal controls.

Unusual and complex transactions and matters where judgment is required are more likely therefore to pose significant risk.

The ISA gives the following examples of the inherent **risk factors** (which we gave above, in the section 'Understanding the entity's system of internal control'). These are the kinds of things that could feature in an exam question and which you therefore need to be able to recognise as risks (*ISA 315: Appendix 2*).

| Risk factor | |
|---|---|
| Complexity | Regulatory - lots of **complex regulation** <br> Business model - **complex alliances** and joint ventures <br> Financial reporting framework - complex accounting measurements <br> Transactions - complex arrangements (eg off-balance sheet finance) |
| Subjectivity | Financial reporting framework: <br> • Wide range of possible accounting estimates (eg depreciation) <br> • **Management choice** of valuation technique |
| Change | Changes in: <br> **Economic conditions** - instability (eg current devaluation) <br> **Markets** - exposure to volatility (eg futures trading) <br> **Customer loss** - going concern / liquidity risk <br> **Industry model** - changes in the industry in which the entity operates <br> **Business model** - change in supply chain, new lines of business <br> **Geography** - expanding into new locations <br> **Entity structure** - for example reorganisations, subsidiaries sold <br> **IT** - IT environment change / new IT systems relevant to FR |
| Uncertainty | Financial reporting - estimation uncertainty <br> Pending litigation and contingent liabilities |
| Management bias or fraud risk | **Opportunities** for fraudulent financial reporting <br> Transactions with **related parties** <br> **Non-routine or non-systemic transactions** <br> Transactions recorded based on **management intentions** |

### 5.1.1 Response to audit risk

The auditor should obtain sufficient appropriate audit evidence regarding the assessed risks of material misstatement, through designing and implementing appropriate responses to those risks (ISA 330: para. 3) .

In the exam you are likely to be asked to explain the auditor's response to each audit risk you have identified in the scenario. Here you are not required to write out specific audit procedures, rather you need to explain:

- the types of enquiries the auditor should make (and of whom)
- the information/documentation they would require
- the correspondence they should review
- the impact on the level of materiality
- the type of testing they should perform
- the calculations they would do/re-perform
- the assets they should inspect

The best way to be able to explain the auditor's response to identified audit risks is to practice past exam questions and build your confidence at explaining the auditor's response. This is because the best response to each risk will depend on the particular circumstances of the audit client and the environment in which it operates.

To help you with this, we have considered some examples of audit risks along with an appropriate response to each risk. Note however, that you should not simply learn a list of responses.

| Audit risk | Auditor's response |
|---|---|
| Risk that inventory has a lower net realisable value than cost and is therefore overstated (eg NRV falls due to the client being in an industry where tastes/fashions change quickly). | Examine the instructions to identify slow moving inventory lines when attending the inventory count. <br><br> Increase the emphasis on reviewing the year end aged inventory analysis for evidence of slow-moving inventory. <br><br> Ascertain sales values for items sold post year end that were in inventory at the year end to ensure their NRV was higher than the cost recorded as part of the inventory value in the financial statements. |
| Assets are desirable / more susceptible to theft leading to a risk that recorded assets do not exist (eg inventory/non-current assets). | Focus on testing internal controls over those assets (including physical controls to prevent theft). <br><br> Increase sample sizes for inspecting recorded assets, ensuring any material assets are verified (in the context of performance materiality). |
| Increased risk of revenue expenditure being incorrectly classified as capital (or vice versa), leading to misstatement of assets/expenses (eg extensive refurbishment of non-current assets where judgement is needed to establish whether the nature of the work is to enhance the asset or repair/replace it). | Obtain a breakdown of related costs and review accounting entries against invoices/details of work done to ensure expenditure is correctly treated as capital/revenue. <br><br> Perform a detailed review of repairs accounts for any items which should be included in non-current assets. <br><br> Review the asset register to ensure only capital items have been included. |
| Increased risk of incomplete or unrecorded income due to fraud or theft (eg large amounts of cash collected and held prior to banking). | Perform analytical procedures focusing on comparing revenue with expected seasonal/monthly patterns. <br><br> If a retail client, perform/reperform a reconciliation of a sample of till records to actual bankings. |
| Receipts/invoicing significantly in advance/arrears of providing services or goods, therefore leading to an increased risk of revenue being in the wrong period (eg deposits received in advance, reservation fees, contracts spanning the year end). | For a sample of revenue entries recorded prior to the year end, agree the transactions as relating to pre year end sales by inspecting the contract / other supporting documentation. <br><br> Trace post year end transactions back to a supporting contract/documentation to test that revenue was recorded in the proper period. <br><br> For a sample of contracts or GDNs, verify the revenue was recognised according to the provision of services/goods. <br><br> Perform analytical procedures where monthly revenue is compared to expectations and budgeted revenue. Unexpected deviations should be investigated. |

| Audit risk | Auditor's response |
|---|---|
| Invoices received (or payments made) in advance/arrears of goods or services delivery date leading to overstatement or understatement of costs and/or liabilities. | Review post year end bank statements / cash book payments for evidence of amounts relating to the financial year but not included in liabilities.<br><br>For a sample of documents pre and post year end indicating date of delivery of goods/services (eg GRNs), verify the cost and liability were recorded in the appropriate period. |
| There is an increased risk of irrecoverable debts (eg due to the nature of the client's industry or customers), resulting in assets being potentially overstated. | Identify year end receivable balances still outstanding at the date of the audit by reviewing post year end receipts from customers. For amounts still outstanding establish whether these are provided for.<br><br>Review aged receivables analysis and customer correspondence files for evidence of disputes with receivables and consider the adequacy of any related receivables allowance. |
| Significant client borrowing and/or overdraft with cash flow problems which may indicate going concern problems. | Review correspondence with the bank/lender for any evidence of withdrawal or extension of facilities.<br><br>If there are bank covenants linked to performance on which facilities depend, review compliance with these, and increase testing on areas where management could manipulate performance indicators (such as provisions).<br><br>Review post year end results and cash flow forecasts (if prepared) for evidence the company can continue as a going concern. |
| New client systems/controls/staff impacting on amounts recorded in the financial statements, increasing the risk of errors and the risk of internal controls not operating effectively. | Undertake additional visits (eg interim audit) to assess the effectiveness of controls operating over areas affected.<br><br>Perform extra work to document and evaluate new systems/controls, performing tests of controls where necessary.<br><br>Increase sample sizes for substantive testing over financial statement areas impacted. |
| Management has an incentive to manipulate performance, increasing the risk of profits being overstated (eg remuneration or bank funding is reliant on performance). | Focus on and increase testing on judgemental areas in the financial statements (eg provisions, revenue recognition accounting policies). |

# 6 Fraud, laws and regulations

## 6.1 Fraud

KEY
TERM

**Fraud:** an "intentional act by one or more individuals among management, those charged with governance, employees, or third parties, involving the use of deception to obtain an unjust or illegal advantage" (ISA 240: para. 11(a)).

**Fraud** may be perpetrated by an individual, or colluded in, with people internal or external to the business.

**Fraud risk factors** are "events or conditions that indicate an incentive or pressure to commit fraud or provide an opportunity to commit fraud" (ISA 240: para. 11(b)).

There are two types of fraud which may cause material misstatement in the financial statements:

(a) **Fraudulent financial reporting** (intentional misstatements, including omissions of amounts or disclosures in financial statements, to deceive financial statement users)

(b) **Misappropriation of assets** (the theft of an entity's assets)

(ISA 240: para. 3)

## Essential reading

See Chapter 6 of the Essential reading for more information on fraudulent financial reporting and misappropriation of assets.

The Essential reading is available as an Appendix of the digital edition of the Workbook.

The **responsibility to prevent and detect fraud** lies with an entity's **management** and those charged with governance. It is their responsibility to establish a culture of honesty and ethical behaviour and to implement a system of internal control to mitigate the risk of fraud.

(ISA 240: para. 4)

ISA 240 *The Auditor's Responsibilities Relating to Fraud in an Audit of Financial Statements* states that the **auditor** is responsible for obtaining reasonable assurance that the financial statements are free from material misstatement, whether caused by fraud or error. (ISA 240: para. 5)

The auditor is responsible for maintaining professional scepticism throughout the audit, considering the possibility of management override of controls, and recognising that the audit procedures effective for detecting errors may not be effective for detecting fraud.

(ISA 240: para. 12)

Where the auditor's risk assessment suggests there is a risk of material misstatement due to fraud the risk should be treated as a significant risk.

In this event the auditor should:

- Assign and supervise audit staff taking into account their knowledge, skill and ability;
- Evaluate whether the client's accounting policies may indicate fraudulent financial reporting; and
- Incorporate unpredictability in the selection of the nature, timing and extent of audit procedures (ISA 240: para.29).

There should be a discussion among audit team members that places particular emphasis on how and where the financial statements may be susceptible to fraud.

Risk assessment procedures to obtain information in identifying the risks of material misstatement due to fraud shall include the following:

(a) **Enquiries of management** regarding:

(i) **Management's assessment** of the risk that the financial statements may be misstated due to fraud

 BPP

(ii) **Management's process** for identifying and responding to the risk of fraud

(iii) **Management's communication to those charged with governance** in respect of its process for identifying and responding to the risk of fraud

(iv) **Management's communication to employees** regarding its views on business practices and ethical behaviour

(v) **Knowledge** of any actual, suspected or alleged fraud

(b) **Enquiries of internal audit** for knowledge of any actual, suspected or alleged fraud, and its views on the risks of fraud

(c) Obtaining an **understanding** of how those charged with governance **oversee** management's processes for identifying and responding to the risk of fraud and the internal control established to mitigate these risks

(d) **Enquiries of those charged with governance** for knowledge of any actual, suspected or alleged fraud

(e) Evaluating whether any unusual relationships have been identified in performing **analytical procedures** that may indicate risk of material misstatement due to fraud

(f) Considering whether any **other information** may indicate risk of material misstatement due to fraud

(g) Evaluating whether any **fraud risk factors** are present

(ISA 240: paras. 17–24)

If the auditor identifies fraud or receives information that a fraud may exist, the auditor shall report this on a **timely basis** to the **appropriate level of management** (ISA 240: para. 40).

If the auditor identifies or suspects fraud involving management, employees with significant roles in internal control, and others where fraud could have a material effect on the financial statements, they shall communicate this on a **timely basis** to **those charged with governance** (ISA 240: para. 41).

The auditor also needs to consider whether there is a responsibility to report to the **regulatory or enforcement authorities** – the auditor's professional duty of **confidentiality** may be **overridden** by **laws and statutes** in certain jurisdictions (ISA 240: para. 43).

## 6.2 Laws and regulations

An entity is likely to be subject to several laws and regulations.

The auditor is not responsible for preventing non-compliance and cannot be expected to detect non-compliance with all laws and regulations (ISA 250 (Revised): para. 4).

The **auditor's responsibility** is to obtain reasonable assurance that the financial statements are **free from material misstatement** whether due to fraud or error and, in this respect, the auditor must take into account the legal and regulatory framework within which the entity operates (ISA 250 (Revised): para. 5).

ISA 250 (Revised) (para. 6) distinguishes the auditor's responsibilities in relation to compliance with two different categories of laws and regulations:

(a) Those that have a **direct effect** on the determination of **material amounts** and disclosures in the financial statements (such as tax or pension laws and regulations)

(b) Those that **do not have a direct effect** on the determination of material amounts and disclosures in the financial statements but where compliance may be fundamental to the **operating aspects**, ability to **continue in business**, or to avoid **material penalties** (such as regulatory compliance or compliance with the terms of an operating licence)

For the first category, the auditor's responsibility is to obtain sufficient appropriate audit evidence about **compliance** with those laws and regulations (ISA 250 (Revised): para. 14).

For the second category, the auditor's responsibility is to undertake specified audit procedures to help **identify non-compliance** with laws and regulations that may have a **material effect** on the financial statements. These include enquiries of management and inspecting correspondence with the relevant licensing or regulatory authorities (ISA 240 (Revised): para. 15).

**Examples of laws and regulations** that may be included in these categories include the following:

- Fraud, corruption and bribery
- Money laundering, terrorist financing and proceeds of crime
- Securities markets and trading
- Banking and other financial products and services
- Data protection
- Tax and pension liabilities and payments
- Environmental protection
- Public health and safety

(ISA 250 (Revised): para. A6)

The responsibility to comply with relevant laws and regulations lies with an entity's management and those charged with governance.

## Essential reading

See Chapter 6 of the Essential reading for more information on laws and regulations.

The Essential reading is available as an Appendix of the digital edition of the Workbook.

# Chapter summary

## Risk assessment

### ISA 200 Overall Objectives of the Independent Auditor and the Conduct of an Audit in Accordance with ISAs

**Overall objectives**
- To obtain reasonable assurance that the financial statements are free from material misstatement
- To express an opinion on the financial statements

**Professional scepticism**
- Questioning mind
- Be alert for contradictory evidence
- Be aware of possible fraud
- Be alert for information the brings reliability of documents/responses into question

**Professional judgement**
- Level of audit risk and setting materiality
- Nature, timing and extent of audit procedures
- Sufficiency and appropriateness of audit evidence
- Management's judgements
- Drawing conclusions

**Risk based approach to audit**
- Identify risk
- Direct audit testing to risky areas

### Audit risk

**Definition**
The risk that the auditor expresses an inappropriate opinion when the financial statements are materially misstated

**Inherent risk**
The susceptibility of an assertion about a class of transaction, account balance or disclosure to a misstatement that could be material, either individually or when aggregated with other misstatements, before consideration of any related internal controls

**Control risk**
The risk that a material misstatement could occur in an assertion about a class of transaction, account balance or disclosure and that could be material, individually or when aggregated with other misstatements, will not be prevented or detected and corrected, on a timely basis by the entity's internal control

**Detection risk**
- The risk that the auditor's procedures will not detect a misstatement that exists in an assertion that could be material either individually or when aggregated with other misstatements
- Sampling risk: the auditor's conclusion based on the sample tested is not appropriate for the population as a whole
- Non-sampling risk: other factors, for example time pressure, new audit, poor planning

### ISA 320 Materiality in Planning and Performing an Audit

**Definition**
Information is material if its omission or misstatement could reasonably be expected to influence the economic decisions of users taken on the basis of the financial statements

**The calculation of materiality**
- Matter of judgement
- Quantitative and qualitative
- Benchmarks:
  - 0.5 to 1% revenue
  - 1 to 2% total assets
  - 5 to 10% PBT

**Performance materiality**
Amount set by the auditor at less than the materiality level for a particular class of transactions or account balance

**Revising materiality as the audit progresses**
Materiality level may need to change as a result of new information or a change in the auditor's understanding

**Documentation of materiality**
- Document materiality and performance materiality
- The reasons for any revisions

### Understanding the entity and its environment

**Objective**

Identify and assess the risks of material misstatement and design and implement a response to them

**Requirements**

- Industry, regulatory and other external factors
- Nature of the entity
- Entity's selection and application of accounting policies
- Objectives and strategies
- Measurement and review of the entity's financial performance
- Internal control
- Via enquiries, analytical procedures and observation and inspection

**ISA 520 *Analytical Procedures***

- The analysis of relationships to identify inconsistencies and unexpected relationships
- Use as part of risk assessment procedures
- Includes comparisons with:
  - Prior periods and budgets
  - Industry information
  - Predictive estimates
  - Ratio analysis, variance analysis, proof in total
  - Relationships between financial and non-financial information

### Assessing the risks of material misstatement

**Significant risks**

- Require special audit consideration
- Include:
  - Risk of fraud
  - Unusual transactions
  - Complex transactions

### Fraud, laws and regulations

**Fraud**

- An intentional act, involving the use of deception to obtain an unjust or illegal advantage
- Management/those charged with governance have responsibility to prevent/detect fraud
- Auditor's responsibility to plan/perform audit with a reasonable chance of **detecting material misstatements**
- Where fraud is suspected, the auditor should:
  - Assign/supervise audit staff taking into account their knowledge, skill and ability
  - Evaluate client's accounting policies
  - Incorporate unpredictability in the selection of audit procedures

**Laws and regulations**

- Management/those charged with governance have responsibility to comply with laws and regulations
- Auditor's responsibility to obtain reasonable assurance that financial statements are **free from material misstatements**

# Knowledge diagnostic

### 1. Professional scepticism and professional judgement

Auditors must carry out their work with professional scepticism and exercise professional judgement.

### 2. Audit risk

Audit risk is the risk that the auditor expresses an inappropriate audit opinion when the financial statements are materially misstated. It has three components: inherent risk, control risk and detection risk (which includes sampling and non-sampling risk).

### 3. Inherent risk and control risk

Inherent risk and control risk are determined by the nature of the entity, the industry in which it operates and its internal control systems. The auditor cannot influence these but must assess whether they are high, medium or low.

### 4. Detection risk

Detection risk is the only component of audit risk over which the auditor has control. The auditor's actions can decrease detection risk, for example by extending sample sizes or using more experienced audit staff.

### 5. Materiality

The auditor must determine a materiality level for the financial statements at the planning stage. Where audit risk is deemed to be high, the level of materiality will be less which in turn increases the amount of audit testing performed.

### 6. Materiality considerations

An item may be material due to its monetary value (quantitative materiality) or by its nature (qualitative materiality). The materiality level may be revised during the course of the audit if information comes to light that indicates the level set at the planning stage is not appropriate.

### 7. Performance materiality

The auditor should also set a level for performance materiality which will be lower than the materiality level set for the financial statements.

### 8. Management's responsibilities for fraud and error

An entity's management and those charged with governance are responsible for the prevention and detection of fraud and error and for non-compliance with laws and regulations.

### 9. Auditor's responsibilities for fraud and error

The auditor should plan and perform their audit so that they have reasonable assurance of detecting material fraud and non-compliance with laws and regulations that may have a material impact on the financial statements.

# Further study guidance

## Question practice

Now try the following from the Further question practice bank [available in the digital edition of the Workbook]:

- Section A Q25, Q27, Q30 and Q31
- Section B Q64 Glo
- Section B Q65 Stone Holidays
- Section B Q66 Parker (a) and (b)
- Section B Q67 Heels (a), (b) and (c)
- Section B Q68 Turbo (a) and (b)

## Further reading

There are technical articles and study support videos on the ACCA website written/recorded by members of the AA examining team and other tutors which are relevant to some of the topics covered in this chapter that you should read:

Technical articles:

- *Risk and understanding the entity* (https://www.accaglobal.com/gb/en/student/exam-support-resources/professional-exams-study-resources/p7/technical-articles/risk-understanding-entity.html)
- *Laws and regulations* (https://www.accaglobal.com/gb/en/student/exam-support-resources/fundamentals-exams-study-resources/f8/technical-articles/laws-and-regulations.html)
- *Audit Risk* (https://www.accaglobal.com/uk/en/student/exam-support-resources/professional-exams-study-resources/p7/technical-articles/audit-risk.html)
- *ISA 330 and Responses to Assessed Risks* (https://www.accaglobal.com/uk/en/student/exam-support-resources/fundamentals-exams-study-resources/f8/technical-articles/ISA330-responses-assessed-risks.html)

## Own research

Identify an industry which interests you and choose a company from that industry. Download the company's financial statements and consider which areas of the financial statements or the nature of the company may pose increased audit risk.

# Activity answers

## Activity 1: Audit risks and auditor's response

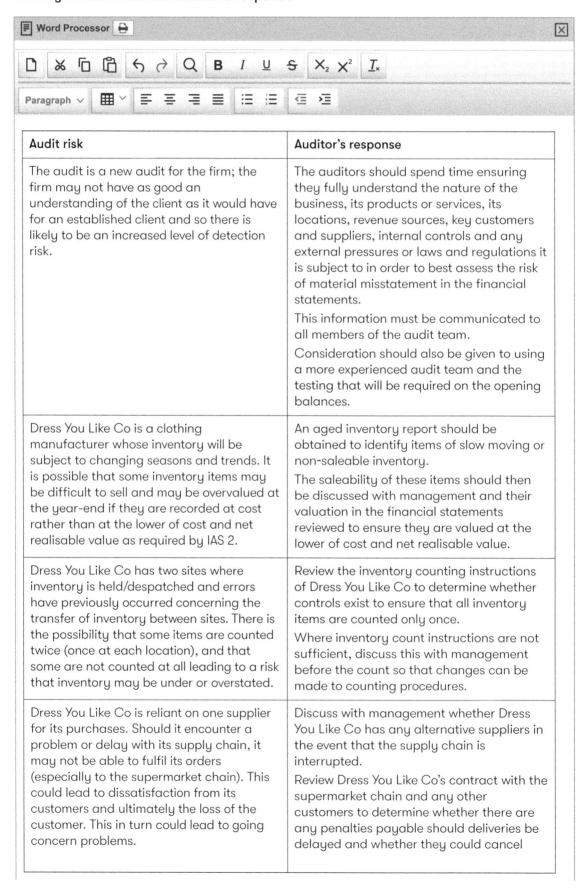

| Audit risk | Auditor's response |
|---|---|
| The audit is a new audit for the firm; the firm may not have as good an understanding of the client as it would have for an established client and so there is likely to be an increased level of detection risk. | The auditors should spend time ensuring they fully understand the nature of the business, its products or services, its locations, revenue sources, key customers and suppliers, internal controls and any external pressures or laws and regulations it is subject to in order to best assess the risk of material misstatement in the financial statements.<br><br>This information must be communicated to all members of the audit team.<br><br>Consideration should also be given to using a more experienced audit team and the testing that will be required on the opening balances. |
| Dress You Like Co is a clothing manufacturer whose inventory will be subject to changing seasons and trends. It is possible that some inventory items may be difficult to sell and may be overvalued at the year-end if they are recorded at cost rather than at the lower of cost and net realisable value as required by IAS 2. | An aged inventory report should be obtained to identify items of slow moving or non-saleable inventory.<br><br>The saleability of these items should then be discussed with management and their valuation in the financial statements reviewed to ensure they are valued at the lower of cost and net realisable value. |
| Dress You Like Co has two sites where inventory is held/despatched and errors have previously occurred concerning the transfer of inventory between sites. There is the possibility that some items are counted twice (once at each location), and that some are not counted at all leading to a risk that inventory may be under or overstated. | Review the inventory counting instructions of Dress You Like Co to determine whether controls exist to ensure that all inventory items are counted only once.<br><br>Where inventory count instructions are not sufficient, discuss this with management before the count so that changes can be made to counting procedures. |
| Dress You Like Co is reliant on one supplier for its purchases. Should it encounter a problem or delay with its supply chain, it may not be able to fulfil its orders (especially to the supermarket chain). This could lead to dissatisfaction from its customers and ultimately the loss of the customer. This in turn could lead to going concern problems. | Discuss with management whether Dress You Like Co has any alternative suppliers in the event that the supply chain is interrupted.<br><br>Review Dress You Like Co's contract with the supermarket chain and any other customers to determine whether there are any penalties payable should deliveries be delayed and whether they could cancel |

BPP

| Audit risk | Auditor's response |
| --- | --- |
| | their contract with Dress You Like Co. |
| Dress You Like Co allows its supermarket customer 60-day credit terms. This may place additional strain on cash flow and lead to potential going concern problems given the deterioration during the year of cash flow and working capital. | Request that management produce cash flow forecasts for the year ahead to identify any deficits in cash flow.<br><br>Consider the reasonableness of the assumptions on which these are based (especially relating to the timing of cash flows from the supermarket).<br><br>Consider whether there are any known concerns about the supermarket's ability to settle its debts.<br><br>Determine from management whether they have access to any short-term finance should any cash flow problems arise. |
| The finance director is suing the company for constructive dismissal but no mention of this has been made in the year-end financial statements (ie no provision or contingent liability).<br><br>The case has been going on for some time which suggests that at least disclosure of a contingent liability is required and so there is a risk that provision/contingent liability disclosures may not be complete. | Review correspondence from both the director and the entity's legal advisers relating to the legal claim in order to establish the likely outcome of the claim.<br><br>Discuss the appropriate accounting treatment for the claim with the directors.<br><br>Review minutes of board meetings and events after the reporting period to determine whether the claim was settled. |
| There has not been a finance director in place for the last six months of the year (since March 20X6). The lack of finance director increases control risk and furthermore there is a lack of experience at this high level and the assistant is also overloaded. The assistant may not have the time or ability to answer queries from the audit team which could lead to difficulty in obtaining sufficient information and explanations required by the auditor. | Determine from management whether there will be appropriate personnel available to answer the audit team's queries and provide the information they require for the audit.<br><br>Particular attention should be paid to judgemental areas to ensure any judgements made are reasonable. |
| The internal audit function used to perform reviews on the bank reconciliation and supplier statement reconciliations which would increase the reliability of the bank and payables balances.<br><br>The fact that there is now no longer any internal audit function means that there is an increased likelihood that material errors in the completeness, accuracy and validity of the bank balance and the completeness of payables may not have been detected by the client staff. | A detailed review of the year-end bank reconciliation and supplier statement reconciliations should be performed in order to determine the accuracy and completeness of bank and payables.<br><br>A larger sample size may be necessary if it is anticipated that there will be a high level of errors.<br><br>A detailed review of reconciling items and payments made in the post year-end period should be conducted. |

## Activity 2: Ratios and risk

1

| | 20X6 | 20X5 |
|---|---|---|
| | | |
| Gross profit margin (supermarket) | 1,650/53,500 | 3,920/49,000 |
| | = 3% | = 8% |
| Gross profit margin (other) | 820/8,200 | 800/6,700 |
| | = 10% | = 12% |
| Receivables collection period (supermarket) | (11,800/53,500) × 365 | (8,300/49,000) × 365 |
| | = 81 days | = 62 days |
| Receivables collection period (other) | (700/8,200) × 365 | (600/6,700) × 365 |
| | = 31 days | = 33 days |
| Inventory holding period | (13,800/59,275) × 365 | (4,900/50,980) × 365 |
| | = 85 days | = 35 days |

\* 59,275 = 51,895 + 7,380
^ 50,980 = 45,080 + 5,900

2

| | |
|---|---|
| The draft financial statement extracts indicate that there may be cash flow problems leading to concern over going concern. | Discuss the going concern status of Dress You Like Co with management. |
| Dress You Like Co has seen falling gross profit margins during the year. For the supermarket customer, these are from 8% in 20X5 to 3% in 20X6 and for other customers 12% (20X5) to 10% (20X6). | Obtain a copy of the cash flow forecasts produced by management and consider whether the assumptions on which they are based are reasonable, particularly in terms of the timings of cash received from customers. |
| The receivables collection period for the supermarket customer is 81 days in 20X6 compared to 62 days in 20X5. For other customers the receivables collection period is largely stable at 31 and 33 days. | Discuss with management whether Dress You Like Co has any alternative funding available in the event that it struggles with cash flow. |
| The inventory holding period has risen from 35 days in 20X5 to 85 days in 20X6 largely due to stockpiling for last minute orders. | Discuss with management whether any disclosures relating to going concern have been made in the financial statements. |
| Overall, the fall in margins, lack of credit control and increased inventory holdings mean that the company has gone from a | |

| cash position of $200,000 in 20X5 to an overdraft of $750,000 in 20X6. This further compounds cash flow and going concern worries and worries that inventory may be overstated. | |
| --- | --- |

# Skills checkpoint 2

## How to approach audit risk questions

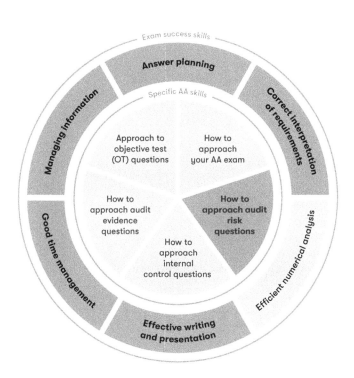

## Introduction

The external auditor must assess the level of audit risk when planning an audit as this impacts the amount and nature of audit procedures they will perform. Consequently, questions on audit risk feature regularly in the Audit and Assurance (AA) exam.

There are two main types of audit risk questions: knowledge based questions where you need to explain audit risk and its components (inherent, control and detection risk), and scenario based questions on audit risk which tend to feature in Section B of the exam.

The Examiner's reports state that candidates' performance in Section B questions on audit risk can often be very mixed. You will be provided with a scenario and the requirement will ask you to 'Describe (for example) seven audit risks and explain the auditor's response to each risk in planning the audit of ABC Co'.

This skills checkpoint will therefore consider how you should approach such questions.

# Skills Checkpoint 2: How to approach audit risk questions

### AA Skill: How to approach audit risk questions

A step-by-step technique for ensuring that your approach to audit risk questions uses the scenario provided in the exam and maximises your marks is outlined below. Each step will be explained in more detail in the following sections and illustrated by answering a requirement from a past exam question.

> **STEP 1:**
>
> Allow some of your allotted time to read the requirements and the scenario.
> Don't rush into starting to write your answer.

> **STEP 2:**
>
> Re-read the scenario and start to develop an answer plan.
> Use the table headings provided (Audit risk and Auditor's response) and as you read through the scenario for the second time, write down a few words or a bullet point each time you identify a potential audit risk in the scenario.
> Use these as headings in your answer.

> **STEP 3:**
>
> Re-read the requirement to confirm how many audit risks you need to describe. You may have written down more headings than required, in which case decide which ideas you can explain most easily and include those in your answer.
>
> When you write your answer the audit risk should describe the specific impact that the issue might have on the financial statements (ie a balance could be under/overstated or a disclosure missing) or the impact on the smooth running of the audit (ie information may not be available). Next explain the practical steps you would expect the auditor to take to address the risks.

# Exam success skills

The following illustration is based on an extract from a past exam question, about a pharmaceutical manufacturer, called 'Abrahams'. This extract was worth 10 marks.

For this question, we will also focus on the following **exam success skills**:

- **Managing information**. It is easy for the amount of information contained in scenario-based questions to feel overwhelming. To manage this, focus on the requirement first, noting the key exam verbs to ensure you answer the question properly. Then, read the rest of the question, noting important and relevant information from the scenario.

- **Correct interpretation of requirements**. Here you need to **both** describe the audit risk **and** explain the auditor's response to each risk.

- **Answer planning**. Everyone will have a preferred style for planning an answer. For example, it may be highlighting or simply making notes. Remember you have a highlighter tool available in the assessment platform and a scratch pad tool is available too for you to make notes as you read through the scenario. Choose the approach that you feel most comfortable with or, if you are not sure, try out different approaches for different questions until you have found your preferred style.

- **Effective writing and presentation**. A blank table will be provided for audit risk and response questions. One column will be for risks and one column for responses. Start each risk or response in a new cell of the table provided in the appropriate column. Enter the related risks

 **BPP**

and responses on the same row. Ensure you explain the impact that audit risk could have on the financial statements or the smooth running of the audit. Use full sentences, ensuring your style is professional.

- **Good time management.** It is essential that you do not overrun on the constructed response questions in Section B and so you must always keep an eye on time. Note down the time you should finish the question.

# Skill Activity

**STEP 1**   Allow some of your allotted time to read the requirement and the scenario. Do not rush into starting to write your answer.

Start by analysing the requirements so that you know what you are looking for when you read the scenario.

### Required

(b)  Using the information provided, describe **FIVE** audit risks, and explain the auditor's response to each risk in planning the audit of Abrahams Co.

**Note.** Prepare your answer using the two columns provided, headed Audit risk and Auditor's response respectively.

**10 marks**

The first part of the requirement is to 'describe **FIVE** audit risks'. Here you need to use the scenario to generate five issues that could cause a problem in the financial statements or affect the smooth running of the audit. Note that where you are asked for *audit* risks, you should not be writing about *business* risks, which are something altogether different. It is important to remember that for a risk to be an audit risk rather than just a general business risk it needs to have an impact on the financial statements being audited. A common mistake by students is listing a risk to a business that doesn't have an impact on the financial statements or without explaining the impact on the financial statements.

Problems in the financial statements could include:

- A balance being over or understated (for example if there is an error in the accounting treatment or cut-off)

- A disclosure being omitted or misleading (for example relating to a contingent liability)

- Uncertainty relating to going concern (for example loss of a key customer or the impending renewal of bank loan/overdraft facilities)

- Loss of client accounting information/systems

Events that might impact the smooth running of the audit include:

- The client is a new audit client (so the auditor is less familiar with the client's business/systems)

- Loss of key client personnel (for example the loss of a finance director/finance officer before the year-end)

- Whether there are time pressures on the audit or a tight reporting schedule

The second part of the requirement is to 'explain the auditor's response to each risk'. This does not mean that you need to provide a list of audit procedures but rather you should explain the practical action the auditor would take. For example, what questions should they ask, what information would they need, what documents would they require access to and which figures might they recalculate?

This requirement is worth 10 marks and at 1.8 minutes a mark, should take 18 minutes to both plan and write the solution.

## Abrahams

Abrahams Co develops, manufactures and sells a range of pharmaceuticals and has a wide customer base across Europe and Asia. You are the audit manager of Nate & Co and you are planning the audit of Abrahams Co whose financial year end is 31 January. You attended a planning meeting with the finance director and audit engagement partner and are now reviewing the meeting notes in order to produce the audit strategy and plan. Revenue for the year is forecast at $25 million.

During the year the company has spent $2.2 million on developing several new products. Some of these are in the early stages of development whilst others are nearing completion. The finance director has confirmed that all projects are likely to be successful and so he is intending to capitalise the full $2.2 million.

Once products have completed the development stage, Abrahams Co begins manufacturing them. At the year-end it is anticipated that there will be significant levels of work in progress. In addition, the company uses a standard costing method to value inventory; the standard costs are set when a product is first manufactured and are not usually updated. In order to fulfil customer orders promptly, Abrahams Co has warehouses for finished goods located across Europe and Asia; approximately one-third of these are third-party warehouses where Abrahams Co just rents space.

In September a new accounting package was introduced. This is a bespoke system developed by the information technology (IT) manager. The old and new packages were not run in parallel as it was felt that this would be too onerous for the accounting team. Two months after the system changeover, the IT manager left the company; a new manager has been recruited but is not due to start work until January.

In order to fund the development of new products, Abrahams Co has restructured its finance and raised $1 million through issuing shares at a premium and $2.5 million through a long-term loan. There are bank covenants attached to the loan, the main one relating to a minimum level of total assets. If these covenants are breached then the loan becomes immediately repayable. The company has a policy of revaluing land and buildings, and the finance director has announced that all land and buildings will be revalued as at the year-end.

The reporting timetable for audit completion of Abrahams Co is quite short, and the finance director would like to report results even earlier this year.

**STEP 2**  Now you should be ready to re-read the scenario and plan your answer using the risks you identify as you read through.

Work through each paragraph of the scenario identifying specific audit risks. Each risk is worth one mark and the auditor's response is also worth one mark, hence why you need five properly explained risks and responses to gain 10 marks.

### Completed answer plan

Having worked through each paragraph, an answer

plan can now be completed. A possible answer plan is

shown here. Note that in the CBE environment you can

use the highlighter tool to pick out the underlined words

while using the scratch pad to make the related notes.

Abrahams Co develops, manufactures and sells a range of pharmaceuticals and has a wide customer base across Europe and Asia. You are the audit manager of Nate & Co and you are planning the audit of Abrahams Co whose financial year end is 31 January. You attended a planning meeting with the finance director and audit engagement partner and are now reviewing the meeting notes in order to produce the audit strategy and plan. Revenue for the year is forecast at $25 million.

During the year, the company has spent $2.2 million on developing several new products. Some of these are in the early stages of development whilst others are nearing completion. The finance director has confirmed that all projects are likely to be successful and so he is intending to capitalise the full $2.2 million[1].

[1] Risk that intangible assets and profit may be overstated if IAS 38 PIRATE criteria not met

Once products have completed the development stage, Abrahams Co begins manufacturing them. At the year-end, it is anticipated that there will be significant levels of work in progress[2]. In addition, the company uses a standard costing method to value inventory; the standard costs are set when a product is first manufactured and are not usually updated.[3] In order to fulfil customer orders promptly, Abrahams Co has warehouses for finished goods located across Europe and Asia; approximately one-third of these are third-party warehouses where Abrahams Co just rents space.[4]

[2] Risk that work in progress may be overvalued/difficult to value – do we have sufficient skills? Expert required?

[3] Standard costs used – must be kept up to date so they approximate to actual costs – inventory may be over/understated

[4] Inventory held at third party locations – any inaccuracies in inventory count may lead to material over/understatement. Which locations should we attend for the inventory count?

In September, a new accounting package was introduced[5]. This is a bespoke system developed by the IT manager. The old and new packages were not run in parallel as it was felt that this would be too onerous for the accounting team. Two months after the system changeover the IT manager left[6] the company; a new manager has been recruited but is not due to start work until January.

[5] New accounting system (and bespoke) – any errors on transfer of information could lead to material errors in fs. Testing required on transfer of balances.

[6] IT manager left, replacement not yet started. Investigate level of errors occuring and support available. Document new internal controls.

In order to fund the development of new products, Abrahams Co has restructured its finance and raised $1 million through issuing shares[7] at a premium and $2.5 million through a long-term loan. There are bank covenants[8] attached to the loan, the main one relating to a minimum level of total assets. If these covenants are breached then the loan becomes immediately repayable. The company has a policy of revaluing[9] land and buildings, and the finance director has announced that all land and buildings will be revalued as at the year-end.

The reporting timetable for audit completion of Abrahams Co is quite short[10], and the finance director would like to report results even earlier this year.

[7] Share issue – risk that transaction not properly disclosed in statement of changes in equity. Recalculate split between nominal value and premium.

[8] Loan covenants exist – risk that financing could be recalled if covenants not met (going concern). Review covenants to determine whether breach has occured and bank correspondence.

[9] Revaluation may be required to satisfy loan covenants – risk that valuation overstated. Consider status of valuer (independent/competent).

[10] Tight reporting timescale may not allow enough time to gather sufficient evidence. Plan to perform work on assets pre year end, use more experienced staff.

**STEP 3** You will see that there are more than five audit risks, therefore choose the five that you can best explain.

You will enter your answer into the table provided in the CBE. Describe each audit risk in detail explaining the potential impact on the financial statements. Also remember to explain the practical steps the auditor would take and the work they would do.

Start each risk and related response in a new row of the table provided in the CBE (in the appropriate column).

**STEP 4** Suggested solution

Note that you would enter each risk and response into each column of a table but the solution below has each risk followed by each response underneath so that tutorial notes can be shown alongside the risks/responses to which they relate.

**Audit risk** — Abrahams Co's finance director intends to capitalise the $2.2 million of development expenditure incurred. This material amount should only be capitalised if the related product can generate future profits as set out in IAS 38 *Intangible Assets*. There is a risk that at least some of the expenditure does not meet the criteria. This will mean assets and profits are overstated[11].

**Auditor's response** — An analysis[12] showing developments costs in relation to each product should be obtained and reviewed. Testing should be carried out to ensure the technical and commercial feasibility of each product and, where it cannot be proven that future economic benefits will result from the product developed, the related costs should be expensed.

[11] Here the requirements of the accounting standard are explained as well as the potential impact on the fs

[12] Response is to obtain a breakdown of costs which have been capitalised and test them to determine whether they meet the IAS 38 criteria

**Audit risk** — At the year-end it is anticipated that there will be significant levels of work in progress, likely to constitute a material balance. The pharmaceuticals production process is likely to be complex and the audit team may not be sufficiently qualified to assess the quantity and value of work in progress. Therefore, they may be unable to gain sufficient evidence[13] over a material area of the financial statements.

[13] Audit risk explains that WIP is a complex/judgemental area so there is risk that the balance may be materially misstated

**Auditor's response** — Nate & Co should assess its ability to gain the required level of evidence and if it is not sufficient, it should approach an independent expert to value the work in progress. This should be arranged after obtaining consent from Abrahams Co's management and in time for the year-end inventory count.

**Audit risk** — In September, a new accounting package was introduced. The fact the two systems were not run in parallel increases the risk that errors occurring during the changeover were not highlighted, and all areas of the financial statements could potentially be affected.[14]

[14] New accounting system brings the risk that data produced by the new system at the year-end may not be reliable

**Auditor's response** — The new system will need to be fully documented[15] by the audit team including relevant controls. Testing should be performed to ensure the closing data on the old system was correctly transferred as the opening data on the new system, and that transactions have not been duplicated on both systems and therefore included twice.

[15] Action: document new system and test changeover of data

**Audit risk** — The loan has covenants[16] attached to it. If these are breached then the loan would be repayable straight away and would need to be classified as a current liability, potentially resulting in a net current liability position on the statement of financial position. If the company did not have sufficient cash available to repay the loan balance the going concern status of the company could be threatened.

[16] Loan covenants pose a going concern risk if breached and also the potential to manipulate fs to ensure breaches do not occur

**Auditor's response** — Obtain and review (or reperform) covenant calculations to identify any breaches. If there are any the likelihood of the bank demanding repayment will need to be assessed and the potential impact on the company considered. The need to avoid breaching the covenants reinforces the audit team's need to maintain professional scepticism[17] in areas that could be manipulated.

**Audit risk** — The already short reporting timetable[18] for Abrahams Co is likely to be reduced. This could increase detection risk because there is pressure on the team to obtain sufficient and appropriate evidence in a shorter timescale, which could adversely influence judgement on the size of samples and the extent of work needed.

**Auditor's response** — If it is confirmed with the finance director that the time available at the final audit is to be reduced then the ability of the team to gather sufficient appropriate evidence should be assessed. If it is not realistically possible to perform all the required work at a final audit then an interim audit[19] should take place in late December or early January to reduce the level of work to be done at the final audit.

[17] Response – be alert for potential manipulation, review covenants for evidence of breaches

[18] Risk that short timescale means we cannot gather all of the evidence that we need to form our opinion

[19] Response is to perform work before the year end to reduce pressure after the year end

## Exam success skills diagnostic

Every time you complete a question, use the diagnostic below to assess how effectively you demonstrated the exam success skills in answering the question. The table has been completed below for the 'Abrahams' activity to give you an idea of how to complete the diagnostic.

| Exam success skills | Your reflections/observations |
|---|---|
| Managing information | Did you identify audit risks in the scenario? |
| Correct interpretation of requirements | Did you identify that you only need five audit risks and five (related) auditor's responses to gain ten marks? |
| Answer planning | Did you draw up an answer plan using your preferred approach (eg, highlighting, notes)? Did your plan help to create a structure for your answer? |
| Effective writing and presentation | Did you use full sentences? And most importantly – did you explain **why** your points constituted an audit risk? |
| Good time management | Did you manage to read, plan and complete your solution in the allotted time? |
| Most important action points to apply to your next question | |

| Exam success skills | Your reflections/observations |
|---|---|
|  |  |

## Summary

You are likely to see a scenario-based question on audit risk in the exam. You cannot prepare for every type of business and all audit risks, however you can equip yourself with the skills to attempt audit risk questions by using the information given in the question to guide the structure of your answer. A key skill is then applying this back to the given scenario. You will not be able to pass these questions unless you explain both the audit risk and the auditor' response. It is therefore essential that you try to create a practical answer that is relevant to the scenario, and/or addresses the issues identified in the scenario, instead of simply producing risks/responses you have learned by heart.

As you move into practising questions as part of your final revision, you will need to practise taking in information from a scenario quickly, accurately understanding the requirements, and creating an answer that fully addresses the requirements in the context of the scenario.

# 7

# Audit planning and documentation

## Learning objectives

On completion of this chapter, you should be able to:

| Syllabus learning outcomes | Syllabus reference no. |
| --- | --- |
| Identify and explain the need for, benefits of and importance of planning an audit | B6 (a) |
| Identify and describe the contents of the overall audit strategy and audit plan | B6 (b) |
| Explain and describe the relationship between the overall audit strategy and the audit plan | B6 (c) |
| Explain the difference between an interim and final audit | B6 (d) |
| Describe the purpose of an interim audit, and the procedures likely to be adopted at this stage in the audit | B6 (e) |
| Describe the impact of the work performed during the interim audit on the final audit | B6 (f) |
| Explain the need for, and the importance of, audit documentation | B6 (g) |
| Describe the form and contents of working papers and supporting documentation | B6 (h) |
| Explain the procedures to ensure safe custody and retention of working papers | B6 (i) |

## Business and Exam context

This chapter covers the more detailed aspects of audit planning and the documentation that is produced at this stage of the audit. It is important to understand why we plan an audit and the purpose, form and content of audit documentation. We will also look at the retention of documentation, who it belongs to and whether we are allowed to show it to anyone else.

# Chapter overview

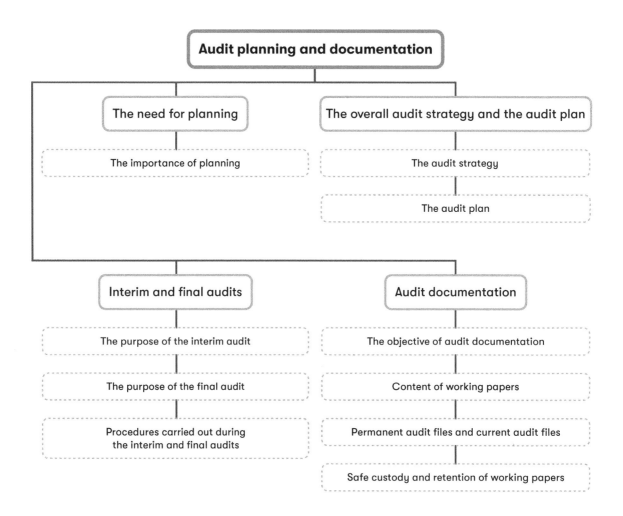

# 1 The need for planning

## 1.1 The importance of planning

An effective and efficient audit relies on proper planning procedures. ISA 300 *Planning an Audit of Financial Statements* states the auditor shall plan the audit work so that the engagement will be performed in an effective manner.

The objectives of planning are:

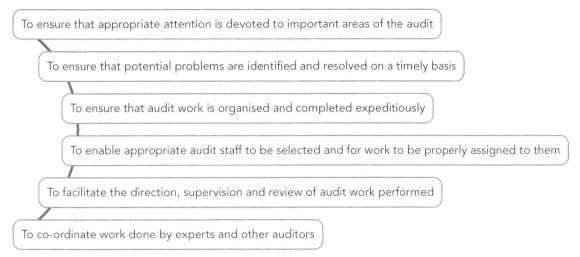

To ensure that appropriate attention is devoted to important areas of the audit

To ensure that potential problems are identified and resolved on a timely basis

To ensure that audit work is organised and completed expeditiously

To enable appropriate audit staff to be selected and for work to be properly assigned to them

To facilitate the direction, supervision and review of audit work performed

To co-ordinate work done by experts and other auditors

The form and nature of planning is different for each audit and is affected by:

- Size of the entity
- Complexity of the audit
- Auditor's experience with the entity and their knowledge of the business
- Commercial environment
- Method of processing transactions
- Reporting requirements

# 2 The overall audit strategy and the audit plan

## 2.1 The audit strategy

**Audit strategy:** The overall audit strategy sets the scope, timing and direction of the audit and guides the development of the more detailed audit plan.

The appendix to ISA 300 sets out the following matters that should be considered when establishing an overall audit strategy:

| Matters to consider | |
|---|---|
| **Characteristics of the engagement** (ISA 300: para. 8(a)) | • Financial reporting framework<br>• Industry-specific reporting requirements<br>• Expected audit coverage<br>• Nature of business segments<br>• Availability of internal audit work<br>• Use of service organisations<br>• Effect of information technology on audit procedures |

| | |
|---|---|
| | • Availability of client personnel and data |
| **Reporting objectives, timing of the audit and nature of communications**<br>(ISA 300: para. 8(b)) | • Entity's timetable for reporting<br>• Organisation of meetings with management and those charged with governance<br>• Discussions with management and those charged with governance<br>• Expected communications with third parties |
| **Significant factors, preliminary engagement activities, and knowledge gained on other engagements**<br>(ISA 300: para. 8(c)–(d)) | • Determination of materiality<br>• Areas identified with higher risk of material misstatement<br>• Results of previous audits<br>• Need to maintain professional scepticism<br>• Evidence of management's commitment to design, implementation and maintenance of sound internal control<br>• Changes within the applicable reporting framework which may involve significant new or revised disclosures<br>• Volume of transactions<br>• Process used by management to identify and prepare disclosures<br>• Significant business developments<br>• Significant industry developments<br>• Significant changes in financial reporting framework<br>• Other significant recent developments |
| **Nature, timing and extent of resources**<br>(ISA 300: para. 8(e)) | • Selection of engagement team<br>• Assignment of work to team members<br>• Engagement budgeting |

Examples of items to include in the overall audit strategy include:
- Industry-specific financial reporting requirements
- Number of locations to be visited
- Audit client's timetable for reporting to its shareholders/members
- Communication between the audit team and the client

## 2.2 The audit plan

**Audit plan:** The audit plan converts the audit strategy into a more detailed plan and includes the nature, timing and extent of audit procedures to be performed by engagement team members in order to obtain sufficient appropriate audit evidence to reduce audit risk to an acceptably low level.

The audit plan sets out the detailed audit procedures which need to be performed in order to implement the audit strategy and includes the following:

- A description of the nature, timing and extent of planned risk assessment procedures
- A description of the nature, timing and extent of planned further audit procedures at the assertion level
- Other planned audit procedures required to be carried out for the engagement to comply with ISAs

(ISA 300: para. 9)

Examples of items included in the audit plan could be:

- Timetable of planned audit work
- Allocation of work to audit team members
- Audit procedures for each major account area (eg inventory, receivables, cash)
- Materiality for the financial statements as a whole and performance materiality

During the audit the auditor may need to modify the overall audit strategy or audit plan, due to unexpected events, changes in conditions or audit evidence obtained. All decisions must be documented and reviewed. (ISA 300: para. 12(c))

# 3 Interim and final audits

Auditors usually carry out their audit work for a financial year in one or more sittings. These are referred to as the **interim audit(s)** and the **final audit.**

Any interim audit visits are carried out **during the period of review** and the final audit visit will take place **after the year end.**

## 3.1 The purpose of the interim audit

The purpose of the interim audit is to **carry out procedures that would be difficult to perform at the year end** because of time constraints.

Work performed during an interim audit tends to focus on **risk assessment** and on **documenting and testing internal controls**.

Some substantive procedures can also be carried out but these are limited because statement of financial position figures will not be the ones reported on.

## 3.2 The purpose of the final audit

During the final audit, the auditor will focus on the audit of the financial statements and issue a report which contains the opinion expressed on the financial statements covering the entire year being audited.

The final audit opinion will take account of conclusions reached at both (or all) audit visits.

Some audit procedures can only be performed at the final audit visit, such as agreeing the financial statements to the accounting records and examining adjustments made during the process of preparing the financial statements.

## 3.3 Procedures carried out during the interim and final audits

The following table shows the procedures performed at the interim and final audits:

| Interim audit procedures may include: | Final audit procedures include: |
|---|---|
| • Inherent risk assessment and gaining an understanding of the entity<br>• Recording the entity's system of internal control<br>• Evaluating the design of internal controls<br>• Carrying out tests of controls on the company's internal controls to ensure they | • Substantive procedures involving verification of statement of financial position balances and amounts in the statement of profit or loss<br>• Obtaining third-party confirmations<br>• Analytical procedures relating to figures in the financial statements |

| Interim audit procedures may include: | Final audit procedures include: |
|---|---|
| are operating as expected<br><br>• Performing substantive testing of transactions/balances to gain evidence that the books and records are a reliable basis for the preparation of financial statements<br><br>• Identification of issues that may have an impact on work to take place at the final audit | • Subsequent events review<br>• Agreeing the financial statements to the accounting records<br><br>• Examining adjustments made during the process of preparing the financial statements<br>• Consideration of the going concern status of the entity<br>• Performing tests to ensure that the conclusions formed at the interim audit are still valid<br>• Obtaining written representations |

### Essential reading

See Chapter 7 of the Essential reading for information on how the work performed at the interim audit impacts the final audit.

The Essential reading is available as an Appendix of the digital edition of the Workbook.

# 4 Audit documentation

### PER alert

Objective 19 of the PER performance objectives is to collect and evaluate evidence for an audit or assurance engagement. One of the ways to demonstrate PO 19 is through the preparation of working papers that document and evaluate audit procedures. The knowledge you gain in this section will be a useful aid in preparing these sorts of working papers.

## 4.1 The objective of audit documentation

KEY TERM

**Audit documentation:** is the record of audit procedures performed, relevant audit evidence obtained, and conclusions the auditor reached (terms such as 'working papers' or 'work papers' are also sometimes used). (ISA 230: para. 6(a))

All audit work must be documented: the working papers are the tangible evidence of the work done to support the audit opinion.

ISA 230 *Audit Documentation* (para. 7), states that 'the auditor shall prepare audit documentation on a **timely basis**'.

Audit documentation is necessary for the following reasons. (ISA 230: para. 3)

> To provide evidence of the auditor's basis for a conclusion about the achievement of the overall objective

> To provide evidence that the audit was planned and performed in accordance with ISAs and other legal/regulatory requirements

> To assist the management team to plan and perform the audit

> To assist team members responsible for supervision to direct, supervise and review audit work

> To enable the audit team to be accountable for its work

> To retain a record of matters of continuing significance (points carried forward)

> To enable quality reviews and inspections to be performed (internal and external)

## 4.2 Content of working papers

Working papers should be sufficiently complete and detailed to **enable an experienced auditor with no previous connection** with the audit subsequently to ascertain from them what work was performed and to support the conclusions reached. (ISA 230: para. 8)

They should record information on the auditor's planning of the audit, the nature, timing and extent of the audit procedures performed, and the results thereof, and the conclusions drawn from the audit evidence obtained.

They should also document the auditor's reasoning on all significant matters requiring exercise of judgement, with auditor's conclusions thereon.

### Essential reading

See Chapter 7 of the Essential reading for examples of working papers and an illustration of a typical audit working paper.

The Essential reading is available as an Appendix of the digital edition of the Workbook.

## 4.3 Permanent audit files and current audit files

Working papers may be divided in to two types:

- Permanent audit files (containing information of **continuing importance** to the audit; and
- Current audit files (containing information relevant to th**e current year's audit**).

Examples of information included in the permanent audit file (PAF) are:

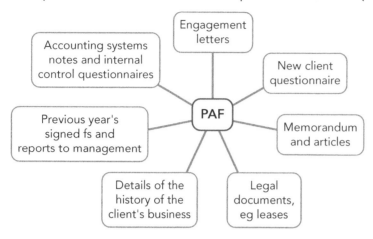

Examples of information included in the current audit file (CAF) are:

The current audit file also contains working papers covering each audit area. These should include a lead schedule for each balance in the financial statements and a list of audit procedures performed along with the results and conclusions of the testing.

An appropriate time limit within which to complete the assembly of the final audit file is ordinarily not more than 60 days after the date of the auditor's report. (ISA 230: para. A21)

## 4.4 Safe custody and retention of working papers

Working papers are the property of the auditors and so the audit firm should establish policies and procedures designed to maintain the confidentiality, safe custody, integrity, accessibility and retrievability of documentation, for example:

- Passwords to restrict access to electronic documentation to authorised users
- Back-up routines
- Confidential storage of hard copy documentation

ISA 230 specifies that the retention period for audit engagements ordinarily is no shorter than five years from the date of the auditor's report, or, if later, the date of the group auditor's report. (ISA 230: para. A23)

Information contained in working papers should not be made available to third parties without the permission of the entity.

# Chapter summary

**Audit planning and documentation**

**The need for planning**

The importance of planning
- To ensure the audit is carried out in an efficient and effective manner
- Objectives:
  - Devote appropriate attention to important areas
  - Identify and resolve potential problems
  - Complete work expeditiously
  - Proper assignment of work to audit staff
  - Facilitate the direction, supervision and review of work performed
  - Co-ordinate work done by experts/other auditors

**The overall audit strategy and the audit plan**

The audit strategy
- Sets the scope, timing and direction of the audit
- Guides the development of the audit plan
- Matters to consider:
  - Characteristics of the engagement
  - Reporting objectives, timing of the audit and nature of communications
  - Significant factors, preliminary engagement activities and knowledge gained on other audits
  - Nature, timing and extent of resources

The audit plan
- Sets out the detailed audit procedures
- Examples include:
  - Timetable of planned audit work
  - Allocation of work to audit staff
  - Audit procedures for each major account area (eg receivables)
  - Materiality and performance materiality
- Any changes to the audit strategy/audit plan must be documented and reviewed

## Interim and final audits

**The purpose of the interim audit**
- Carried out during the period of review
- Focus on risk assessment and internal controls

**The purpose of the final audit**
- Carried out after the year end
- Focus on substantive audit procedures

**Procedures carried out during the interim and final audits**
- Interim audit:
  - Assess inherent risk
  - Understand the entity
  - Record and evaluate internal controls
  - Perform tests of control
  - May perform some substantive procedures
- Final audit:
  - Substantive procedures on SOFP and SPL
  - Obtain third party confirmations
  - Analytical procedures
  - Subsequent events review
  - Agree fs to accounting records
  - Examining adjustments
  - Going concern review
  - Obtain written representations

## Audit documentation

**The objective of audit documentation**
- Record of work done by the auditor in order to support their audit opinion
- Also known as 'working papers'

**Content of working papers**
- Sufficiently complete and detailed to enable an experienced auditor with no previous connection with the audit to ascertain what work was performed and to support the conclusions reached
- Must document the auditor's reasonings on all significant matters regarding the exercise of judgement

**Permanent audit files and current audit files**
- PAF: Contains information of continuing importance to the audit
- Examples:
  - Engagement letters
  - Legal documents
  - Information on client's business
  - Previous year's signed fs
- CAF: Contains information relevant to the current year's audit
- Examples:
  - Financial statements
  - Accounts checklist
  - Planning memo
  - Accounting systems notes and I/C questionnaires
  - Written representations
  - Report to management
  - Notes of board minutes

**Safe custody and retention of working papers**
- Auditor's responsibility to maintain the safe custody of working papers

# Knowledge diagnostic

## 1. Objectives of planning

An auditor must plan their audit work in order to ensure that the audit engagement is performed in an effective manner. This will mean that appropriate attention is devoted to each area, that work is directed, supervised and reviewed and that appropriate audit staff are allocated to the audit team.

## 2. Audit strategy

The overall audit strategy sets the scope, timing and direction of the audit and guides the development of the more detailed audit plan. It should consider the characteristics of the engagement; the reporting objectives, timing of the audit and nature of communications; the significant factors, preliminary engagement activities; knowledge gained on other engagements and the nature, timing and extent of resources.

## 3. Audit plan

The audit plan is more detailed than the audit strategy and includes the nature, timing and extent of audit procedures that will be performed in order to obtain sufficient appropriate audit evidence. It will show the timetable of planned work; allocation of work to audit team members; audit procedures for each major account area and materiality for the financial statements as a whole and performance materiality.

## 4. Interim and final audits

Audit work is normally carried out over the course of more than one sitting. Audit work performed during the period of review is called interim audit work and audit work performed after the year end is called final audit work.

## 5. Interim audit: procedures

Audit procedures performed during an interim audit focus on risk assessment, internal controls testing and identification of issues that may affect the final audit.

## 6. Final audit: procedures

Audit procedures performed during the final audit focus on substantive audit procedures (including analytical procedures), subsequent events review, going concern review and obtaining written representations.

## 7. Audit documentation

Audit documentation forms a record of the work performed by the auditor and the basis of conclusion for their opinion on the financial statements.

## 8. Permanent and current audit files

There are two main types of audit documentation: the permanent audit file contains information of continuing importance to the audit and the current audit file contains information relevant to the current year's audit.

# Further study guidance

## Question practice

Now try the following from the Further question practice bank [available in the digital edition of the Workbook]:

- Section A Q28 and Q32
- Section B Q69 Audit planning and documentation

## Further reading

There are technical articles and study support videos on the ACCA website written/recorded by members of the AA examining team and other tutors which are relevant to some of the topics covered in this chapter that you should read:

Technical articles:

- *Audit working papers* (https://www.accaglobal.com/gb/en/student/exam-support-resources/fundamentals-exams-study-resources/f8/technical-articles/effective-audit-service.html)

## Own research

Imagine the situation whereby an auditor is taken to court and accused of not having performed an audit properly. What sort of information do you think the auditor should have documented in order to demonstrate that they had conducted their audit in accordance with ISAs?

# 8

## Introduction to audit evidence

## Learning objectives

On completion of this chapter, you should be able to:

| Syllabus learning outcomes | Syllabus reference no. |
|---|---|
| Explain the assertions contained in the financial statements about classes of transactions and events and related disclosures; and account balances and related disclosures at the period end. | D1 (a) |
| Describe audit procedures to obtain audit evidence, including inspection, observation, external confirmation, recalculation, re-performance, analytical procedures and enquiry. | D1 (b) |
| Discuss the quality and quantity of audit evidence. | D1 (c) |
| Discuss the relevance and reliability of audit evidence. | D1 (d) |
| Discuss substantive procedures for obtaining audit evidence. | D2 (a) |
| Discuss and provide examples of how analytical procedures are used as substantive procedures. | D2 (b) |
| Discuss the difference between tests of control and substantive procedures. | D2 (e) |

## Business and Exam context

This chapter is an introductory chapter to the next ten chapters where we consider what audit evidence is and the methods the auditor uses to gather that evidence. We will look at the type and quantity of evidence that we need to gather to support the opinions we make. We want to ensure that we have enough, in other words sufficient, evidence and the right type of evidence, in other words appropriate evidence. So, we will consider what exactly is meant by sufficient, appropriate evidence in a bit more detail.

We will then learn about the financial statement assertions. These are the statements that management make about the financial statements that we are auditing. For example, when management include an amount for property, plant and equipment in the statement of financial position they are asserting that, amongst other things, the assets exist. As auditors, we need to make sure that this is really the case and so will need to gather evidence relating to the existence of property, plant and equipment. Similarly, auditors need to gather evidence over several other assertions, so it is essentially we understand what these actually are.

We will also discuss the procedures auditors can use to gather audit evidence. There are five main types of procedures which can be remembered with the mnemonic **AEIOU**: Analytical procedures, enquiry (both internal and external), inspection, observation and recalculation (including re-performance).

# Chapter overview

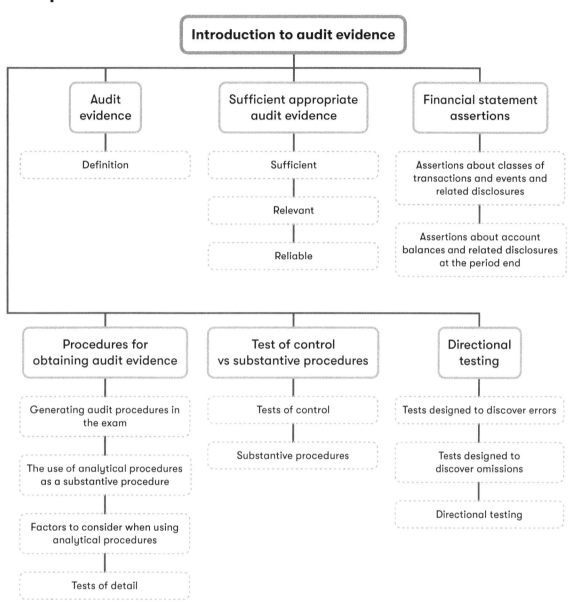

# 1 Audit evidence

## 1.1 Definition

The objective of an audit of financial statements is to enable the auditor to express an opinion on whether the financial statements are prepared, in all material respects, in accordance with an identified financial reporting framework (ISA 200: para. 3).

> **Audit evidence:** is all the information used by the auditor in arriving at the conclusions on which the auditor's opinion is based **Audit evidence** (ISA 500: para. 5(c)).

# 2 Sufficient appropriate audit evidence

The auditor should obtain **sufficient appropriate** audit evidence to be able to draw reasonable conclusions on which to base the audit opinion (ISA 500: para. 4).

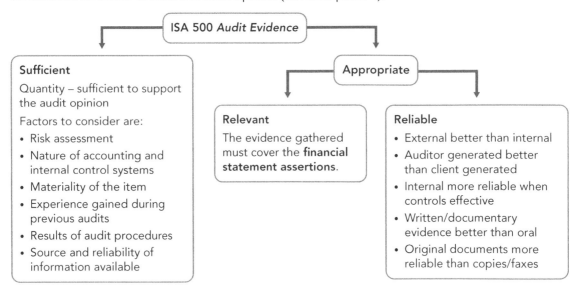

ISA 500 *Audit Evidence*

**Sufficient**

Quantity – sufficient to support the audit opinion

Factors to consider are:

- Risk assessment
- Nature of accounting and internal control systems
- Materiality of the item
- Experience gained during previous audits
- Results of audit procedures
- Source and reliability of information available

**Appropriate**

**Relevant**

The evidence gathered must cover the **financial statement assertions**.

**Reliable**

- External better than internal
- Auditor generated better than client generated
- Internal more reliable when controls effective
- Written/documentary evidence better than oral
- Original documents more reliable than copies/faxes

⚠️ **PER alert**

Objective 19 of the PER performance objectives is to collect and evaluate evidence for audit or assurance engagement. You can apply the knowledge you gain from this and subsequent chapters to assist in achieving this objective.

# 3 Financial statement assertions

> **Assertions:** Representations, explicit or otherwise, with respect to the recognition, measurement, presentation and disclosure of information in the financial statements which are inherent in management representing that the financial statements are prepared in accordance with the applicable financial reporting framework. Assertions are used by the auditor to consider the different types of potential misstatements that may occur when identifying, assessing and responding to the risks of material misstatement (ISA 315: para. 12a).

Evidence must be relevant to the particular financial statement **assertion** the auditor is trying to test. There are two categories:

 BPP

| Assertions about classes of transactions and events and related disclosures<br><br>O<br>C<br>C<br>C<br>A<br>P | **Occurrence:**<br>Transactions and events that have been recorded or disclosed have occurred and pertain to the entity.<br>**Completeness:**<br>All transactions and events that should have been recorded have been recorded and all related disclosures that should have been included in the financial statements have been included.<br>**Cut-off:**<br>Transactions and events have been recorded in the correct accounting period.<br>**Classification:**<br>Transactions and events have been recorded in the proper accounts. **Accuracy:**<br>Amounts and other data relating to recorded transactions and events have been recorded appropriately, and related disclosures have been appropriately measured and described.<br>**Presentation:**<br>Transactions and events are appropriately aggregated or disaggregated and are clearly described, and related disclosures are relevant and understandable in the context of the requirements of the applicable financial reporting framework. |
|---|---|
| Assertions about account balances and related disclosures at the period end<br><br>C<br>O<br>V<br>E<br>C<br>P | **Completeness:**<br>All assets, liabilities and equity interests that should have been recorded have been recorded and all related disclosures that should have been included in the financial statements have been included.<br>**Obligations and rights:**<br>The entity holds or controls the rights to assets, and liabilities are the obligations of the entity.<br>**Valuation, accuracy and allocation:**<br>Assets, liabilities, and equity interests are included in the financial statements at appropriate amounts and any resulting valuation or allocation adjustments are appropriately recorded, and related disclosures have been appropriately measured and described.<br>**Existence:**<br>Assets, liabilities, and equity interests exist.<br>**Classification:**<br>Assets, liabilities, and equity interests have been recorded in the proper account.<br>**Presentation:**<br>Assets, liabilities and equity instruments are appropriately aggregated or disaggregated and are clearly described, and related disclosures are relevant and understandable in the context of the requirements of the applicable financial reporting framework. |

Sometimes an entity will use an **expert**, for example a chartered surveyor, to assist them in the preparation of the financial statements.

**Management's expert:** an individual or organisation possessing expertise in a field other than auditing or accounting, whose work is used by the entity to assist in the preparation of the financial statements.

ISA 500 states that when wanting to rely on the work of the expert, the auditor must evaluate the competence, capabilities and objectivity of the expert, obtain an understanding of the work done, and evaluate the appropriateness of the work done as audit evidence.

If the auditor is unable to obtain sufficient appropriate evidence, then they should consider the implications for the auditor's report (Chapter 20).

# 4 Procedures for obtaining audit evidence

There is rarely one piece of audit evidence that gives sufficient appropriate evidence over a class of transactions, account balance or presentation and disclosure. Rather, audit evidence is obtained by performing an appropriate mix of audit procedures.

There are two types of audit procedure:

> **Tests of controls:** audit procedures designed to **evaluate the operating effectiveness of controls** in preventing, or detecting and correcting, material misstatements at the assertion level (ISA 330: para. 4(b)).
>
> **Substantive procedures:** audit procedures designed to detect material misstatements at the assertion level. Substantive procedures comprise:
>
> (a) Tests of details (of classes of transactions, account balances, and disclosures); and
>
> (b) Substantive analytical procedures
>
> (ISA 330: para. 4(a))

## 4.1 Generating audit procedures in the exam

Exam questions will often ask you to describe audit procedures for specific items, for example additions to property, plant and equipment. The mnemonic **AEIOU** may be useful in helping you to generate audit procedures.

| Audit procedure | Description | Type of procedure |
| --- | --- | --- |
| **A**nalytical procedures | The evaluation of financial information by a comparison to financial and non-financial data and the investigation of significant differences and relationships which are inconsistent with other information | Substantive procedure |
| **E**nquiry (and confirmation) | Seeking information of knowledgeable persons throughout the entity or outside the entity (enquiry) and obtaining representations directly from a third party (confirmation) | Enquiry – both substantive procedure and a test of controls<br>Confirmation – substantive procedure |
| **I**nspection | Examining records, documents and tangible assets | Both |
| **O**bservation | Looking at a process or procedure being performed by others | Test of controls |
| **R**ecalculation (and re-performance) | Verifying the arithmetical accuracy of documents or records and the auditor's | Recalculation – substantive procedure |

| Audit procedure | Description | Type of procedure |
| --- | --- | --- |
| | independent execution of procedures and the **re-performance** of controls | Re-performance – test of controls |

## 4.2 The use of analytical procedures as a substantive procedure

There are three main types of analytical procedures which an auditor can use:

 **Variance analysis**
- the review of current year financial information in comparison to prior period or budgeted information

 **Ratio analysis**
- the calculation of ratios and analysis and investigation of **significant differences**

**Proof in total**
- the use of interrelationships between data (financial and non-financial) to estimate an expected value in the financial statements, again with the investigation of significant differences

## 4.3 Factors to consider when using analytical procedures

The auditor will need to consider:

The suitability of analytical procedures to a particular **assertion**

The **reliability of the data** from which the expected amounts or ratios are developed

Whether the expectation is sufficiently precise to identify a **material** misstatement

The amount of any **difference that is acceptable** without further investigation being required

## 4.4 Tests of details

Tests of details are a further type of substantive procedure and describe the process of gathering audit evidence through detailed inspection of invoices, documents and assets.

Examples include:

- **Inspection of invoices** to verify the accuracy of the amounts recorded in the financial statements
- **Physical inspection** of non-current assets and inventory to verify their existence
- Review of **board meeting minutes** for evidence of any provisions for legal claims which should be included in the financial statements
- **Review of after-date monies received** per the cash book in order to gain evidence over the valuation of receivables

 ### Essential reading

See Chapter 8 of the Essential reading for more information on audit procedures to obtain audit evidence.

The Essential reading is available as an Appendix of the digital edition of the Workbook.

## Activity 1: Analytical procedures

You are an audit senior of Check & Co and are currently conducting the audit of HMA for the year ended 30 September 20X6.

HMA Co (HMA) is a marketing company that designs advertisements which are then placed in newspapers and magazines and on websites. During the course of the audit a number of events and issues have been brought to your attention.

### Expenses

HMA rents an office in an upmarket location in order to promote itself as a fashionable and quality marketing company. HMA currently has a Human Resource team, Accounts department and Sales team and also employs a significant number of design staff.

On 1 January 20X6 HMA decided that it needed to occupy a second floor in its current office premises in order to be able to create a specialist publishing department so that the designers' adverts can be modified in-house which would then allow them to be used across different publishing platforms (both published products and online). The directors decided to take out a loan to help fund the cost of this in the short term.

The following information is available in relation to the loan:

|  | $ |
|---|---|
| Finance charge in the statement of profit or loss | 81,000 |
| Opening loan liability on 1 January 20X6 | 400,000 |

The loan carries a fixed rate of interest of 2% per month and interest is paid at the end of each month. HMA repaid capital of $50,000 on 1 April 20X6. In order to verify the finance charge for the year, you have been asked to perform a proof in total.

### Required

What is the expected finance charge for the above loan for the year ended 30 September 20X6 and the resultant impact on profit for the period?

- O Finance charge should be $96,000, profit is overstated
- O Finance charge should be $72,000, profit is understated
- O Finance charge should be $67,000, profit is understated
- O Finance charge should be $66,000, profit is understated

## Activity 2: Analytical procedures

In relation to the rent expense for the office premises:

### Required

Which of the following audit procedures would provide the auditor with the MOST reliable audit evidence regarding the rent expense?

- O Calculate the rent expense variance this year compared to last year and discuss any significant differences with management.
- O Obtain a copy of the latest rental agreement and recalculate the expected rent expense for the year.
- O Agree the rent expense to copies of invoices provided by management
- O Determine the general level of rent increases during the year for offices near to HMA's location and recalculate the expected rent expense. Discuss any significant differences with management.

### Activity 3: Analytical procedures

The audit assistant who has been assigned to help you appears to be unsure as to which audit procedures provide audit evidence in relation to different financial statement assertions.

**Required**

Which of the following audit procedures provide evidence over the CUT OFF assertion for revenue?

○ Obtain a breakdown of revenue for the period and vouch a sample of revenue values to sales invoices.

○ Calculate the gross profit margin for the years ended 30 September 20X6 and 20X5 and investigate any significant differences in the ratio with management.

○ Review credit notes issued post year end to determine the levels of returns and whether any adjustment is required in the financial statements.

○ Review cash book receipts during the post year end period to determine whether any sales need to be removed due to irrecoverable debts.

## 5 Tests of control vs substantive procedures

Gaining audit evidence through tests of controls is very different from gaining audit evidence through substantive procedures.

For example, consider audit procedures to test the **completeness** of the **payables** balance:

```
┌─────────────────────┐                    ┌─────────────────────────┐
│  Tests of controls  │                    │ Substantive procedures  │
└─────────────────────┘                    └─────────────────────────┘
           │                                            │
           ▼                                            ▼
┌─────────────────────────────┐          ┌─────────────────────────────┐
│ These focus on the auditor  │          │ These focus on the auditor  │
│ confirming their            │          │ performing detailed         │
│ understanding of the control│          │ procedures on the numbers   │
│ being in place and testing  │          │ in the financial statements.│
│ that it has operated        │          │ Source documentation →      │
│ effectively throughout the  │          │ financial statements        │
│ period                      │          │                             │
└─────────────────────────────┘          └─────────────────────────────┘
           │                                            │
           ▼                                            ▼
┌─────────────────────────────┐          ┌─────────────────────────────┐
│ This includes:              │          │ This includes:              │
│ • Observing the control     │          │ • AEIOU                     │
│   taking place              │          │                             │
│ • Reperforming the control  │          │                             │
│ • Inspecting evidence that  │          │                             │
│   the control has taken     │          │                             │
│   place                     │          │                             │
└─────────────────────────────┘          └─────────────────────────────┘
           │                                            │
           ▼                                            ▼
```

**Enquire** from management the process used to reconcile supplier statements.

For a sample of supplier statement reconciliations, **inspect** the reconciliation to see evidence that the reconciliation has been performed and any differences investigated and resolved. Verify that any necessary changes to the accounting system have been authorised and processed.

**Reperform** the reconciliation to ensure it has been completed accurately.

**Inspect** the reconciliation to verify it has been reviewed by an appropriate level of management.

**Observe** a supplier statement reconciliation being performed.

Perform **analytical procedures** on the amounts owed to major suppliers at the year end compared to the prior period.

**Enquire** from management the reasons for any significant differences.

Circularise a sample of year-end payables and request them to **confirm** the balance owed at the year end.

**Inspect** the cash book payments in the post year end period for any significant payments to suppliers to ensure the year-end liability is accurately recorded.

**Calculate** the payables payment ratio and compare to the prior period. Discuss any significant differences with management.

Does the control operate efficiently?
This will depend on the level of errors in the sample, ie the **number of times** the control did not operate.

Is the balance complete?
This will depend on the level of errors in the sample, ie the **monetary value** of any errors.

# 6 Directional testing

Substantive tests are designed to discover errors or omissions. Broadly speaking, substantive procedures can be said to fall into two categories.

(a) Tests to discover **errors** (resulting in over- or understatement)

(b) Tests to discover **omissions** (resulting in understatement)

## 6.1 Tests designed to discover errors

These tests will start with the **accounting records** in which the transactions are recorded to supporting documents or other evidence. Such tests should detect any overstatement and also any understatement through causes other than omission. For example, if a test is designed to ensure that sales are priced correctly, it would begin with a sales invoice selected from the receivables ledger. Prices would then be checked to the official price list.

## 6.2 Tests designed to discover omissions

These tests must start from **outside the accounting records** and then matched back to those records. Understatements through omission will never be revealed by starting with the account itself, as there is clearly no chance of selecting items that have been omitted from the account. For example, if a test is designed to discover whether all raw material purchases have been properly processed, it would start with goods received notes to be agreed to the inventory records or payables ledger.

## 6.3 Directional testing

For most systems, auditors would include tests designed to discover both errors and omissions. The type of test, and direction of the test, should be recognised before selecting the test sample. If the sample which tested the accuracy and validity of the receivables ledger was chosen from a file of sales invoices then it would not substantiate the fact that there were no errors in the receivables ledger.

Directional testing is particularly appropriate when testing the financial statement assertions of existence, completeness, rights and obligations, and valuation.

The concept of directional testing derives from the principle of double-entry bookkeeping, in that for every **debit** there should be a **corresponding credit**. Therefore, any **misstatement** of a **debit entry** will result in either a corresponding **misstatement** of a **credit entry** or a **misstatement** in the opposite direction, of **another debit entry**.

By designing audit procedures carefully the auditors are able to use this principle in drawing audit conclusions, not only about the debit or credit entries that they have directly tested, but also about the corresponding credit or debit entries that are necessary to balance the books.

Audit procedures are therefore designed in the following way:

| Test item | Example |
| --- | --- |
| Test **debit items** (expenditure or assets) for overstatement by selecting debit entries recorded in the nominal ledger and confirming value, existence and ownership. | If a non-current asset entry in the nominal ledger of $1,000 is selected, it would be overstated if it should have been recorded at anything less than $1,000 or if the company did not own it, or indeed if it did not exist (eg it had been sold or the amount of $1,000 in fact represented a revenue expense). |
| Test **credit items** (income or liabilities) for understatement by selecting items from appropriate sources independent of the nominal ledger and ensuring that they result in the correct nominal ledger entry. | Select a goods despatched note and agree that the resultant sale has been recorded in the nominal ledger revenue account. Revenue would be understated if the nominal ledger did not reflect the transaction at all (completeness) or reflected it at less than full value (say, if goods valued at $1,000 were recorded in the revenue account at $900, there would be an understatement of $100). |

A test for the overstatement of an asset simultaneously gives comfort on understatement of other assets, overstatement of liabilities, overstatement of income and understatement of expenses.

So, by performing the primary tests, the auditors obtain audit assurance in other audit areas. Successful completion of the primary tests will therefore result in them having tested all account areas for both overstatement and understatement.

# Chapter summary

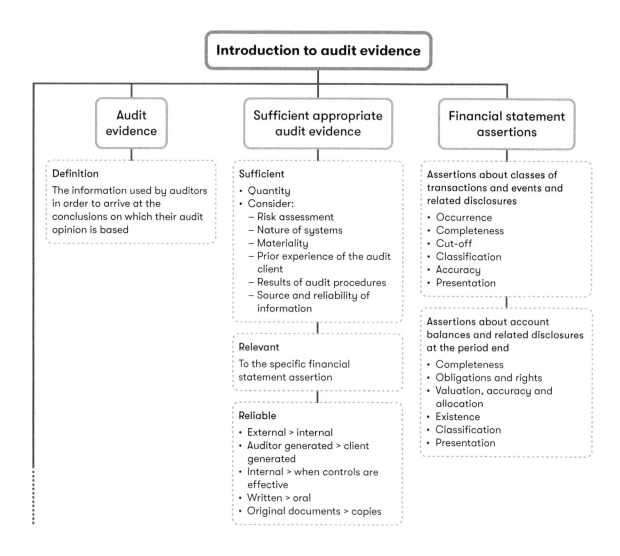

**Introduction to audit evidence**

## Audit evidence

**Definition**

The information used by auditors in order to arrive at the conclusions on which their audit opinion is based

## Sufficient appropriate audit evidence

**Sufficient**

- Quantity
- Consider:
  - Risk assessment
  - Nature of systems
  - Materiality
  - Prior experience of the audit client
  - Results of audit procedures
  - Source and reliability of information

**Relevant**

To the specific financial statement assertion

**Reliable**

- External > internal
- Auditor generated > client generated
- Internal > when controls are effective
- Written > oral
- Original documents > copies

## Financial statement assertions

**Assertions about classes of transactions and events and related disclosures**

- Occurrence
- Completeness
- Cut-off
- Classification
- Accuracy
- Presentation

**Assertions about account balances and related disclosures at the period end**

- Completeness
- Obligations and rights
- Valuation, accuracy and allocation
- Existence
- Classification
- Presentation

## Procedures for obtaining audit evidence

**Generating audit procedures in the exam**

- Analytical procedures
- Enquiry (and confirmation)
- Inspection
- Observation
- Recalculation (and re-performance)

**The use of analytical procedures as a substantive procedure**

- Variance analysis
- Ratio analysis
- Proof in total

**Factors to consider when using analytical procedures**

- Suitability to the assertion
- Reliability of source data
- Whether expectation is sufficiently precise to identify a material misstatement
- The amount of difference that is acceptable

**Tests of detail**

- Type of substantive procedure
- Examples:
  - Inspection of invoices/assets
  - Review of board meeting minutes
  - Review of cash book

## Test of control vs substantive procedures

**Tests of control**

Confirm the auditor's understanding of the control and test whether it has operated effectively throughout the period

**Substantive procedures**

- Detailed procedures on the numbers in the financial statements
- AEIOU

## Directional testing

**Tests designed to discover errors**

Test from accounting records to source documentation

**Tests designed to discover omissions**

Test from source documentation to accounting records

**Directional testing**

- Test debit items for overstatement
- Test credit items for understatement

# Knowledge diagnostic

### 1. Reasons for obtaining evidence

Auditors need to gain audit evidence in order to support the conclusions on which they base their auditor's opinion.

### 2. Quantity and quality of evidence

The auditor should obtain **sufficient appropriate** audit evidence. Evidence is appropriate if it is both **relevant** (to the **financial statement assertion** being tested) and **reliable**.

### 3. Financial statement assertions

There are two categories of financial statement assertions: assertions about **classes of transactions and events and related disclosures** and assertions about **account balances and related disclosures at the period**.

### 4. Types of substantive procedures

There are two types of audit procedures: tests of controls and substantive procedures. Substantive procedures are broken down into two further categories: tests of details and analytical procedures.  The mnemonic **AEIOU** serves to remind you of the ways in which you can generate audit procedures.

### 5. Tests of controls

Tests of controls involve identifying and repeatedly testing an entity's internal controls in order to determine whether they have operated effectively throughout the period under audit.

### 6. Substantive procedures

Substantive procedures are used by the auditor to detect material misstatements.

# Further study guidance

## Question practice

Now try the following from the Further question practice bank (available in the digital edition of the Workbook):

- Section A Q29
- Section B Q60 Audit evidence considerations

## Further reading

There are technical articles on the ACCA website written/recorded by members of the AA examining team and other tutors which are relevant to some of the topics covered in this chapter that you should read:

- *The audit of assertions:* https://www.accaglobal.com/gb/en/student/exam-support-resources/fundamentals-exams-study-resources/f8/technical-articles/assertions.html
- *Analytical procedures:* https://www.accaglobal.com/gb/en/student/exam-support-resources/professional-exams-study-resources/p7/technical-articles/analytical-procedures.html

## Own research

Consider the entity that you work for and talk to some of the staff in the finance department who deal with the auditors when they visit. Do the auditors focus mainly on tests of controls or substantive procedures?

# Activity answers

### Activity 1: Analytical procedures

The correct answer is: Finance charge should be $66,000, profit is understated

|  | $ |
|---|---:|
| 1.1.X6 - 31.3.X6 | |
| ($400,000 × 2%) = $8,000 × 3 months | 24,000 |
| 1.4.X6 - 30.9.X6 | |
| ($400,000 - $50,000) × 2% = $7,000 × 6 months | 42,000 |
| Total | 66,000 |

### Activity 2: Analytical procedures

The correct answer is: Obtain a copy of the latest rental agreement and recalculate the expected rent expense for the year.

The latest rental agreement is documented evidence from a third party and should stipulate the rental charge for both floors which are now occupied by HMA

### Activity 3: Analytical procedures

The correct answer is: Calculate the gross profit margin for the years ended 30 September 20X6 and 20X5 and investigate any significant differences in the ratio with management.

Generally speaking, an entity's gross profit margin tends to remain relatively stable and so any unexpected changes should be investigated as they could indicate that material misstatements exist. For example, an unexpected increase in gross profit margin could indicate a cut-off error where sales after the year end have been included in the year-end figures.

# 9 — Internal control

## Learning objectives

On completion of this chapter, you should be able to:

| Syllabus learning outcomes | Syllabus reference no. |
|---|---|
| Explain why an auditor needs to obtain an understanding of the components of internal control relevant to the preparation of the financial statements. | C1 (a) |
| Describe and explain the five components of a system of internal control: the control environment; the entity's risk assessment process; the entity's process to monitor the system of internal control; the information system and communication; control activities. | C1 (b) |
| Describe why smaller entities may have different control environments and describe the types of evidence likely to be available in smaller-entities. | D2 (d) |
| Explain how auditors record systems of internal control system including the use of narrative notes, flowcharts and questionnaires. | C2 (a) |
| Evaluate internal control components, including deficiencies and significant deficiencies in internal control. | C2 (b) |
| Discuss the limitations of internal control components. | C2 (c) |
| Describe computer systems controls including general IT controls and information processing controls. | C3 (a) |

## Business and Exam context

This chapter looks at internal control systems, but what is internal control? Let's take the example of a fast food outlet. One of their aims is to make sure that the food that they sell is sold as soon as possible after it has been prepared so that customers enjoy it and return to buy more, and consequently the outlet makes money. They do not want food sitting behind the counter for too long in case it goes stale and makes customers ill. In addition to this, there are health and safety regulations which they need to adhere to in terms of how long food can be left out before being thrown away, assuming that it is not sold. The fast food outlet wants to make sure that they achieve their aims of selling more food and managing the risks, such as selling stale food or not adhering to health and safety regulations. As such, they will design, implement and maintain processes to make sure that the chance of these problems happening are kept to a minimum. These processes and who is responsible for them describes the entity's system of internal controls.

The auditor generally seeks to rely on the internal controls within the entity in order to reduce the amount of substantive procedures they perform. The initial evaluation of a client's system is essential as the auditor gains an understanding of the entity, as we outlined in Chapter 6. In this chapter, we shall look at some of the detailed requirements of ISA 315 with regard to internal controls, and also set out control issues that the auditor may come across.

The auditor will assess the risks of material misstatement arising and, as we discussed in Chapter 6, may respond to those risks by carrying out tests of controls. If they conclude that they can rely on the controls in place, the level of substantive audit testing required can be reduced.

In this chapter, we also look at the ways in which auditors can document the internal control systems using narrative notes, flowcharts, questionnaires and checklists, focusing particularly on the use of questionnaires.

# Chapter overview

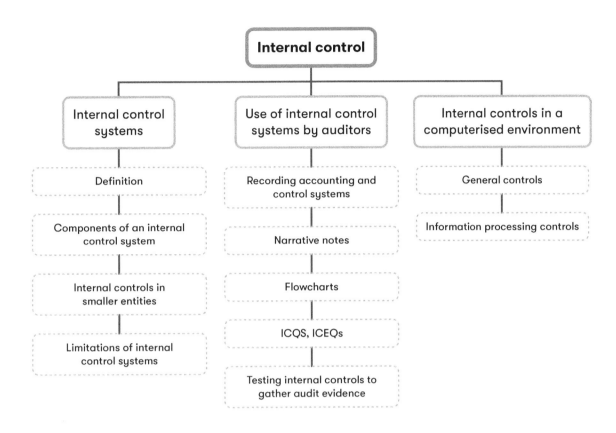

# 1 Systems of internal control

## 1.1 Definition

> **System of internal control:** The system designed, implemented and maintained by those charged with governance, management and other personnel, to provide reasonable assurance about the achievement of an entity's objectives with regard to reliability of financial reporting, effectiveness and efficiency of operations, and compliance with applicable laws and regulations (ISA 315: para. 12(m)).

## 1.2 Components of a system of internal control

ISA 315 *Identifying and Assessing the Risks of Material Misstatement* (paras. 21 – 26) describes **five components** of an internal control system:

| Component | Description |
|---|---|
| Control environment | • Governance and management functions<br>• Attitudes, awareness and actions of management<br>• Sets the tone by creating a culture of honest and ethical behaviour<br>• Provides an appropriate foundation for the other components of internal control |
| The entity's risk assessment process | • How management identifies risks and decides upon actions to manage them |
| The entity's process to monitor the system of internal control | • Assess the design and operation of controls over time<br>• Ongoing monitoring is part of regular management activity<br>• Separate monitoring may be performed by the internal audit function |
| The information system and communication | • Consists of infrastructure, software, people, procedures and data<br>• The related accounting records, supporting information and specific accounts in the financial statements that are used to record, process and report transactions |
| Control activities | • The policies and procedures that help ensure that management directives are carried out<br>The categories most relevant to an audit are:<br>• Performance reviews<br>• Information processing<br>• Physical controls<br>• Segregation of duties |

**Prominent Note**

The ACCA examining team has said to BPP that students should know that this 5-point understanding of the system of internal control was amended by the 2019 revision of ISA 315 and differed from what went before it.

## Essential reading

See Chapter 9 of the Essential reading for more information on the components of an internal control system.

The Essential reading is available as an Appendix of the digital edition of the Workbook.

### 1.3 Internal controls in smaller entities

Many of the controls which would be relevant to a large entity are neither practical nor appropriate for the smaller entity.

Two key issues arise:

- Smaller entities are likely to have **less segregation of duties** due to limited numbers of staff.
- **Management override of controls** is likely to be an increased risk as a result of the close involvement of directors/owners.

To compensate for these issues, management should instigate additional physical authorisation, arithmetical, accounting and supervisory procedures.

The attitudes, awareness and actions of management are of particular importance to the auditor's understanding and assessment of the control environment in a smaller entity.

If an auditor is satisfied that the internal control system in a smaller entity is robust, and the auditor can test that direct controls are operating effectively, then the level of substantive procedures can be reduced.

However, because of the key issues discussed above, the auditor will often choose or be forced to turn to substantive procedures to gain sufficient appropriate audit evidence when auditing a smaller entity. This can often mean use of:

- Confirmations
- Agreeing samples related to different financial statement areas to source documents
- Analytical procedures where these are considered suitable

## Activity 1: Examples of internal control

Consider each of the following examples. What checks (internal controls) would you expect to be carried out in each situation?

| (1) | The postman knocks at your front door and hands you a letter which has been sent by recorded delivery. |
|-----|---|
| (2) | You submit a claim for expenses to your line manager. |
| (3) | You need to work an extra day over and above your normal hours to clear a backlog of work and will expect to be paid overtime for this. |
| (4) | You are responsible for maintaining the cash book and have just been passed the latest bank statement. |
| (5) | You have just received a monthly statement from your main supplier. |
| (6) | You are responsible for payroll processing and you have just received notification from human resources that an employee wants to take advantage of a season ticket loan |

| | | |
|---|---|---|
| | | offered by your company. Your password does not give you permission to amend employee deductions. |
| (7) | | You have just returned from a three-month holiday and are trying to log on to your computer. |
| (8) | | You are preparing to pay an invoice received from a supplier. |
| (9) | | You have prepared a bank reconciliation for your supervisor. |
| (10) | | You are entering 75 sales invoices into the accounting records and want to check the accuracy of your posting. |
| (11) | | You have been working on the computer but have now gone away to make a cup of tea, leaving the computer inactive for a period of time. |
| (12) | | You have a Saturday job operating the till in a small corner shop which is closing for the night. |
| (13) | | You work in a shop that sells diamond jewellery; the jeweller is very keen to keep their inventory secure. |

**Solution**

## 1.4 Limitations of systems of internal control

Even with the best system of internal control, there is no guarantee that an entity will be able to fulfil all of its objectives and be fully protected from fraud and error. This is due to the inherent limitations of internal control systems:

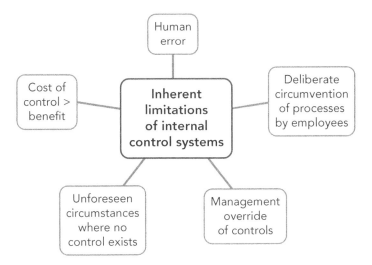

The inherent limitations of internal control systems mean that an auditor cannot rely solely on audit evidence from tests of control, they will always need to conduct some substantive procedures.

# 2 Use of systems of internal control by auditors

ISA 315 requires the auditor to understand the system of internal control insofar as it is relevant to the preparation of the financial statements.

The auditor shall:

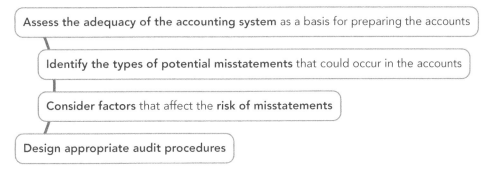

## 2.1 Recording accounting and control systems

The auditor must obtain and document an understanding of the entity's internal controls **regardless** of whether they want to gain audit evidence by relying on the internal controls.

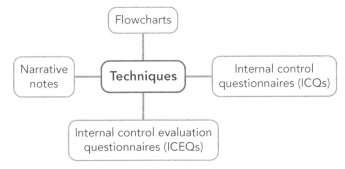

## 2.2 Narrative notes

Narrative notes tend to be used to document simple internal control systems; they are usually typed, and detail and explain each stage of the entity's systems.

| Advantages | Disadvantages |
|---|---|
| Relatively **simple** to record and can facilitate understanding by all audit team members | Describing a process in narrative notes can be a lot more time consuming than, say, representing it as a simple flowchart, particularly where the system follows a logical flow. |
| Can be used for any system due to the method's **flexibility** | Awkward to update if written manually |
| Editing in future years can be relatively easy if they are computerised | Potential difficulty in **identifying missing internal controls** because notes record the detail of systems but may not identify control exceptions clearly |

## 2.3 Flowcharts

Flowcharts are generally a graphic illustration of the physical flow of information through the accounting system. Flowlines represent the sequences of processes, and other symbols represent the inputs and outputs to a process.

| Advantages | Disadvantages |
|---|---|
| Can be prepared quickly by an **experienced user** | They are most **suitable for describing standard systems**. Procedures for dealing with unusual transactions will normally have to be recorded using narrative notes. |
| **Easy to follow and review** due to information being presented in a standard form | **Major amendment is difficult without redrawing.** |
| Ensures that the system is recorded in its entirety, as all document flows have to be traced from beginning to end. Any 'loose ends' will be apparent from a cursory examination | Time can sometimes be wasted by charting areas that are of no audit significance. |
| Eliminates the need for extensive narrative and can be of considerable help in **highlighting the salient points of control and any deficiencies in the system** | |

### Essential reading

See Chapter 9 of the Essential reading for an example of a flowchart.

The Essential reading is available as an Appendix of the digital edition of the Workbook.

## 2.4 Internal control questionnaires (ICQs)

Internal control questionnaires (ICQs) comprise a series of questions designed to help the auditor to assess the strength of the system of controls.

Generally, ICQs conform to the following basic principles:

(a) They **comprise a list of questions** designed to determine whether desirable controls are present for each major transaction cycle (for example. sales, purchases).

(b) They are formulated so that there is one list of questions to **cover each of the major transaction cycles**.

One of the most effective ways of designing the questionnaire is to phrase the questions so that all the answers can be given as 'YES' or 'NO' and a 'NO' answer indicates a deficiency in the system.

Examples of questions on an ICQ are:

| | |
|---|---|
| 'Is a bank reconciliation performed each month?' | Yes / No |
| 'Is the bank reconciliation reviewed by a supervisor or member of management?' | Yes / No |

### Essential reading

See Chapter 9 of the Essential reading for a further example of an ICQ.

The Essential reading is available as an Appendix of the digital edition of the Workbook.

## 2.5 Internal control evaluation questionnaires (ICEQs)

Internal control evaluation questionnaires (ICEQs) are slightly more robust in that they ask questions which concentrate on the significant errors or omissions that could occur at each phase of the appropriate cycle if controls are weak. This, in turn, enables the auditor to elicit the controls which exist.

An example of a question on an ICEQ is:

Is there reasonable assurance that 'Goods cannot be received without an associated liability being recorded in the accounting records?'

The idea behind the above question is that the person responsible for this part of the purchases cycle will answer:

'Yes, because a **sequentially numbered**, **multi-part** goods received note is generated upon receipt of the goods and one copy passed to the accounts department. This is then filed whilst we wait for the supplier's invoice. This **file is then reviewed** at the end of each month and an **accrual made** for any goods received which have not yet been invoiced.'

| ICQs and ICEQs | |
|---|---|
| **Advantages** | **Disadvantages** |
| If drafted thoroughly, questionnaires can ensure **all controls** are **considered**. | Can be **drafted vaguely**, hence **misunderstood** and important controls not identified |
| **Quick** to **prepare** | May contain a large number of **irrelevant controls** |
| **Easy** to **use** and **control** and can therefore be given to junior staff to complete | May not include **unusual controls**, which are nevertheless effective in particular circumstances |
| **ICEQs** are easier to apply to a variety of systems than **ICQs** because they are drafted in terms of **objectives** rather than specific controls. | Can give a distorted view of the entity's internal controls as there is **no weighting of more important controls**. In many systems, one 'NO' answer (for example lack of segregation of duties) will cancel out a string of 'YES' answers. |
| Answering ICEQs should enable auditors to | The client may be able to **overstate controls**. |

| ICQs and ICEQs | |
|---|---|
| **Advantages** | **Disadvantages** |
| **identify the direct controls** which they are most likely to test during control testing. | |
| ICEQs can **highlight deficiencies** where extensive substantive procedures will be required. | |

### Essential reading

See Chapter 9 of the Essential reading for a further example of an ICEQ.

The Essential reading is available as an Appendix of the digital edition of the Workbook.

## 2.6 Confirming understanding

In order to confirm their understanding of the control systems, auditors will often carry out **walk-through tests**. This is where they pick up a transaction and follow it through the system to see whether all the controls they anticipate being in existence were in operation with regard to that transaction.

## 2.7 Testing internal controls to gather audit evidence

The auditor would **only** ever test internal controls to gain audit evidence if the initial assessment indicates that the controls are relevant to the financial statement assertions and appear to exist and have operated effectively throughout the period:

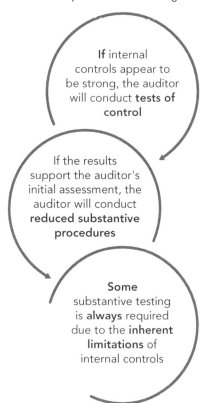

**If** internal controls appear to be strong, the auditor will conduct **tests of control**

If the results support the auditor's initial assessment, the auditor will conduct **reduced substantive procedures**

**Some** substantive testing is **always** required due to the **inherent limitations** of internal controls

Where the results of the tests of control indicate that the internal controls are not effective, the auditor will:

- Report the deficiencies in internal controls to those charged with governance (Chapter 10); and

*   Perform full substantive testing.

# 3 Internal controls in the IT environment

As part of the obtaining an understanding of the entity's information system and communication, the auditor should understand how the entity has responded to the risks arising from information technology (IT). Fundamentally, this will be a matter of assessing whether the entity's IT controls address the risks that arise from IT.

The IT controls which the auditor would expect to find can be considered in two categories:

*   General IT controls
*   Information processing controls

A rough way to grasp this distinction could be by way of an analogy with a computer - the general IT controls might be the operating system, with the information processing controls being the specific apps being used.

General IT controls and information processing controls are interrelated. Strong general IT controls contribute to the assurance which may be obtained by an auditor in relation to information processing controls. Unsatisfactory general IT controls may undermine strong information processing controls.

## 3.1 General IT controls

KEY
TERM

**General IT controls:** Controls over the entity's IT processes that support the continued proper operation of the IT environment, including the continued effective functioning of information processing controls and the integrity of information (ie, the completeness, accuracy and validity of information) in the entity's information system (ISA 315: para. 12(d)).

General IT controls commonly include:

| General IT controls | Examples |
| --- | --- |
| Development of computer applications | <ul><li>Standards over systems design, programming and documentation</li><li>Full testing procedures using test data</li><li>Approval by computer users and management</li><li>**Segregation of duties** so that those responsible for design are not responsible for testing</li><li>Installation procedures so that data is not corrupted in transition</li><li>**Training of staff** in new procedures and availability of adequate documentation</li></ul> |
| Prevention or detection of unauthorised changes to programs | <ul><li>Segregation of duties</li><li>Full records of program changes</li><li>**Password protection** of programs so that access is limited to computer operations staff</li><li>**Restricted access** to central computer by locked doors, keypads</li><li>Maintenance of programs logs</li><li></li></ul> |

| General IT controls | Examples |
|---|---|
| | • Virus checks on software: use of anti-virus software and policy prohibiting use of non-authorised programs or files |
| | • **Back-up copies** of programs being taken and stored in other locations |
| | • Control copies of programs being preserved and regularly compared with actual programs |
| | • Stricter controls over certain programs (utility programs) by use of read-only memory |
| Testing and documentation of program changes | • Complete testing procedures |
| | • Documentation standards |
| | • Approval of changes by computer users and management |
| | • Training of staff using programs |
| Controls to prevent wrong programs or files being used | • Operation controls over programs |
| | • Libraries of programs |
| | • Proper **job scheduling** |
| Controls to prevent unauthorised amendments to data files | • Password protection |
| | • **Restricted access** to authorised users only |
| Controls to ensure continuity of operation | • Storing extra copies of programs and data files off-site |
| | • Protection of equipment against fire and other hazards |
| | • Back-up power sources |
| | • **Disaster recovery** procedures eg availability of back-up computer facilities |
| | • **Maintenance agreements** and insurance |

## 3.2 Information processing controls

> **Information processing controls:** Controls relating to the processing of information in IT applications or manual information processes in the entity's information system that directly address risks to the integrity of information (ie, the completeness, accuracy and validity of transactions and other information) (ISA 315: para. 12(e)).

Information processing controls ensure that all transactions are authorised and recorded, and are processed completely, accurately and on a timely basis - or as the ISA puts it, they 'support the effective implementation of the entity's implementation policies' (ISA 315: para. A6).

They may include the following.

| Control | Examples |
|---|---|
| Controls over input: **completeness** | • Manual or programmed agreement of **control totals** |
| | • **Document counts** |

| Control | Examples |
|---|---|
| | • **One-for-one checking** of processed output to source documents<br>• **Programmed matching** of input to an expected input control file<br>• Procedures over resubmission of rejected controls |
| Controls over input: **accuracy** | Programs to **check data** fields (for example value, reference number, date) on input transactions for plausibility:<br><br>• Digit verification (eg reference numbers are as expected)<br>• Reasonableness test (eg sales tax to total value)<br>• Existence checks (eg customer name)<br>• Character checks (no unexpected characters used in reference)<br>• Necessary information (no transaction passed with gaps)<br>• Permitted range (no transaction processed over a certain value)<br>**Manual scrutiny** of output and reconciliation to source<br>Agreement of **control totals** (manual/programmed) |
| Controls over input: **authorisation** | **Manual checks** to ensure information input was:<br><br>• Authorised<br>• Input by authorised personnel |
| Controls over **processing** | • Similar controls to input must be in place when input is completed, for example **batch reconciliations**<br>• **Screen warnings** can prevent people logging out before processing is complete |
| Controls over **master files and standing data** | • **One-for-one checking**<br>• **Cyclical reviews** of all master files and standing data<br>• **Record counts** (number of documents processed) and hash totals (for example, the total of all the payroll numbers) used when master files are used to ensure no deletions<br>• **Controls** over the deletion of accounts that have no current balance |

# Chapter summary

```
                        ┌─────────────────────┐
                        │  Internal control   │
                        └─────────────────────┘
              ┌──────────────────┴──────────────────────────┐
    ┌───────────────────┐              ┌────────────────────────────────────────┐
    │  Internal control │              │ Use of internal control systems by      │
    │      systems      │              │              auditors                   │
    └───────────────────┘              └────────────────────────────────────────┘
```

## Internal control systems

**Definition**

The process designed, implemented and maintained by those charged with governance, management and other personnel to provide reasonable assurance that an entity will achieve its objectives with regard to:

- The reliability of financial reporting
- The effectiveness and efficiency of operations
- Compliance with applicable laws/regulations

**Components of an internal control system**

- The control environment
- The entity's risk assessment process
- The entity's process to monitor the system of internal control
- The information system and communication
- The control activities

**Internal controls in smaller entities**

- Limited segregation of duties
- Risk of management override of controls
- Audit approach: most likely substantive procedures including:
  - Confirmations
  - Agreeing samples to source documents
  - Analytical procedures

**Limitations of internal control systems**

- Human error
- Deliberate circumvention of I/C
- Management override
- Unforeseen circumstances
- Cost of control > benefit

## Use of internal control systems by auditors

**Recording accounting and control systems**

- Narrative notes
- Flowcharts
- ICQs, ICEQs

**Narrative notes**

- Advantages:
  - Simple
  - Flexible
  - Editable
- Disadvantages:
  - Time consuming
  - Awkward
  - Difficult to identify missing controls

**Flowcharts**

- Advantages:
  - Quick to prepare (experienced user)
  - Easy to follow/review
  - Highlights controls and any deficiencies
- Disadvantages:
  - Only suitable for standard systems
  - Major amendments require redrawing
  - May chart areas of no audit significance

**ICQS, ICEQs**

- Advantages:
  - Ensures all controls are considered
  - Quick to prepare
  - Easy to delegate
  - ICEQs identify direct controls and highlight deficiencies
- Disadvantages:
  - Important controls can be missed if not drafted specifically
  - May contain irrelevant controls
  - May not include unusual controls
  - No weighting of the importance of different controls

**Testing internal controls to gather audit evidence**

- Test controls to determine whether:
  - Controls exist
  - Control have operated effectively throughout the period
- If yes, reduced substantive procedures
- If no, full substantive testing

```
                    Internal controls in a computerised environment
```

**General controls**

- Development of computer applications:
  - Installation and testing procedures
  - Segregation of duties
- Prevention/detection of unauthorised change to programs:
  - Segregation of duties
  - Password protection
  - Restricted access
  - Virus checks
  - Back-up copies
- Testing and documentation of program changes:
  - Testing procedures
  - Approval
  - Training
- Controls to prevent wrong programs/files being used:
  - Operation controls
  - Libraries
  - Job scheduling
- Controls to prevent unauthorised amendments to data files:
  - Password protection
  - Restricted access
- Controls to ensure continuity of operation:
  - Off-site storage
  - Disaster recovery
  - Maintenance agreements

**Information processing controls**

- Controls over input - completeness:
  - Control totals
  - Document counts
  - One-for-one checking
- Controls over input - accuracy:
  - Digit verification
  - Reasonableness test
  - Existence checks
  - Character checks
  - Permitted range
- Controls over input - authorisation:
  - Manual authorisation checks
- Controls over processing:
  - Batch reconciliations
  - Screen warnings
- Controls over master files and standing data:
  - One-for-one checking
  - Record counts

# Knowledge diagnostic

### 1. Components of a system of internal control

A company's **system of internal control** is the board of directors' responsibility and comprises:

(a) Control environment

(b) The entity's risk assessment process

(c) The entity's process to monitor internal control

(d) The information system and communication

(e) Control activities

### 2. Examples of internal controls

Examples of internal controls include approval, authorisation, reconciliations, computer controls (passwords, sequence checks), review and physical controls.

### 3. Inherent limitations of systems of internal control

There are inherent limitations in any system of internal control which include human error, deliberate circumvention of controls, management override and unforeseen circumstances where no control exists. There are also occasions where the cost of implementing a control outweighs the potential benefit of having the control.

### 4. Auditor's responsibility relating to internal control

The auditor must **obtain an understanding** of internal control to:

(a) Assess the adequacy of the accounting systems as a basis for preparing the accounts

(b) Identify types of potential **misstatement**

(c) Assess **risks**

(d) Design appropriate **audit procedures**

### 5. Documenting controls

The auditor must document their understanding of the company's internal controls using narrative notes, flowcharts, ICQs and/or ICEQs.

### 6. Use of internal controls in the audit

Where controls appear to operate effectively, the auditor will test the controls to gain audit evidence. Some substantive testing must **always** be done due to the inherent limitations of internal controls.

### 7. Internal controls in a computerised environment

The auditor needs to consider both **general IT** and **information processing** controls in their assessment of control risk. General IT controls need to be designed and implemented to mitigate risks arising from information technology. Information processing controls are needed to prevent and detect errors that can arise when data is input and processed.

# Further study guidance

## Question practice

Now try the following from the Further question practice bank [available in the digital edition of the Workbook]:

* Section A Q33 and Q34
* Section B Q71 Internal control systems

## Further reading

There are technical articles and study support videos on the ACCA website written/recorded by members of the AA examining team and other tutors which are relevant to some of the topics covered in this chapter that you should read:

Technical article:

* *Risk and understanding the entity. (https://www.accaglobal.com/gb/en/student/exam-support-resources/professional-exams-study-resources/p7/technical-articles/risk-understanding-entity.html)*

## Own research

Consider the internal controls that operate in your place of work (or even your home). What are the processes and policies that you need to follow and what documentation are you required to complete? Are any checks made to determine whether the processes and policies have been accurately followed?

# Activity answers

## Activity 1: Examples of internal control

| | | |
|---|---|---|
| 1 | The postman knocks at your front door and hands you a letter which has been sent by recorded delivery. | You should be required to sign for the letter on the postman's handset. |
| 2 | You submit a claim for expenses to your line manager. | You should need to evidence the claim by presenting the receipt; the line manager should sign the claim form to authorise payment. |
| 3 | You need to work an extra day over and above your normal hours to clear a backlog of work and will expect to be paid overtime for this. | You should submit a request that the overtime be authorised prior to it being completed and this authorisation request should be signed by your line manager. |
| 4 | You are responsible for maintaining the cash book and have just been passed the latest bank statement. | You should perform a bank reconciliation to verify the completeness and accuracy of the cash book. |
| 5 | You have just received a monthly statement from your main supplier. | You should reconcile the balance per the supplier statement to the purchase ledger balance. |
| 6 | You are responsible for payroll processing and you have just received notification from human resources that an employee wants to take advantage of a season ticket loan offered by your company. Your password does not give you permission to amend employee deductions. | You should be provided with a copy of the letter signed by the employee which authorises the deductions and a hierarchical password should be required to amend the standing data. |
| 7 | You have just returned from a three month holiday and are trying to log on to your computer. | Your password should have expired, and the computer should automatically require you to change your password. |
| 8 | You are preparing to pay an invoice received from a supplier. | You should verify that the goods have been received by checking to a goods received note, vouch the prices to the supplier's price list and recalculate the sales tax and addition of the invoice. The invoice should then be authorised for payment and this evidenced by a signature. |
| 9 | You have prepared a bank reconciliation for your supervisor. | Your supervisor should review the bank reconciliation to verify it has been done properly and sign to evidence that the |

| | | review has taken place. |
|---|---|---|
| 10 | You are entering 75 sales invoices into the accounting records and want to check the accuracy of your posting. | You should perform a batch reconciliation whereby you manually count the number of invoices posted and verify to the system or manually total the value of the invoices and verify that the revenue, sales tax and receivables accounts have increased by the corresponding amounts.

Provided that the invoices are sequentially numbered, you should also perform a sequence check to determine whether any invoice numbers have been omitted. |
| 11 | You have been working on the computer but have now gone away to make a cup of tea, leaving the computer inactive for a period of time. | You should log out/lock your computer prior to leaving your work station.

If you do not lock your computer then the computer should 'time out' after a certain period of time and require you to re-enter your login/ password details before you can resume work. |
| 12 | You have a Saturday job operating the till in a small corner shop which is closing for the night. | The cash in the till should be counted at the end of the day and reconciled to the till receipt. Money should be kept in a safe overnight. |
| 13 | You work in a shop that sells diamond jewellery; the jeweller is very keen to keep their inventory secure. | The shop should have CCTV in operation, the front door should be locked with a doorbell which must be rung to gain entry, jewellery should be kept in locked cabinets and stored overnight in a safe/secure vault and grilles pulled down over the shop windows. |

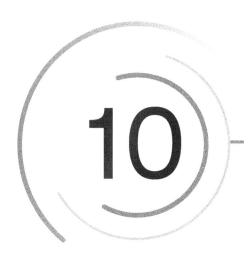

# 10

# Tests of controls

## Learning objectives

On completion of this chapter, you should be able to:

| Syllabus learning outcomes | Syllabus reference no. |
|---|---|
| Describe control objectives, control procedures, control activities, direct controls, indirect controls and tests of controls in relation to:<br><br>• The sales system<br>• The purchases system<br>• The payroll system<br>• The inventory system<br>• The bank and cash system<br>• Non-current assets | C3 (b) |
| Discuss the requirements and methods of how reporting significant deficiencies in internal control are provided to management and those charged with governance. | C4 (a) |
| Explain, in a format suitable for inclusion in a management letter, significant deficiencies within a system of internal control and provide control recommendations for overcoming these deficiencies to management. | C4 (b) |
| Discuss the need for auditors to communicate with those charged with governance. | C4 (c) |
| Describe the format and content of internal audit review reports and make appropriate recommendations to management and those charged with governance. | C6 (e) |

# Business and Exam context

We have already seen that the external auditor is required to understand a client's accounting and internal control systems. Having documented the system, the auditors will decide which controls, if any, they wish to rely on and plan tests of controls to obtain audit evidence to determine whether the controls are properly designed and have operated effectively throughout the period to be audited.

The syllabus examines six systems: sales, purchases, payroll, inventory, cash and non-current assets. The first three of these are covered in the main chapter whilst the final three are included in Chapter 10 of the Essential Reading which is available in Appendix 2 of the digital edition of the Workbook.

For each system, we will identify the main risks which relate to the systems, then look at the controls that the business could put in place to minimise the risks identified. Finally, we will consider the different tests of controls that auditors will carry out to determine whether these controls have operated effectively.

We end this chapter by considering the report to management submitted to the directors and management of an entity and the reports that may be issued by the internal auditors. The report to management summarises the significant deficiencies the auditor has identified in the entity's systems during their testing. It should explain the deficiency and its implication for the entity as well as recommending the appropriate action that should be taken by management and those charged with governance.

# Chapter overview

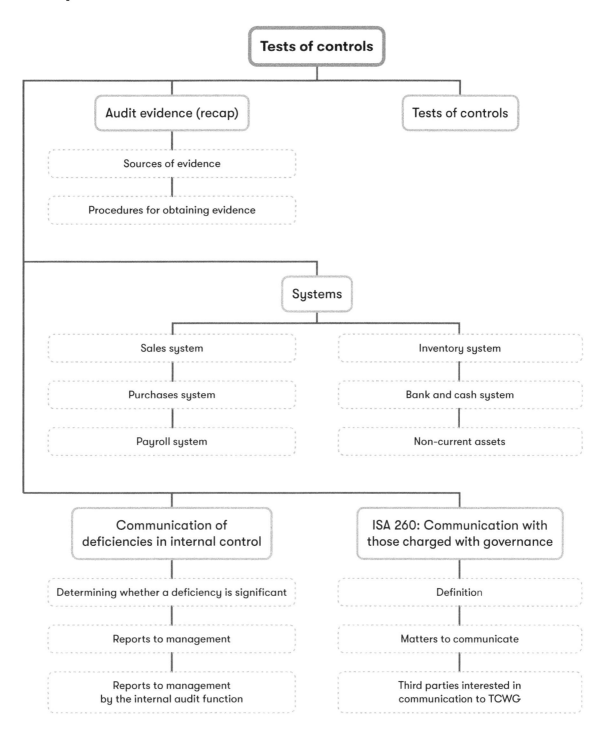

**Tests of controls**

- Audit evidence (recap)
  - Sources of evidence
  - Procedures for obtaining evidence
- Tests of controls

- Systems
  - Sales system
  - Purchases system
  - Payroll system
  - Inventory system
  - Bank and cash system
  - Non-current assets

- Communication of deficiencies in internal control
  - Determining whether a deficiency is significant
  - Reports to management
  - Reports to management by the internal audit function

- ISA 260: Communication with those charged with governance
  - Definition
  - Matters to communicate
  - Third parties interested in communication to TCWG

# 1 Audit evidence (recap)

## 1.1 Sources of evidence

In Chapter 8 we saw that there are two main ways in which an auditor can gather audit evidence. These were:

- Tests of controls
- Substantive procedures (tests of detail and analytical procedures)

## 1.2 Procedures for obtaining evidence

The mnemonic **AEIOU** can help generate different audit procedures.

| Audit procedure | Description | Type of procedure |
|---|---|---|
| **A**nalytical procedures | The evaluation of financial information by a comparison to financial and non-financial data and the investigation of significant differences and relationships which are inconsistent with other information | Substantive procedure |
| **E**nquiry (and confirmation) | Seeking information of knowledgeable persons throughout the entity or outside the entity (enquiry) and obtaining representations directly from a third party (confirmation) | Enquiry – both substantive procedure and a test of controls<br>Confirmation – substantive procedure |
| **I**nspection | Examining records, documents and tangible assets | Both |
| **O**bservation | Looking at a process or procedure being performed by others | Test of controls |
| **R**ecalculation (and re-performance) | Verifying the arithmetical accuracy of documents or records and the auditor's independent execution of procedures and the **re-performance** of controls | Recalculation – substantive procedure<br>Re-performance – test of controls |

This chapter will focus on **tests of controls**.

# 2 Tests of controls

We saw in Chapter 9 that internal controls are implemented by management and those charged with governance to prevent or detect fraud and error. The auditor must have an understanding of an entity's accounting and internal control systems but will only ever carry out tests of controls if their initial risk assessment suggests that the entity's internal controls **operate effectively**.

If this is the case, the auditor will perform tests of controls to gather audit evidence about relevant financial statement assertions.

The auditor must test that the control:

- Is properly designed;
- Exists; and
- Has operated throughout the period.

Failures of internal controls (or **deviations**) should be recorded and investigated **regardless of the monetary amount involved**. The auditor must assess whether deviations are **isolated departures** or indicate existence of errors in accounting records.

If the results of the tests of control are unsatisfactory, then the auditor's preliminary assessment of control risk is not supported and the auditor must perform extensive substantive procedures.

Tests of controls include **enquiry** in combination with other audit procedures, for example:

(a) **Inspection** of documents supporting controls or events to gain audit evidence that controls have operated effectively, for example verifying that a transaction has been authorised

(b) **Observation** of the entity's control procedures, for example observing an inventory count to ensure it is being conducted in accordance with the inventory count instructions

(c) **Re-performance** of the application of a control to ensure it was performed correctly, for example reperforming a bank reconciliation to verify that it has been done properly

(d) **Examination** of evidence of management reviews, for example minutes of board meetings

(e) **Testing of the control activities performed by a computer**, using for example computer-assisted audit techniques (CAATs)

# 3 Systems

There are six systems detailed in the syllabus:

## 3.1 Sales system

The sales system consists of four main stages. Each stage has its own key documentation.

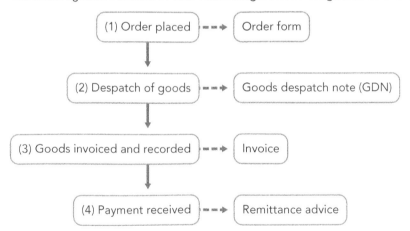

## Activity 1: Sales system (deficiencies)

Dress You Like Co is a clothing manufacturer, based in the UK, which has been trading for over ten years. It operates from two sites: a factory where the clothes are made and a head office where the administration is carried out. Completed inventory orders are despatched from both the factory and the head office.

In an effort to reduce costs, Dress You Like Co now imports its material from one sole supplier based overseas.

Dress You Like Co sells its finished products to small independent retailers and also one major supermarket chain. The supermarket chain often requires additional deliveries without much prior notice and so Dress You Like Co has to maintain a high level of inventory should this occur. Credit terms are normally 30 days, but the supermarket is given 60-day credit terms.

You are an audit senior in Check and Co and you are carrying out the controls work on the sales system for the year ended 30 September 20X6. You have access to the systems notes that Dress You Like Co provided to its previous auditors for the year ended 30 September 20X5 and you have spoken to several members of Dress You Like Co staff to obtain more information about the sales system.

**Extract from Dress You Like Co's sales systems notes for the year ended 30 September 20X5**

### Order Placed

Customers contact Dress You Like Co by phone or email and inform the sales team which products they require. A member of the sales team completes a standard form with all of the customer details and forwards this to the warehouse for despatch to the customer.

### Despatch of Goods

The warehouse manager collates all of the orders from the previous day and passes them to the picking team. This team then picks the items, packages them and produces a goods despatch note detailing all of the products. The warehouse manager then organises delivery of the products for the following day.

### Goods Invoiced and Recorded

Each day the finance team receives copies of the GDNs completed by the warehouse staff and uses these to generate invoices. Each invoice has the customer details, the products despatched and the standard prices. The supermarket chain has its own price list, which is significantly discounted on the other retailer prices.

### Payment Received

Customers can pay by cash, cheque or BACS and should return a remittance advice with all payments. There is no formal process for monitoring old debts. Bank reconciliations are performed on a weekly basis by the accounts team and monthly by the internal audit department.

**Transcripts of conversations with Dress You Like Co staff**

### Interview with Jenny Bristow, sales team

**You:** So Jenny, can you tell me a little more about the standard form that you complete when you receive an order?

**Jenny:** Sure. The order form is three-part; we complete it by hand using the information the customer has provided by phone or email. We refer back to the standard product list, which all our customers have a copy of, to ensure that we have the correct product codes for each item. Once the form is complete, we send one copy to the customer (either by post or scanned and emailed), one copy is sent to the warehouse and we retain one copy here.

**You:** OK, is the process any different for the supermarket?

**Jenny:** No, not really. For the supermarket we send the order straight to the despatch team in the warehouse so the order can be sent quickly, rather than sending it to the warehouse manager.

**You:** Thanks. Oh, one more question. What happens with new customers?

**Jenny:** How do you mean?

**You:** Well, do you have any specific checks on new customers or any prescribed credit limits?

**Jenny:** Umm, no not really. We just record their details on the form as normal and then pass the order on to the warehouse.

**You:** Brilliant, thanks very much.

**Jenny:** You're welcome.

### Interview with David Furber, Warehouse Manager

**You:** Hi David, thank you for taking the time to help me today.

**David:** Fine, but this had better be quick, I'm very busy.

**You:** OK. Can you tell me how the process for despatching goods works?

**David:** Well, I get the orders from the sales team through the day, then at the beginning of the next day I allocate them to the boys in the warehouse to pick and pack while I sort out delivery drivers for the day after. Simple really.

**You:** Good, well can you give me a bit more detail on the picking and packing? What happens if you are out of stock of any item?

**David:** The boys pick the goods that are on the customer order and they put them in boxes. Then they write a GDN based on what is in the box. If there is something out of stock they mark it on the customer order and then pass it back to me. I can then allocate that order back out to someone to pick tomorrow or the next day. I keep a file with all of the orders that haven't been fully despatched, and I check it every day. The customer might have to wait a few days, but they always get the whole order in the end.

**You:** OK, do you check this outstanding file back to any other information?

**David:** Yes, at the end of each month I sit down with Jenny from the sales team. We go through the outstanding orders file and copies of all of the GDNs to make sure all orders have been captured.

**You:** Lovely, thank you very much.

**David:** Great, I can get back to some proper work now.

### Interview with Edward Times, Finance Assistant

**You:** Hi Ed, is now a good time to talk about the invoicing process?

**Ed:** Sure, no problem, what would you like to know?

**You:** Well, I understand that you get copies of the GDNs from the warehouse team and you use them to generate invoices, can you give me a bit more detail?

**Ed:** OK. Every day I get a pile of GDNs from the warehouse for the stuff despatched the day before and I copy the details from here into the invoicing software. I copy across the products despatched and the customer details and then the system automatically applies prices.

**You:** Does everyone pay the same price?

**Ed:** No, the supermarket has a special price structure which the system automatically applies when I record the customer details and everyone else pays the same.

**You:** OK, can you override the prices in any way, say to offer a special discount?

**Ed:** No, I can't do that, but Katie can.

**You:** Katie?

**Ed:** Yes, Katie Escombe, the acting Finance Director/Chief Finance Officer.

**You:** Oh yes. So, how does she do that?

**Ed:** She has a special login to the system which then allows her to amend prices; I don't really know much more than that except that any changes she makes are reviewed by another director.

**You:** Great. I think that's all for now, thanks very much.

**Ed:** OK, see you later.

### Interview with Claire Wilson, Accounts Receivable Clerk

**You:** Thanks for taking the time to meet me, Claire. I was hoping to find out a bit more about the process for receiving payment for invoices.

**Claire:** OK. Well, customers send us money either in the post or put it straight into the bank. They should send us remittance advices, so we know what the money is for, but they don't always do it, especially for the payments direct into the bank.

**You:** So, what do you do if they don't send a remittance advice?

**Claire:** Well, we try to guess what the amount is for, so if it matches the most recent statement etc we allocate it to those invoices, but if we can't guess we just allocate it to the oldest invoices.

**You:** Right, so what do you do to make sure old debts are paid?

**Claire:** Well, I don't really have any formal process. I just look out for customers who haven't paid in a long time and give them a call when I have a chance.

**You:** Do you send statements or do any aged receivables analysis?

**Claire:** Oh, I've heard about aged receivables analysis, but I don't know if our system will produce one, I've never tried.

**You:** OK, one final thing. Do you do bank reconciliations?

**Claire:** Not me personally but Simon does them each week.

**You:** Great, I think that's it. Thanks.

**Claire:** Thanks.

**Required**

In respect of the internal controls relating to the sales system of Dress You Like Co:

(1)   Identify and explain **THREE** deficiencies; and

(2)   Recommend a control to address each of these deficiencies.

| Control deficiency | Control recommendation |
|---|---|
|  |  |
|  |  |
|  |  |

Solution

## Activity 2: Sales system (test of controls)

In respect of the internal controls relating to the sales system of Dress You Like Co:

(1) Identify and explain **THREE** direct controls within the sales system; and

(2) Describe TEST OF CONTROLS the external auditors should perform to assess if each of these controls is operating effectively.

| Control | Test of controls |
| --- | --- |
|  |  |
|  |  |
|  |  |

| Control | Test of controls |
|---------|------------------|
|         |                  |

Solution

In **exam questions,** it is important to **use the scenario** to generate your answer rather than to learn lots of internal controls and tests of controls by heart.

You have just seen two activities where the first asked for control deficiencies and recommendations, then the next asked for direct controls and tests of controls. These are common requirements in the exam. You could also see both of these appear in the same exam question with one requirement asking for direct controls and associated tests, and a second asking for deficiencies and associated recommendations.

You should try to complete as many practice questions on this area as possible. To help you in this, we have included some other examples of control objectives, internal controls and tests of controls below.

| Stage: Order Placed | | | |
|---------------------|---|---|---|
| Risk | Control objectives | Controls | Tests of controls |
| That an order is accepted from and goods despatched to a customer who is not creditworthy | To ensure that goods and services are only supplied to customers with good credit ratings | Conduct a credit check on all new customers **prior** to accepting an order. The credit check should be undertaken by someone separate from sales department.<br><br>Once accepted, new customers should be given a credit limit – these | Inspect a sample of new customer accounts to ensure that credit checks/ references were obtained before the order was accepted.<br><br>For a sample of customer accounts, attempt to process an order that will take a customer over their |

 **BPP**

| Stage: Order Placed | | | |
|---|---|---|---|
| **Risk** | **Control objectives** | **Controls** | **Tests of controls** |
| | | should be reviewed regularly. | credit limit to determine whether the order is rejected. |
| That an order is not fulfilled leading to loss of future business from dissatisfied customers | To ensure that all goods ordered are despatched/fulfilled | Orders should be completed on sequentially numbered order forms and sequentially numbered goods despatched notes (GDN) generated from the same information. A copy of the GN should be passed to the sales department by the warehouse team once the order is despatched. The sales team should regularly review any order forms which are not matched to GDNs. | Using a computer (or manually) test the numerical sequence to ensure it is complete. Review a sample of unfulfilled orders and enquire as to why these remain outstanding. |
| That the wrong items, wrong quantity or damaged goods are despatched | To ensure that the correct items are despatched in terms of item, quantity and condition | Spot checks should be conducted on goods once they have been packed to ensure the goods packed are in good condition and agree to the order form. | Vouch a sample of items packed to the GDNs and order form to ensure the goods packed are accurate. Physically inspect a sample of goods which have been packed. Review customer complaint files for evidence of incorrectly despatched goods. |

| Stage: Despatch of goods | | | |
|---|---|---|---|
| **Risk** | **Control objectives** | **Controls** | **Tests of controls** |
| That goods are not despatched to the required destination | To ensure that goods are despatched to the required destination | On receipt of the goods, the customer signs the multi-part GDN. One copy should then be left with the customer and the others returned with the delivery driver (and one copy passed to the sales team, one retained in the warehouse and one passed to the invoicing department). | Review a sample of GDNs for evidence of the customer's signature. |

## Stage: Goods Invoiced and Recorded

| Risk | Control objectives | Controls | Tests of controls |
|---|---|---|---|
| That goods despatched are not invoiced/not invoiced correctly | To ensure that all goods despatched are correctly invoiced | Invoices should be sequentially numbered and generated using the information on the GDNs.<br><br>All invoices should be authorised and details agreed to price lists/credit terms. | Match a sample of GDNs with the corresponding invoice.<br>Perform a sequence check of invoices to ensure all invoices are recorded.<br>Compare a sample of invoices with the authorised price list and credit terms to ensure they are accurate. |
| That invoices are posted to the wrong customer account | To ensure that invoices are posted to the correct customer account | Periodically review customer accounts for any unpaid amounts.<br>Send statements to customers on a monthly basis. | Review customer correspondence files for evidence of any complaints/instances of incorrect invoices being applied to a customer's account. |

## Stage: Payment Received

| Risk | Control objectives | Controls | Tests of controls |
|---|---|---|---|
| That cash is not received | To ensure that monies are received for invoices raised | Produce an aged receivables report on a monthly basis and actively pursue old/overdue balances. | Review the aged receivables report and discuss the action taken on old/ overdue balances with credit control. |
| That payments received are misappropriated | To ensure that monies received are safeguard and banked promptly | There should be segregation of duties between those who update receivables ledger and those who:<br><br>• Raise invoices<br><br>• Raise credit notes<br><br>• Follow up statement queries<br><br>• Open and count cash<br>Cash/cheques should be kept securely and banked promptly. | Observe the procedures in place to ensure segregation of duties.<br><br><br><br>Observe the procedures for banking cash/cheques. |

## 3.2 Purchases system

As with the sales system, the purchases system also consists of four main stages and has key documentation at each stage.

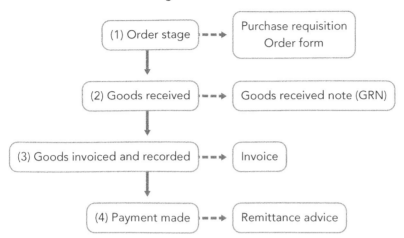

### Activity 3: Purchases system (deficiencies)

You are now carrying out the work on the purchases system at Dress You Like Co. You again have access to the systems notes that Dress You Like Co provided to its previous auditors for the year ended 30 September 20X5 and you have spoken to several members of Dress You Like Co staff to obtain more information about the purchases system.

**Extract from Dress You Like Co's purchases systems notes for the year ended 30 September 20X5**

**Order Stage**

Reorder levels exist for all items of inventory. When the level of inventory falls to the reorder level, a standard order form is automatically generated by the inventory system to order a set quantity of material. The order form details the name of the buyer responsible for that inventory line and a copy of the order is forwarded to the warehouse where goods are received.

**Goods Received**

On receipt of the goods, the quality of the materials is checked and then the warehouse manager generates a sequentially numbered, multi-part goods received note.

**Goods Invoiced and Recorded**

Each day the finance team receives copies of the GRNs completed by the warehouse staff. These are filed in sequential number order to await receipt of the associated invoice.

**Payment Made**

All invoices in the file are automatically paid at the end of each month. The overseas supplier sends a monthly statement but this is not reconciled to the purchase ledger account. Bank reconciliations are performed on a weekly basis by the accounts team and monthly by the internal audit department.

**Transcripts of conversations with Dress You Like Co staff**

*Interview with Ivan Higster, purchasing department*

**You:** So Ivan, can you give me some more information about the reorder levels that are set?

**Ivan:** Yes, it's quite simple really: because we're involved in the fashion industry we need to make sure our products meet current trends so every season the buyers monitor which items sell well and then adjust the reorder levels for each product in the current season based on our past experience.

**You:** Thanks. So, what checks do the buyers perform when orders are generated for their inventory lines?

**Ivan:** None really, we just get the order through and then place it with our supplier. We do forward a copy of the order to the warehouse, though.

**You:** Great, thanks for your time.

**Ivan:** No worries!

### Interview with David Furber, Warehouse Manager

**You:** Hi David, sorry to be asking you some more questions but I'm looking at the purchases system now. Have you got five minutes?

**David:** I wish you auditors would get organised and do all your questions in one go!

**You:** Sorry David, it shouldn't take long. Would you talk me through what happens when an order for goods is received into the warehouse?

**David:** Well, the goods arrive with a list of what's in each crate and I get the boys to unpack it. They check the condition of each roll of material and make sure the quality looks satisfactory and that it was packaged securely. Once they've confirmed to me what was received, I generate a sequentially numbered, multi-part goods received note. I send one part of this to the finance team.

**You:** OK, do you check the details on the goods received note back to any other information?

**David:** No, all of our deliveries come from our overseas supplier so I don't need to make any checks.

**You:** Right, thanks then.

**David:** That's OK.

### Interview with Sadie Thomas, Finance Assistant

**You:** Hi Sadie, would it be OK to have a quick chat about the process for recording purchase invoices?

**Sadie:** Hi, yes, I was expecting you!

**You:** Thanks! David tells me that you get copies of the GRNs from the warehouse team. Can you tell me what happens next in the process?

**Sadie:** Sure, each day David passes me the GRNs generated by the warehouse for items that have been received from our overseas supplier the day before. I file these in sequential number order so I have them ready for when the supplier invoice arrives.

**You:** What happens when the invoice arrives?

**Sadie:** I identify the GRN that it relates to and check the details to the GRN so I know that we've been invoiced for the right items in terms of product code, quantity and price. I initial the invoice to show that this has been checked and enter the invoice into the accounting system. I allocate each invoice the same number as the related GRN and then staple them together in the file.

**You:** That sounds very comprehensive. Thanks Sadie.

**Sadie:** No problem!

### Interview with Lauren White, Accounts Payable Clerk

**You:** Hi Lauren, Sadie gave me your name and said you would be the best person to speak to about the process for paying invoices. Have you got a few minutes?

**Lauren:** Sure.

**You:** Great, can you explain to me how invoices get paid?

**Lauren:** Yes, at the end of each month, I have a look in Sadie's file and identify all of the invoices which are matched to GRNs which are unpaid and then pay them.

**You:** How do you know which invoices are unpaid?

**Lauren:** Well there's two ways of knowing really – firstly once I pay an invoice I mark it with a stamp saying 'paid'. Secondly, we always pay all of the invoices received in the month so, for example, at the end of June I would know that all of the invoices received in June that have been matched to GRNs need to be paid.

**You:** Do you have set credit terms with the supplier?

**Lauren:** Yes, they give us 30 days' credit from the end of the month so an invoice dated 14 June would have to be paid by the end of July.

**You:** OK. Does the supplier send statements?

**Lauren:** Yes, they send us a statement each month which details all of the transactions we have had with them during the month. I file this in their correspondence file.

**You:** So how is the actual payment made?

**Lauren:** We pay by bank transfer. I prepare a schedule detailing the invoices and the total amount we need to pay. Each of the buyers sign off to say that they authorise the payments. I then prepare the bank payment authorisation and give all of this information to Katie to check and authorise the bank transfer.

1   From a review of the information above, your audit assistant has highlighted some potential deficiencies in respect of the purchases system at Dress You Like Co.

One such deficiency is that the goods received into the warehouse are not checked back to the order form and your audit assistant feels this deficiency could have implications for the company.

**Required**

Which TWO of the following statements describe valid implications of the above deficiency?

☐   Goods may be accepted which have not been ordered and therefore are not needed by the business.

☐   Goods may be accepted by the business which are of insufficient quality.

☐   Goods which are actually required for production may have been omitted from the delivery which could lead to stock outs and business interruption.

☐   Orders may be placed for goods which are not required

2   A second deficiency relates to the fact that the balance per the purchase ledger account is not reconciled to supplier statements.

**Required**

Which of the following recommendations would NOT be appropriate to address this deficiency?

○   The accounts payable clerk should reconcile the balance per the purchase ledger to the balance per the supplier statement each month.

○   Invoices on the supplier statement which relate to goods received but not invoiced should not be included in the purchase ledger to avoid the payables balance being overstated at the year-end.

○   Any journals processed as a result of the reconciliation should be authorised by the department supervisor.

○   The reconciliation performed by the accounts payable clerk should be reviewed by the department supervisor.

3   The report to those charged with governance at Dress You Like Co will recommend that a notification is added to the accounting system which identifies when an invoice is due for payment.

**Required**

Which of the deficiencies in Dress You Like Co's purchases system will this recommendation BEST address?

○   That supplier invoices are not recorded accurately in the purchase ledger

○   That supplier invoices are incorrectly coded

○ That supplier invoices are paid too late

○ That supplier invoices are paid too early

---

## Activity 4: Purchases system (test of controls)

The following questions relate to the information in Activity 3.

1 In order to ensure that Dress You Like Co is only invoiced for items which have been received the finance assistant vouches the details on the invoices to the goods received note.

**Required**

Which of the following statements is a valid test of controls that the auditor could perform in order to conclude whether this control operates effectively?

○ Observe a sample of goods being received in the warehouse to ensure that the goods received note is completed accurately.

○ Inspect a sample of invoices recorded in the ledger to verify that they have been allocated the correct product code.

○ For a sample of invoices which have been matched to goods received notes, reperform the calculations to ensure they have been done properly.

○ Analytically review the level of purchases made each month to the budget and investigate any significant variances.

2 Your audit assistant is planning to inspect a sample of the bank payment authorisation documents for evidence of the Finance Director's signature.

**Required**

For which of the following internal control objectives would this provide sufficient, appropriate audit evidence?

○ That payments to the supplier are made on a timely basis

○ That payments to the supplier are reviewed and authorised prior to payment

○ That payments to the supplier are accurately recorded in the ledger

○ That payments to the supplier are for valid business expenses only

---

In **exam questions,** it is important to **use the scenario** to generate your answer rather than learn lots of internal controls and tests of controls by heart.

You should try to complete as many practice questions on this area as possible. To help you in this, we have included some other examples of control objectives, internal controls and tests of controls below.

| Stage: Order Stage | | | |
|---|---|---|---|
| **Risk** | **Control objectives** | **Controls** | **Tests of controls** |
| That an order is unauthorised and not for business use | To ensure that orders are only placed once authorised and vetted to ensure they are for business use | Orders should only be raised on receipt of an authorised purchase requisition which is approved by the department manager. | Review a sample of orders for evidence that the purchase requisition was authorised and the goods are for business use. |
| That the entity does not buy | To ensure that the entity buys | Orders should only be placed with a supplier | For a sample of orders, vouch that the suppliers |

| Stage: Order Stage | | | |
|---|---|---|---|
| **Risk** | **Control objectives** | **Controls** | **Tests of controls** |
| items at the most competitive price | items at the most competitive price | which is on the entity's list of preferred suppliers which have been approved in terms of cost and quality.<br><br>For non-standard items, separate quotations may be required. | used are on the preferred supplier listing. |

| Stage: Goods Received | | | |
|---|---|---|---|
| **Risk** | **Control objectives** | **Controls** | **Tests of controls** |
| That goods ordered are not received, potentially leading to stock outs | To ensure that all goods ordered are received | On receipt of goods the warehouse should raise a multi-part, sequentially numbered goods received note (GRN). One part of the GRN should be passed to the purchasing department to be matched to the order form.<br><br>Unmatched orders should be reviewed on a periodic basis and suppliers chased | Observe the receipt of goods into the warehouse to ensure all goods are recorded and a GRN generated.<br>Verify that the GRN is matched to the order form by the purchasing department.<br>Enquire as to the action taken where orders are unfulfilled and reperform this process. |
| That faulty goods are accepted | To ensure that goods are only accepted if they are of the correct quality | On receipt of goods, all items are to be verified to ensure they are in satisfactory condition. | Observe the receipt of goods by staff to confirm the control is carried out. |

| Stage: Goods Invoiced and Recorded | | | |
|---|---|---|---|
| **Risk** | **Control objectives** | **Controls** | **Tests of controls** |
| That the liability for goods received is not recognised in the accounting records | To ensure that liabilities for goods received are recognised in the accounting records | Another part of the GRN should be passed to the accounts department.<br>Invoices received from suppliers should then be matched to the GRN.<br>Unmatched GRNs should be reviewed periodically and an accrual posted for the associated liability. | For a sample of GRNs trace through to corresponding invoice and verify that the invoice has been recorded in the accounting records.<br>Where no invoice has been received verify that the relevant accrual has been recorded. |

| Stage: Goods Invoiced and Recorded | | | |
|---|---|---|---|
| **Risk** | **Control objectives** | **Controls** | **Tests of controls** |
| That a liability is recognised for goods which have not been received | To ensure that a liability is only recognised for goods which have been received | Upon receipt of a supplier invoice, it should be matched to the sequentially numbered GRN and order form. The invoice should be allocated the same sequential number. | For a sample of invoices recorded, vouch the details back to the GRN and order form to verify that the goods were received. |

| Stage: Payment Made | | | |
|---|---|---|---|
| **Risk** | **Control objectives** | **Controls** | **Tests of control** |
| That payments are made to the wrong supplier | That payments are only made to the correct supplier for bona fide purchases | All invoices should be authorised for payment and coded to the relevant supplier by the appropriate budget holder. Authorisation/coding should be evidenced by a signature.<br><br>Statements received from suppliers should be reconciled to the relevant purchase ledger account on a monthly basis. Any subsequent changes to the accounting records must be authorised. | Inspect a sample of invoices for authorisation and appropriate coding.<br><br><br>Review a sample of supplier reconciliations to ensure that they have been completed accurately and any resultant changes authorised. |
| That an invoice is paid twice/is for the wrong amount | To ensure that suppliers are paid accurately | Prior to being paid all invoices should be agreed to the GRN and order form and calculations such as unit price, sales tax, quantities and discounts agreed to the appropriate records.<br>Once paid the invoice should be stamped 'paid'. | Inspect a sample of invoices for evidence that calculations have been reperformed and the invoice stamped as 'paid'. |

## 3.3 Payroll system

The payroll system has two main areas to consider:

| Human Resources (HR) function | Payroll processing function |
|---|---|
| Includes:<br>Staff appointment<br>Staff removal | Includes:<br>Monthly processing of payroll |

| Human Resources (HR) function | Payroll processing function |
|---|---|
| Staff appraisal<br>Notifications of salary changes | |

Ideally, these two distinct roles would be **carried out by different** members of staff/ departments; however, this may not be possible in smaller businesses where we have seen that it can be difficult to have sufficient segregation of duties.

There are inherent risks within a payroll system, including:

**Fraud**
- Establishing fake payroll records
- Changing pay rates without authorisation
- Claiming payment for more hours than genuinely worked
- Theft (if wages are paid in cash (rare))

**Errors**
- Complexities relating to tax
- Other deductions

The payroll system consists of three main stages with documentation at each stage:

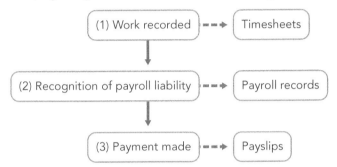

 ## Activity 5: Payroll system (deficiencies)

You are now carrying out the work on the wages system at Dress You Like Co. You have been given the following information concerning the wages system for the year ended 30 September 20X6.

(1) The factory and warehousing staff record the number of hours worked using a clocking in/out system which is observed by a supervisor. On arrival at work each morning and at the end of each day's work, each worker enters their unique employee number on a keypad. Any employee who does not clock out at the end of their shift is automatically clocked out by the system.

(2) In order to claim overtime, employees need to complete an 'overtime claim' form and submit it to the wages clerk.

(3) The Wages Clerk, Jake Newman, works in the finance team and is responsible for making amendments to the computerised wages system in respect of employee holidays and illness. He also sets up and maintains all employee records and processes the monthly payroll.

(4) The computerised wages system calculates deductions from gross pay, such as employee taxes and net pay. Each month a list of net cash payments for each employee is produced and this is reviewed and authorised by the acting finance director before the employees are paid by BACS transfer. Deductions are checked by Jake Newman on a periodic basis.

**Required**

In respect of the internal controls relating to the payroll system of Dress You Like Co.

(1) Identify and explain **TWO** deficiencies; and

(2) Recommend a control to address each of these deficiencies.

| Control deficiency | Control recommendation |
|---|---|
| | |
| | |

---

## Activity 6: Payroll system (test of controls)

In respect of the internal controls relating to the payroll system of Dress You Like Co:

(1) Identify and explain **TWO** controls within the payroll system; and

(2) Describe **TEST OF CONTROLS** the external auditors should perform to assess if each of these controls is operating effectively.

| Control | Test of controls |
|---|---|
| | |
| | |

---

In **exam questions,** it is important to **use the scenario** to generate your answer rather than learn lots of internal controls and tests of controls by heart.

You should try to complete as many practice questions on this area as possible. To help you in this, we have included some other examples of control objectives, internal controls and tests of controls below.

## Stage: Work recorded

| Risk | Control objectives | Controls | Tests of controls |
|------|-------------------|----------|-------------------|
| That hours worked are not recorded accurately | To ensure that hours worked are accurately recorded | Hours worked should be recorded using timesheets or a clocking in and out system.<br><br>Hours recorded to be reviewed by responsible official. | Observe a sample of employees clocking in and out to ensure it is done according to the entity's procedures.<br>Inspect a sample of timesheets for evidence that they have been reviewed by a responsible official. |
| That additional hours are recorded which have not been worked | To ensure that only overtime which has been completed is recorded and paid | Overtime must be authorised by an appropriate supervisor/manager in advance of the overtime being carried out and an overtime authorisation form completed. | For a sample of overtime payments, trace back to the overtime authorisation form and inspect the form for evidence of the overtime being authorised. |

## Stage: Recognition of payroll liability

| Risk | Control objectives | Controls | Tests of controls |
|------|-------------------|----------|-------------------|
| That fictitious employees are paid | To ensure that only individuals which are bona fide employees are paid | Where new joiners are taken on/ current employees leave Human Resources (HR)/staff manager should complete and sign a joiners/leavers form which should be passed to payroll. Payroll must acknowledge receipt of the form/changes to the payroll system should be made and amendments to the system subsequently reviewed by a supervisor.<br><br>Personnel files should be held for all employees.<br><br>Assign unique employee numbers to each employee | Obtain a list of joiners/leavers during the period and trace a sample through to ensure that appropriate HR documentation was completed and the payroll system amendment was made accurately.<br><br>Select a sample of starters and leavers during the period and determine whether they were genuine employees by tracing employee details back to personnel files.<br><br>Review procedures for entering and removing employee numbers from the payroll master file. |

**BPP**

## Stage: Recognition of payroll liability

| Risk | Control objectives | Controls | Tests of controls |
|---|---|---|---|
| | | in the payroll master file. Only employees with valid employee numbers can be paid. | |
| That wages are paid/deductions made at the wrong rate | To ensure that wages are paid/deductions are made at the appropriate rate | Any changes to standing data for payroll (employee salaries/hourly rates/deductions from gross wages/tax codes etc) should be authorised by HR/staff manager using appropriate documentation.<br><br>A report of changes to standing data should be printed on a monthly basis and reviewed by an appropriate manager to ensure all changes are *bona fide* and accurately made. | Review a sample of the reports showing changes made to standing data to ensure that changes made were appropriately authorised and accurately made.<br><br>Recalculate PAYE and other deductions to ensure they have been correctly calculated. |

## Stage: Payment made

| Risk | Control objectives | Controls | Tests of controls |
|---|---|---|---|
| That employees are not paid the amount that they are due to receive per payroll records/their payslip | To ensure that employees are paid the correct amount according to payroll records/their payslip | Each month, a printout of all amounts due to be paid to employees should be printed and reviewed for any unusual amounts/employees.<br><br>The total of the amount to be paid should be recast.<br><br>If employees are paid by BACS transfer then the employees' bank account number should be verified and the amount due to each employee agreed back to the payroll system and payslip. | Review the printout to determine whether any unusual items were followed up. Discuss the outcome with management.<br><br>Recast the schedule in order to ensure it has been accurately cast.<br><br>For a sample of employees reperform the controls in place to ensure they have been completed accurately.<br><br>Vouch the authorisation of the payroll manager/ finance director. |

| Stage: Payment made | | | |
|---|---|---|---|
| **Risk** | **Control objectives** | **Controls** | **Tests of controls** |
| | | The BACS transfer should then be authorised by the payroll manager/ finance director. | Observe cash payment process. |
| | | If employees are paid in cash then an additional check should be made that the amount included in the wage packet agrees back to the payslip. Wage packets should be made up by two payroll staff and employees required to sign to confirm receipt of the wage packet. | |

## 3.4 The inventory system

The fourth system included in the syllabus is the inventory system.

The main objectives/stages of the internal controls in this system are to ensure:

- Only goods required by the entity are accepted and are accurately recorded
- Damaged goods are not accepted and inventory is appropriately valued
- The business is not interrupted due to stock outs
- Inventory is kept securely (not damaged or stolen)

Many of these objectives overlap to a large extent with the middle stages of the purchases cycle.

| Stage: Only goods required by the entity are accepted and are accurately recorded | | | |
|---|---|---|---|
| **Risk** | **Control objectives** | **Controls** | **Tests of controls** |
| That goods which have not been ordered are accepted | To ensure that only goods which have been ordered are accepted | A copy of the authorised order form should be passed to the warehouse. When goods are received, they should be matched to the order form and only accepted if they were ordered. The GRN should be signed to evidence that it has been vouched back to the order form. | Inspect a sample of GRNs for evidence of a signature verifying that the goods received were traced back to an authorised order form. |
| That purchases and sales of inventory are recorded in the | To ensure that all purchases and sales of inventory are | All GDNs and GRNs are processed on a daily basis to record the despatch and receipt of inventory. | Inspect documentation to confirm that daily processing of GDNs and GRNs occurs. |

| Stage: Only goods required by the entity are accepted and are accurately recorded | | | |
|---|---|---|---|
| **Risk** | **Control objectives** | **Controls** | **Tests of controls** |
| wrong accounting period | recorded in the correct accounting period | | |

| Stage: Damaged goods are not accepted and inventory is appropriately valued | | | |
|---|---|---|---|
| **Risk** | **Control objectives** | **Controls** | **Tests of controls** |
| That damaged/ faulty goods are accepted | To ensure that goods are only accepted if they are of the appropriate quality | On receipt of goods, all items are to be verified to ensure they are in satisfactory condition. | Observe the receipt of goods by staff to confirm the control is carried out. |
| That inventory is not valued at the lower of cost and net realisable value | To ensure that inventory is properly stated at the lower of cost and net realisable value | Standard costs are to be regularly reviewed by management to ensure they are kept up to date. | Review the entity's procedures for updating standard costs and test a sample of standard costs to determine whether they approximate to current cost. |
| | | Inventory managers should review inventory regularly to identify slow-moving, obsolete and excess inventory. | Discuss the procedure for reviewing inventory with management and observe the review process/inspect any reports which management have issued after the review has taken place. |

| Stage: The business is not interrupted due to stock outs | | | |
|---|---|---|---|
| **Risk** | **Control objectives** | **Controls** | **Tests of controls** |
| That goods ordered are not received, potentially leading to stock outs | To ensure that goods ordered are received | On receipt of goods, the warehouse should raise a multi-part, sequentially numbered goods received note (GRN). One part of the GRN should be passed to the purchasing department to be matched to the order form. | Observe the receipt of goods into the warehouse to ensure all goods are recorded and a GRN generated. Verify that the GRN is matched to the order form by the purchasing department. |

## Stage: The business is not interrupted due to stock outs

| Risk | Control objectives | Controls | Tests of controls |
|---|---|---|---|
| | | Unmatched orders should be reviewed on a periodic basis and suppliers chased. | Enquire as to the action taken where orders are unfulfilled and reperform this process. |

## Stage: Inventory is kept securely (not damaged or stolen)

| Risk | Control objectives | Controls | Tests of controls |
|---|---|---|---|
| That inventory is damaged/stolen | To ensure that inventory is safeguarded | Inventory should be stored in an appropriate environment (for example, perishable inventory should be kept at the right temperature/ refrigerated if necessary).<br><br>Access to inventory should only be granted to the appropriate personnel.<br><br>Items should only be issued from inventory if accompanied by a copy of a customer sales order form. | Inspect the environment in which inventory is stored to ensure it is suitable for the nature of the inventory.<br><br>Inspect the identity cards of employees working within the inventory area.<br><br>Inspect a sample of GDNs to verify that they relate to bona fide customer orders. |
| That inventory movements are not adequately monitored | To ensure that all inventory movements are authorised and recorded | Inventory should only be moved if it is accompanied by a pre-numbered GDN or GRN.<br><br>Regular reconciliations performed of inventory records with the general ledger.<br><br>Segregation of duties to exist in terms of the responsibilities for the maintenance of inventory records and the custodianship of inventory. | For a sample of inventory movements, inspect GDNs and GRNs to determine whether inventory is being moved for valid reasons.<br><br>Review a sample of reconciliations to confirm that they have been accurately prepared and reviewed by a manger/supervisor.<br><br>Observe the recording of inventory and discuss inventory procedures with relevant staff to ensure that proper segregation of duties is operating. |

## 3.5 The bank and cash system

The fifth system included in the syllabus is the cash system.

The main objectives/stages of the internal controls in this system are to ensure:

- All monies received are recorded
- All monies received are banked
- Cash and cheques are safeguarded against loss or theft
- All payments are authorised, made to correct payees and recorded
- Payments are not made twice for the same liability

Many of these objectives overlap to a large extent with the final stages of the sales and purchases systems.

| Stage: All monies received are recorded | | | |
|---|---|---|---|
| **Risk** | **Control objectives** | **Controls** | **Tests of controls** |
| That monies are received but not recorded | That all monies received are recorded | There should be a segregation of duties in place between those receiving the monies and those recording them in the accounting system. | Observe the process of the post being opened and monies received recorded to ensure that the entity's internal controls are being adhered to. |
| | | Two people should open the post and record the amounts received on a 'receipts listing'. This information should then be passed to another member of staff who will then record the entries in the cash book and write out the bank paying in slip. | Inspect documentation such as the bank paying in slip for evidence of each staff member carrying out their separate part of the process. |
| | | Another member of staff should be responsible for banking any monies received. | |

## Stage: All monies received are banked

| Risk | Control objectives | Controls | Tests of controls |
|---|---|---|---|
| That monies received are not banked | To ensure that monies received are banked | Bank reconciliations should be performed on a weekly/monthly basis by someone not responsible for the banking and the reconciliation reviewed by a supervisor/manager. | Reperform the bank reconciliation to ensure it has been done accurately. Review the bank reconciliation for evidence of the supervisor/manager review being performed. |
| | | Customer statements should be prepared and sent out on a regular (monthly) basis. | Enquire from management as to whether customer statements are sent out on a regular basis and review customer correspondence in order to determine the level of errors identified as a result of customer statements being sent out. |

## Stage: Cash and cheques are safeguarded against loss or theft

| Risk | Control objectives | Controls | Tests of controls |
|---|---|---|---|
| That cash/cheques are misappropriated | To ensure that cash/cheques are safeguarded against loss or theft. | Unbanked receipts should be kept in a locked safe at all times. Cheque books should be kept by a supervisor/manager and stored in a secure location such as a locked drawer/cash tin or safe. | Physically verify the location of unbanked receipts/cheque books to ensure they are kept securely. |

## Stage: All payments are authorised, made to correct payees and recorded

| Risk | Control objectives | Controls | Tests of controls |
|---|---|---|---|
| That invoices are paid without being authorised/paid to the wrong supplier and not recorded accurately in the accounting records | To ensure that invoices are only paid once authorised and that payment is made to the correct payee and recorded | All invoices should be authorised for payment and coded to the relevant supplier by the appropriate budget holder prior to the invoice being paid. Authorisation/coding should be evidenced by a signature. | Inspect a sample of invoices for authorisation and appropriate coding. |

| Stage: All payments are authorised, made to correct payees and recorded | | | |
| --- | --- | --- | --- |
| Risk | Control objectives | Controls | Tests of controls |
| | | Statements received from suppliers should be reconciled to the relevant purchase ledger account on a monthly basis. Any subsequent changes to the accounting records must be authorised. | Review a sample of supplier statement reconciliations to ensure that they have been completed accurately and any resultant changes authorised. |

| Stage: Payments are not made twice for the same liability | | | |
| --- | --- | --- | --- |
| Risk | Control objectives | Controls | Tests of controls |
| That an invoice is paid twice | To ensure that invoices are not paid twice for the same liability | Once paid the invoice should be stamped 'paid'. | Inspect a sample of invoices for evidence that calculations have been reperformed and the invoice stamped as 'paid'. |
| | | Purchase invoices should be sequentially numbered and the invoice recorded as 'paid' on the system so that the computer will not allow the same invoice to be paid twice. | Attempt to process a payment for an invoice which has previously been paid to determine whether the system will block the payment. |

## 3.6 Non-current assets

The sixth system included in the syllabus is non-current assets. This system relates to capital expenditure.

Many of the objectives overlap with the initial stage of the purchases system where an entity must ensure that only goods required are ordered and that all orders are authorised.

The principal internal controls in this system which have not already been detailed in the purchases system are to ensure:

- That capital expenditure is appropriately classified in the accounting records
- That capital items are recorded in the non-current asset register
- That there is safe custody of assets

| Stage: That capital expenditure is appropriately classified in the accounting records | | | |
| --- | --- | --- | --- |
| **Risk** | **Control objectives** | **Controls** | **Tests of controls** |
| That revenue expenditure is recorded as capital expenditure or vice versa | To ensure that capital expenditure is appropriately classified in the accounting records | Separate order forms should be used for the purchase of inventory items (see purchases cycle) and capital items.<br><br>For capital items, the order should be authorised by one or two managers/ directors depending on the value of items ordered. The order should be coded to the appropriate non-current asset account.<br><br>Periodically, review the revenue and capital expenditure nominal ledger accounts for evidence of large/unusual items which may have been incorrectly recorded. | Inspect a sample of orders for capital items.<br><br>Vouch that the appropriate level of authorisation has been made and evidenced by a signature. Verify that the account code relates to the item ordered.<br><br>Discuss with management the outcome of the nominal ledger reviews. Inspect any journals made to correct errors to ensure that they have been authorised. |

| Stage: That capital items are recorded in the non-current asset registe | | | |
| --- | --- | --- | --- |
| **Risk** | **Control objectives** | **Controls** | **Tests of controls** |
| That capital items are not recorded in the non-current asset register | To ensure that capital items are recorded in the non-current asset register | Periodically review the non-current assets held by the business and trace them through to verify that they are recorded in the non-current asset register.<br><br>On a monthly basis, reconcile the totals on the non-current asset nominal ledger codes to the balance per the non-current asset register. Investigate any differences. Authorise all adjustments. | For a sample of non-current assets, inspect the non-current asset register to ensure that they have been included.<br><br>Review the reconciliation to see the level of adjustments required. Discuss with management why errors have occurred and the action being taken to reduce future errors. |

| Stage: That there is safe custody of assets | | | |
|---|---|---|---|
| **Risk** | **Control objectives** | **Controls** | **Tests of controls** |
| That capital items are misappropriated | To ensure that there is safe custody of assets | Establish physical safeguards over non-current assets such as locks, safes, keypads, CCTV, security guards in order to reduce the risk of theft.<br><br>Maintain adequate insurance over non-current assets. | Test the operation of the physical controls, for example obtain to gain access to a restricted area without following security procedures.<br><br>For a sample of assets, inspect insurance documents to determine whether insurance is adequate and up to date. |

# 4 Communication of deficiencies in internal control

ISA 265 *Communicating Deficiencies in Internal Control to Those Charged with Governance and Management* states that **significant deficiencies in internal control** should be communicated in writing to those charged with governance.

This will take the form of a **report to management**.

A **significant deficiency** in internal control is a deficiency or combination of deficiencies in internal control that, in the auditor's professional judgement, is of sufficient importance to merit the attention of those charged with governance.

## 4.1 Determining whether a deficiency is significant

The auditor should consider the following matters when determining whether a deficiency in internal control is a significant deficiency:

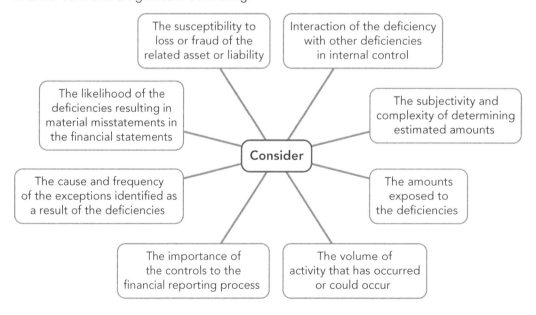

## 4.2 Reports to management

Once the auditor has decided that there are significant deficiencies which need to be communicated to those charged with governance, they should include this information in a **report to management**.

In the exam you may be asked **only** to identify and explain deficiencies in internal control and to make a recommendation to address these.

Alternatively, you may be asked to include the above information in a report to management.

An example format for a report to management is included below:

| | Check and Co Auditor's Address |
|---|---|
| Board of Directors Dress You Like Co | |
| | Date: exam date |

Dear Sirs,

**Audit of Dress You Like Co for the year ended 30 September 20X6**

Please find enclosed the report to management on significant deficiencies in internal controls identified during the audit for the year ended 30 September 20X6.

The Appendix to the report identifies and explains deficiencies in the sales system and provides recommendations to address those deficiencies.

Please note that this report only addresses any significant deficiencies identified during the audit and if further testing had been performed then more deficiencies may have been reported. It is not therefore a comprehensive list of all deficiencies.

This report is solely for the use of management and if you have any further questions then please do not hesitate to contact us.

Yours faithfully,
Check and Co

**Appendix:**

| Control deficiency | Control recommendation |
|---|---|
| No credit checks are made before new customers are accepted and credit limits are not prescribed. The company may well accept an order and despatch goods to a bad credit risk. This may mean that goods are sold to a customer who cannot pay for them, leading to a loss of revenue and inventory. | A standard new customer form should be created which must be completed before orders are accepted from new customers. This form should require a credit check to be made in relation to the customer and a credit limit allocated. Standard tiers of credit limits could be applied for different customers. All completed new customer forms should be authorised by Edward Times or Katie Escombe prior to goods being despatched. The authorisation should be evidenced on the form. |

## 4.3 Reports to management by the internal audit function

In the example above, the report to management was produced by the external auditor.

In Chapter 5 we saw that one of the roles of the internal audit function is often to review an entity's internal controls and to report their findings (including any deficiencies) to management.

It is very possible therefore that a report on deficiencies, implications and recommendations might be prepared by the internal audit function. The format of such a report will be determined by management and is much more flexible than the above report by the external auditor.

**Essential reading**

See Chapter 10 of the Essential reading for an example internal auditor's report.

The Essential reading is available as an Appendix of the digital edition of the Workbook.

# 5 ISA 260 (Revised): *Communication with those charged with governance*

In this chapter and also Chapters 3 and 4, we have seen that there are often occasions where the external auditor needs to communicate audit matters with those charged with governance.

## 5.1 Definition

**KEY TERM**

> **Those charged with governance:** are the person(s) or organisation(s) with responsibility for **overseeing the strategic direction** of the entity and obligations relating to the **accountability** of the entity (ISA 260 (Revised): para. 10a).

## 5.2 Matters the auditor would communicate to those charged with governance

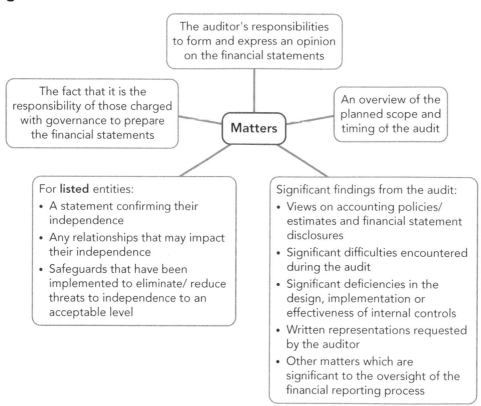

## 5.3 Third parties interested in communications to those charged with governance

Occasionally, those charged with governance may wish to provide third parties, for example bankers or certain regulatory authorities, with copies of a written communication from the auditors.

It is important that the auditor ensures that third parties who see the communication understand that it was not prepared with them in mind.

To that effect, written communication from the auditors will include certain caveats:

- The report has been prepared for the sole use of the entity;
- It must not be disclosed to a third party, or quoted or referred to, without the written consent of the auditors; and
- No responsibility is assumed by the auditors to any other person.

# Chapter summary

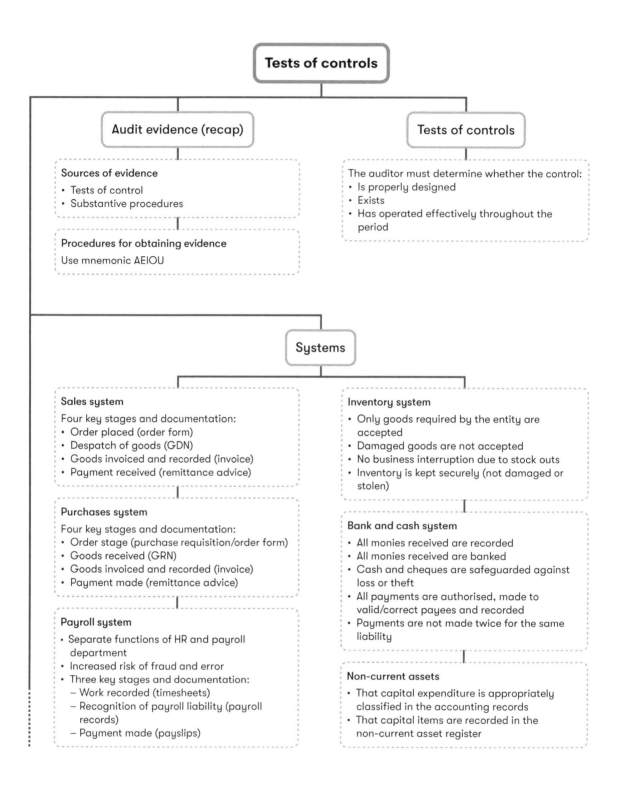

**Tests of controls**

**Audit evidence (recap)**

Sources of evidence
- Tests of control
- Substantive procedures

Procedures for obtaining evidence
Use mnemonic AEIOU

**Tests of controls**

The auditor must determine whether the control:
- Is properly designed
- Exists
- Has operated effectively throughout the period

**Systems**

Sales system
Four key stages and documentation:
- Order placed (order form)
- Despatch of goods (GDN)
- Goods invoiced and recorded (invoice)
- Payment received (remittance advice)

Purchases system
Four key stages and documentation:
- Order stage (purchase requisition/order form)
- Goods received (GRN)
- Goods invoiced and recorded (invoice)
- Payment made (remittance advice)

Payroll system
- Separate functions of HR and payroll department
- Increased risk of fraud and error
- Three key stages and documentation:
  - Work recorded (timesheets)
  - Recognition of payroll liability (payroll records)
  - Payment made (payslips)

Inventory system
- Only goods required by the entity are accepted
- Damaged goods are not accepted
- No business interruption due to stock outs
- Inventory is kept securely (not damaged or stolen)

Bank and cash system
- All monies received are recorded
- All monies received are banked
- Cash and cheques are safeguarded against loss or theft
- All payments are authorised, made to valid/correct payees and recorded
- Payments are not made twice for the same liability

Non-current assets
- That capital expenditure is appropriately classified in the accounting records
- That capital items are recorded in the non-current asset register

 BPP

## Communication of deficiencies in internal control

Report significant deficiencies in internal control to those charged with governance

### Determining whether a deficiency is significant

- Likelihood of the deficiency resulting in material misstatements in the fs
- Susceptibility to loss or fraud
- Subjectivity/complexity of determining estimated amounts
- The amounts exposed to the deficiencies
- The volume of activity
- The importance of the controls to the financial reporting process
- The cause and frequency of the exceptions identified

### Reports to management

- Form of communication to be agreed at planning stage
- Contents to be discussed with management
- Addressed to audit committee/board
- Structure:
  - Identify and explain deficiency
  - Control recommendation
- Caveats:
  - Not for external use
  - Not a comprehensive list of all deficiencies

### Reports to management by the internal audit function

- More varied reporting
- Flexible format

## ISA 260: Communication with those charged with governance

### Definition

Person(s) or organisation(s) with responsibility for overseeing the strategic direction of the entity and obligations relating to the accountability of the entity

### Matters to communicate

- Auditor's responsibilities (to express an opinion)
- Responsibility of those charge with governance (to prepare fs)
- Overview of planned scope/timing of the audit
- Significant findings from the audit
- For listed entities:
  - Statement to confirm independence
  - Relationships that may impact independence
  - Safeguards that have been implemented

### Third parties interested in communication to TCWG

- Auditor's report is for sole use of entity
- Report must not be disclosed without prior, written consent
- No responsibility assumed to third parties by the auditor

 **BPP**

# Knowledge diagnostic

### 1. Types of audit procedures

Audit evidence can be gained using tests of controls and/or substantive procedures.

### 2. Tests of controls

Tests of controls involve repeatedly testing specific internal controls to ensure that they are properly designed, exist and have operated throughout the period.

### 3. Methods to test controls

Internal controls can be tested using enquiry, inspection, observation and reperformance.

### 4. Examinable systems

There are six systems in the syllabus: sales, purchases, payroll, inventory, cash and non-current assets. A business should establish internal controls in each system.

### 5. Exam questions

Questions on this area will be **scenario based** and so you need to be able to identify internal controls and/or internal control deficiencies from a given scenario.

### 6. Significant deficiencies

Significant deficiencies in internal control noted by the auditor will be communicated via a report to management. You may need to produce this in the exam and so will need to be familiar with its contents.

### 7. Reports on internal control deficiencies

Reports on internal control deficiencies may also be one of the areas of work undertaken by the internal audit function.

### 8. Internal auditor's reports

Whenever the internal audit function carries out an assignment, they are likely to produce a report which details their findings. The reports will vary according to the type of assignment the internal audit function has performed. You should be able to describe the form and content of internal auditor's reports.

### 9. Communicating with those charged with governance

There are many different matters which the external auditor may communicate with those charged with governance. These range from responsibilities for the financial statements, planning issues, audit issues, internal control deficiencies and the auditor's independence.

# Further study guidance

## Question practice

Now try the following from the Further question practice bank [available in the digital edition of the Workbook]:

*   Section A Q35 to Q39
*   Section B Q72(a) Fenton Distributors
*   Section B Q73 Cheque payments and petty cash

## Further reading

Please refer to the exam success site at the end of the eBook for details on how to access videos of the interviews contained within this Chapter.

There is a technical article on the ACCA website which is relevant to some of the topics covered in this chapter that you should read:

Technical article:

*   *The audit of wages. (https://www.accaglobal.com/gb/en/student/exam-support-resources/fundamentals-exams-study-resources/f8/technical-articles/the-audit-of-wages.html)*

## Own research

As we saw in Chapter 9, it would be helpful for you to consider the internal controls that operate in your place of work (or even your home). What are the processes and policies that you need to follow and what documentation are you required to complete? Are any checks made to determine whether the processes and policies have been accurately followed?

# Activity answers

## Activity 1: Sales system (deficiencies)

| Control deficiency | Control recommendation |
|---|---|
| Many parts of the sales system process are completed by hand/manually. For example, the order form is completed by hand and is then passed (by hand) to the warehouse. Completing items by hand could lead to an increased risk of manual error in filling out the form, or errors in processing if handwriting cannot easily be read. Additional time is also taken photocopying/scanning orders which are then posted/emailed to customers. There could also be delays in passing the order to the warehouse. | The computer system should generate a blank, sequentially numbered standard order form for the sales team to complete electronically which will ensure all required information is captured. Once completed, this should be emailed to the customer and sent electronically to the warehouse. Periodic sequence checks should be undertaken in order to ensure that all orders have been recorded. |
| The goods despatched note (GDN) is not generated from the order form but is simply written up from what is packed in the boxes. There is also no double-check that the items on the GDN are those items packed in the boxes. If errors are made in the packing process, the customer could be despatched items that they did not order or may not receive items they did order, even if they are not out of stock. | The GDN should be generated as an electronic copy of the order form and detail the product code and quantity ordered. Where an item is not in stock this should be recorded on the GDN to provide a record of items which are missing. Spot checks should be carried out to verify that the contents packed agree to the order form. |
| Monies received from customers are not always accompanied by a remittance advice and so cannot always be allocated to specific outstanding invoices. Sometimes monies are simply allocated to the oldest invoices. The company does not have an accurate record of outstanding invoices and so cannot chase overdue amounts efficiently. This will also mean that disputed invoices are not necessarily identified. This could lead to a loss of cash flow and/or irrecoverable debts. | Monies received with remittance advices should be allocated against the specific invoices which are being paid. Where a remittance advice is not received, the accounts receivables clerk should contact the customer by telephone to determine the breakdown of invoices being paid. |
| **Note.** Only **THREE** deficiencies were required for this activity. However, there were many other deficiencies in the activity and these are detailed below for completeness: | |
| The order form is not pre-numbered. The situation may arise where more than one order is given the same order number causing confusion in the sales team when dealing with customer queries. If the order forms are not pre-numbered then | Order forms should be pre-numbered and sequentially numbered in order to be able to determine whether any order forms are missing. |

| Control deficiency | Control recommendation |
|---|---|
| it is also more difficult to file them in a logical order and thus resolve any customer queries quickly and efficiently. | |
| Orders for the supermarket chain are sent directly to the despatch team and not to the warehouse manager.<br><br>The warehouse manager has responsibility to ensure that all orders received are allocated to a team of pickers. He also monitors that orders are subsequently fulfilled where items are initially out of stock.<br><br>Passing the order directly to the despatch team may mean that these unfulfilled orders are not later despatched leading to dissatisfaction from the company's major customer. | All orders should be passed to the warehouse manager who can then allocate the jobs to the despatch team on a timely basis. |
| No credit checks are made before new customers are accepted and credit limits are not prescribed.<br><br>The company may well accept an order and despatch goods to a bad credit risk. This may mean that goods are sold to a customer who cannot pay for them, leading to a loss of revenue and inventory. | A standard 'new customer' form should be created which must be completed before orders are accepted from new customers. This form should require a credit check to be made in relation to the customer and a credit limit allocated. Standard tiers of credit limits could be applied for different customers. All completed 'new customer' forms should be authorised by Edward Times or Katie Escombe prior to goods being despatched. The authorisation should be evidenced on the form. |
| The invoice process is also completed manually and the items to be invoiced are manually input from the details on the GDN.<br><br>Any errors in the GDN will result in errors on the invoice. This will lead to staff time being taken up to correct the errors and could lead to customer dissatisfaction if the level of errors is high. | An electronic invoice should be generated from the electronic order form and GDN using the standard product codes and prices in order to improve the accuracy of information. |
| The prices charged to the supermarket are automatically generated by the system without any checks being made.<br><br>Any errors in the pricing standing data will mean that the supermarket could be charged for goods at too low a price, thus losing the entity revenue, or at too high a price which would potentially lead to customer dissatisfaction. | Each time that prices change, a report showing the pricing standing data should be generated and reviewed by a supervisor/manager to ensure all changes are accurate and to reduce the risk of unauthorised changes being made. This review should be evidenced by a signature. |
| There is no formal process to monitor overdue amounts.<br><br>Customer statements are not sent each month and no aged receivables analysis is produced.<br><br>If overdue amounts are not chased as soon as they fall overdue then there is an increased | A formal process should be adopted to chase outstanding customer balances.<br><br>Statements should be prepared on a monthly basis and sent to each customer detailing the transactions with the customer during the month and the balance outstanding at the |

| Control deficiency | Control recommendation |
|---|---|
| risk of non-payment. | end of the month. |
| | The aged receivables report should also be produced on a monthly or at least quarterly basis to identify amounts which have been overdue for some time. |
| | Customers with overdue accounts should be contacted by telephone as soon as possible and a letter requesting payment sent if no payment is received. |
| | Accounts should be placed 'on stop' if a customer exceeds their credit limit until such time that the balance is repaid. |

## Activity 2: Sales system (test of controls)

| Control | Test of controls |
|---|---|
| When completing an order form, the sales team refer to the standard product list in order to verify that the correct product codes have been used and that the order is accurate. | For a sample of orders throughout the year, vouch the product codes on the order form to the standard product list to verify that the correct product codes have been used. |
| Any changes to standard data, such as discounts, require hierarchical authorisation by the acting finance director. This will prevent unauthorised changes being made to the standard data. | For a sample of customers who are not entitled to a discount, attempt to process a discount to determine whether a prompt will be received requesting an appropriate login. |
| Bank reconciliations are performed each week to monitor the completeness, accuracy and validity of the information held in the cash book. The reconciliations are also performed by someone other than the accounts receivables clerk which strengthens the control due to the segregation of duties. | For a sample of bank reconciliations, reperform the reconciliation to ensure it has been completed properly. Vouch the balances per the bank statement and cash book to the bank statement and the accounting records and recast the arithmetical accuracy of the reconciliation. Trace through any reconciling items to ensure that they are reasonable. If the bank reconciliation was reviewed, inspect the reconciliation for evidence of the review taking place. |
| **Note.** Only **three** controls were required for this activity. However, there were several other controls in the activity and these are detailed below for completeness. | |
| Orders which have been received but have not been completed because the item is out of stock are reviewed daily to ensure that customer orders are completed as efficiently as possible. A full review of outstanding orders is also done each month with the sales team. | Observe the warehouse manager review these orders and follow up to ensure that they have been allocated to a picking team and fulfilled within an appropriate timescale. Observe the review of outstanding orders to ensure it is conducted each month. |
| Invoicing is carried out daily once the GDNs are received from the warehouse. This ensures that goods despatched are invoiced on a | For a sample of GDNs trace through to the related invoice and vouch the date to ensure that the invoice was sent out shortly after the |

| Control | Test of controls |
|---|---|
| timely basis thus improving cash flow. | goods were despatched. |

## Activity 3: Purchases system (deficiencies)

1   The correct answers are:

- Goods may be accepted which have not been ordered and therefore are not needed by the business.
- Goods which are actually required for production may have been omitted from the delivery which could lead to stock outs and business interruption.

Goods received should be vouched to the order form in order to ensure that the business receives exactly what it ordered; however, this process will not stop orders being processed unnecessarily. Furthermore, a separate quality check should be performed on the goods received.

2   The correct answer is: Invoices on the supplier statement which relate to goods received but not invoiced should not be included in the purchase ledger to avoid the payables balance being overstated at the year-end.

Where goods have been received before the month-end/year-end a corresponding liability should be recognised even if the invoice has not been received.

3   The correct answer is: That supplier invoices are paid too early

At Dress You Like Co supplier invoices are currently being paid in the month in which they are received rather than when they fall due. Therefore, having some sort of prompt/notification in the accounting system which identifies when each invoice needs to be paid according to the supplier's credit terms will reduce the risk that invoices are paid too early.

## Activity 4: Purchases system (test of controls)

1   The correct answer is: For a sample of invoices which have been matched to goods received notes, reperform the calculations to ensure they have been done properly.

Reperforming the calculations will enable the auditor to conclude whether the finance assistant has accurately vouched the details on the invoice to the goods received note.

Note that analytical review is a substantive procedure, not a test of controls.

2   The correct answer is: That payments to the supplier are reviewed and authorised prior to payment

The Finance Director signs the bank payment authorisation to demonstrate that she has reviewed the list of invoices being paid and approves the payment.

## Activity 5: Payroll system (deficiencies)

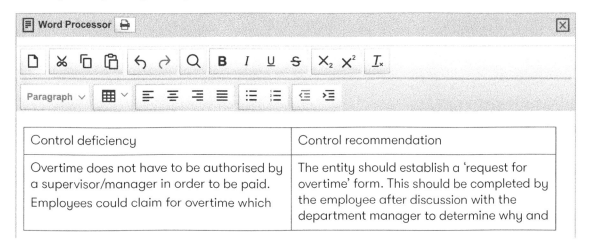

| Control deficiency | Control recommendation |
|---|---|
| Overtime does not have to be authorised by a supervisor/manager in order to be paid. Employees could claim for overtime which | The entity should establish a 'request for overtime' form. This should be completed by the employee after discussion with the department manager to determine why and |

 BPP

| Control deficiency | Control recommendation |
|---|---|
| has not been worked.<br><br>Also, the entity cannot budget its cash flow properly if overtime is not planned in advance and authorised. | whether overtime is necessary. The department manager should sign to evidence their authorisation for the overtime to be performed which will prevent unauthorised overtime being completed/paid.<br><br>Once the overtime has been completed, both the 'request for overtime' and 'overtime claim' forms should be signed by the department manager and forwarded to the wages clerk. |
| The wages clerk is able to amend the standing data on the payroll system and also processes payroll on a day-to-day basis.<br><br>The wages clerk has too much influence over the payroll system and could carry out fraudulent activity such as setting up fictitious employees and changing rates of pay if he wanted to. | At least two people should be involved in the payroll process. One person should have responsibility for amending standing data and joiners and leavers and the second person should process the day-to-day payroll in order to improve segregation of duties and increase the likelihood of errors being detected.<br><br>All amendments to standing data should be authorised before they are made and an exception report of changes made should be printed each month and reviewed for any unexpected changes in order to reduce the risk of unauthorised changes being made. |

## Activity 6: Payroll system (test of controls)

| Control | Test of controls |
|---|---|
| Hours worked are recorded by a clocking in/out system, with each employee using their unique employee number. Employees are automatically clocked out at the end of their shift, reducing the risk that employees are paid for hours not worked. | Observe the clocking in/out process to ensure that each employee has to enter their own employee number.<br><br>Attempt to clock in using an incorrect employee number to verify that the system will not allow the entry.<br><br>For a valid employee number, do not clock out at the end of the day and inspect the system records to ensure that the employee has been logged out by the system. |
| The listing of employee pay details is reviewed by the acting finance director before payments are made to the employees. This reduces the risk of fraudulent/erroneous payments. | Observe the monthly payroll being processed and reviewed by the acting finance director. Inspect a copy of the payroll listing to vouch the finance director's signature authorising the payment. |

# Skills checkpoint 3

# How to approach internal control questions

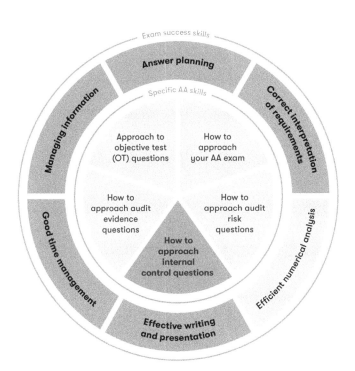

## Introduction

Both the external auditor and the internal auditor have a role to play in relation to an entity's internal control systems.

The external auditor needs to have an understanding of an entity's internal control relevant to the audit. This means that they need an understanding of the policies and procedures which are relevant to the financial statements regardless as to whether or not they want to gather audit evidence via tests of controls.

The internal auditor may be involved in developing an entity's internal control system or in testing the system.

Whatever their involvement, it is likely that both the external and the internal auditors will be in a position to identify deficiencies in an entity's internal control systems and they should report those deficiencies to management/those charged with governance. Conversely, they are both in a position to be able to identify direct controls which operate within the internal control system and can then test them.

Consequently, questions on internal control feature regularly in the Audit and Assurance exam. There are several types of questions which may be tested:

- Identify and explain control deficiencies and make recommendations to address each deficiency;

- Explain direct controls and describe tests of control to ensure the controls are operating effectively; and
- Control deficiencies, recommendations and tests of control.

Where such questions feature in Section B of the exam, they tend to be scenario based.

The Examiner's reports imply that candidates' performance in Section B questions on internal control is better than that on audit risk but that there is still room for improvement in terms of fully explaining both deficiencies and controls.

This skills checkpoint will therefore consider how you should approach such questions. We will use the example of the first type of question although the same approach should be applied to all three types.

# Skills Checkpoint 3: How to approach internal control questions

## AA Skill: How to approach internal control questions

A step-by-step technique for ensuring that your approach to internal control questions uses the scenario provided in the exam and maximises your marks is outlined below. Each step will be explained in more detail in the following sections, and illustrated by answering a requirement from a past exam question.

> **STEP 1:**
>
> Allow some of your allotted time to read the requirements and the scenario.
> Don't rush into starting to write your answer.

> **STEP 2:**
>
> Re-read the scenario and start to develop an answer plan.
> Use the table headings provided (Control deficiency and Control recommendation) and as you read through the scenario for the second time, write down a few words or a bullet point each time you identify a potential internal control deficiency in the scenario.
> Use these as headings in your answer.

> **STEP 3:**
>
> Re-read the requirement to confirm how many control deficiencies you need to explain. You may have written down more headings than required, in which case decide which ideas you can explain most easily and include those in your answer.
> When you write your answer the deficiency should describe the specific impact that the issue might have on the entity (ie they may pay employees for more hours than have been worked). Next describe the internal control you would recommend management implement to address the deficiency.

# Exam success skills

The following illustration is based on an extract from a past exam question, about a pharmaceutical manufacturer, called 'Oregano'. This extract was worth 12 marks.

For this question, we will also focus on the following **exam success skills**:

- **Managing information**. It is easy for the amount of information contained in scenario-based questions to feel overwhelming. To manage this, focus on the requirement first – noting the key exam verbs to ensure you answer the question properly. Then read the rest of the question, noting important and relevant information from the scenario

- **Correct interpretation of requirements**. Here you need to **both** identify and explain the deficiency **and** recommend an internal control to address the deficiency.

- **Answer planning.** Everyone will have a preferred style for planning an answer. For example, it may be highlighting or simply making notes. Remember you have a highlighter tool available in the assessment platform and a scratch pad tool is available too for you to make notes as you read through the scenario. Choose the approach that you feel most comfortable with or, if you are not sure, try out different approaches for different questions until you have found your preferred style.

- **Effective writing and presentation**. A blank table will be provided for control deficiencies and recommendations to address them. One column will be for deficiencies and one column for recommendations. Start each deficiency or recommendation in a new cell of the table provided in the appropriate column. Enter the related deficiencies and recommendations on the same row. Ensure you fully explain the internal control that would address the deficiency. Use full sentences, ensuring your style is professional.

- **Good time management**. It is essential that you do not overrun on the constructed response questions in Section B and so you must always keep an eye on time. Note down the time you should finish the question.

**STEP 1**  Allow some of your allotted time to read the requirement and the scenario. Don't rush into starting to write your answer.

Start by analysing the requirements so that you know what you are looking for when you read the scenario.

(c)  Identify and explain SIX deficiencies in Oregano Co's sales and dispatch system and provide a recommendation to address each of these deficiencies.

**Note.** Prepare your answer using two columns headed Control deficiency and Control recommendation respectively.

**12 marks**

### Required

The first part of the requirement is to 'identify and explain SIX deficiencies'. Here you need to use the scenario to generate six issues that could impact the smooth running of the business. It may be that the entity should have an internal control but no control is operational (if a control is not mentioned in the scenario then assume that it does not operate) or that the entity has an internal control but it doesn't operate effectively.

The second part of the requirement is to 'provide a recommendation to address each deficiency'. Here you should describe in detail the internal control that management should implement to prevent the deficiency recurring or to detect it should it happen again.

This requirement is worth 12 marks and at 1.8 minutes a mark, should take 21 minutes to both plan and write the solution.

## Question – Oregano (12 marks)

You are a member of the recently formed internal audit department of Oregano Co (Oregano). The company manufactures tinned fruit and vegetables which are supplied to large and small food retailers. Management and those charged with governance of Oregano have concerns about the effectiveness of their sales and dispatch system and have asked internal audit to document and review the system.

### Sales and dispatch system

Sales orders are mainly placed through Oregano's website but some are made via telephone. Online orders are automatically checked against inventory records for availability; telephone orders, however, are checked manually by order clerks after the call. A follow-up call is usually made to customers if there is insufficient inventory. When taking telephone orders, clerks note down the details on plain paper and afterwards they complete a three-part pre-printed order form. These order forms are not sequentially numbered and are sent manually to both dispatch and the accounts department.

As the company is expanding, customers are able to place online orders which will exceed their agreed credit limit by 10%. Online orders are automatically forwarded to the dispatch and accounts department.

A daily pick list is printed by the dispatch department and this is used by the warehouse team to dispatch goods. The goods are accompanied by a dispatch note and all customers are required to sign a copy of this. On return, the signed dispatch notes are given to the warehouse team to file.

The sales quantities are entered from the dispatch notes and the authorised sales prices are generated by the invoicing system. If a discount has been given, this has to be manually entered by the sales clerk onto the invoice. Due to the expansion of the company, and as there is a large number of sales invoices, extra accounts staff have been asked to help out temporarily with producing the sales invoices. Normally it is only two sales clerks who produce the sales invoices.

**STEP 1** Now you should be ready to re-read the scenario and plan your answer using the deficiencies you identify as you read through.

Work through each paragraph of the scenario identifying specific deficiencies. Each deficiency is worth one mark and the recommendation is also worth one mark, hence why you need six properly explained deficiencies and recommendations to gain 12 marks.

## Completed answer plan

Having worked through each paragraph, an answer plan can now be completed.

A possible answer plan is shown here. Note that in the CBE environment you can use the highlighter tool to pick out the underlined words while using the scratch pad to make the related notes.

You are a member of the recently formed internal audit department of Oregano Co (Oregano). The company manufactures tinned fruit and vegetables which are supplied to large and small food retailers. Management and those charged with governance of Oregano have concerns about the effectiveness of their sales and dispatch system and have asked internal audit to document and review the system.

### Sales and dispatch system

Sales orders are mainly placed through Oregano's website but some are made via telephone. Online orders are automatically checked against inventory records for availability; telephone orders, however, are checked manually[20] by order clerks after the call. A follow-up call is usually made to customers if there is insufficient inventory. When taking telephone orders, clerks note down the details on plain paper and afterwards[21] they complete a three-part pre-printed order form.

[20] Deficiency – manual check (risk of errors) after order taken (risk of goods being unavailable and dissatisfied customers) Recommendation - use same system for both types of order

[21] Deficiency – order form not completed at time of order (risk of errors/lost orders) Recommendation - complete order form at time of order and confirm details with customer

These order forms are not sequentially numbered[22] and are sent manually to both dispatch and the accounts department.

As the company is expanding, customers are able to place online orders which will exceed their agreed credit limit by 10%[23]. Online orders are automatically forwarded to the dispatch and accounts department.

A daily pick list[24] is printed by the dispatch department and this is used by the warehouse team to dispatch goods. The goods are accompanied by a dispatch note and all customers are required to sign a copy of this. On return, the signed dispatch notes are given to the warehouse team[25] to file.

The sales quantities are entered from the dispatch notes and the authorised sales prices are generated by the invoicing system. If a discount[26] has been given, this has to be manually entered by the sales clerk onto the invoice. Due to the expansion of the company, and as there is a large number of sales invoices, extra accounts staff have been asked to help out temporarily[27] with producing the sales invoices. Normally it is only two sales clerks who produce the sales invoices.

[22] Deficiency – order forms not sequentially numbered (risk of lost orders as can't check completeness) Recommendation - create sequentially numbered system

[23] Deficiency – exceeding credit limits increase risk of non-payment Recommendation - orders to be rejected if they cause credit limits to be exceeded

[24] Deficiency – pick list not agreed to order forms (wrong goods could be sent) Recommendation - pick list to be supported by order forms

[25] Deficiency – no copy of GDN to accounts dept (delays in invoicing) Recommendation - multi=part document, copy sent to accounts dept on dispatch of goods

[26] Deficiency – discounts entered manually (scope for fraud/error) Recommendation - discount levels authorised by mgt and recorded on customer file

[27] Deficiency – lack of experience/training increases scope for error Recommendation - consider secondment/recruitment of staff

**STEP 2** You will see that there are more than six deficiencies, therefore choose the six for which you can provide a recommended control.

You will enter your answer into the table provided in the CBE. Explain each deficiency in terms of its impact on the entity. Also remember to explain the recommendation, what internal control should be implemented and by whom.

Start each deficiency and related recommendation in a new row of the table provided in the CBE (in the appropriate column).

### Suggested solution

Note that you would enter each risk and response into each column of a table but the solution below has each deficiency followed by each recommendation underneath so that tutorial notes can be shown alongside the deficiency/recommendation to which they relate.

**Control deficiency** — Telephone orders are checked manually[28] after an order has been placed.

[28] Identify – manual process Explain - unfulfilled orders/customer dissatisfaction

This creates a risk of goods for which orders have been placed being unavailable, leading to unfulfilled orders. This gives rise to dissatisfaction from customers and has a negative impact on the company's reputation.

**Control recommendation** — Orders should not be confirmed before the availability of the product has been checked.

To ensure that orders are fulfilled consistently, telephone orders and online orders should ideally be processed through the same system[29], with automatic notifications to the customer who has placed the order once product availability has been checked.

[29] Practical recommendation

**Control deficiency** — Order forms for telephone orders are completed after[30] an order has been placed.

[30] Identify – completed AFTER Explain - risk of errors

This increases the risk that information on the order forms is incorrect or incomplete, leading to errors in fulfilling the order.

**Control recommendation** — All order forms should be completed at the time the order is placed. For telephone orders, the order clerk should confirm with the customer[31] that all details are correct.

[31] Practical recommendation

**Control deficiency** — Customers are able to exceed their agreed credit limit by 10%[32] when they place their orders online.

[32] Identify – exceed credit limit by 10% Explain - risk of irrecoverable debts

This increases the risk that customers with bad credit histories are accepted, leading to slow-moving or irrecoverable debts.

**Control recommendation** — The online ordering system should be modified to reject orders[33] which would cause credit limits to be exceeded.

[33] Practical recommendation

Customers' credit limits should be assessed on a regular basis by a responsible official. Credit limits could be extended for customers with good credit histories.

**Control deficiency** — The signed dispatch notes are not sent to the accounts department.

This could result in delays in invoicing[34], leading to loss of revenue.

[34] Identify – dispatch note not sent to accounts Explain - delays in invoicing

**Control recommendation** — Copies of the signed dispatch notes should be forwarded to the accounts department[35] once the goods have been delivered. Invoices should be raised based on the dispatch notes in a timely manner, and the dispatch notes filed by the accounts team along with evidence that the related invoices have been processed.

[35] Practical recommendation

**Control deficiency** — Discounts are manually entered by the sales clerk onto the invoice.

This creates the risk of discounts being omitted by error.

More importantly, the lack of authorisation[36] process increases the risk of unauthorised discounts being given, leading to loss of revenue.

[36] Identify – manual entry, not authorised Explain - risk of fraud/error

**Control recommendation** — Discounts should be approved by a responsible official. The authorised discount levels should be recorded automatically[37] in the customer master file, so that they appear on the invoices without manual input.

[37] Practical recommendation

The invoicing system should be modified to prevent the manual processing of discounts.

**Control deficiency** — Extra accounts staff have been allocated to produce the sales invoices.

The extra staff's lack of experience and training increases the risk of errors[38] on the invoices, resulting in customers being over- or undercharged.

[38] Identify – lack of appropriately trained staff. Explain - risk of errors

**Control recommendation** — Only sales clerks with the appropriate experience should be allowed to produce sales invoices. Oregano could consider recruiting and training[39] permanent staff with the appropriate experience.

[39] Practical recommendation

## Exam success skills diagnostic

Every time you complete a question, use the diagnostic below to assess how effectively you demonstrated the exam success skills in answering the question. The table has been completed below for the 'Oregano' activity to give you an idea of how to complete the diagnostic.

| Exam success skills | Your reflections/observations |
|---|---|
| Managing information | Did you identify internal control deficiencies in the scenario? |

| Exam success skills | Your reflections/observations |
|---|---|
| Correct interpretation of requirements | Did you identify that you only need six deficiencies and six (related) recommendations to gain 12 marks? |
| Answer planning | Did you draw up an answer plan using your preferred approach (eg highlighting, notes)?<br>Did your plan help to create a structure for your answer? |
| Effective writing and presentation | And most importantly –did you explain why your points constituted a deficiency? |
| Good time management | Did you manage to read, plan and complete your solution in the allotted time? |
| Most important action points to apply to your next question | |

## Summary

You are likely to see a scenario-based question on internal control deficiencies and recommendations, direct controls and tests of control or deficiencies, recommendations and tests of control in the exam. You cannot prepare for every type of business and all internal controls but you can equip yourself with the skills to attempt internal control questions, by using the information given in the question to guide the structure of your answer. A key skill is then applying this back to the given scenario. You will not be able to pass these questions unless you answer ALL parts of the question (for example explain both the deficiency and provide a recommendation). It is therefore essential that you try to create a practical answer that is relevant to the scenario, and/or addresses the issues identified in the scenario, instead of simply producing rote-learned deficiencies/controls/tests of control.

As you move into practising questions as part of your final revision, you will need to practise taking in information from a scenario quickly, accurately understanding the requirements, and creating an answer that addresses the requirements in the context of the scenario.

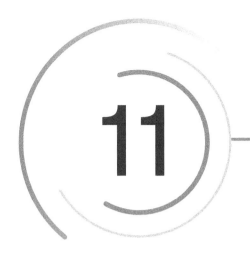

# 11 Audit sampling and automated tools and techniques

## Learning objectives

On completion of this chapter, you should be able to:

| Syllabus learning outcomes | Syllabus reference no. |
|---|---|
| Define audit sampling and explain the need for sampling. | D3 (a) |
| Identify and discuss the differences between statistical and non-statistical sampling. | D3 (b) |
| Discuss and provide relevant examples of the application of the basic principles of statistical sampling and other selective testing procedures. | D3 (c) |
| Discuss the results of statistical sampling, including consideration of whether additional testing is required. | D3 (d) |
| Explain the use of automated tools and techniques in the context of an audit, including the use of audit software, test data and other data analytics tools. | D5 (a) |
| Discuss and provide relevant examples of the use of automated tools and techniques including test data, audit software and other data analytics tools. | D5 (b) |

## Business and Exam context

In this chapter, we look at the use of audit sampling and automated tools and techniques.

We will look in detail at audit sampling, which is an important aspect of the audit. We consider different types of audit sampling and the evaluation of errors.

Automated tools and techniques are an important tool in the audit and we examine the two main types: audit software and test data. Use of computers on audits is common practice. In answering questions on obtaining evidence, remember to include reference to automated tools and techniques if they seem relevant.

Your AA syllabus does not require you to have a detailed knowledge of data analytics, but this is a topical area. The AA examining team has stated that candidates will only be expected to have a broad understanding of what data analytics is, how it may be used in an audit and how it may improve audit efficiency.

Both sampling and the use of automated tools and techniques could come up in OTQs in Section A, or as part of Section B. Questions could require you to explain different sampling methods, for example.

# Chapter overview

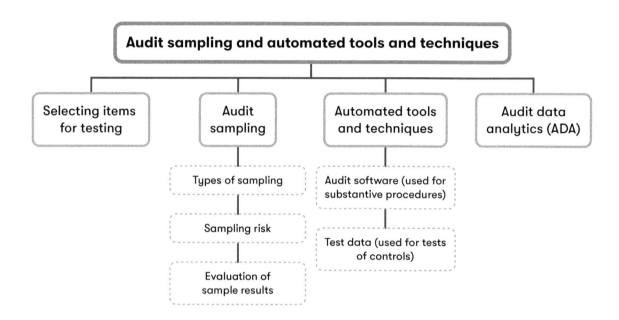

# 1 Selecting items for testing

The overall aim of the external audit is for the auditor to give an opinion as to whether the financial statements are free from material misstatement (present fairly).

The auditor does not test everything as it would be impractical to do so and so they need to decide on the extent of testing they will perform.

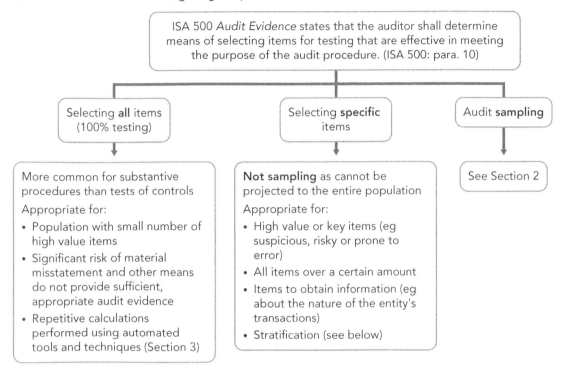

Sometimes, the auditor may want to ensure that they test certain items within a population. For example, they may decide they want to review the monies received post year-end from the client's 10 largest receivables balances in order to gather evidence over the valuation of receivables. The receivables population is then divided into two discrete sub-populations. One sub-population has the ten largest balances in it and each of these will be tested. The second sub-population contains all remaining receivables and the auditor may also test a sample of these balances. This is called **stratification**.

# 2 Audit sampling

KEY
TERM

**Audit sampling:** means "the application of audit procedures to **less than 100%** of the items within a population of audit relevance such that all sampling units have **an equal chance of selection,** in order to provide the auditor with a reasonable basis on which to draw conclusions about the entire population" (ISA 530: para. 5(a)).

**Population:** is "the entire set of data from which a sample is selected and about which the auditor wishes to draw conclusions" (ISA 530: para. 5(b)).

## 2.1 Types of sampling

There are two types of sampling: **statistical** sampling and **non-statistical** sampling.

**Non-statistical** sampling does not use any mathematical basis for selecting a sample. Examples of non-statistical sampling include:

| Haphazard selection | Block selection |
|---|---|
| Here the auditor selects the items to be included in the sample without following a structured technique but which avoids any conscious bias or predictability (for example the auditor should not exclude items which are difficult to locate from the sample purely because of the inconvenience). | This may be used to check whether certain items have particular characteristics. For example, an auditor may use a sample of 50 consecutive cheques to test whether cheques are signed by authorised signatories rather than picking 50 single cheques throughout the year. However, block sampling may produce samples that are not representative of the population as a whole, particularly if errors only occurred during a certain part of the period, and therefore the errors found cannot be projected onto the rest of the population. |

**Statistical** sampling uses:

- Mathematical number tables to choose a sample which is **free from bias**; and
- Probability theory to evaluate the results of the testing.

Examples of statistical sampling methods include:

| Random selection | Systematic selection | Value weighted selection (or monetary unit sampling (MUS)) |
|---|---|---|
| This process uses random number tables (or a computerised random number generator) to select the items in the sample. It ensures that all items in the population have an equal chance of selection | This involves selecting items using a constant interval between selections, the first interval having a random start. For example, if the auditor has a population with 1,000 items and requires a sample containing 200 items then the sampling interval is 5 (1,000 ÷ 200). A random starting point within the first 5 is then determined (say 2) and the auditor will test every 5th item after item number 2 (ie 2 then 7 and so on). | Here the population is randomly ordered and items are selected for sampling by weighting the items in proportion to their value. |

The difference between the two types of sampling is that, with statistical sampling, the sampling risk can be measured and controlled (we look at sampling risk in Section 2.2). With non-statistical sampling, it cannot be measured.

Although the audit procedures performed on the items in the sample will be the same whether a statistical or non-statistical approach is used, meaningful extrapolation can only occur from a statistical sample which has been selected randomly.

## Activity 1: Preparation

Check & Co is intending to audit the trade receivables of Dress You Like Co by circularising a sample of the year-end balances. This audit test involves obtaining a written confirmation of the balance owing from a sample of Dress You Like's trade receivables (you will learn about this test in more detail in Chapter 14).

Trade receivables at Dress You Like Co total $12.5m at the year end, of which $11.8m relate to one large supermarket. Check & Co have decided to use stratification for selecting their sample. The $11.8m relating to the supermarket will be circularised and a sample of seven other trade receivables will be selected for circularisation from the remaining $0.7m using value weighted selection (MUS).

The overall materiality level for the audit is $100,000.

The trade receivables listed below have been randomly tabulated.

**Required**

State which receivable balances will be selected for sampling using value weighted selection (MUS).

| Customer | Balance $'000 | Cumulative total $'000 | Selected (Y/N) |
|---|---|---|---|
| Safari Schoolwear | 28 | | |
| Clothing Terrain | 33 | | |
| Everyday Wear | (6) | | |
| All About Clothes | 21 | | |
| Jim's Jumpers | 38 | | |
| Look the Part | 124 | | |
| Freya's Threads | 8 | | |
| Holly Aristocrat | 73 | | |
| Girls on the Go | 13 | | |
| Odd One Out | 67 | | |
| Upward Trends | 17 | | |
| Ivory Gowns | 2 | | |
| Skirts and all sorts | 57 | | |
| Dress for the Occasion | 92 | | |
| Holiday Accessories | 5 | | |
| Ties with a Difference | 12 | | |
| Up and Out | 9 | | |
| In all Weather | 16 | | |
| Duncan's Dresses | 3 | | |
| Ewan Trading | 29 | | |
| We're Going Exploring | 12 | | |
| Fred's Fashions | 47 | | |
| | 700 | | |

Solution

### 2.1.1 Advantages and disadvantages of monetary unit sampling (MUS)

| Advantages | Disadvantages |
|---|---|
| • The auditor can design and evaluate the sample quickly and in a cost-effective way using automated tools and techniques (Section 3). <br><br> • All material items are automatically selected ensuring all material items are tested. | • Selecting the sample can be time consuming if automated tools and techniques cannot be used to select the sample. <br><br> • MUS does not cope where there are negatively valued items in the population. <br><br> • MUS will not be effective if the population is not randomly ordered. |

## 2.2 Sampling risk

> **Sampling risk:** is the risk that the auditor's conclusion, based on a sample, may be different from the conclusion if the entire population were subjected to the same audit procedure. (ISA 530: para. 5(c))

The auditor must determine a sample size that will reduce sampling risk to an **acceptably low level**.

If the auditor judges that sampling risk is high then they will need to select a larger sample in order to have reasonable assurance that the results are free from material misstatement. There is therefore a direct relationship between sampling risk and sample size.

Other factors which affect **sample size** include:

| Factor | Effect on sample size |
|---|---|
| Risk of material misstatement | If the auditor assesses the level of inherent risk and control risk to be high, then detection risk needs to be low in order to reduce audit risk to an acceptably low level. <br><br> Detection risk includes both sampling and |

| Factor | Effect on sample size |
|---|---|
| | non-sampling risk and in order for sampling risk to be low a larger sample size is needed. |
| Required confidence level | This describes how confident the auditor needs to be that the sample results are representative of the population as a whole. |
| | The greater the degree of confidence the auditor requires, the larger the sample size needs to be. |
| Expected error | This relates to the level of errors the auditor expects to find in the population. |
| | If the level of expected error is high then the sample size will need to be larger in order to make a reasonable estimate of the actual amount of the error in the population. |
| Tolerable error/ misstatement | This relates to the level of error or misstatement that the auditor can accept in the population before he is concerned that there is a material misstatement. |
| | The lower the level of tolerable errors that can be accepted, the larger the sample size needs to be. |

## 2.3 Evaluation of sample results

Once the audit procedures have been carried out on the sample, the auditor should evaluate the sample results to determine whether they are satisfactory or whether further work is required.

Where there are **errors** in the sample, the auditor should consider:

- The nature and cause of the error
- Whether the error is a 'one-off' (anomalous) error or a recurrent issue
- Whether the error effects the purpose of the audit procedure
- Whether the error affects other areas of the audit

> **Anomaly:** "a misstatement or deviation that is demonstrably not representative of misstatements or deviations in a population" (ISA 530: para. 5(e)).
>
> **Tolerable misstatement:** "a monetary amount set by the auditor in respect of which the auditor seeks to obtain an appropriate level of assurance that the monetary amount set by the auditor is not exceeded by the actual misstatement in the population" (ISA 530: para. 5(i)).
>
> **Tolerable rate of deviation:** "a rate of deviation from prescribed internal control procedures set by the auditor in respect of which the auditor seeks to obtain an appropriate level of assurance that the rate of deviation set by the auditor is not exceeded by the actual rate of deviation in the population" (ISA 530: para. 5(j)).

### 2.3.1 Tests of details

Where sampling has been used to perform tests of details, the auditor should project the **monetary errors** found in the sample to the population as a whole and compare this to the level of tolerable misstatement.

Where an error has been established as an anomaly, it may be excluded when projecting sample errors to the population (but it still needs to be considered overall in addition to the projection of the non-anomalous errors).

## Activity 2: Results – tests of detail

For this activity **only**, imagine that Dress You Like Co was a much smaller manufacturer and did not have the supermarket as a major customer. Hypothetically, the entire trade receivables would total $700,000 at 30 September 20X6. As stratification would not be used, any error could be projected to the entire population.

You have obtained the following results based on your sample:

| | |
|---|---:|
| Total value of the population | $700,000 |
| Number of items in the population | 22 |
| Number of items tested | 7 |
| Value of items tested | $407,000 |
| Error in the sample | $20,000 |

### Required

Consider the results of the testing as follows:

1   Assuming the errors are not anomalous ones, calculate the expected error in the population.

2   Assuming that tolerable misstatement was set at $30,000, explain what action should be taken.

### Solution

---

### 2.3.2   Tests of controls

When sampling has been used to test controls, no explicit projection of errors is necessary since the sample **deviation (or error) rate** is also the projected deviation rate for the population as a whole.

For example, if the auditor has performed tests of controls on a sample of 20 items and has found two deviations, this represents an error rate of 10% ($^2/_{20}$ × 100). The auditor must then decide if this error rate is acceptable.

## Activity 3: Tests of controls

You are auditing the internal controls relating to the authorisation of adjustments made to Dress You Like Co's inventory system in order to determine the accuracy and validity of the adjustments. You have obtained the following results based on your sample:

| | |
|---|---|
| Total number of adjustments made to inventory records during the year | 1,500 |
| Number of adjustments tested in the sample | 225 |
| Number of occasions when adjustments tested were not authorised | 18 |

**Required**

Consider the results of the testing as follows:

(1) Assuming the errors are not anomalous ones, calculate the error rate in the population.

(2) Assuming that tolerable rate of deviation was set at 13%, explain what action should be taken.

**Solution**

If the evaluation of sample results indicates that there may be significant issues, the auditor may:

(a) Request management to investigate identified errors and the potential for further errors and make any necessary adjustments;

(b) Modify the nature, timing and extent of further audit procedures; and/or

(c) Consider the effect on the auditor's report

### PER alert

Being able to apply the techniques of audit sampling discussed in this section will assist you in achieving PER Objective 19 on preparing for and collecting evidence for audit.

### Essential reading

See Chapter 11 of the Essential reading for further details on the requirements of ISA 530 *Audit Sampling*.

The Essential reading is available as an Appendix of the digital edition of the Workbook.

# 3 Automated tools and techniques

> **Automated tools and techniques:** are "applications of auditing procedures using the computer as an audit tool".

Automated tools and techniques involve using a computer to perform audit work. Computers can be used to perform either substantive procedures or tests of controls. There are two particularly common types: **audit software** and **test data**.

## Activity 4: Automated tools and techniques

Can you think of any advantages or disadvantages of using automated tools and techniques in an audit?

| Advantages | Disadvantages |
|---|---|
| [ ] | [ ] |
| [ ] | [ ] |
| [ ] | [ ] |
| [ ] | [ ] |
| [ ] | |

## 3.1 Audit software (used for substantive procedures)

> **Audit software:** consists of computer programs used by the auditor, as part of their auditing procedures, to process data of audit significance from the entity's accounting system. Audit software is used to conduct substantive procedures. It may consist of **generalised audit software** or **custom audit software**.
>
> **Generalised audit software:** allows auditors to perform tests on computer files and databases, such as reading and extracting data from a client's systems for further testing, selecting data that meets certain criteria, performing arithmetic calculations on data, facilitating audit sampling and producing documents and reports. Examples of generalised audit software are ACT and IDEA.
>
> **Custom audit software:** is written by auditors for specific tasks when generalised audit software cannot be used.

 BPP

Audit software can be used to:

<table>
<tr><td>

**Select information**

*Examples*

- A sample of suppliers to circularise to test completeness of the payables balance (perhaps using MUS)
- To identify missing, large or unusual items or items outside specified parameters

</td><td>

**Perform calculations**

*Examples*

- To calculate variances and ratios used in analytical review
- To check the accuracy of the casting of the trial balance or ledger listings

</td></tr>
<tr><td>

**Read and extract data from a client's system and produce a report in a specified format**

*Examples*

- The auditor could download the client's sales ledger onto their own software, and use their own (trusted) software to produce an aged receivables listing; this can then be used as a basis for testing the valuation of receivables
- Or an aged inventory report

</td><td>

**Print reports in specified formats**

*Example*

- Letters to be sent out in a receivables confirmation

</td></tr>
</table>

## 3.2 Test data (used for tests of controls)

**Test data:** techniques are used in conducting audit procedures by entering data (eg a sample of transactions) into an entity's computer system, and comparing the results obtained with pre-determined results. Test data is used for tests of controls.

Test data is a fictitious set of test transactions which are input into the client's system in order to determine whether the internal controls within the entity's computer systems have operated effectively throughout the period.

Should an auditor wish to gather audit evidence using test data, they will need significant co-operation from their client, especially in terms of the time required to access their computer systems.

There are two typical uses of test data:

(a)  Test data used to test specific controls in computer programs

For example, an auditor could try to access data or areas of the computer system which are password protected in order to determine whether the control is operating effectively.

(b)  Test transactions

Here the auditor processes a series of transactions and monitors the output from the computer systems in order to determine whether the transactions have been processed correctly.

This can be conducted 'live' (when the computer systems are operational) or 'dead' (when the computer system is not in business use). Test transactions normally involve submitting both **valid and invalid data** for processing.

Invalid data could include, for example, zero quantity items, negative prices or extraordinarily high prices. The auditor would expect the valid data to be processed properly and the invalid data to be rejected.

Some computer systems have an **embedded test facility**. This may comprise a 'dummy unit' to which test transactions are posted throughout the period or a systems control and review file (SCARF) where real transactions are replicated and stored for later review by the auditor.

## PER alert

Two of the PER performance objectives require the use information and communications technology (PO2 and PO5). The use of automated tools and techniques by you during an audit assignment will help to achieve this objective.

## Essential reading

See Chapter 11 of the Essential reading to read about using automated tools and techniques plus the benefits and difficulties of using audit software and test data.

The Essential reading is available as an Appendix of the digital edition of the Workbook.

# 4 Audit data analytics (ADA)

**KEY TERM**

**Big data:** is a broad term for the larger, more complex datasets that can be held by modern computers. The term refers to a qualitative shift in the amount of data that is available in comparison with the past.

**Data analytics:** is the examination of data to try to identify patterns, trends or correlations. As the quantity of data has increased, it has become more and more necessary to evolve ways of processing and making sense of it.

In recent years, many fields have undergone a revolution at the hands of big data, and the audit profession is no different. The introduction of big data in the form of audit data analytics (ADA) routines has the potential to revolutionise the audit process. Current ISAs are based on a risk management approach to audit, whereby the auditor does not test 100% of an entity's transactions, but instead focuses audit work on the riskiest areas. In contrast to this, data analytics offers the chance of examining all of an entity's data. This could eventually revolutionise the way audits are conducted, together with the approach advocated by auditing standards.

The use of data analytics software will initially involve **significant costs** on the part of the auditor and **extensive training**, however it could offer auditors the ability to **examine all of an entity's data** and **test entire populations**. This in turn should improve both **audit efficiency** and **audit quality**. Large quantities of data can be interrogated relatively quickly, allowing auditors to focus immediately on the riskiest areas, and thus obtain evidence to reduce audit risk.

Examples of how auditors might use data analytics include:

- Analyse patterns relating to revenue or costs per product or per customer
- Trace the matching of orders to goods despatched/goods received documentation and to the invoice, in order to determine whether revenue and costs should be recognised
- Interrogate journals to determine whether there are any patterns (regarding who has processed certain journals) where fraud is suspected

## Activity 5: Data analytics

Which TWO of the following are examples of how data analytics might be used by audit firms?

☐ To predict market trends

☐ To calculate inventory ageing and how many days inventory is in stock by item

☐ Detailed recalculations of depreciation on non-current assets by item

☐ To analyse customer feedback in relation to products sold

## Essential reading

See Chapter 11 of the Essential reading for further information on audit data analytics.

The Essential reading is available as an Appendix of the digital edition of the Workbook.

# Chapter summary

**Audit sampling and automated tools and techniques**

## Selecting items for testing

- Select all items (100% examination): more common for substantive procedures
- Select specific items: stratification, not sampling
- Audit sampling

## Audit sampling

Application of audit procedures to < 100% of population

**Types of sampling**
- Non-statistical: Haphazard selection, block selection
- Statistical – random selection, systematic selection, value weighted selection (MUS)

**Sampling risk**

Sampling risk or ROMM or required confidence level or expected error or tolerable misstatement = high = larger sample size

**Evaluation of sample results**
- Are any errors one-off/anomolous?
- Tests of details: Project any monetary errors to the population as a whole
- Tests of controls: Calculate error rate

## Automated tools and techniques

Using computers to perform audit work

**Audit software (used for substantive procedures)**

Generalised or custom

**Test data (used for tests of controls)**

Ficticious/test transactions input into the client system

## Audit data analytics (ADA)

- Offer the chance to examine all a client's data
- May render sampling unnecessary in future

# Knowledge diagnostic

### 1. Selecting items for testing

The auditor needs to decide which items they will select for testing. It is most common for the auditor to carry out sampling; however, there may be situations where they test 100% of items or where they stratify the population in order to test specific items.

### 2. Sampling

Sampling relates to the application of audit procedures to less than 100% of the population in order to form a conclusion on the population as a whole.

### 3. Statistical sampling

Statistical sampling methods provide more comfort that the sample is free from bias and the sampling results representative of the population as a whole.

### 4. Extrapolating errors

Any errors identified in the sample must be **extrapolated** and the impact on the population as a whole considered.

### 5. Automated tools and techniques

Automated tools and techniques describe any process where the auditor uses a computer to help them carry out their audit procedures.

### 6. Different types of automated tools and techniques

Automated tools and techniques used to perform tests of details (substantive procedures) are known as **audit software** whilst automated tools and techniques used to carry out tests of controls are called **test data.**

### 7. Data analytics

**Data analytics** is the examination of data to try to identify patterns, trends or correlations

### 8. The impact of data analytics on the audit

The emergence of **data analytics** should lead to increased auditor efficiency and reduced audit risk.

 **BPP**

# Further study guidance

## Question practice

Now try the following from the Further question practice bank [available in the digital edition of the Workbook]:

- Section A Q42
- Section B Q75 'Elsams'

## Further reading

There are some technical articles on the ACCA website written by members of the AA examining team which are relevant to some of the topics covered in this chapter that you should read:

- *Audit sampling* (https://www.accaglobal.com/gb/en/student/exam-support-resources/fundamentals-exams-study-resources/f8/technical-articles/audit-sampling.html)
- *Specific aspects of auditing in a computer-based environment* (https://www.accaglobal.com/gb/en/student/exam-support-resources/professional-exams-study-resources/p7/technical-articles/auditing-computer-environment.html)
- *Auditing in a computer-based environment (2)* (https://www.accaglobal.com/gb/en/student/exam-support-resources/professional-exams-study-resources/p7/technical-articles/auditing-computer-based-environment2.html)

## Own research

The IAASB set up a Data Analytics Working Group (DAWG) in 2015. In 2018, this group published a Feedback Statement entitled 'Exploring the Growing Use of Technology in the Audit, with a Focus on Data Analytics'.

You can read the Feedback Statement at https://www.iaasb.org/publications-resources/feedback-statement-exploring-growing-use-technology-audit-focus-data

Note that this is not an examinable document for AA.

# Activity answers

## Activity 1: Preparation

| Customer | Balance $'000 | Cumulative total $'000 | Selected (Y/N) |
|---|---|---|---|
| Safari Schoolwear | 28 | 28 | N |
| Clothing Terrain | 33 | 61 | N |
| Everyday Wear | (6) | 55 | N |
| All About Clothes | 21 | 76 | N |
| Jim's Jumpers | 38 | 114 | Y |
| Look the Part | 124 | 238 | Y |
| Freya's Threads | 8 | 246 | N |
| Holly Aristocrat | 73 | 319 | Y |
| Girls on the Go | 13 | 332 | N |
| Odd One Out | 67 | 399 | N |
| Upward Trends | 17 | 416 | Y |
| Ivory Gowns | 2 | 418 | N |
| Skirts and all sorts | 57 | 475 | N |
| Dress for the Occasion | 92 | 567 | Y |
| Holiday Accessories | 5 | 572 | N |
| Ties with a Difference | 12 | 584 | N |
| Up and Out | 9 | 593 | N |
| In all Weather | 16 | 609 | Y |
| Duncan's Dresses | 3 | 612 | N |
| Ewan Trading | 29 | 641 | N |
| We're Going Exploring | 12 | 653 | N |
| Fred's Fashions | 47 | 700 | Y |
| | 700 | 700 | |

## Activity 2: Results – tests of detail

1   Error rate in sample × total value of population: ($20,000/$407,000) × $700,000 = $34,398

2   **Action to be taken**

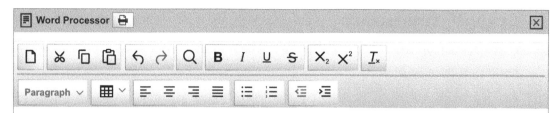

The projected misstatement is above the tolerable misstatement limit. This means that further evidence is needed. This could be done by:

- Extending the sample tested in the procedure and then reperforming the extrapolation; or

- Designing and performing additional substantive procedures.

If further evidence allows the auditor to conclude that the actual misstatement in the population does not exceed tolerable misstatement, then the auditor will conclude that no adjustment is necessary, although the error of $20,000 will be noted on a schedule of uncorrected misstatements.

If the further evidence indicates that there is a misstatement that exceeds tolerable misstatement then the auditor will ask the client to make an adjustment to the financial statements.

## Activity 3: Tests of controls

Error rate in sample

$$(18/225) = 8\%$$

This means that the internal control is believed to have operated effectively throughout the period and the auditor can rely on it when assessing the accuracy and validity of adjustments made to the inventory system.

No further testing is required; however, any monetary errors resulting from the 18 failures of the internal control should be noted on the schedule of uncorrected misstatements.

## Activity 4: Automated tools and techniques

| Advantages | Disadvantages |
|---|---|
| Auditors can test program controls as well as general internal controls associated with computers. | Setting up the software needed for automated tools and techniques can be time consuming and expensive. |
| Auditors can test a greater number of items more quickly and accurately than would be the case otherwise. | Audit staff will need to be trained so they have a sufficient level of IT knowledge to apply automated tools and techniques. |
| Auditors can test transactions rather than paper records of transactions that could be incorrect. | Not all client systems will be compatible with the software used with automated tools and techniques. |
| Automated tools and techniques are cost effective in the long term if the client does not change its systems. | There is a risk that live client data is corrupted and lost during the use of automated tools and techniques. |
| Results from automated tools and techniques can be compared with results from traditional testing – if the results correlate, overall confidence is increased. | |

## Activity 5: Data analytics

The correct answers are:

- To calculate inventory ageing and how many days inventory is in stock by item
- Detailed recalculations of depreciation on non-current assets by item

The other two options are examples of how data analytics may be used in a business and not by auditors.

# Non-current assets

## Learning objectives

On competition of this chapter, you should be able to:

| Syllabus learning outcomes | Syllabus reference no. |
| --- | --- |
| Explain the audit objectives and the audit procedures to obtain sufficient, appropriate evidence in relation to: Tangible and intangible non-current assets <br><br> (a) Evidence in relation to non-current assets, <br> (b) Depreciation, and <br> (c) Profit/ loss on disposal | D4 (e) |
| Discuss why auditors rely on the work of others | D6 (a) |
| Discuss the extent to which external auditors are able to reply on the work of experts, including the work of internal audit the extent to which external auditors are able to reply on the work of experts, including the work of internal audit. | D6 (b) |
| Discuss the problems associated with the audit and review of accounting estimates. | D2 (c) |

## Business and Exam context

Many candidates who sit the ACCA Audit and Assurance (AA) exam do not work in audit practice. This can make it harder to see the practical nature of the subject and to learn to apply the knowledge learned. Consequently, we have tried to make this chapter relating to substantive procedures as practical as possible, so that you can apply your knowledge to exam scenarios.

This chapter, Non-current assets, highlights the key objectives for each major component of non-current assets. You must understand what objectives the various audit procedures are designed to achieve in relation to the financial statement assertions.

Assertions could be the focus of questions: you could be asked to describe audit procedures to test one particular assertion, or to identify the assertions relevant to the audit of tangible non-current assets, or indeed both. Both audit procedures and assertions can be tested in the form of OTQs in Section A as well as in the long scenario questions in Section B. Make sure you can distinguish the assertions relating to the statement of financial position and statement of profit and loss.

Valuation is an important assertion. The auditors will concentrate on testing any external valuations made during the year, and also whether other values appear reasonable given asset usage and condition. An important aspect of testing valuation is reviewing depreciation rates. A topic we cover, using the work of an expert, may well be important in the audit of non-current assets in respect of valuation.

You will need knowledge of the accounting standards you learnt in your Fundamentals in Financial Accounting (FFA) relating to tangible and intangible non-current assets for this chapter.

# Chapter overview

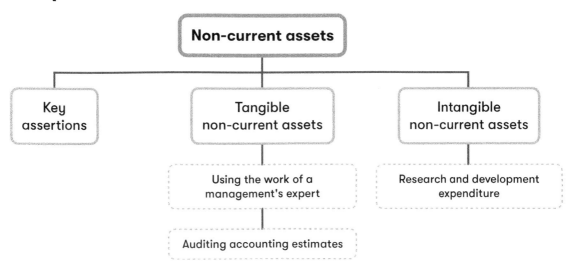

# 1 Key assertions

You have already studied assertions in Chapter 8 of this workbook, Introduction to Audit Evidence. In this chapter you will learn which of these assertions relate to non-current assets and the audit procedures required to cover these assertions. These can apply to both tangible or intangible non-current assets.

## Essential reading

See Chapter 12 of the Essential reading for the assertions that apply to non-current assets.

The Essential reading is available as an Appendix of the digital edition of the Workbook.

## Activity 1: Assertions

1   Which of the following audit procedures would provide audit evidence as to the existence of a tangible non-current asset?

- ○ Inspecting board minutes approving authorisation of the asset
- ○ Physically inspecting the asset
- ○ Reviewing the non-current asset register for inclusion of the asset
- ○ Inspecting the invoice and purchase order documentation of the asset

2   Inspecting the title deeds of a building provides audit evidence concerning which one of the following financial statement assertions?

- ○ Existence
- ○ Valuation
- ○ Rights and obligations
- ○ Completeness

# 2 Tangible non-current assets

## Activity 2: Opening balances

Throughout this chapter, we will continue to use the audit of Dress You Like Co for the year ended 30 September 20X6. The audit team has prepared the following lead schedule for the audit of non-current assets of Dress You Like Co for the current year:

| | Land and buildings | Plant and machinery | IT equipment | Motor vehicles | Total |
|---|---|---|---|---|---|
| | $'000 | $'000 | $'000 | $'000 | $'000 |
| **Cost or valuation** | | | | | |
| As at 1 October 20X5 | 7,520 | 775 | 215 | 41 | 8,551 |
| Additions | | 65 | 31 | 80 | 176 |
| Disposals | | | | (41) | (41) |
| Revaluation increase | 1,200 | | | | 1,200 |
| **As at 30 September 20X6** | **8,720** | **840** | **246** | **80** | **9,886** |
| | | | | | |
| **Depreciation** | | | | | |
| As at 1 October 20X5 | 3,057 | 485 | 70 | 24 | 3,636 |
| Depreciation charge for the year | 201 | 75 | 62 | 10 | 348 |
| Disposals | | | | (24) | (24) |
| **As at 30 September 20X6** | **3,258** | **560** | **132** | **10** | **3,960** |
| | | | | | |
| Carrying amount | | | | | |
| **As at 30 September 20X6** | **5,462** | **280** | **114** | **70** | **5,926** |
| | | | | | |
| **As at 30 September 20X5** | **4,463** | **290** | **145** | **17** | **4,915** |

## Required

Can you suggest an audit procedure for the balances given in the two lines on the schedule which are labelled 'As at 1 October 20X5' documenting the reason for this procedure?

## Solution

## Example – The non-current assets register

An entity's non-current assets are listed on a 'non-current asset register' which exists outside the double entry system and reconciles to the balances on the statement of financial position.

The following is an extract of the non-current asset register of Dress You Like Co:

EXTRACT – NON-CURRENT ASSET REGISTER FOR DRESS YOU LIKE CO

YEAR END 30 SEPTEMBER 20X6

| Asset | Purchase date | Depreciation rate | Cost | Accumulated depreciation | Carrying amount |
|---|---|---|---|---|---|
| | | | $ | $ | $ |
| Computer A | 1.1.X5 | 3 years SL | 3,000 | 1,000 | 2,000 |
| Computer B | 1.1.X4 | 3 years SL | 3,000 | 2,000 | 1,000 |
| Computer C | 1.1.X5 | 3 years SL | 3,000 | 1,000 | 2,000 |
| Machinery A | 1.1.X2 | 5 years SL | 50,000 | 40,000 | 10,000 |
| Office furniture | 1.1.X3 | 5 years SL | 25,000 | 15,000 | 10,000 |
| | | | **84,000** | **59,000** | **25,000** |

As part of their substantive procedures, Check & Co should compare non-current assets in the general ledger with the non-current assets register and obtain explanations for differences.

For a sample of assets which physically exist Check & Co should agree that they are recorded in the non-current asset register to ensure completeness.

They should also agree a sample of assets from the non-current asset register to the physical assets to ensure existence.

## Activity 3: Additions

Dress You Like Co has provided the following listing of all additions to non-current assets in the year:

| Description | Date | Cost | Notes |
|---|---|---|---|
| Photocopier/printer | 16/11/20X5 | 4,000 | |
| Software | 20/12/20X5 | 5,000 | |
| Server equipment | 2/01/20X6 | 12,000 | |
| Cutting machinery | 25/01/20X6 | 15,000 | |
| Cutting machinery - set up cost | 25/01/20X6 | 2,500 | |
| Cutting machinery – training cost | 30/01/20X6 | 2,500 | |
| Delivery vehicle × 4 | 08/03/20X6 | 80,000 | |
| Laptops | 16/04/20X6 | 10,000 | |

| Description | Date | Cost | Notes |
|---|---|---|---|
| | | | Deposit of $20,000 paid on 1/09/20X6 |
| | | | Outstanding $25,000 paid on delivery of machine on |
| Sewing equipment | 1/09/20X6 | 45,000 | 10/10/20X6 |
| **Total** | | **176,000** | |

### Required

Consider the above information with regards to additions at Dress You Like Co.

1. Identify two additions where the accounting treatment may be incorrect and explain why an adjustment to the financial statements may be required.

2. Describe the substantive procedures Check & Co should perform to obtain sufficient and appropriate evidence in relation to Dress You Like Co's additions to non-current assets. Ensure you document the reason for each procedure.

### Solution

---

## Activity 4: Disposals

During the year ending 30 September 20X6, Dress You Like Co replaced all its delivery vehicles with electric vans. The old delivery vehicles were purchased for a total of $41,000 in March 20X0 and had accumulated depreciation of $24,000 on their disposal in March 20X6 when they were sold for $10,000.

### Required

Describe the substantive procedures Check & Co should perform to obtain sufficient and appropriate evidence in relation to the disposal of the old delivery vehicles. Ensure you document the reason for each procedure.

Solution

---

## 2.1 Using the work of a management's expert

Sometimes an entity will use an **expert**, for example an actuary or chartered surveyor to assist them in the preparation of the financial statements.

> **Management's expert:** an individual or organisation possessing expertise in a field other than accounting or auditing, whose work in that field is used by the entity to assist the entity in preparing the financial statements (ISA 500: para. 5(d)).

The auditors may be able use the work of a management's expert as audit evidence for the valuation of non-current assets as well as other areas of the audit such as inventory valuation.

ISA 500 (para. 8) considers the use of a management's expert by management and states that if information to be used as audit evidence has been prepared by a management's expert, the auditor must:

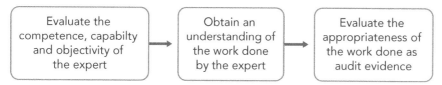

Evaluate the competence, capabilty and objectivity of the expert → Obtain an understanding of the work done by the expert → Evaluate the appropriateness of the work done as audit evidence

If the auditors find they are unable to rely on a management's expert, they may consider hiring their own expert to get the audit evidence required. This expert is called an auditor's expert. We will cover the use of auditor's experts in Chapter 13.

### Essential reading

See Chapter 12 of the Essential reading for further information on using the work of a management's expert.

The Essential reading is available as an Appendix of the digital edition of the Workbook.

---

## Activity 5: Revaluation

During the year ended 30 September 20X6, Dress You Like Co engaged a specialist to revalue its factory and head office sites. The revaluation resulted in a total increase of $1.2m to Dress You Like Co's properties.

**Required**

Describe the substantive procedures Check & Co should perform to obtain sufficient and appropriate evidence in relation to the revaluation of the factory and head office sites. Ensure you document the reason for each procedure.

**Solution**

## 2.2 Auditing accounting estimates

Ascertaining an estimated useful life for a non-current asset is an example of an accounting estimate. Other examples of accounting estimates are:

- Allowance for receivables
- Provisions for litigation settlements
- Inventory obsolescence
- Accrued revenue
- Warranty obligations

Management often make these estimates in conditions of uncertainty over outcomes and with the use of judgement. The risk of misstatement is increased, and the evidence available to detect a material misstatement will often be more difficult to obtain and less persuasive than that relating to other items in the financial statements.

The auditor is required to obtain sufficient appropriate evidence about whether the accounting estimates and related disclosures are reasonable. ISA 540 (Revised) *Auditing Accounting Estimates and Related Disclosures* provides guidance on the audit of accounting estimates contained in financial statements.

## Essential reading

See Chapter 12 of the Essential reading for further information on how to audit accounting estimates.

The Essential reading is available as an Appendix of the digital edition of the Workbook.

## Activity 6: Depreciation

Dress You Like Co calculates depreciation on a straight-line basis over the estimated useful life of its assets. Estimated useful lives are as follows:

Buildings – 50 years

Plant and machinery – 10 years

IT equipment – 4 years

Motor vehicles – 8 years

**Required**

Describe the substantive procedures Check & Co should perform to obtain sufficient and appropriate evidence in relation to the depreciation charge for the year ended 30 September 20X6 at Dress You Like Co. Ensure you document the reason for each procedure.

**Solution**

## Essential reading

See Chapter 18 of the Essential reading for a summary of the accounting knowledge relevant to IAS 16: *Property, plant and equipment* which is brought forward to this paper from your earlier Fundamentals in Financial Accounting studies.

The Essential reading is available as an Appendix of the digital edition of the Workbook.

# 3 Intangible non-current assets

Intangible assets are identifiable non-monetary assets without physical substance. Examples of intangible assets include patents, franchises, licences, computer software and royalties. The accounting for intangibles is prescribed in IAS 38 *Intangible Assets*. Intangible assets with finite useful lives will be amortised.

The key assertions relating to intangibles are existence (not so much 'do they exist?', but 'are they genuinely assets?') and valuation. They will therefore be audited with reference to criteria laid down in IAS 38. As only purchased goodwill or intangibles with a readily ascertainable market value can be capitalised, audit evidence should be available (purchase invoices or specialist valuations). The audit of amortisation will be similar to the audit of depreciation.

## 3.1 Research and development expenditure

Accounting for research and development is included within IAS 38.

> **Research:** original and planned investigation undertaken with the prospect of gaining new scientific or technical knowledge and understanding.
>
> **Development:** the application of research findings or other knowledge to a plan or design for the production of new or substantially improved materials, devices, products, processes, systems or services before the start of commercial production or use.

Research **cannot** be capitalised as an intangible asset and must be **expensed** to the statement of profit or loss.

Remember that, under IAS 38, an entity **must** capitalise development expenditure if it satisfies **all** of the following criteria:

| | |
|---|---|
| **P** | **P**robable future economic benefits |
| **I** | **I**ntention to complete and use/sell asset |
| **R** | **R**esources adequate and available to complete and use/sell asset |
| **A** | **A**bility to use/sell the asset |
| **T** | **T**echnical feasibility of completing asset for use/sale |
| **E** | **E**xpenditure can be measured reliably |

The audit work undertaken must serve to ensure that any development expenditure meets the IAS 38 *Intangible Assets* criteria.

### Example - Intangible Assets

Company A is a packaging company which has been in operation for 30 years. The company has been developing a new form of packaging for fruits and vegetables as an alternative to the plastics commonly used in supermarkets. Several large supermarket chains have expressed an interest in using the packaging when it becomes available. Company A expects the packaging will be available for sale in one year.

The substantive procedures the auditors need to perform are as follows:

- Review the accounting records to ensure that the expenditure can be readily measured, eg separate cost centre or nominal ledger code.
- Review invoices to verify expenditure by Company A on the project.
- Verify wages' costs to supporting documentation such as timesheets.
- Discuss the stage of development of the new packaging with Company A's directors.
- Discuss the technical feasibility of the project with Company A's technical staff.
- Consider probability of future economic benefits (ie commercial viability) and ability to sell or use the packaging in relation to market research results, advance orders, budgets and forecasts.
- Review budgeted revenues and costs. Ensure that they are reasonable based on results to date, discussion with directors, production forecasts and advance orders.
- Review cash flow forecasts to ensure that adequate resources exist to complete the project. Discuss any shortfalls with the directors of Company A.

- Obtain written representations from management of their intention to complete the packaging and either use or sell it.
- Ensure any development costs capitalised are disclosed and presented in line with the requirements of IAS 38 *Intangible Assets*

### Essential reading

See Chapter 18 of the Essential reading for a summary of the accounting knowledge relevant to IAS 38: *Intangible assets* which is brought forward to this paper from your earlier Fundamentals in Financial Accounting studies.

The Essential reading is available as an Appendix of the digital edition of the Workbook.

## 3.2 Audit procedures for non-current assets

The following table contains audit procedures for non-current assets (tangible and intangible) matched to the financial statement assertions they test. This table is for reference only, the procedures should not be learned by heart, but may be useful when practising exam questions.

**Tangible non-current assets:**

| Financial statement assertion | Audit procedure |
|---|---|
| Completeness | • **Obtain** or **prepare** a **summary** of tangible non-current assets showing how the following **reconcile** with the **opening position**.<br>  - **Gross carrying amount**<br>  - **Accumulated depreciation**<br>  - **Carrying amount**<br>• **Compare non-current assets** in the general ledger with the **non-current assets register** and **obtain explanations** for **differences**.<br>• For a sample of assets which physically exist, agree that they are **recorded** in the **non-current asset register**.<br>• If a non-current asset register is not kept, **obtain** a **schedule** showing the original costs and present depreciated value of major non-current assets.<br>• **Reconcile** the **schedule** of non-current assets with the **general ledger**. |
| Existence | • **Confirm** that the **company physically inspects** all items in the non-current asset register each year.<br>• **Inspect assets**, concentrating on high value items and additions in-year. Confirm that items inspected:<br>  - Exist<br>  - Are in use<br>  - Are in good condition<br>  - Have correct serial numbers<br>• **Review records** of **income-yielding assets**.<br>• |

| Financial statement assertion | Audit procedure |
|---|---|
| | • **Reconcile** opening and closing **vehicles** by numbers as well as amounts. |
| Valuation | • **Verify valuation** to valuation certificate.<br>• **Consider reasonableness** of **valuation**, reviewing:<br>  – Experience of valuer<br>  – Scope of work<br>  – Methods and assumptions used<br>  – Valuation bases are in line with accounting standards<br>• **Reperform** calculation of revaluation surplus.<br>• Confirm whether valuations of all assets that have been revalued have been **updated regularly** so that the asset's carrying amount is not materially different from its fair value by asking the Finance Director and inspecting the previous financial statements.<br>• **Inspect** draft accounts to check that client has recognised revaluation losses in the statement of profit or loss unless there is a credit balance in respect of that asset in equity, in which case it should be debited to equity to cancel the credit. All revaluation gains should be credited to equity.<br>• **Review insurance policies** in force for all categories of tangible non-current assets and consider the adequacy of their insured values and check expiry dates. |
| Valuation - depreciation | • **Review depreciation** rates applied in relation to:<br>  – Asset lives<br>  – Residual values<br>  – Replacement policy<br>  – Past experience of gains and losses on disposal<br>  – Consistency with prior years and accounting policy<br>  – Possible obsolescence<br>• **Review** non-current assets register to ensure that **depreciation** has been **charged on all assets** with a finite useful life.<br>• For **revalued assets**, ensure that the charge for **depreciation** is based on the revalued amount by recalculating it for a sample of revalued assets.<br>• Reperform calculation of depreciation rates to ensure it is accurate.<br>• **Compare ratios** of depreciation to non-current assets (by category) with:<br>  – Previous years<br>  – Depreciation policy rates<br>• |

| Financial statement assertion | Audit procedure |
|---|---|
| | • **Scrutinise** draft accounts to ensure that **depreciation policies** and rates are **disclosed** in the accounts. |
| Rights and obligations | • **Verify title** to land and buildings by inspection of:<br>  - Title deeds<br>  - Land registry certificates<br>  - Leases<br>• Obtain a certificate from solicitors/bankers:<br>  - **Stating purpose** for which the deeds are being held (custody only)<br>  - **Stating deeds** are **free** from **mortgage** or **lien**<br>• **Inspect registration documents** for vehicles held, confirming that they are in client's name.<br>• **Confirm** all vehicles are used for the **client's business**.<br>• **Examine documents** of **title** for other assets (including purchase invoices, architects' certificates, contracts, hire purchase or lease agreements).<br>• **Review for evidence** of charges in statutory books and by company search.<br>• **Review leases** of leasehold properties to ensure that company has fulfilled covenants therein.<br>• **Examine invoices received after year end, orders** and **minutes** for evidence of capital commitments. |
| Additions: rights and obligations, valuation and completeness | • Verify additions by inspection of architects' certificates, solicitors' completion statements, suppliers' invoices etc.<br>• **Review** capitalisation of expenditure by examining for non-current assets additions and items in relevant expense categories (repairs, motor expenses, sundry expenses) to ensure that:<br>  - Capital/revenue distinction is correctly drawn<br>  - Capitalisation is in line with consistently applied company policy<br>• **Inspect** non-current asset accounts for a sample of purchases to ensure they have been **properly allocated**.<br>• Verify that **additions** have been **recorded** by **scrutinising** the non-current asset register and general ledger. |
| Disposals: rights and obligations, completeness and accuracy | • **Verify disposals** with supporting documentation, checking transfer of title, sales price and dates of completion and payment<br>• **Recalculate** gain or loss on disposal.<br>• Consider whether proceeds are reasonable.<br>• If the asset was **used as security**, ensure **release from security** has been correctly made. |

| Financial statement assertion | Audit procedure |
| --- | --- |
| Classification | • **Review** non-current asset disclosures in the financial statements to ensure they meet IAS 16 criteria.<br>• For a sample of **fully depreciated assets**, inspect the register to ensure no further depreciation is charged. |

**Intangible non-current assets:**

| Financial statement assertion | Audit procedure |
| --- | --- |
| Goodwill | • Agree the consideration to sales agreement by **inspection**.<br>• Consider whether asset valuation is reasonable.<br>• Agree that the calculation is correct by **recalculation**.<br>• **Review** the impairment review and **discuss** with management.<br>• Ensure valuation of goodwill is reasonable / there has been no impairment not adjusted through **discussion** with management. |
| Research and development (R&D) costs | • Confirm that capitalised development costs conform to IAS 38 criteria by **inspecting** details of projects and **discussions** with technical managers.<br>• Confirm feasibility and viability by **inspection** of budgets.<br>• **Recalculate** amortisation calculation to ensure it commences with production / is reasonable.<br>• **Inspect** invoices to verify expenditure incurred on R&D projects. |
| Other intangibles | • Agree purchased intangibles to purchase documentation agreement by **inspection**.<br>• **Inspect** specialist valuation of intangibles and ensure it is reasonable.<br>• Review amortisation calculations and ensure they are correct by **recalculation**. |

# Chapter summary

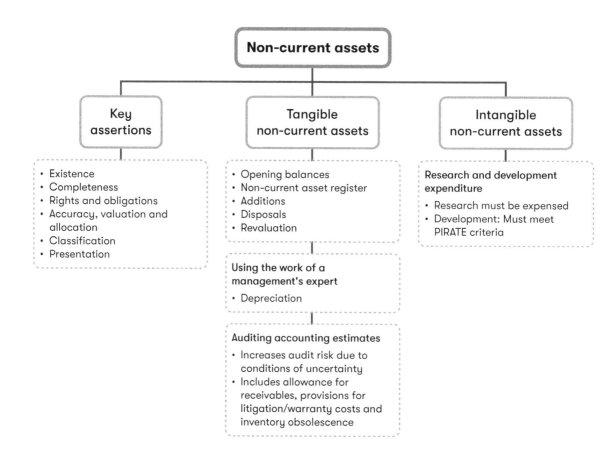

**Non-current assets**

**Key assertions**
- Existence
- Completeness
- Rights and obligations
- Accuracy, valuation and allocation
- Classification
- Presentation

**Tangible non-current assets**
- Opening balances
- Non-current asset register
- Additions
- Disposals
- Revaluation

**Using the work of a management's expert**
- Depreciation

**Auditing accounting estimates**
- Increases audit risk due to conditions of uncertainty
- Includes allowance for receivables, provisions for litigation/warranty costs and inventory obsolescence

**Intangible non-current assets**

Research and development expenditure
- Research must be expensed
- Development: Must meet PIRATE criteria

 **BPP**

# Knowledge diagnostic

### 1. Key financial statement assertions

Completeness, existence, valuation and rights and obligations are the key tangible non-current asset assertions.

### 2. Non-current assets register

Entities should have a tangible non-current assets register that lists all the tangible non-current assets owned.

### 3. Key audit areas

Key areas of tangible non-current assets for auditors to test are additions, disposals, revaluations and depreciation.

### 4. Management's expert

Auditors may need to place reliance on the work of a management's expert when auditing a revaluation of a non-current asset.

### 5. Accounting estimates

Accounting estimates such as depreciation and amortisation involve judgements and so can be high-risk items in the financial statements.

### 6. Intangible assets

The audit of intangible non-current assets is likely to focus on development expenditure and the capitalisation criteria of IAS 38.

# Further study guidance

## Question practice

Now try the following from the Further question practice bank (available in the digital edition of the Workbook):

- Section A Q6, Q7 and Q45 cover tangible non-current assets
- Section A Q52 examines intangible assets
- Section B Q67 (d) and (e) 'Heels' look at estimates
- Section B Q77 'Boston Manufacturing' focuses on tangible non-current assets

## Further reading

There is a technical article on the ACCA website written by a member of the AA examining team which is relevant to some of the topics covered in this chapter that you should read:

- *The audit of assertions: https://www.accaglobal.com/gb/en/student/exam-support-resources/fundamentals-exams-study-resources/f8/technical-articles/assertions.html*

## Own research

Obtain a recent set of financial statements for an organisation and look for the non-current asset notes.

Are there any figures in the financial statements where management might need to have used an expert?

Can you find any figures in the financial statements that have been estimated?

# Activity answers

## Activity 1: Assertions

1 The correct answer is: Physically inspecting the asset

2 The correct answer is: Rights and obligations

## Activity 2: Opening balances

The opening balances should be agreed to the signed financial statements and any breakdown provided by the client to ensure they have been carried forward accurately from the previous year.

We would normally also agree the opening balances to the previous year's audit file, however, given that this is the first year that we have audited Dress You Like Co and so it is not possible to conduct this audit procedure.

Non-current assets comprise a cumulative figure in the statement of financial position. If the balances from the prior year have not been brought forward accurately to the current year, there may be a material misstatement in the non-current assets balance in the financial statements. The depreciation charge may also be calculated incorrectly and could be over or understated on the statement of financial position.

## Activity 3: Additions

1 IAS 16 states that training costs are not allowed to be included in the cost of any non-current assets. The cutting machinery training costs of $2,500 should not be included as an addition to non-current assets. If this cost is not removed, non-current assets will be overstated in the statement of financial position and expenses will be understated in the statement of profit or loss. The sewing equipment was not actually in the company's possession and use at the year end. The deposit of $20,000 should not have been shown as plant and machinery, but rather as a payment on account. If the amount was considered to be material, a note to the accounts should give details of this prepayment. The balance of $45,000 must be removed from the additions listing or non-current assets will be overstated.

2 Substantive procedures – additions to non-current assets

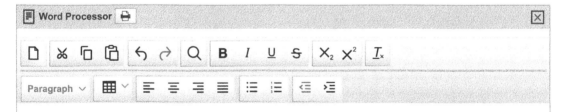

- The total of the list of additions should be recalculated to ensure its accuracy.

- The total of Dress You Like's additions list should be agreed to the non-current asset note in the financial statements.

- A sample of additions should be selected and their cost should be traced to invoices or contracts to confirm that the value of the addition is accurate. Inspect invoice/contract to confirm the amount capitalised, excludes any recoverable sales tax.

- A sample of additions should be selected and Check & Co should inspect whether invoices or contracts are addressed to Dress You Like Co to ensure the company holds the rights and obligations for the assets.

- Check & Co should examine motor vehicle registration documentation and inspect whether it is in Dress You Like Co's name to ensure the company holds the rights and obligations for the delivery vehicles.

- A sample of additions should be selected and physically verified to confirm their existence and condition.

- For a sample of additions, confirm that they have been included in the non-current assets register at Dress You Like Co to ensure they have been recorded properly.

- Review the additions listing to ensure there are no other items that have been capitalised which should have been expensed.

- Review items in relevant expense categories (such as repairs, motor expenses, sundry expenses) to ensure that items have not been expensed which should have been capitalised to ensure completeness of additions.

- Examine invoices received after year end, orders and board minutes for evidence of capital commitments which may not have been included in the financial statements. This test ensures the completeness of non-current assets.

> **Tutorial note.** Note that just like a normal word processor you have the option on the CBE platform to enter your text as bullet points using the bullet point icon above the area you type your answer into.

## Activity 4: Disposals

### Substantive procedures – disposals

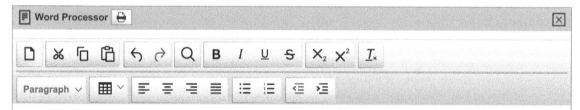

- Obtain a list of all disposals from Dress You Like Co and cast to ensure accuracy.

- Agree the total of the disposals listing to the financial statements.

- Confirm that all disposals have been removed from Dress You Like Co's non-current asset register to ensure existence.

- Verify the valuation of the disposals with supporting documentation such as an invoice issued to the buyer of the delivery vehicles, checking transfer of title, sales price and dates of completion and payment.

- Check & Co should recalculate the loss on disposal and agree this amount to the nominal ledger and financial statements of Dress You Like Co. On disposal, the delivery vehicles had a carrying amount of $17,000 ($41,000 – $24,000). Since the vehicles were sold for $10,000, this results in a loss on disposal of $17,000.

- Consider whether proceeds from disposal of the delivery vehicles are reasonable.

- Recalculate the depreciation up to the date of disposal, based on the company's accounting policy to ensure this has been calculated correctly.

- Trace the proceeds from sale of the vehicles to the cash book and the bank statement.

## Activity 5: Revaluation

- Trace the revalued amount to the valuer's report and confirm that the surplus is $1,200,000.

- Agree that the $1,200,000 has been transferred to a revaluation reserve through scrutiny of the nominal ledger.

- Agree the basis of valuation to the valuer's report. Verify the disclosure of this to the notes to the financial statements.

- Assess the competence, capability and objectivity of the specialist engaged to perform the revaluation by considering:

- Experience of the specialist
- Qualifications of the specialist
- Reputation of the specialist
- Scope of work
- Methods and assumptions used
- Whether the basis of the valuation is in line with accounting standards

- Assess the reasonableness of the valuation by comparison with any similar properties which may have recently changed hands on the open market.
- Recalculate depreciation to confirm that it is based on the revalued amount.
- Review the notes to the financial statements to confirm that the revaluation has been disclosed in line with the requirements of IAS 16.

## Activity 6: Depreciation

- Obtain details of the depreciation accounting policy from the notes to the financial statements and confirm that there have been no changes to this policy.
- Review the depreciation policy disclosure in the notes to the financial statements to confirm this is presented in accordance with the requirements of IAS 16.
- Review the depreciation rates in the policy and consider whether they are reasonable. Take the following into consideration:
  - Asset lives
  - Residual values
  - Replacement policy
  - Past experience of gains and losses on disposal
  - Consistency with prior years and accounting policy
  - Possible obsolescence
- Compare ratios of depreciation to non-current assets (by category) with:
  - Previous years
  - Depreciation policy rates
- Review the non-current assets register to ensure that depreciation has been charged on all assets with a limited useful life.
- Recalculate the depreciation on a sample of assets. Compare the calculations to the depreciation charge in the non-current assets register for each item in the sample.
- For the two revalued sites, ensure that the charge for depreciation is based on the revalued amount by recalculating it.
- Alternatively perform a proof in total of depreciation charge for each category of asset by taking the average cost balance ((opening cost + closing cost)/2) and multiplying by depreciation rate. Enquire of management the reason for any significant differences to the actual depreciation charged.

# 13

# Inventory

## Learning objectives

On completion of this chapter, you should be able to:

| Syllabus learning outcomes | Syllabus reference no. |
| --- | --- |
| Explain the audit objectives and the audit procedures to obtain sufficient, appropriate evidence in relation to: <br> Inventory <br> (a) Inventory counting procedures in relation to year-end and continuous inventory systems <br> (b) Cut-off testing <br> (c) Auditor's attendance at inventory counting <br> (d) Direct confirmation of inventory held by third parties <br> (e) Valuation, and <br> (f) Other evidence in relation to inventory | D4 (b) |
| Discuss the extent to which external auditors are able to rely on the work of experts, including the work of internal audit. | D6 (b) |
| Explain the extent to which reference to the work of others can be made in the independent auditor's report. | D6 (d) |

## Business and exam context

No area of the statement of financial position creates more potential problems for the auditors than that of inventory. Closing inventory does not normally form an integrated part of the double entry bookkeeping system and hence a misstatement (under or overstatement) may not be detected from tests in other audit areas.

Many candidates who sit the ACCA AA exam do not work in audit practice. This can make it harder to see the practical nature of the subject and to learn to apply the knowledge learned. Consequently, we have tried to make this chapter relating to substantive procedures as practical as possible, so that you can apply your knowledge to exam scenarios.

You may be asked to list and explain audit procedures you would perform to confirm specific assertions relating to inventory.

You could be asked to do the following, for example:

- Describe the audit procedures to perform before, during and after attending the inventory count.
- Describe the audit procedures to be applied in respect of specific financial statement assertions related to inventory (including work in progress).

- The financial statement assertions and their related audit procedures could also constitute the subject of mini-case OT questions in Section A.

The requirement to consider valuation of inventory is also a topic which is regularly examined. If asked for procedures in this area, restrict your answer to only those procedures related to valuation. The examining team has noted that in previous exams, some candidates provided procedures related to other assertions, therefore wasting valuable time.

# Chapter overview

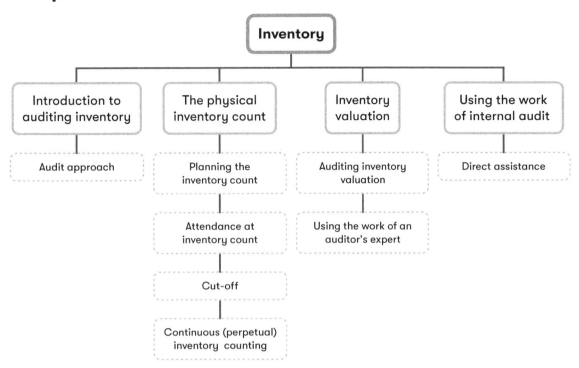

# 1 Introduction to auditing inventory

## 1.1 Assertions

You have already studied assertions in Chapter 8 of this workbook, Introduction to Audit Evidence. In this chapter you will learn which of these assertions relate to inventory and the audit procedures undertaken to provide audit evidence to support these assertions.

### Essential reading

See Chapter 13 of the Essential reading for the assertions that apply to inventory.

The Essential reading is available as an Appendix of the digital edition of the Workbook.

## 1.2 Audit approach

The audit approach must consider the following with regards to inventory:

**Quantity** – normally arrived at by a year-end inventory count (unless solely a perpetual system)

**Valuation** – must apply IAS 2 *Inventories*

Disclosure

We saw in Chapter 10 that the approach taken to the audit of inventory depends on the control system in place over inventory.

Remember, if the entity has a perpetual inventory system in place (where inventory is counted continuously throughout the year) and a year-end count is not undertaken, a **controls-based approach** is feasible as long as the controls over the system are appropriately designed. In fact, a controls-based approach may actually be more efficient.

However, where inventory quantities will be determined by an inventory count at the year-end date, a largely **substantive approach** is taken. We look at both year-end inventory counts and periodic counts in support of perpetual inventory systems in this chapter.

### Exercise: Inventory lead schedule

Throughout the chapter, we will continue to use the audit of Dress You Like Co for the year ended 30 September 20X6.

The audit team has prepared the following lead schedule for the audit of inventory of Dress You Like Co for the current year.

Reference:

Client: Dress You Like Co

Prepared by:

Reviewed by:

Date: 30/10/X6

|  | Draft 20X6 | Dr | Cr | Final 20X6 | Actual 20X5 |
|---|---|---|---|---|---|
|  | $'000 | $'000 | $'000 | $'000 | $'000 |
| Inventories: |  |  |  |  |  |
| Raw materials (at cost) | 12,952 |  |  |  | 4,600 |
| Work in progress (at cost) | 20,699 |  |  |  | 15,201 |

| | Draft 20X6 | Dr | Cr | Final 20X6 | Actual 20X5 |
|---|---|---|---|---|---|
| | $'000 | $'000 | $'000 | $'000 | $'000 |
| Finished goods | 13,800 | | | | 4,900 |
| Total inventory | 47,451 | | | | 24,701 |

# 2 The physical inventory count

## 2.1 Introduction

A particular technique to verify **quantity and conditions** of inventories is for the auditor to attend the client's inventory count. Physical inventory count procedures are vital, as they provide evidence which cannot be obtained elsewhere or at any other time about the quantities and conditions of inventories and work-in-progress.

ISA 501 Audit Evidence – Specific Considerations for Selected Items (para. 4) provides guidance for auditors on attending the physical inventory count. It states that where inventory is **material**, auditors shall obtain sufficient appropriate audit evidence regarding its **existence** and **condition** by attending the physical inventory count (unless this is impracticable). The following process is to be performed:

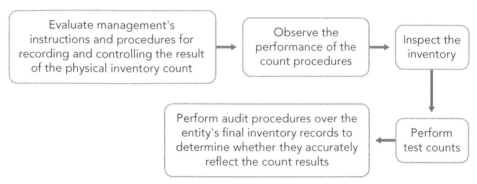

Attendance at the inventory count can serve as **either substantive procedures or tests of controls**, depending on the auditor's risk assessment, planned approach and specific procedures carried out.

## 2.2 Planning the inventory count

Before the physical inventory count the auditors should ensure audit **coverage** of the count is appropriate, and that the client's count instructions have been reviewed.

Factors to consider when planning attendance at the inventory count include the following:

- The **risks of material misstatement** of inventory
- **Internal controls** related to inventory
- Whether **adequate procedures** are expected to be established and **proper instructions** issued for counting
- The **timing** of the count
- Whether the entity maintains a **perpetual inventory system**
- **Locations** at which inventory is held (including any material **amounts held by third parties**)
- Whether the assistance of an **auditor's expert** is required

(ISA 510: para. A3)

### 2.2.1 Inventory held by third parties

Where the entity has inventory that is held by third-parties and which is **material** to the financial statements, the auditor shall obtain sufficient appropriate audit evidence by performing one or both of the following:

- Direct confirmation from the third-party regarding quantities and condition (in accordance with ISA 505 *External Confirmations*)
- Inspection or other appropriate audit procedures (if third party's integrity and objectivity are doubtful, for example) (ISA 501: para. 8)

### Essential reading

See Chapter 13 of the Essential reading for further considerations of the auditor when planning to attend the inventory count. This section also explains the other audit procedures the auditor might need to plan and perform where a material portion of the audit client's inventory is located with a third-party.

The Essential reading is available as an Appendix of the digital edition of the Workbook.

### Activity 1: Inventory count instructions

Check & Co have been provided with the following inventory count instructions by Dress You Like Co:

- Sadie Thomas, Finance Assistant, has overall responsibility for the inventory count but she is to be assisted by Mr David Furber, the warehouse manager, to whom the inventory counting teams are to report, and who will be responsible for the detailed organisation of the count.
- Five inventory count teams are to carry out the actual count, each team to be responsible for a predetermined section of the warehouse. Each team comprises two persons: one from the accounting department and the other from the warehouse.
- Each inventory count team is to meet David Furber at 07:30am on 30 September 20X6 and will be provided with pre-numbered and pre-printed inventory sheets for the section of the warehouse for which they are responsible. These inventory sheets have been prepared by the inventory control department and show the balance of each inventory item on hand as shown on the inventory records held independently of the warehouse.
- Each inventory count sheet is to be signed by the senior member of the count team and the bin or rack cards held in the warehouse are to be adjusted, if necessary, to actual quantities counted. All cards are to be initialled to show that the count has been made.
- Any goods that appear to be in poor condition are to be noted on the inventory sheets, such action to be supported by initials of the senior member of the count team.
- Any queries during the count are to be referred to David Furber to whom inventory sheets are to be returned at the conclusion of the count. David Furber is responsible for ensuring that all inventory count sheets have been returned and forwarded to Sadie Thomas for valuation.

**Required**

Identify THREE matters that will require action by management if the inventory count is to be effective. Explain how the matters could be rectified.

Solution

---

## 2.3 Attendance at inventory count

During the inventory count the auditors should **observe** whether the count is being carried out according to instructions, carry out **test counts**, and watch out for **third-party inventory** and **slow-moving inventory** and **cut-off problems**.

### 2.3.1 Audit procedures during attendance at the inventory count

Audit procedures include:

- **Observe** whether the **client's staff are following inventory count instructions** to ensure the count is complete and accurate
- **Perform test counts** to ensure procedures and internal controls are operating effectively, and to gain evidence over the existence and completeness of inventory
- Ensure that the **procedures for identifying damaged, obsolete and slow-moving inventory** operate effectively to confirm **valuation** of inventory:
    - Obtain information about the inventory's condition, age and usage
    - Obtain information concerning the stage of completion of work-in-progress
- **Confirm** that **inventory held on behalf of third parties is separately identified and accounted for** to ensure that inventory is not overstated
- **Obtain** copies of the **last goods received note (GRN) and the last goods despatch note (GDN)** in order to confirm **cut-off** of inventory
- Conclude whether any amendment is necessary to subsequent audit procedures
- Gain an **overall impression** of the levels and values of inventories held in order to be able to judge whether the inventory figure in the financial statements appears reasonable

### 2.3.2 Performing test counts

The auditors **perform test counts** to ensure procedures and internal controls are working properly. The auditor should test counts from the inventories to the inventory sheets (to gain evidence of **completeness**) and from the inventory sheets to the inventories (to prove **existence**). Tests should concentrate on **high value** inventory. If the results of the test counts are not satisfactory, the auditors may request that inventory be **recounted**.

### 2.3.3 Documentation of audit work performed during the count

The auditors' working papers should include the following:

- Details of their **observations** and **procedures performed**
- The manner in which points that are relevant and material to the inventory being counted or measured have been dealt with by the client
- Instances where the **client's procedures have not been satisfactorily carried out**
- **Items for subsequent testing**, such as photocopies of (or extracts from) rough inventory sheets
- **Details of the sequence of inventory sheets**
- The **auditors' conclusions**

## Activity 2: Completeness

You are the audit manager at Check & Co and are planning the audit procedures for inventory for the year ending 30 September 20X6.

**Required**

Which ONE of the following audit procedures provides evidence of the completeness of inventory?

- ○ Test counts from inventory in the warehouse to the inventory records
- ○ Review an aged inventory listing and identify any slow moving items of inventory
- ○ Test counts from the inventory records to the inventory in the warehouse
- ○ Observe the location of any inventories held by third parties and that they are not being included in the inventory count

## 2.4 After the inventory count

After the count the auditors should check that **final inventory sheets** have been **properly compiled** from count records and that **book inventory** has been **appropriately adjusted.**

Key tests include the following:

- **Trace items** that were **test counted** to final inventory sheets.
- **Agree sequence** of inventory sheets
- **Observe** whether all count records have been included in final inventory sheets.
- Inspect final inventory sheets to ensure they are supported by count records.
- Confirm that continuous inventory records have been adjusted to the amounts physically counted or measured, and that differences have been investigated.
- Confirm cut-off by using details of the last serial number of GRN and GDN and details of movements during the count.
- Review replies from third parties about inventory held by or for them.
- Reperform client's computation of the final inventory figure to ensure it has been calculated correctly.
- Follow up queries and notify problems to management.
- Confirm necessary adjustments to book inventories have been made by inspecting the client's ledgers.

## Activity 3: Test counts

The following are extracts from the inventory count sheets of Dress You Like Co for the year ending 30 September 20X6:

### COUNT SHEET 45

Date: 30 September 20X6

Counter: AL

Approved by: DF

Location: Factory, Aisle 14, shelf B7

| Inventory code | Quantity as per inventory records | Quantity counted | Notes |
|---|---|---|---|
| DYL563536P | 12 | 12 | |
| DYL455666L | 50 | 50 | |
| DYL883722G | 125 | 50 | |
| DYL829427T | 78 | 78 | |
| DYL879239X | 100 | 100 | Blue dye has rubbed onto all these White shirts from nearby denim. (Noted DF) |
| DYL875621P | 65 | 65 | |
| DYL261567L | 87 | 88 | |
| DYL822782K | 150 | 150 | |

### Required

Answer the following questions:

1   Note down any items from the inventory count sheet that might require investigation. Why have you chosen these items?

2   Rewrite the information above as an audit procedure, documenting the reason for the procedure.

### Solution

## 2.5 Cut-off

Cut-off testing is a specific audit procedure performed after the inventory count to ensure that all of the company's transactions have been **included in the correct period**. Cut-off is usually tested by obtaining a sample of GRNs and GDNs either side of the year end and then matching them to purchase/sales invoices to ensure they have been included in the correct account balance(s). The auditor should have obtained the samples of GRNs and GDNs when attending the inventory count.

**Purchases cut-off**
- All purchases for which goods have been received before the year end must be included in the financial statements as a liability, expense and closing inventories.
- Goods received after the year end should not be included in the financial statements.

**Revenue cut-off**
- Revenue for where the goods have left the warehouse should be included within the revenue and trade receivables at the year end, but not in closing inventories.
- Revenue made after the year end must not be included in the financial statements but should be included in closing inventories.

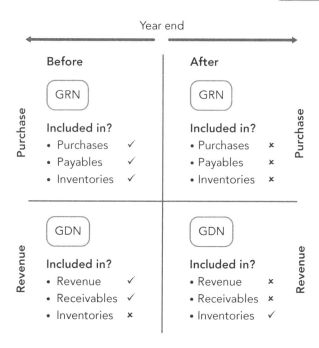

### Essential reading

See Chapter 13 of the Essential reading for further details on the importance of cut-off testing and management's cut-off procedures.

The Essential reading is available as an Appendix of the digital edition of the Workbook.

## 2.6 Continuous (perpetual) inventory counting

A business may count inventory by one or a combination of the following methods:

> **Physical inventory counts at the year end**
> - From the viewpoint of the auditor, this is often the best method.

> **Physical inventory counts before or after the year end**
> - This will provide audit evidence of varying reliability depending on:
> - The length of time between the physical inventory count and the year-end (the greater the time period, the less the value of audit evidence)
> - The business's system of internal controls
> - The quality of records of inventory movements in the period between the physical inventory count and the year end (the auditors will need to perform roll back or roll forward tests on these records)

> **Continuous (or perpetual) inventory**
> - Management has a programme of inventory counting throughout the year.
> - Continuous systems make use of modern computing power to link inventory records to information about sales and purchases, as well as to management information such as an item's location within the entity.
> - This is the preferred method of monitoring inventory levels throughout the year, but its weakness is that over time the **actual inventory level** will tend to **diverge from what** the computer says it **should be**, as a result of unrecorded transactions or theft.
> - As a result of this divergence, it will be necessary to perform physical inventory counts of selected inventory lines throughout the year to determine the extent of the system's divergence from actual inventory levels. All inventory lines should be subject to a physical count at least once a year.

The audit work when continuous (or perpetual) inventory counting is used focuses on tests of controls rather than substantive audit work. Nevertheless, the auditor will also need to do some further substantive audit work on completeness and existence at the year end.

### Essential reading

See Chapter 13 of the Essential reading for further details on the auditor's actions when attending a physical inventory count where an audit client uses a continuous system.

The Essential reading is available as an Appendix of the digital edition of the Workbook.

# 3 Inventory valuation

## 3.1 Accounting for inventory

IAS 2 *Inventories* requires inventory to be stated at the **lower of cost and net realisable value** (IAS 2: para. 9).

> **Cost:** Cost is defined by IAS 2 (para. 10) as comprising all costs of purchase and other costs incurred in bringing inventory to its present location and condition.
>
> **Net realisable value (NRV):** Net realisable value (NRV) is the estimated selling price in the ordinary course of business, less the estimated cost of completion and the estimated costs necessary to make the sale (IAS 2: para. 6).

 **BPP**

Broadly speaking, this means that inventory should be stated at cost, because companies tend to sell inventory for more than it costs. It is possible, however, that the inventory is not worth what it costs – perhaps because it is damaged or obsolete – in which case it should be stated at what it is worth, ie its net realisable value.

Auditors must understand how the company determines the cost of an item for inventory valuation purposes. Costs should include an appropriate proportion of overheads, in accordance with IAS 2 (para. 12).

An entity may use **standard costs** to value inventory provided that the standard costs **approximate to actual cost**.

## 3.2 Auditing inventory valuation

Auditing the **valuation** of inventory has the following aims.

Ensuring the method of determining cost and the **allocation of overheads** is appropriate

Confirming inventory is carried at the **lower** of **cost** and **net realisable value**

### Essential reading

See Chapter 13 of the Essential reading for further details on inventory accounting as per IAS 2 and auditing the valuation of inventory.

The Essential reading is available as an Appendix of the digital edition of the Workbook.

**Estimating** the net realisable value of inventory requires **judgement** and can involve **uncertainty**. The rules of ISA 540 (Revised) *Auditing Accounting Estimates and Related Disclosures* will apply to the audit of NRV. The standard mentions that inventory obsolescence is an example of an accounting estimate. The audit of accounting estimates has already been studied in Chapter 12 *Non-current Assets*.

### Activity 4: Cost of inventory

The following is an extract of Dress You Like Co's breakdown of the cost of finished inventory for the year ending 30 September 20X6. The full breakdown lists the same information for the several thousand product lines held in finished inventory.

| Inventory Code | Quantity | Raw material cost ($) | Labour cost ($) | Overheads ($) | Total cost ($) | Total cost per unit ($) |
| --- | --- | --- | --- | --- | --- | --- |
| DYL120004P | 1,000 | 5,648 | 1,010 | 500 | 7,158 | 7 |
| DYL120005P | 5,000 | 20,597 | 5,641 | 2,500 | 28,738 | 6 |
| DYL120006P | 750 | 3,652 | 800 | 350 | 4,802 | 6 |
| DYL120007P | 2,500 | 12,456 | 2,900 | 1,755 | 17,111 | 7 |
| DYL120008P | 800 | 6,054 | 1,655 | 5,000 | 12,709 | 16 |
| DYL120009P | 500 | 2,648 | 544 | 250 | 3,442 | 7 |

**Required**

List the audit procedures you would perform on the full breakdown of the cost of finished inventory when auditing the valuation of inventory. Document the reason for each procedure.

## Activity 5: Cost vs NRV

The following is an extract from a schedule prepared by Dress You Like Co for year ending 30 September 20X6. The schedule details the total cost per unit of inventory versus the actual price at which the inventory was sold per unit after the year-end.

| Inventory Code | Total cost per unit ($) | Selling price per unit ($) |
|---|---|---|
| DYL120004P | 7 | 20 |
| DYL120005P | 6 | 15 |
| DYL120006P | 6 | 16 |
| DYL120007P | 7 | 14 |
| DYL120008P | 16 | 10 |
| DYL120009P | 7 | 20 |

### Required

Answer the following questions:

1. Note down any items from this schedule that might require investigation. Why have you chosen these items?

2. Rewrite the information above as an audit procedure, documenting the reason for the procedure.

### Solution

### 3.2.1 Audit procedures for inventory

The following table contains audit procedures for inventory matched to the financial statement assertions they test. This table is for reference only, the procedures should not be learned by heart, but may be useful when practising exam questions.

| Financial statement assertion | Audit procedure |
|---|---|
| Completeness | • **Trace** test counts to the detailed inventory listing.<br><br>• Where inventory is held in **third-party locations**, **physically inspect** this inventory or **review confirmations** received from the third party and match to the general ledger.<br><br>• **Compare** the gross profit percentage to the previous year or industry data and investigate any unexpected variations. |
| Existence | • Observe the **physical inventory count** |
| Rights and obligations | • Verify that any **inventory held for third parties** is not included in the year-end inventory figure by being appropriately segregated during the inventory count.<br><br>• For any **'bill and hold' inventory** (ie where the inventory has been sold but is being held by the entity until the customer requires it), identify such inventory and ensure that it is segregated during the inventory count so that it is not included in the year-end inventory figure.<br><br>• Confirm that any inventory held at **third-party locations** is included in the year-end inventory figure by reviewing the inventory listing. |
| Accuracy, valuation and allocation | • Obtain a copy of the inventory listing and **agree** the totals to the general ledger.<br><br>• **Cast** the inventory listing to ensure it is mathematically correct.<br><br>• **Vouch** a sample of inventory items to suppliers' invoices to ensure it is correctly valued.<br><br>• Where **standard costing** is used, obtain a copy of the standard cost card, vouch a sample of purchases costs to invoices and labour rates to payroll records and discuss the amount of labour time taken per unit/batch with production staff to ensure the standard cost is correctly valued.<br><br>• For **materials**, agree the valuation of raw materials to invoices and price lists.<br><br>• Confirm that an appropriate **basis of valuation** (eg FIFO) is being used by discussing with management.<br><br>• For **labour** costs, agree costs to wage records.<br><br>• **Review** standard labour costs in the light of actual costs and production.<br><br>• **Reconcile** labour hours to time summaries.<br><br>• Where inventory relates to work in progress, discuss the stage of completion with production management and recalculate inventory values. Consider whether an expert is required.<br><br>• Make **enquiries of management** to ascertain any slow-moving or obsolete inventory that should be written down.<br><br>• |

| Financial statement assertion | Audit procedure |
| --- | --- |
| | • **Examine prices** at which finished goods have been sold after the year end to ascertain whether any finished goods need to be written down. |
| | • If significant levels of finished goods remain unsold for an unusual period of time, **discuss** with management and consider the need to make allowance. |
| | • **Compare** the gross profit percentage to the previous year or industry data. |
| | • **Compare** raw material, finished goods and inventory collection period to the previous year and industry averages. |
| | • **Compare** inventory holding period with the previous year and industry average. |
| | • **Compare** the current year standard costs to the previous year after considering current conditions. |
| | • **Compare** actual manufacturing overhead costs with budgeted or standard manufacturing overhead costs. |
| | • Obtain a copy of the inventory listing and **cast** it, and test the mathematical extensions of quantity multiplied by price. |
| | • **Trace** test counts back to the inventory listing. |
| | • If the entity has adjusted the general ledger to agree with the physical inventory count amounts, **agree** the two amounts. |
| | • Where a **continuous (perpetual) inventory system** is maintained, agree the total on the inventory listing to the continuous inventory records, using automated tools and techniques. |
| Cut-off | • Note the numbers of the **last GDNs and GRNs** before the year end and the **first GDNs and GRNs** after the year end and check that these have been included in the correct financial year. |
| Classification | • **Review** the inventory listing to ensure that inventory has been properly classified between raw materials, work-in-progress and finished goods.<br>• **Read** the notes to the accounts relating to inventory to ensure they are understandable. |
| Presentation | • Complete the **disclosure checklist** to ensure that all the disclosures relevant to inventory have been made.<br>• **Review** the financial statements to confirm whether the cost method used to value inventory is accurately disclosed.<br>• **Read** the notes to the financial statements to ensure that the information is accurate and properly presented at the appropriate amounts. |

### 3.3 Using the work of an auditor's expert

An expert may be used to assist with auditing the valuation of inventory, for example in valuing precious stones or assessing the stage of completion of WIP. You have already studied the use of a management's expert in Chapter 12 on non-current assets. In this section, we will look at the situation where an expert is employed by the auditor, rather than the audit client. Guidance on this area is provided by ISA 620 *Using the Work of an Auditor's Expert*.

**Auditor's expert:** An Auditor's expert is "an individual or organisation possessing expertise in a field other than accounting or auditing, whose work in that field is used by the auditor to assist the auditor in obtaining sufficient appropriate audit evidence. An auditor's expert may be either an auditor's internal expert (who is a partner or staff, including temporary staff, of the auditor's firm or a network firm) or an auditor's external expert" (ISA 620: para. 6(a)).

Be mindful that auditors' experts can be employed to assist with areas other than inventory valuation, such as the valuation of land and buildings or legal opinions concerning interpretations of agreements, statutes and regulations, or on the outcome of litigation or disputes .

The auditor must **not refer to the work of an auditor's expert in the auditor's report** containing an unmodified opinion (unless required by law or regulation).

### Essential reading

See Chapter 13 of the Essential reading for further details on using an auditor's expert.

The Essential reading is available as an Appendix of the digital edition of the Workbook.

# 4 Using the work of internal audit

Another party that the auditors can rely upon in the audit of inventory is the internal audit function at a client (note that the internal auditors will cover many areas, not just inventory). During the course of their planning, the external auditors should perform an assessment of the internal audit function if they consider that it may be possible, and desirable, to rely on some of internal audit's work. If the external auditor can rely on the work conducted by the internal auditor, the volume of detailed work undertaken by the external auditor may be reduced.

**Internal audit function:** Internal audit function is "a function of an entity that performs assurance and consulting activities designed to evaluate and improve the effectiveness of the entity's governance, risk management and internal control processes" (ISA 610 (Revised): para. 14(a)).

ISA 610 (Revised) *Using the Work of Internal Auditors* provides guidance for the external auditor when the external auditor expects to use the work of the internal audit function to modify the nature or timing, or reduce the extent, of audit procedures to be performed directly by the external auditor.

Although the work of internal audit may be used for the purposes of the external audit, it is important to note that the external auditor has **sole responsibility** for the audit opinion expressed on the financial statements (ISA 610 (Revised): para. 11). The external auditor cannot make reference to work done by the internal auditor in their auditor's report.

ISA 610 ((Revised): para. 22) requires the external auditor to read the reports of the internal audit function relating to the work the external auditor plans to use. This is to obtain an understanding of the nature and extent of audit procedures the internal audit function performed, as well as understanding the related findings.

Before using the work of internal audit, the external auditors need to **evaluate** and **perform audit procedures** on the entirety of the work that they plan to use, in order to determine its adequacy for the purposes of the audit.

The evaluation includes the following:

| |
|---|
| Whether the work was **properly planned, performed, supervised, reviewed** and **documented** |
| Whether **sufficient appropriate evidence** was obtained to allow the internal auditors to draw reasonable conclusions |
| Whether the **conclusions** reached are **appropriate** in the circumstances and the reports prepared are **consistent** with the results of the work done |

(ISA 610 (Revised): para. 23)

The **nature and extent** of the audit procedures performed on specific work of the internal auditors will depend on the external auditor's assessment of:

| The amount of **judgement** involved | The assessed **risk** of material misstatement | How well the audit function's organisational status and relevant policies and procedures support the **objectivity of the internal auditors** | The level of **competence** of the function |
|---|---|---|---|

Note that ISA 610 ((Revised): para. 24) requires the external auditor's procedures to include **reperformance** of some of the internal audit work used.

Audit procedures might include:

- Examination of items **already examined** by the internal auditors
- Examination of **other similar items**
- **Observation of procedures** performed by the internal auditors

(ISA 610 (Revised): para. A30)

As the work of internal audit is reviewed, the external auditor must consider whether the initial conclusions reached when deciding whether to use (and to what extent to use) internal audit work in the first place are still valid, and should tailor audit procedures accordingly (ISA 610 (Revised): para. 25).

## 4.1 Direct assistance

> **Direct assistance:** Direct assistance refers to "the use of internal auditors to perform audit procedures under the direction, supervision and review of the external auditor" (ISA 610 (Revised): para. 14(b)).

ISA 610 ((Revised): para. 30) **prohibits** the use of internal auditors to provide direct assistance to perform procedures that:

| |
|---|
| Involve making **significant judgements** in the audit |
| Relate to **higher assessed risks of material misstatement** where more than a limited degree of **judgment** is required: for example, in assessing the valuation of accounts receivable, internal auditors may be assigned to check the accuracy of receivables ageing, but they must not be involved in evaluating the adequacy of the provision for irrecoverable receivables |
| Relate to work with which the **internal auditors have been involved** |
| Relate to **decisions** the external auditor makes **regarding the internal audit function** and the use of its work or direct assistance |

## Essential reading

See Chapter 13 of the Essential reading for further details on using the work of internal audit including the use of direct assistance.

The Essential reading is available as an Appendix of the digital edition of the Workbook.

## Activity 6: Reliance on internal audit

For the first eight months of the year ended 30 September 20X6, Dress You Like Co outsourced their internal audit function to Pricey & Co, an external audit firm. Callum Lewis, the son of Gary Lewis, the Chair of Dress You Like Co, is an audit junior at Pricey & Co.

During the eight months to February 20X6, Dress You Like Co specifically requested the internal auditor's document and test the controls that ensure all customers receive their goods within one week of making an order. No other controls over inventory were tested.

**Required**

Which of the following statements, if any, are true?

(1)  Check & Co cannot use the work of the internal auditor because they were not engaged by Dress You Like Co for the entire year being audited.

(2)  Check & Co cannot rely on the work of Pricey & Co because Callum Lewis is an audit junior there and they lack objectivity.

(3)  Check & Co can rely on the work of Dress You Like Co for auditing the existence and completeness of inventory.

O  (1) only

O  (3) only

O  (1) and (2)

O  Neither (1) nor (2) nor (3)

## Essential reading

See Chapter 18 of the Essential reading for a summary of the accounting knowledge relevant to IAS 2: *Inventories* which is brought forward to this paper from your earlier Financial Accounting studies.

The Essential reading is available as an Appendix of the digital edition of the Workbook.

# Chapter summary

**Inventory**

## Introduction to auditing inventory

**Audit approach**
- Consider quantity, valuation and disclosure
- Substantive procedures or controls testing or a mix of both?

## The physical inventory count

**Planning the inventory count**
- Include inventory held by third parties
- Is an expert required?

**Attendance at inventory count**
- Observe count procedures being performed
- Inspect inventory
- Perform test counts

**Cut-off**
Check GRNs and GDNs from before & after year end

**Continuous (perpetual) inventory counting**
= inventory counting throughout the year – focus on controls testing

## Inventory valuation

**Auditing inventory valuation**
- Appropriate allocation of overheads?
- Appropriate method of determining cost?
- Valued at lower of cost and NRV?
- NRV is an estimated figure

**Using the work of an auditor's expert**
- Evaluate competence, capability and objectivity
- Do not refer to their work in an unmodified auditor's report

## Using the work of internal audit

- External auditor has sole responsibility for audit opinion
- Is the internal auditor competent, objective and do they use a systematic and disciplined approach?

**Direct assistance**
Direct assistance prohibited for significant judgements, high ROMM, areas where internal auditors have performed work, decisions external auditors makes regarding the internal audit function and its work

# Knowledge diagnostic

### 1. Inventory quantity

Procedures to verify the quantity of inventory will depend on whether the client uses a **year-end** inventory count or a **continuous** inventory system.

### 2. Inventory count

**Physical inventory count procedures** are vital, as they provide evidence which cannot be obtained elsewhere or at any other time about the quantities and conditions of inventory and WIP.

### 3. Auditor attendance at the inventory count

The auditor will **attend** the inventory count to:

(a) Perform tests of controls (observation)

(b) Obtain substantive evidence of quantity (test counts, cut-off details)

(c) Obtain preliminary evidence of valuation (note damaged or obsolete inventories)

### 4. Inventory cut-off

**Cut-off tests** are used to ensure that transactions have been recorded in the correct accounting period.

### 5. Cut-off testing

Auditors should test cut-off by noting the serial numbers of GDNs and GRNs received and despatched just before and after the year-end, and subsequently testing that they have been included in the correct period.

### 6. IAS 2 *Inventories*

The **valuation** and **disclosure** rules for inventory are laid down in IAS 2 *Inventories*. Inventory should be valued at the **lower of cost and net realisable value.**

### 7. Inventory valuation

Auditing the valuation of inventory includes:

(a) Testing the **allocation of overheads** is appropriate

(b) Confirming inventory is carried at the lower of cost and net realisable value

### 8. Using the work of an expert

External auditors may make use of the work of an auditor's expert or internal audit when carrying out audit procedures.

 BPP

# Further study guidance

## Question practice

Now try the following from the Further question practice bank [available in the digital edition of the Workbook]:

- Section A Q44 on the external auditor's reliance on the internal audit function
- Section A Q46 on cut off
- Section B Q74(b) on using the work of an auditor's expert
- Section B Q75(a) 'Elsams' on use of computers when auditing inventory
- Section B Q76 'ZPM' on using the work of internal auditors
- Section B Q78 'Wandsworth Wholesalers' on the inventory count
- Section B Q79 'Snu' on perpetual inventory counting
- Section B Q80 'Sitting Pretty' on the inventory count, inventory valuation and cut-off

## Further reading

There are technical articles on the ACCA website written by members of the AA examining team which are relevant to some of the topics covered in this chapter that you should read:

- *https://www.accaglobal.com/gb/en/student/exam-support-resources/fundamentals-exams-study-resources/f8/technical-articles/assertions*.html
- https://www.accaglobal.com/gb/en/student/exam-support-resources/fundamentals-exams-study-resources/f8/technical-articles/internal-auditors.html

## Own research

- Obtain a recent set of financial statements for an organisation and look for the inventory balance. Do you think the auditors might have used an expert to audit the valuation of this inventory?
- The tools and techniques auditors use to audit inventory are changing with the development of new technologies. This article looks at how drones can be used to in the audit of inventory: www.accaglobal.com/us/en/student/sa/features/drones.html

# Activity answers

## Activity 1: Inventory count instructions

Matters requiring action – inventory count

Three matters which will require action by management if the inventory count is to be effective together with corrective action are:

1.  By allowing David Furber to take responsibility for the detailed organisation of the count, the present instructions permit the person with day-to-day responsibility for the inventory area to supervise one of the most important control checks on that area. This represents a deficiency in the company's system of internal control, since the opportunity is afforded to David Furber to cover up any inadequacies there may be in the operational efficiency of controls in the area of inventories.

Sadie Thomas should take more direct responsibility for the detailed organisation of the count.

2.  By giving to those members of staff responsible for the physical count of the inventories an indication of the quantity, which is expected to be in inventory, there is a risk that this may prejudice their opinion in the event of there being a discrepancy. More importantly, it will tend to reduce the benefits which it is intended to derive from having an independent check on the inventory records by having to reconcile them with the quantities determined by a physical count.

The pre-printed inventory sheets should not show the balance of each inventory item on hand as shown on the inventory records held independently of the warehouse.

3.  There are no members of staff recounting a sample of inventory that has already been counted. This is an important control over the inventory count.

A number of teams of checkers (two or three) should be appointed to go around after the counters. The task of these checkers would be to:

*   Carry out sample tests on the accuracy of the original counters
*   Ensure that inventory count completion tags have been left by the counters at each inventory location

The appointment of checkers will improve the efficiency of the overall count by acting as a check on both the accuracy and completeness of the count.

## Activity 2: Completeness

The correct answer is: Test counts from inventory in the warehouse to the inventory records

## Activity 3: Test counts

1   The quantity of item DYL883722G is 125 in the inventory records but only 50 items have been counted. This item will need investigating as it could be indicative of an overstatement of inventory in the statement of financial position.

Item DYL879239X appears to have been damaged. This will need investigating since the inventory may need to be written off if the blue dye cannot be removed from the white shirts. If the inventory cannot be brought back to a saleable standard then it might be overstated in the statement of financial position and an adjustment may need to be made.

A total of 88 items was counted for inventory code DYL261567L but only 87 items are recorded in the inventory records. This small difference may be a counting error and should be looked into to ensure the completeness of the inventory balance.

2    Inspect the inventory count sheets for any notes on damaged inventory and enquire with management as to whether this inventory has been sold or scrapped since the year end. If any of this inventory has been sold since the year end, agree to sales invoices to ensure the accuracy of the valuation. If neither sold or scrapped, discuss the saleability of the damaged inventory with management to ensure the valuation of inventory is the lower of cost and net realisable value

Inspect the inventory count sheets and note any differences between the quantities recorded in the inventory records and the quantities counted in the inventory count. Enquire whether management has followed up on any differences and agree that any necessary adjustments have been made in the client's ledgers. This will ensure the existence and completeness of the inventory balance.

### Activity 4: Cost of inventory

- Recalculate the total of the breakdown to ensure it has been calculated correctly.

- Agree the total of the breakdown to the finished goods figure to the trial balance and financial statements to ensure the accuracy, completeness and existence of the figure in the financial statements.

- For a sample of inventory codes, agree the cost of raw materials to purchase invoices to ensure the valuation of the raw material cost is accurate.

- For a sample of inventory codes, agree the labour cost to underlying documentation, such as time sheets, to ensure the valuation of the labour cost is accurate.

- Enquire of management as to the basis of the overhead calculation and compare this to previous years in order to assess the reasonableness of the calculation.

- For a sample of inventory codes, agree the overhead cost to supporting documentation such as invoices for electricity. Ensure that any overhead costs included are attributable to production.

### Activity 5: Cost vs NRV

1    Item DYL120008P cost $16 to manufacture but only sold for $10. The cost is greater than the net realisable value and so the item needs to be written down or inventory will be overstated in the statement of financial position.

2    For a sample of inventory codes, agree the selling price after year-end to sales invoices and recalculate the unit price to ensure it is calculated correctly.

Compare the cost of the inventory per unit to the selling price per unit to assess whether any inventory needs to be written down to net realisable value.

### Activity 6: Reliance on internal audit

The correct answer is: Neither (1) nor (2) nor (3)

Check & Co could use the work of the internal auditors for the first 8 months of the year, if they were found to be objective, competent and having a systematic and disciplined approach during that time. As long as Callum Lewis was not in the internal audit team, the objectivity of Pricey & Co should not be affected. The tests performed by Pricey & Co do not provide evidence of the completeness or existence of inventory.

# Receivables

## Learning objectives

On completion of this chapter, you should be able to:

| Syllabus learning outcomes | Syllabus reference no. |
|---|---|
| Explain the audit objectives and the audit procedures to obtain sufficient, appropriate evidence in relation to: Receivables | D4 (a) |
| (a) Direct confirmation of accounts receivable | |
| (b) Other evidence in relation to receivables and prepayments | |
| (c) Other evidence in relation to current assets | |
| (d) Completeness and occurrence of revenue | |

## Business and Exam context

Many candidates who sit the ACCA AA exam do not work in audit practice. This can make it harder to see the practical nature of the subject and to learn to apply the knowledge learned. Consequently, we have tried to make this chapter relating to substantive procedures as practical as possible, so that you can apply your knowledge to exam scenarios.

Receivables can be tested in Section A or Section B of the exam. Section B of the exam may ask you to describe the substantive audit procedures you would perform to obtain sufficient and appropriate evidence for assertions relating to receivables. Alternatively, a Section A question could ask you to select an appropriate procedure from a list of procedures to provide evidence over a particular assertion.

It is worth noting that where an exam question asks specifically for audit procedures for receivables, no marks would be awarded if you identify audit procedures relevant only for prepayments, for example.

You must ensure that you are fully conversant with the 'standard' procedures, such as the confirmation of receivables. The receivables confirmation is primarily designed to test the client's entitlement to receive the debt, not the customer's ability to pay. Auditors also need to consider cut-off for receivables. Revenue testing is often carried out in conjunction with the audit of receivables, as the two are linked. We also briefly consider the audit of prepayments.

You will need knowledge of the accounting standards you learnt in your Fundamentals in Financial Accounting (FFA) exam relating to receivables for this chapter.

# Chapter overview

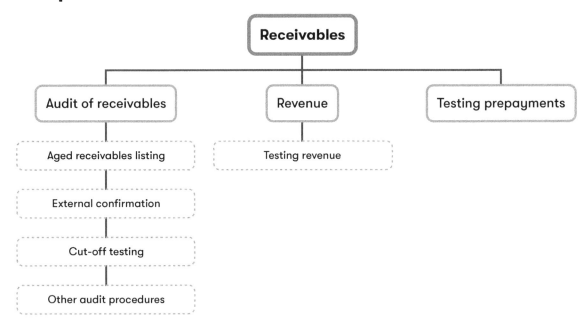

BPP

# 1 Audit of receivables

## 1.1 Assertions

You have already studied assertions in Chapter 8 of this workbook, Introduction to Audit Evidence. In this chapter you will learn which of these assertions relate to receivables and the audit procedures required to cover these assertions. These can cover the receivables balance at the year-end or allowances for receivables.

### Essential reading

See Chapter 14 of the Essential reading for the assertions that apply to receivables.

The Essential reading is available as an Appendix of the digital edition of the Workbook.

Throughout this chapter, we will continue to use the audit of Dress You Like Co for the year ended 30 September 20X6. Remember that the company normally allows credit terms of 30 days, but the supermarket is given 60-day credit terms.

The audit team has prepared the following lead schedule for the audit of receivables of Dress You Like Co for the current year.

Reference:

Client: Dress You Like Co

Prepared by:

Reviewed by:

Date: 30/10/X6

|  | Draft 20X6 | Dr | Cr | Final 20X6 | Actual 20X5 |
|---|---|---|---|---|---|
|  | $'000 | $'000 | $'000 | $'000 | $'000 |
| Trade receivables: |  |  |  |  |  |
| Supermarket | 11,800 |  |  |  | 8,300 |
| Other | 700 |  |  |  | 600 |
|  | 12,500 |  |  |  | 8,900 |

## 1.2 Aged receivables listing

### Activity 1: Aged receivables listing

The following is a copy of the aged receivables listing of Dress You Like Co as at 30 September 20X6:

| Customer | Total | 30 days | 60 days | 90 days | > 90 days |
|---|---|---|---|---|---|
|  | $'000 | $'000 | $'000 | $'000 | $'000 |
| Jasco Supermarket | 11,800 | 3,100 | 2,800 | 3,600 | 2,300 |
| All About Clothes | 21 | 4 | 12 | 5 | - |
| Clothing Terrain | 33 | 26 | 5 | - | 2 |
| Dress for the Occasion | 92 | 41 | 39 | 12 | - |

| Customer | Total $'000 | 30 days $'000 | 60 days $'000 | 90 days $'000 | > 90 days $'000 |
|---|---|---|---|---|---|
| Duncan's Dresses | 3 | 3 | - | - | - |
| Everyday Wear | (6) | - | - | - | (6) |
| Ewan Trading | 29 | 14 | 15 | - | - |
| Fred's Fashions | 47 | 37 | 6 | - | 4 |
| Freya's Threads | 8 | 8 | - | - | - |
| Girls on the Go | 13 | 4 | 9 | - | - |
| Holly Aristocrat | 73 | 41 | 19 | 1 | 12 |
| Holiday Accessories | 5 | - | 5 | - | - |
| In all Weather | 16 | 2 | 13 | 1 | - |
| Ivory Gowns | 2 | - | - | - | 2 |
| Look the Part | 124 | 79 | 38 | 7 | 1 |
| Jim's Jumpers | 38 | 30 | 8 | - | - |
| Odd One Out | 67 | 52 | 15 | - | - |
| Safari School wear | 28 | - | 28 | - | - |
| Skirts and all sorts | 57 | 15 | 30 | 12 | - |
| Ties with a Difference | 12 | 12 | - | - | - |
| Upward Trends | 17 | 17 | - | - | - |
| Up and Out | 9 | - | 9 | - | - |
| We're Going Exploring | 12 | 5 | - | 7 | - |
| | 12,500 | 3,490 | 3,051 | 3,645 | 2,314 |

**Required**

1   Note down any items in the aged receivables listing that might require investigation. Why have you chosen these items?

2   Rewrite the information in part (1) as an audit procedure, documenting the reason for the audit procedure.

**Solution**

### 1.2.1 Monies received post year end

The auditor review after date cash received to test existence and valuation of receivables.

## Activity 2: Post year end cash receipts

Below is an extract from the cash book receipts of Dress You Like Co during October and November 20X6. All the following amounts received have also cleared on the bank statement:

| Customer | Amount received | Balance owed at year-end |
|---|---|---|
| | $'000 | $'000 |
| Jasco Supermarket | 5,680 | 11,800 |
| All About Clothes | 21 | 21 |
| Clothing Terrain | 31 | 33 |
| Dress for the Occasion | 92 | 92 |
| Duncan's Dresses | 3 | 3 |
| Everyday Wear | 0 | (6) |
| Ewan Trading | 29 | 29 |
| Fred's Fashions | 43 | 47 |
| Freya's Threads | 8 | 8 |
| Girls on the Go | 13 | 13 |
| Holly Aristocrat | 63 | 73 |
| Holiday Accessories | 5 | 5 |
| In all Weather | 16 | 16 |
| Ivory Gowns | 0 | 2 |
| Look the Part | 124 | 124 |
| Jim's Jumpers | 38 | 38 |
| Odd One Out | 62 | 67 |
| Safari School wear | 28 | 28 |
| Skirts and all sorts | 57 | 57 |
| Ties with a Difference | 12 | 12 |
| Upward Trends | 17 | 17 |
| Up and Out | 9 | 9 |
| We're Going Exploring | 5 | 12 |
| | 6,356 | 12,500 |

### Required

1   Consider the information above in relation to the balances owed by each customer at the year-end.  Which balances might require further investigation?

2   Rewrite the information in part (1) as an audit procedure stating the objective of the audit procedure.

**Solution**

### 1.2.2 Credit notes issued post year-end

## Activity 3: Post year end credit notes

The following is a list of the credit notes issued by Dress You Like Co during October and November 20X6:

| Customer | Total $'000 | Description |
|---|---|---|
| Jasco Supermarket | 220 | Issued in relation to a disputed invoice (invoice no 126425) which was due > 90 days |
| Holly Aristocrat | 10 | Issued in relation to the amount of $12,000 due > 90 days |
| Odd One Out | 5 | Issued in relation to an invoice sent in error |

**Required**

1 Consider the information above. What further evidence does it provide about the receivables balance at the year-end?

2 Write out the audit procedure you have conducted in part (1) stating the objective of the audit procedure.

**Solution**

## 1.3 External confirmation

A specific technique used to test for the existence and rights and obligations of receivables is an external confirmation (alternatively called 'circularisation'). ISA 505 *External Confirmations* covers the confirmation of amounts by third parties, including the confirmation of amounts by receivables.

**External confirmations:** Audit evidence obtained as a direct written response to the auditor from a third-party (the confirming party), in paper form, or by electronic or other medium.

An external confirmation will produce a written statement from each respondent that the amount owed at the date of the confirmation is correct. The audit evidence obtained is reliable since it is from an **independent source** and in **documentary** form.

The confirmation letter must be written on the client's headed paper and signed by the client with a copy of the current statement attached. It shall request that the **reply be sent directly to the auditor** and a prepaid envelope is included for this purpose.

There are two types of confirmation:

| | |
|---|---|
| A **positive** confirmation request is where the confirming party responds directly to the auditor, indicating whether they agree with the information in the request or provides the requested information | A **negative** confirmation request is where the confirming party responds directly to the auditor only if they disagree with the information in the request |

The positive method is generally preferable, as it is designed to encourage definite replies from those contacted.

The negative method provides less persuasive audit evidence and shall not be used as the sole substantive procedure to audit receivables unless all of the following are present:

*   The risk of material misstatement has been assessed as low.
*   The auditor has obtained sufficient appropriate audit evidence on the operating effectiveness of relevant controls.
*   The population consists of a large number of small, homogeneous account balances.
*   A very low exception rate is expected.
*   The auditor is not aware of circumstances or conditions that would cause customers to disregard the requests.

(ISA 505: para. 15)

An external confirmation for receivables is conducted as follows:

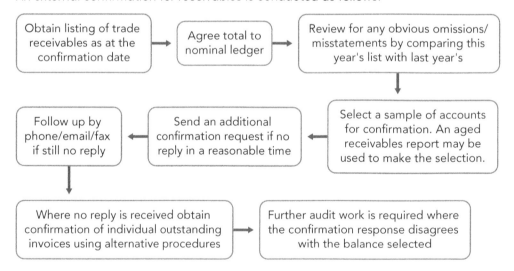

The following balances should be included in the sample of accounts for confirmation:

*   Old, unpaid accounts
*   Accounts written-off during the period under review
*   Accounts with credit balances
*   Accounts settled by round sum payments
*   Accounts with large balances
*   Accounts with nil balances

## Essential reading

See Chapter 14 of the Essential reading for an example of a positive confirmation request letter, and details of the auditor's response when management refuses to send a confirmation request.

The Essential reading is available as an Appendix of the digital edition of the Workbook.

## Activity 4: Audit procedures

The audit assistant at Check & Co is about to begin testing of the receivables balance for Dress You Like Co and you are keen for them to use automated tools and techniques in order to save time and cost. They have approached you with a list of procedures they intend to perform using automated tools and techniques.

### Required

Which of the following procedures could NOT be performed using automated tools and techniques?

O   Selection of a sample of receivables for confirmation

O   Calculation of receivables days

O   Evaluation of the adequacy of the allowance for receivables

O   Production of receivables confirmation letters

### 1.3.1 Exceptions and non-responses

**Exception:** "A response that indicates a difference between information requested to be confirmed, or contained in the entity's records, and information provided by the confirming party." *(ISA 505: para. 6(e))*

**Non-response:** "A failure of the confirming party to respond, or fully respond, to a positive confirmation request, or a confirmation request returned undelivered." (ISA 505: para. 6d))

| | |
|---|---|
| **External confirmation response disagrees** with the **balance stated** (positive and negative confirmation), resulting in an **exception** | • Exceptions may indicate **misstatements** or potential misstatements in the financial statements and must be **investigated** by the auditor <br> • The auditor must evaluate whether misstatements identified are **indicative of fraud** (in line with ISA 240) <br> • Exceptions might also indicate a **deficiency in internal control** <br> • Not all exceptions represent misstatements (eg timing or clerical errors) |
| **Non-response** to external confirmation | • Where no response is received, the auditor shall perform **alternative audit procedures** to obtain relevant and reliable audit evidence <br>    – Verify outstanding items to back up documentation, eg invoices, GDNs and customer orders <br>    – Review cash received after year end <br>    – Discuss with responsible company official |

## Essential reading

Chapter 14 of the Essential reading examines the reasons why exceptions may occur and the appropriate response from the auditor. It also looks at the appropriate response from the auditor where the reply is unreliable.

The Essential reading is available as an Appendix of the digital edition of the Workbook.

## Activity 5: External confirmation

The following are the results from the external confirmation carried out at 30 September 20X6 for Dress You Like Co:

| Customer | Balance per ledger $'000 | Balance per response $'000 | Reason for the difference |
|---|---|---|---|
| Dress for the Occasion | 92 | 53 | Cash in transit ($39,000) |
| Ewan Trading | 29 | 29 | – |
| Fred's Fashions | 47 | 43 | Disputed invoice ($4,000) |
| Girls on the Go | 13 | 11 | Goods not received at year end (GDN no.127057) |
| In all Weather | 16 | 16 | – |
| Look the Part | 124 | 124 | – |
| Upward Trends | 17 | 8 | Goods not received at year end (GDN |

| Customer | Balance per ledger | Balance per response | Reason for the difference |
|---|---|---|---|
| | $'000 | $'000 | |
| | | | no.127058) |
| Jasco Supermarket | 11,800 | 11,580 | Disputed invoice (invoice no.126425) |

**Required**

Detail the audit procedures you would perform on each of these responses.

**Solution**

## 1.4 Cut-off testing

If a set of financial statements is to 'present fairly' the activities of a business, it is important that transactions and events have been recorded in the correct accounting period. Consequently, an auditor would perform ' cut-off' testing . Cut-off testing for receivables and revenue is linked. You will cover the audit of revenue in Section 2 of this chapter.

### Example

The following is a schedule which summarises the results of the 'cut-off' testing performed in relation to Dress You Like Co's revenue at 30 September 20X6:

**Details of the last three goods despatched notes (GDNs) issued on 30 September 20X6**

| GDN # | Date | Invoice # | Date | Accounted for in y/e | Correctly recorded ? |
|---|---|---|---|---|---|
| 127056 | 30.9.X6 | 127056 | 30.9.X6 | 30.9.X6 | Y |
| 127057 | 30.9.X6 | 127057 | 30.9.X6 | 30.9.X6 | Y |
| 127058 | 1.10.X6 | 127058 | 1.10.X6 | 30.9.X6 | N |

**Details of the first three goods despatched notes (GDNs) issued on 1 October 20X6**

| GDN # | Date | Invoice # | Date | Accounted for in y/e | Correctly recorded ? |
|-------|------|-----------|------|---------------------|----------------------|
| 127059 | 1.10.X6 | 127059 | 1.10.X6 | 30.9.X6 | N |
| 127060 | 1.10.X6 | 127060 | 1.10.X6 | 30.9.X7 | Y |
| 127061 | 2.10.X6 | 127061 | 2.10.X6 | 30.9.X7 | Y |

## 1.5 Other audit procedures

The external confirmation is not the only means by which evidence is gained.

The best way to generate a wide range of audit procedures relating to receivables is to:

The following table contains substantive audit procedures (other than external confirmation) for receivables matched to the financial statement assertions they test. This table is for reference only, the procedures should not be learned by heart, but may be useful when practising exam questions.

It is worth noting that some of the audit procedures test for **more than one assertion**. For example:

(a) Reviewing after-date cash receipts is an excellent test for both valuation and existence.

(b) Comparing the gross profit per product line with the previous year tests for the existence and completeness of receivables, as well as the occurrence and accuracy of sales and the completeness, occurrence, accuracy and classification of cost of sales.

| Completeness | • Obtain a breakdown of the trade receivables figure per customer for both the current and the previous period and compare the level of trade receivables year on year. Discuss any obvious omissions/ unusual trends with management. (Note that this procedure can also be carried out in relation to items such as prepayments). |
|---|---|
| | • Select a sample of GDNs issued during the year and vouch them to the relevant sales invoice. Inspect the revenue and receivables accounts in the nominal ledger to ensure that the invoice has been accurately recorded in the correct accounting period. |
| | • Obtain a copy of the aged receivables listing, re-cast the total to ensure it is accurate. Agree the balance on the aged receivables listing to the nominal ledger and trace through to the financial statements to ensure all balances are recorded. |
| Rights and obligations | • Review monies received post year-end for evidence of the balance owed being paid to the audit client, therefore confirming that the debt was due to them. |
| | • Inspect the responses from the direct confirmation for evidence of the customer's name and address to verify that the customer has confirmed that the outstanding balance is due to the audit client. |
| | • For a sample of balances due at the year-end vouch the outstanding balance back to sales invoices and GDNs to verify that the goods were delivered and that the amount is due to the |

| | |
|---|---|
| | audit client. |
| Accuracy, valuation and allocation | • Inspect the aged receivables listing for old and overdue amounts. Discuss the recoverability of these amounts with management and consider whether any write offs or allowances are necessary. |
| | • Compare the receivables collection period ratio for the current and prior year and discuss any significant variations with management. |
| | • Agree monies received post year end from receivables at the year to the cash book, therefore confirming that the balance is recoverable. |
| | • Examine credit notes issued post year end and determine whether they relate to pre year sales and if so whether an allowance should be made against that balance. |
| | • Review the adequacy of the allowance for receivables through discussion with management and the review of correspondence from customers. |
| Existence | • For a sample of balances owed at the year-end, carry out a direct confirmation of receivables, investigate any balances which do not agree and vouch explanations to supporting documentation. |
| | • Review monies received post year-end to confirm that the balance existed at the year-end. |
| | • Inspect customer correspondence/complaints files to identify any concerns over the existence of receivables. |

# 2 Revenue

Receivables will often be tested in conjunction with revenue. The audit of revenue requires an awareness of IFRS 15 *Revenue from Contracts with Customers* which sets out the process of recognising revenue using the following five steps:

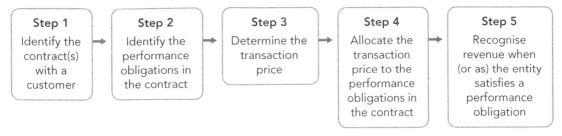

| Step 1 | Step 2 | Step 3 | Step 4 | Step 5 |
|---|---|---|---|---|
| Identify the contract(s) with a customer | Identify the performance obligations in the contract | Determine the transaction price | Allocate the transaction price to the performance obligations in the contract | Recognise revenue when (or as) the entity satisfies a performance obligation |

The key assertions for revenue are occurrence, completeness and accuracy. Auditors are seeking to obtain evidence that revenue exists and pertains to the entity (**occurrence**) and is completely and accurately recorded **(completeness and accuracy)**.

It is also important to test that revenue is recorded in the correct period **(cut-off).** This has already been covered in Section 1.4 of this chapter.

## 2.1 Testing revenue

**Analytical procedures** are important when testing completeness of revenue. A client is likely to have a great deal of information about company revenue and should be able to explain any fluctuations and variances. Auditors should consider the following:

• The **level of revenue** over the year, compared on a month-by-month basis with the previous year

• The effect on revenue value of **changes in quantities** sold

- The effect on revenue value of **changes in products or prices**
- The level of goods **returned, allowances** and **discounts**
- The **efficiency of labour** as expressed in revenue or profit before tax per employee
- Reasons for changes in the **gross profit margin** (analysis of the gross profit margin should be as detailed as possible, ideally broken down by **product area** and **month** or **quarter)**

As well as analytical procedures, auditors may feel that they need to carry out a directional test on **completeness of recording** of individual sales in the accounting records. To do this, auditors should start with the documents that first record revenue (**GDNs** or **till rolls** for example) and trace revenue recorded in these through intermediate documents such as sales summaries to the **sales ledger**. Auditors must ensure that the population of documents from which the sample is originally taken is itself complete, by checking for example the **completeness** of the **sequence** of GDNs.

You must remember the direction of this test. Since we are checking the completeness of recording of revenue in the sales ledger, we cannot take a sample from the ledger because the sample would not include what has not been recorded.

## Example - Revenue completeness testing

The following is a schedule which summarises the results of the completeness testing performed in relation to Dress You Like Co's revenue at 30 September 20X6:

| Standard Order Form # | Standard Order Form $ | GDN # | GDN $ | Sales invoice # | Sales invoice $ | Revenue correctly recorded in receivables ledger? | Notes |
|---|---|---|---|---|---|---|---|
| 125847 | 10,600 | 154845 | 10,600 | 100652 | 10,600 | Y | |
| 126245 | 6,500 | 155352 | 6,500 | 101542 | 6,500 | Y | |
| 127546 | 2,699 | 156875 | 2,699 | 102356 | 2,699 | Y | |
| 128362 | 8,125 | 157545 | 8,125 | 103222 | 8,152 | N | $27 difference |
| 128998 | 25,800 | 158005, 158966 | 17,800 7,000 | 103965 | 24,800 | N | Order was delivered by 2 deliveries $1,000 difference |
| 129875 | 17,775 | 159655 | 17,775 | 104567 | 17,775 | Y | |
| 130055 | 5,225 | 160058 | 5,225 | 105278 | 5,225 | Y | |
| 130854 | 21,600 | 160847 | 21,600 | 106147 | 21,600 | Y | |

The following table contains substantive audit procedures (other than those discussed previously) for revenue matched to the financial statement assertions they test. This table is for reference only, the procedures should not be learned by heart, but may be useful when practising exam questions.

| Completeness | • Obtain a breakdown of revenue for the period on a month by month basis, a product by product basis and/or per customer and compare to prior period/budget. Discuss any significant differences with management. |
|---|---|
| | • Compare the gross product percentage by product line with the previous year and/or industry data. Discuss any significant differences with management. |
| Accuracy | • For a sample of sales invoices, compare the prices and terms to the authorised price list and terms of trade documentation. |
| | • Test whether discounts have been properly applied by recalculating them for a sample of invoices. |

| | • Test the correct calculation of tax on a sample of invoices. |
|---|---|
| Cut-off | • For a sample of invoices around the year end, inspect the dates and compare with the dates of despatch and the dates recorded in the ledger for application of correct cut-off.<br><br>• For sales returns, select a sample of returns documentation around the year end and trace to the related credit entries.<br><br>• Perform analytical procedures on sales returns, comparing the ratio of sales returns to sales. |
| Occurrence | • For a sample of sales transactions recorded in the ledger, vouch the sales invoice back to customer orders and despatch documentation. |

# 3 Testing prepayments

The following procedures should be considered when testing prepayments:

**Completeness**
- **Compare** the level of prepayments to the previous year to ensure the figure is reasonable and complete
- **Review detailed statement of financial position** to ensure all likely prepayments have been included

**Accuracy, valuation and allocation**
- For a sample of prepayments from the prepayments' listing, **recalculate** the amount prepaid to ensure that it has been accurately calculated

**Existence**
- Verify by reference to invoices, cash book and correspondence

# Chapter summary

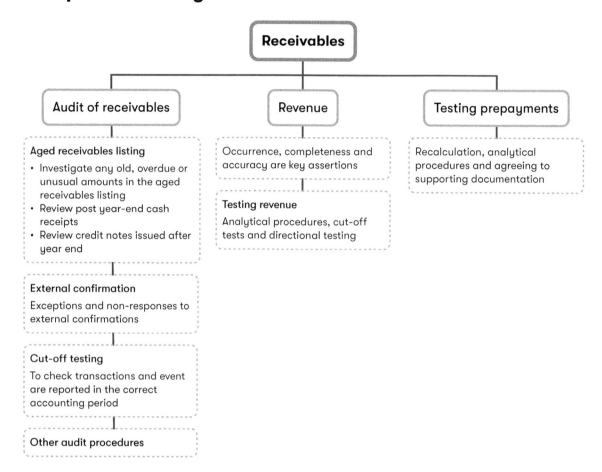

**Receivables**

**Audit of receivables**

**Aged receivables listing**
- Investigate any old, overdue or unusual amounts in the aged receivables listing
- Review post year-end cash receipts
- Review credit notes issued after year end

**External confirmation**
Exceptions and non-responses to external confirmations

**Cut-off testing**
To check transactions and event are reported in the correct accounting period

**Other audit procedures**

**Revenue**

Occurrence, completeness and accuracy are key assertions

**Testing revenue**
Analytical procedures, cut-off tests and directional testing

**Testing prepayments**

Recalculation, analytical procedures and agreeing to supporting documentation

BPP

# Knowledge diagnostic

### 1. Receivables confirmation

External confirmation of receivables is a key procedure. Exceptions must be investigated as these may indicate misstatements. Further audit procedures must be performed for any non-response.

### 2. Other procedures

External confirmation does not give evidence on all the relevant assertions. Other important procedures are cut-off tests and tests to determine recoverability such as looking at cash receipts after the year-end.

### 3. Key assertions

Key assertions for revenue are occurrence, completeness and accuracy.

### 4. Key audit procedures for revenue

Analytical procedures are a way of detecting unexpected fluctuations or variances that could indicate misstatements in revenue. Other key tests are cut-off tests and directional testing (for completeness).

### 5. Key audit procedures for prepayments

Key procedures for prepayments are recalculation, analytical procedures and vouching to supporting documentation such as external invoices.

# Further study guidance

## Question practice

Now try the following from the Further question practice bank [available in the digital edition of the Workbook]:

Section A Q9, Q10, and Q43 on trade receivables

Section A Q40 on revenue

Section B Q81 'Bright Sparks' on trade receivables procedures

## Further reading

There is one technical article on the ACCA website written by members of the AA examining team which are relevant to some of the topics covered in this chapter that you should read:

* *The audit of assertions* https://www.accaglobal.com/gb/en/student/exam-support-resources/fundamentals-exams-study-resources/f8/technical-articles/assertions.html

## Own research

You could read ISA 505 *External Confirmations* available on the IFAC website.

# Activity answers

## Activity 1: Aged receivables listing

1    The balance of $11,800,000 due from Jasco Supermarket is the largest balance owed and $5,900,000 of this has been outstanding for 90 days or more. The supermarket gets 60-days credit but any issues with the recoverability of this amount could impact the financial statements.

There are old balances due from:

- Clothing Terrain ($2,000)
- Fred's Fashions ($4,000)
- Holly Aristocrat ($12,000)
- Ivory Gowns ($2,000)
- Look the Part ($1,000)

These balances would need to be investigated to assess the likelihood of payment being received.

Everyday Wear has a credit balance of $6,000 of their account. Why is this and should this amount be shown as a payable rather than a receivable?

2    Inspect/review the aged receivables listing for old, overdue and unusual amounts. Discuss the recoverability/accounting treatment of these items with management to ensure that receivables are appropriately valued in the financial statements.

## Activity 2: Post year end cash receipts

1    Jasco Supermarket has only paid $5,680,000 out of the $11,800,000 owed at the year-end. However, because the supermarket gets 60-days credit, the amount which should have been paid in October and November is $5,900,000 ($2,300,000 + $3,600,000). This means that there is an amount of $220,000 which should have been paid but which has not.

Clothing Terrain has paid all but $2,000 of the amount due at the year-end. The $2,000 outstanding may well relate to the balance due > 90 days and so the recoverability of this amount could be doubtful.

There has been no movement on the $6,000 credit balance of Everyday Wear.

Fred's Fashions Terrain has paid all but $4,000 of the amount due at the year-end. The $4,000 outstanding may well relate to the balance due > 90 days and so the recoverability of this amount could be doubtful.

Holly Aristocrat has paid all but $10,000 of the amount due at the year-end. There was a balance of $12,000 due > 90 days at the year end. Again, the recoverability of this amount could be doubtful.

Ivory Gowns has not paid any of the $2,000 due at the year-end. This balance is already due > 90 days and it does not look like there has been any continued trade with the customer. The recoverability of this amount is likely to be doubtful.

Odd One Out has paid all but $5,000 of the amount due at the year-end. There does not appear to be any particular reason for this.

We're Going Exploring does not appear to have paid the $7,000 which has been due for 90 days. The reason for this needs to be investigated.

2    Review post year-end cash receipts for evidence that the balance exists, is due to the audit client and is recoverable.

## Activity 3: Post year end credit notes

1    **Further evidence – receivables**

The $220,000 which should have been paid by Jasco Supermarket in October/November but was not related to a disputed invoice. Given that a credit has been issued for this amount post year-end, the balance was not an asset at the year-end and an adjustment should be made to the financial statements to reduce both revenue and receivables by $220,000. The same point applies to the credit notes issued to Holly Aristocrat and Odd One Out. These amounts should be removed from revenue and receivables at the year-end.

2   Review credit notes issued to customers post year-end. Where the credit note relates to a pre year-end invoice, discuss the need for an adjustment in the financial statements in order to ensure that receivables are appropriately valued at the year-end.

## Activity 4: Audit procedures

The correct answer is: Evaluation of the adequacy of the allowance for receivables

Automated tools and techniques can be used to extract samples and perform calculations but they cannot evaluate this information.

## Activity 5: External confirmation

Dress for the Occasion:

- Trace the cash in transit of $39,000 to the cash receipts book post year-end. Vouch that it was received within a few days of the year-end.

Fred's Fashions and Jasco Supermarket:

- Discuss the reason for the disputed invoice with management and review the customer correspondence file for any additional information.

- Enquire from management whether a credit note has been issued post year-end in relation to this and physically verify the credit note.

- If no credit note has been issued, discuss recoverability of the amount with credit control/management.

Girls on the Go and Upward Trends:

- Inspect the GDNs numbers 127057 and 127058, and determine the date on which the goods were dispatched. If goods were not dispatched until after the year-end, request that management remove the amount from revenue and receivables and record the goods as inventory at the year-end.

# 15

# Bank and cash

## Learning objectives

On completion of this chapter, you should be able to:

| Syllabus learning outcomes | Syllabus reference no. |
| --- | --- |
| Explain the audit objectives and the audit procedures to obtain sufficient, appropriate evidence in relation to: Bank and cash: | D4 (d) |
| (a) Bank confirmation reports used in obtaining evidence in relation to bank and cash | |
| (b) Other evidence in relation to bank | |
| (c) Other evidence in relation to cash | |

## Business and Exam context

Many candidates who sit the ACCA Audit and Assurance (AA) exam do not work in audit practice. This can make it harder to see the practical nature of the subject and to learn to apply the knowledge learned. Consequently, we have tried to make this chapter relating to substantive procedures as practical as possible, so that you can apply your knowledge to exam scenarios.

Work on cash and bank will concentrate on the completeness and valuation assertions using the bank reconciliation, bank confirmation letter and counting of cash as key audit tests.

In the exam you may be asked to identify and explain audit procedures you would perform to confirm specific assertions relating to cash and bank. Shorter constructed response question requirements and OT questions in Section A may also ask for audit procedures specifically used to obtain bank confirmation letters.

Remember that the bank confirmation letter contains the balance held by the client at the bank **per the bank's records**. This must be **reconciled** to the balance held with the bank **per the client's records**. When suggesting audit procedures for verifying bank balances, although the bank confirmation letter is important, do **not forget to suggest other procedures** related to the year-end bank reconciliation. Previous candidates have lost out on marks for not focusing enough on these procedures.

# Chapter overview

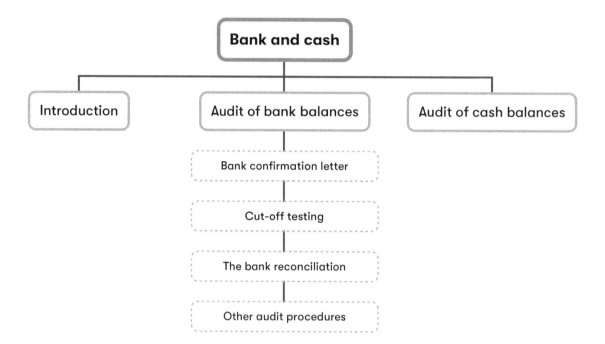

BPP

# 1 Introduction

'Cash' in the financial statements represents cash in hand and cash on deposit in bank accounts. Most accounting transactions pass through the cash account, so cash is affected by all of the entity's business processes. In this chapter, we will consider the substantive audit testing applied to the year-end cash figure.

**Essential reading**

See Chapter 15 of the Essential reading for the assertions that apply to bank and cash.

The Essential reading is available as an Appendix of the digital edition of the Workbook.

# 2 Audit of bank balances

Throughout the chapter, we will continue to use the audit of Dress You Like Co for the year ended 30 September 20X6. The audit team has prepared the following lead schedule for the bank balances of Dress You Like Co for the current year audit:

Reference:

Client: Dress You Like Co

Prepared by:

Reviewed by:

|  | Draft 20X6 $'000 | Dr $'000 | Cr $'000 | Final 20X6 $'000 | Actual 20X5 $'000 |
|---|---|---|---|---|---|
| Bank | 0 |  |  |  | 200 |
| Bank overdraft | (750) |  |  |  | 0 |
|  | (750) |  |  |  | 200 |

## 2.1 Bank confirmation letter

A common procedure for the audit of an entity's bank balances is for the auditor to obtain direct confirmation from the entity's banker(s) of balances and other amounts which appear in the statement of financial position and of other information which may be disclosed in the notes to the financial statements, for example guarantees.

Bank confirmation letters are a valuable source of audit evidence because they come directly from an **independent source** and, therefore, provide greater assurance of reliability than evidence obtained solely from the client's own records. They are mentioned in ISA 505 *External Confirmations* (para. A1).

The procedure is carried out as follows:

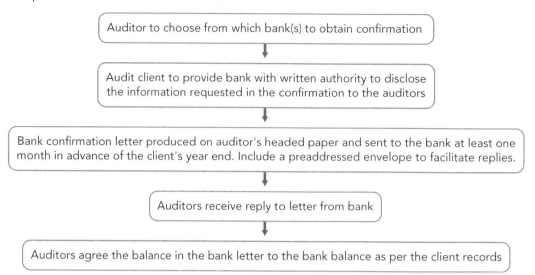

### 2.1.1 Choosing where to send a confirmation request

The following matters will impact the auditor's decision as to which of the audit client's bank or banks to send a bank confirmation letter to:

- Size of balance
- Volume of activity
- Degree of reliance on internal control
- Materiality to the financial statements

### 2.1.2 Written authority

Banks require written authority from their customers to disclose the information requested by the auditors in a bank confirmation letter. This often takes the form of an ongoing standing authority rather than a separate authority each time information is requested.

The auditors' request must refer to the client's letter of authority and the date given in it. Alternatively, it may be countersigned by the client or it may be accompanied by a specific letter of authority. In the case of joint bank accounts, letters of authority signed by all parties will be necessary.

### 2.1.3 Preparation and despatch of the bank confirmation letter

Control over the content and dispatch of confirmation requests is the responsibility of the auditor.

The auditors should determine which of the following approaches is the most appropriate in seeking confirmation of balances or other information from the bank.

| **Listing balances** and other information, and requesting confirmation of their accuracy and completeness | **Requesting details of balances** and other information, which can then be compared with the requesting client's records |
|---|---|

In determining which of the above approaches is the most appropriate, the auditors should weigh the **quality** of **audit evidence** they require in the particular circumstances against the **practicality** of obtaining a reply from the confirming bank. The most commonly requested information is in respect of balances due to, or from, the client entity on current, deposit, loan and other accounts. The request letter should provide the account description number and the type of currency for the account.

It may also be advisable to request information about nil balances on accounts, and accounts which were closed in the 12 months prior to the chosen confirmation date. The client entity may ask for confirmation not only of the balances on accounts but also, where it may be helpful, of other information, such as the maturity and interest terms on loans and overdrafts, unused facilities, lines of credit/standby facilities, any offset or other rights or encumbrances, and details of any collateral given or received.

The client entity and its auditors are likely to request confirmation of contingent liabilities, such as those arising on guarantees, comfort letters and bills. Banks often hold securities and other items in safe custody on behalf of customers. A request letter may therefore ask for confirmation of such items held by the bank.

## Essential reading

See Chapter 15 of the Essential reading for further details and an example of a bank confirmation request letter.

The Essential reading is available as an Appendix of the digital edition of the Workbook.

### 2.1.4 Replies

Replies should be returned directly to the auditors and the auditors should check that the bank's response covers all the information requested. Difficulty may be encountered in obtaining a satisfactory response even where the client company submits information for confirmation to the confirming bank. It is important that a response is sought for all confirmation requests. Auditors should not request a response only if the information submitted is incorrect or incomplete.

### 2.1.5 Agreement to client records

For any response received, the auditors must agree the amounts in the bank confirmation letter to the bank balance in the client's accounting records. Any differences will need to be investigated as they could indicate a misstatement in the cash figure given in the financial statements.

## 2.2 Cut-off testing

When auditing cash balances, care must be taken to ensure that there is no **window dressing**, by auditing **cut-off** carefully. Window dressing in this context is usually manifested as an attempt to overstate the liquidity of the company by:

(a) Keeping the cash book open to take credit for remittances actually received after the year end, thus **enhancing the balance at bank** and reducing receivables

(b) Recording cheques paid in the period under review which are not actually despatched until after the year end, thus **decreasing the balance at bank** and reducing liabilities

A combination of (a) and (b) can contrive to present an artificially healthy looking current ratio.

With the possibility of (a) above in mind, where lodgements have not been cleared by the bank until the new period, the auditors should **examine the paying-in slip** to ensure that the amounts were actually paid into the bank on or before the period-end date.

As regards (b) above, where there appears to be a particularly **large number of outstanding cheques** at the year end, the auditors should check whether these were **cleared within a reasonable time** in the new period. If not, this may indicate that despatch occurred after the year end.

As you can see, performing cut-off testing for transactions at the end of the reporting period gives assurance over the **completeness** and **existence** of cash balances at that date.

## Activity 1: Bank reconciliation

Below is the bank reconciliation of Dress You Like Co as at 30 September 20X6:

Dress You Like Co

Bank Reconciliation 30 September 20X6

|  | $ | $ |
|---|---|---|
| Balance per bank statement 30 September 20X6 | | (758,389) |
| Add: deposits outstanding | | |
| 29 September (ref 1122) | 10,222 | |
| 30 September (ref 1123) | 25.000 | 35,222 |
| | | (723,167) |
| Less: outstanding cheques | | |
| 2411 | 10,250 | |
| 2721 | 2,300 | |
| 2722 | 5,000 | |
| 2723 | 1,345 | |
| 2724 | 1,900 | |
| 2726 | 2,200 | |
| 2728 | 1,006 | |
| 2729 | 1,577 | |
| 2730 | 1,255 | 26,833 |
| Balance per bank in the general ledger | | (750,000) |

1   Consider the information in the bank reconciliation above.

   **Required**

   (a)  Which of the outstanding cheques might require investigation and why?

   (b)  Describe an audit procedure you would perform in relation to the outstanding cheques, documenting the reason for this procedure.

2   Describe audit procedures you would perform in relation to the deposits outstanding, documenting the reason for these procedures.

3   Describe any other audit procedures you would carry out on the bank reconciliation of Dress You Like Co, making sure you document the reason for each procedure.

**Solution**

## 2.3 Audit procedures for bank

The following table contains audit procedures for bank matched to the financial statement assertions they test. This table is for reference only, the procedures should not be learned by heart, but may be useful when practising exam questions.

| Financial statement assertion | Audit procedure |
|---|---|
| Completeness and existence | • **Obtain standard bank confirmations** from each bank with which the client conducted business during the audit period.<br><br>• **Trace cheques shown as outstanding** from the bank reconciliation to the cash book prior to the year end and to the **after-date bank statements** and **obtain explanations** for any **large orunusual items** not cleared at the time of the audit.<br><br>• **Compare cash book(s)** and **bank statements** in detail for the last month of the year, and **match items outstanding** at the reconciliation date to bank statements.<br><br>• Obtain satisfactory explanations for **all items** in the **cash book** for which there are **no corresponding entries** in the **bank statement** and vice versa by **discussion** with finance staff. |
| Valuation | • **Reperform** arithmetic of bank reconciliation.<br><br>• **Review bank reconciliation** previous to the year-end bank reconciliation and test whether **all items** are **cleared** in the last period or **taken forward** to the year-end bank reconciliation.<br><br>• **Verify contra items** appearing in the cash book or bank statements with the original entry.<br><br>• Verify by **inspecting** paying-in slips that **uncleared bankings** are **paid in** prior to the year end.<br><br>• **Examine all lodgements** in respect of which payment has been refused by the bank; ensure that they are cleared on re-presentation or that other appropriate steps have been taken to effect recovery of |

| Financial statement assertion | Audit procedure |
|---|---|
| | the amount due. <br> • **Verify** the **bank balances** with reply to **standard bank letter** and with the **bank statements**. <br> • **Inspect** the cash book and bank statements before and after the year end for **exceptional entries** or **transfers** which have a material effect on the balance shown to be in-hand. |
| Rights and obligations | • Determine whether the bank accounts are **subject** to any **restrictions** by **enquiries** with management. |
| Classification | • Identify whether any **accounts** are **secured** on the **assets** of the company by **discussion** with management. <br> • **Consider** whether there is a **legal right** of **set-off** of overdrafts against positive bank balances. <br> • **Review draft accounts** to ensure that disclosures for bank are complete and accurate and in accordance with accounting standards. |

# 3  Audit of cash balances

Cash balances/floats are often individually immaterial but they may require some audit emphasis because of the opportunities for fraud that could exist where internal control is weak and because they may be material in total.

However, in enterprises such as hotels and retail organisations, the amount of cash-in-hand at the period end could be considerable. Cash counts may be important for internal auditors, who have a role in fraud prevention.

Auditors will be concerned that the cash **exists**, is **complete**, belongs to the company (**rights and obligations**) and is stated at the correct **value**.

Where the auditors determine that cash balances are potentially material they may conduct a **cash count**, ideally at the period end. Rather like attendance at an inventory count, the conduct of the count falls into three phases: planning, the count itself, and follow-up procedures.

### Essential reading

See Chapter 15 of the Essential reading for details of planning, performing and following up a cash count.

The Essential reading is available as an Appendix of the digital edition of the Workbook.

# Chapter summary

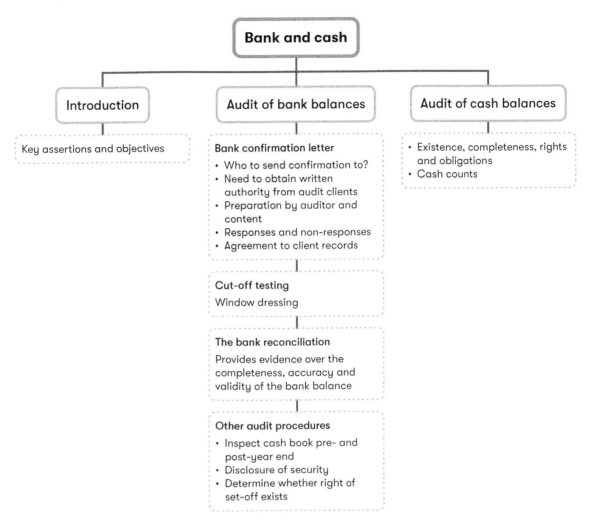

**Bank and cash**

**Introduction**

Key assertions and objectives

**Audit of bank balances**

Bank confirmation letter
- Who to send confirmation to?
- Need to obtain written authority from audit clients
- Preparation by auditor and content
- Responses and non-responses
- Agreement to client records

Cut-off testing

Window dressing

The bank reconciliation

Provides evidence over the completeness, accuracy and validity of the bank balance

Other audit procedures
- Inspect cash book pre- and post-year end
- Disclosure of security
- Determine whether right of set-off exists

**Audit of cash balances**
- Existence, completeness, rights and obligations
- Cash counts

# Knowledge diagnostic

### 1. Definition of cash

'Cash' in the financial statements represents cash-in-hand and cash on deposit in bank accounts.

### 2. Bank confirmation letters

Bank confirmation letters are a reliable source of evidence in respect of the main financial statement assertions relating to bank and cash.

### 3. Bank authority letter

Audit clients must provide **written authority** to their banks so the banks can respond to the auditor's confirmation request.

### 4. Bank reconciliation

The client's **bank reconciliation** must also be tested in detail, in order to verify that reconciling items are genuine.

### 5. Cash counts

If cash-in-hand is material the auditor will perform a cash count.

# Further study guidance

## Question practice

Now try the following from the Further question practice bank [available in the digital edition of the Workbook]:

- Section B Q82 on the audit of cash and bank

## Further reading

There is one technical article on the ACCA website written by members of the AA examining team which are relevant to some of the topics covered in this chapter that you should read:

- *The audit of assertions* (https://www.accaglobal.com/gb/en/student/exam-support-resources/fundamentals-exams-study-resources/f8/technical-articles/assertions.html)

## Own research

After you have read the essential reading, read section of ISA 505 External confirmations (on the IAASB website) called 'Management's Refusal to Allow the Auditor to Send a Confirmation Request' to see what the auditor should do when management doesn't give permission to the auditor to send a bank confirmation letter.

 **BPP**

# Activity answers

## Activity 1: Bank reconciliation

1 Considerations:

(a) The outstanding cheque for $10,250 has a reference (2411) which appears to suggest it was raised much earlier in the year than the others and the fact it has not cleared is unusual. Enquiries should be made in respect of this outstanding cheque.

(b) Trace the cheques shown as outstanding on the bank reconciliation to the cash book prior to the year end. Ensure they have cleared the bank by looking at the after-date bank statements to ensure that the bank balance is not understated. Obtain explanations for any that have not cleared at the time of the audit.

2 Verify that the uncleared bankings (deposits outstanding – ref 1122 and 1123) were paid in prior to the year-end by checking paying-in slips to ensure that they should be recorded in the year being audited.

Review whether the uncleared bankings cleared quickly after the year end. Any that have not cleared soon after the year end should be investigated as they could indicate window-dressing and an overstatement of the cash balance.

3 **Further audit procedures – bank reconciliation**

- Agree the balance per bank statement at 30 September 20X6 as shown on the reconciliation ($758,389) to the bank statement and to the amount for that account shown on the bank confirmation letter.

- Test arithmetic of bank reconciliation by recasting it.

- Review the bank reconciliation previous to the year-end bank reconciliation (31 August 20X6 reconciliation if carried out monthly) and test whether items shown on it cleared in the last period or have been taken forward to the bank reconciliation at 30 September 20X6.

- Verify that the year-end balance per the general ledger according to the reconciliation ($750,000) agrees with the general ledger account balance at 30 September 20X6 and that this has been properly reflected in the financial statements.

# 16

# Payables and accruals

## Learning objectives

On completion of this chapter, you should be able to:

| Syllabus learning outcomes | Syllabus reference no. |
|---|---|
| Explain the audit objectives and the audit procedures to obtain sufficient, appropriate evidence in relation to: Payables and accruals: | D4 (c) |
| (a) Supplier statement reconciliations and direct confirmation of accounts payable | |
| (b) Obtain evidence in relation to payables and accruals | |
| (c) Obtain evidence in relation to current liabilities | |
| (d) Purchases and other expenses, including payroll | |
| Explain the audit considerations relating to entities using service organisations. | D6 (c) |

## Business and Exam context

Many candidates who sit the ACCA AA exam do not work in audit practice. This can make it harder to see the practical nature of the subject and to learn to apply the knowledge learned. Consequently, we have tried to make this chapter relating to substantive procedures as practical as possible, so that you can apply your knowledge to exam scenarios.

In this chapter, we examine the audit of payables, purchases, accruals and payroll. When auditing payables, the auditor must test for understatement (ie completeness). Rather than circularising payables, it is more common to obtain audit evidence from suppliers' statements.

You may be asked to identify and explain audit procedures you would perform to confirm specific assertions relating to payables and accruals. For example, you may be asked for the substantive audit procedures in respect of payroll or administrative expenses.

Every type of liability covered in this chapter can form the basis of a constructed response question in the exam, either in full or in part. The audit procedures and financial statement assertions can also be tested in the form of OT questions in Section A.

# Chapter overview

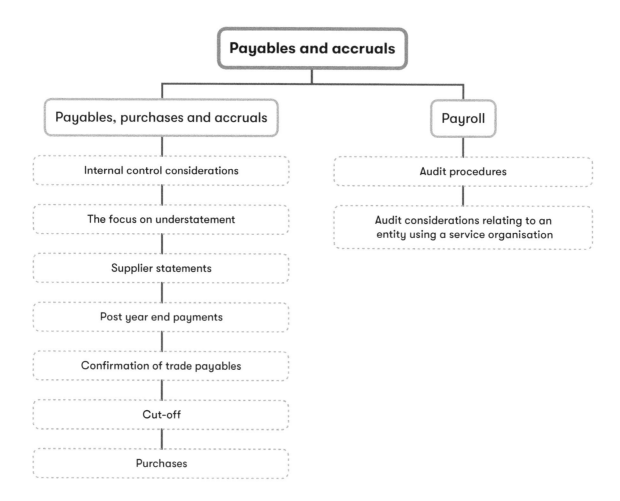

BPP

# 1 Payables, purchases and accruals

## 1.1 Internal control considerations

The audit of payables is closely linked to the purchases system. We looked at controls over the purchases system in Section 3 of Chapter 10, where we saw that they were based around ensuring purchases were authorised, the segregation of duties, matching GRNs with invoices, and prompt recording to minimise cut-off issues.

A specific control often operated by clients over the completeness of trade payables balances is the reconciliation of month-end balances to supplier statements. If the client has carried out this reconciliation at the year-end for all suppliers, the auditor can review these reconciliations.

However, if the client has not carried out these reconciliations, the auditor will need to compare supplier statements with year-end payables balances and investigate differences, so this becomes a substantive procedure that the auditor must undertake.

## 1.2 The focus on understatement

As with accounts receivable, accounts payable are likely to be a material figure in the statement of financial position of most enterprises. The tests of controls on the purchases cycle (Chapter 10) will have provided the auditors with some assurance as to the completeness of liabilities.

However, auditors should be particularly aware, when conducting their work on the statement of financial position, of the possibility of **understatement** of **liabilities** to improve liquidity and profits (by understating the corresponding purchases). The primary objective of their work will therefore be to ascertain whether **liabilities** existing at the year-end have been **completely** and **accurately recorded**.

As regards **trade accounts payable**, this primary objective can be subdivided into two detailed objectives:

| | |
|---|---|
| Is there a **satisfactory cut-off** between goods received and invoices received, so that purchases and trade accounts payable are recognised in the correct year? | Do trade accounts payable represent the *bona fide* amounts due by the company? |

### Essential reading

See Chapter 16 of the Essential reading for further details on the assertions that apply to trade payables, purchases and accruals.

The Essential reading is available as an Appendix of the digital edition of the Workbook.

Throughout this chapter we will continue to use the audit of Dress You Like Co for the year ended 30 September 20X6. The audit team has prepared the following lead schedule for the audit of payables and accruals of Dress You Like Co for the current year:

Reference:

Client: Dress You Like Co

Prepared by:

Reviewed by:

Date: 1/11/X6

|  | Draft 20X6 | Dr | Cr | Final 20X6 | Actual 20X5 |
|---|---|---|---|---|---|
|  | $'000 | $'000 | $'000 | $'000 | $'000 |
| Payables: |  |  |  |  |  |
| Trade | 2,060 |  |  |  | 1,470 |
| Other | 500 |  |  |  | 450 |
|  | 2,560 |  |  |  | 1,920 |

## 1.3 Supplier statements

### Activity 1: Supplier statements

Dress You Like Co receives supplier statements on a monthly basis from all suppliers, including the main overseas supplier LHT Co. Other small suppliers provide mainly sundry items such as zips, buttons and threads. The supplier statement from LHT Co is reconciled to the purchase ledger account but supplier statements from the other suppliers are not. Check & Co have selected balances from a sample of suppliers as at 30 September 20X6.

| Supplier name | Supplier statement balance | Purchase ledger balance |
|---|---|---|
|  | $'000 | $'000 |
| Freda's Fabrics | 155 | 92 |
| Threads for You | 78 | 78 |
| Material Matters | 85 | 85 |
| Wickhams Wools | 33 | 33 |
| David Designs | 32 | 32 |
| Fabricated | 200 | 106 |
| Sang Silks | 25 | 25 |
| Dot's Cottons | 102 | 102 |
| Three Linens Co | 100 | 65 |
| Penelope Prints Shop | 198 | 142 |
| LHT Co | 1,300 | 1,300 |
| Total | 2,308 | 2,060 |

**Required**

1   Which of the payables balances would you investigate and why?

2   Write out the audit procedure you have conducted above documenting the reason for the audit procedure.

Solution

## Essential reading

See Chapter 16 of the Essential reading for further details on supplier statement testing.

The Essential reading is available as an Appendix of the digital edition of the Workbook.

## 1.4 Post year end payments

### Activity 2: Post year end payments

The following is a schedule of work performed on post year end payments by the audit team at Dress You Like Co. The work covers the period immediately after the year-end:

| Date of payment | Amount paid $'000 | Explanation | Included in purchase ledger or accruals? |
|---|---|---|---|
| 1/10/20X6 | 25 | | Yes |
| 1/10/20X6 | 36 | Payment for invoice to Freda's Fabrics dated 12/09/20X6 | No |
| 2/10/20X6 | 44 | | Yes |
| 2/10/20X6 | 21 | | Yes |
| 3/10/20X6 | 15 | | Yes |
| 3/10/20X6 | 98 | | Yes |
| 4/10/20X6 | 63 | | Yes |
| 4/10/20X6 | 51 | | Yes |
| 5/10/20X6 | 35 | Payment for invoice to Three Linens Co dated 29/09/20X6 | No |
| 5/10/20X6 | 79 | Payment for invoice to Fabricated | No |

| Date of payment | Amount paid $'000 | Explanation | Included in purchase ledger or accruals? |
|---|---|---|---|
| | | dated 1/10/20X6 | |
| 6/10/20X6 | 20 | | Yes |
| 6/10/20X6 | 75 | | Yes |
| 7/10/20X6 | 65 | | Yes |
| 7/10/20X6 | 8 | Payment for internet, July–September 20X6 | No |

**Required**

1 Consider the information in the schedule above. What evidence does it provide about the payables balance at the year end?

2 Write out the audit procedure you have conducted above documenting the reason for the audit procedure.

**Solution**

## 1.5 Confirmation of trade payables

We have already discussed the receivables confirmation in Chapter 14. It is also possible to undertake confirmation of trade payables, although this is not used a great deal in practice because the auditor can test trade payables by examining **reliable, independent** evidence in the form of suppliers' invoices and statements.

However, where an entity's internal controls are assessed as deficient, suppliers' statements may not be available, and, in this situation, it may be relevant to undertake **confirmation** procedures. Confirmation of trade payables provides evidence primarily for the completeness assertion.

| Entity **has strong controls** in place to ensure all liabilities are recorded<br>• Confirm large balances | or | Entity **does not have strong controls** in place to ensure all liabilities are recorded<br>• Confirm large balances<br>• Confirm other suppliers with a small or zero balance<br>• Confirm a sample of other accounts |
|---|---|---|

Auditors use a **positive** confirmation, referred to as a **blank** or **zero-balance** confirmation. This confirmation **does not state the balance owed** but requires the supplier to declare the amount owed at the year-end and to provide a detailed statement of the account. When the confirmation is received back, the amount must be reconciled with the entity's records. Differences between the balance confirmed and that on the payables ledger are likely to be for reasons that are similar to those for the receivables confirmation, ie goods in transit, cash in transit, or disputed invoices. Any differences should be **investigated** and **reconciled**.

The selection and sending out of accounts payables' confirmations should be controlled using the same procedures as for the receivables' confirmation that we discussed in Chapter 14.

## 1.6 Cut-off

If a set of financial statements is to 'present fairly' the activities of a business, it is important that transactions and events have been recorded in the correct accounting period. Consequently, an auditor would perform 'cut-off' testing. Cut-off testing for trade payables is similar to the cut-off testing for revenue and inventory you have already learnt about in earlier chapters.

### Example - Cut-off testing

From the inventory count working papers of Dress You Like Co, the number of the last GRN that was issued before the year-end was noted. Check & Co selected a sample of GRNs issued in the period at least two weeks either side of the year-end.

Before year end

| GRN # | Date | Included in purchases ledger at 30/09/20X6 | Correctly recorded |
|---|---|---|---|
| 165258 | 30.9.X6 | Yes | Yes |
| 165259 | 30.9.X6 | Yes | Yes |
| 165260 | 30.9.X6 | No | No |

**After year end**

| GRN # | Date | Included in purchases ledger at 30/09/20X6 | Correctly recorded |
|---|---|---|---|
| 165261 | 1.10.X6 | Yes | No |
| 165262 | 1.10.X6 | No | Yes |
| 165263 | 2.10.X6 | No | Yes |

### 1.6.1 Other audit procedures: payables and accruals

The following table contains audit procedures for payables and accruals matched to the financial statement assertions they test. This table is for reference only, the procedures should not be learned by heart, but may be useful when practising exam questions.

| Financial statement assertion | |
|---|---|
| Completeness and existence | • Perform analytical procedures comparing payables and accruals to previous year-end, budgets or industry data, eg calculating payables payment period or compare accruals listing to prior year |
| Rights and obligations | • Vouch selected amounts from the trade accounts payables listing and accruals listing to supporting documentation such as purchase orders and suppliers' invoices |
| Valuation | • For a sample of accruals, recalculating the amount of the accrual to ensure the amount accrued is correct |
| Classification | • Review the trade accounts payables listing to identify and large debits (which should be reclassified as receivables or deposits) or long-term liabilities which should be disclosed separately |
| Presentation | • Read the disclosure notes relevant to payables and accruals in the draft financial statements to ensure the information is accurate and properly presented at the appropriate amounts |

## 1.7 Purchases

Auditing payables provides some evidence over the purchases expense but we would also perform other procedures such as analytical procedures.

### Example – Analytical review of purchases

Check & Co have prepared the below schedule which compares the purchases of Dress You Like Co for the year ending 30 September 20X6 with the purchases for the year ending 30 September 20X5. Performing analytical procedures on expenses can enable Check & Co to identify areas where further audit procedures may be required.

| Purchase | 30/09/20X6 | 30/09/20X5 | Difference | Difference |
|---|---|---|---|---|
| | $'000 | $'000 | $'000 | % |
| Fabric | 45,276 | 37,912 | 7,364 | 19% |
| Buckles, hooks and clips | 75 | 75 | – | 0% |
| Thread | 185 | 180 | 5 | 3% |
| Buttons | 89 | 89 | – | 0% |
| Zips | 50 | 75 | (25) | -33% |
| Beads and sequins | 102 | 66 | 36 | 55% |
| Payroll | 12,677 | 11,721 | 956 | 8% |
| Telephone and internet | 50 | 49 | 1 | 2% |
| Electricity | 85 | 82 | 3 | 4% |
| Insurance | 33 | 32 | 1 | 3% |

| Purchase | 30/09/20X6 | 30/09/20X5 | Difference | Difference |
|---|---|---|---|---|
| | $'000 | $'000 | $'000 | % |
| Equipment maintenance | 39 | 25 | 14 | 56% |
| Transportation costs | 145 | 189 | (44) | -23% |
| Other purchases | 469 | 485 | 16 | -3% |
| **Total cost of sales** | **59,275** | **50,980** | **8,295** | **16%** |

Looking at the schedule, we can see that the largest purchase for Dress You Like Co is fabric. This has increased by 19% since the prior year. The auditors will need to ascertain why this is. Perhaps the cost of fabrics has increased or Dress You Like Co is manufacturing more products and extra fabric is required. Or alternatively, there has been a misstatement and the figure for purchases of fabric is too high, due to an issue with cut-off of purchases, for example. Check & Co need to obtain evidence that the increase is genuine.

Further down the schedule, we can see that the purchases of zips have fallen by 33% which is unusual. Transportation costs have also fallen by 23% which seems strange. Both these variances will need further investigation by the auditors. There may be some costs missing which have been allocated incorrectly.

The figure for equipment maintenance has increased by 56% year on year. This may be a legitimate increase as the company's equipment ages over time. Or the increase might be due to a misclassification of costs from another area that should not be included in cost of sales. The same applies to the 55% increase in the cost of beads and sequins. Check & Co will need to look into both these increases.

Payroll has increased by 8% year on year and will be covered in the next section of this workbook.

### 1.7.1 Other audit procedures: purchases and other expenses

The following are procedures specifically related to the audit of purchases and other expenses:

- Inspect a sample of purchase invoices to ensure they agree to the amount posted to the general ledger.
- Compare expenses making up administrative expenses to the prior year charge and to expectations on a line by line basis. Where differences from expectations are discovered they should be investigated.
- Enquire of management whether there are any unsettled claims or obligations arising before the year end and ensure these are provided for (to give evidence over the completeness of the charge in the related expense category in the statement of profit or loss)
- Recalculate accruals and prepayments to gain evidence that other expenses are not over or understated.
- Compare gross profit margin with the previous year, the gross margin per the budget and expectations. Investigate any unexpected fluctuations.

## 2 Payroll

One expense that may make up a significant proportion of expenses is the wages cost included in the statement of profit or loss. It is important you know procedures that can be used when auditing this area.

## Activity 3: Payroll Expense

The management accounts of Dress You Like Co contain the following schedule which compares the payroll expense for the years ending 30 September 20X6 and 30 September 20X5:

### Payroll expense

|  | Oct | Nov | Dec | Jan | Feb | Mar |
| --- | --- | --- | --- | --- | --- | --- |
|  | $'000 | $'000 | $'000 | $'000 | $'000 | $'000 |
| 20X4-20X5 | 933 | 1,165 | 1,180 | 936 | 937 | 937 |
| 20X5-20X6 | 980 | 1,254 | 1,508 | 990 | 995 | 989 |

|  | Apr | May | Jun | Jul | Aug | Sep | Total |
| --- | --- | --- | --- | --- | --- | --- | --- |
|  | $'000 | $'000 | $'000 | $'000 | $'000 | $'000 | $'000 |
| 20X4-20X5 | 937 | 937 | 937 | 940 | 942 | 940 | 11,721 |
| 20X5-20X6 | 988 | 991 | 992 | 993 | 999 | 998 | 12,677 |

### Required

1 Consider the information in the above schedule. Explain any matters that might require investigation.

2 Write out the audit procedure you have conducted above stating the objective of the audit procedure.

3 Can you suggest any other audit procedures you would perform on this schedule?

### Solution

## Activity 4: Payroll

The audit team at Check & Co have selected a sample of employees from the payroll records at Dress You Like Co. For each employee selected, Check & Co has agreed the monthly remuneration in the payroll records to the personnel records detailing salaries.

**Required**

Over which of the following assertions would the audit procedure detailed above provide evidence?

- ○ Completeness
- ○ Rights and obligations
- ○ Occurrence
- ○ Existence

## 2.1 Other audit procedures: payroll

Other audit procedures that auditors may perform on payroll are as follows:

(a) Reconcile the gross costs on the payroll to the wages cost in the financial statements.

(b) Reperform casts of payroll records to confirm completeness and accuracy of costs used as a basis for the journals to the financial statements.

(c) Confirm payment of net pay per payroll records to cheque or bank transfer summary.

(d) Inspect payroll for unusual items and investigate them further by discussion with management.

(e) Perform proof-in-total (analytical procedures) on payroll by multiplying estimated average wage (using last year's figures plus expected increases) by average number of employees (therefore incorporating starters and leavers) and compare to figure in draft financial statements to assess reasonableness. Investigate any significant differences by discussing with management.

(f) Reperform calculations of statutory deductions to establish whether valid deductions have been included in the payroll expense

(g) Select a sample of employees from the payroll and recalculate their gross and net pay.

(h) Select a sample of employees from the payroll and agree their pay in the payroll records to personnel records such as employment contracts

(i) Select a sample of employees who have joined or left the organisation during the year. Agree their start/leaving date to supporting documentation such as an employment contract or resignation letter. Ensure that the employee has been added to/removed from the payroll in the correct month. Recalculate the payroll for the month of joining/leaving to ensure its accuracy.

## 2.2 Audit considerations relating to an entity using a service organisation

Many companies now outsource some aspects of their business activities to external service organisations, including payroll.

**KEY TERM**

> **Service organisation:** "A third-party organisation that provides services to user entities that are part of those entities' information systems relevant to financial reporting." (ISA 402: para. 8(e))
>
> **User entity:** "An entity that uses a service organisation and whose financial statements are being audited." (ISA 402: para. 8(i))
>
> **User auditor:** "An auditor who audits and reports on the financial statements of a user entity." (ISA 402: para. 8(h))
>
> **Service auditor:** "An auditor who, at the request of the service organisation, provides an assurance report on the controls of a service organisation." (ISA 402: para. 8(d))

Other examples of where service organisations may be used include the maintenance of accounting records, credit control and data entry or information processing.

ISA 402 *Audit Considerations Relating to an Entity Using a Service Organisation* provides guidance to auditors whose clients use such an organisation.

 ## Essential reading

See Chapter 16 of the Essential reading for further details regarding audit considerations relating to an entity using a service organisation.

The Essential reading is available as an Appendix of the digital edition of the Workbook.

# Chapter summary

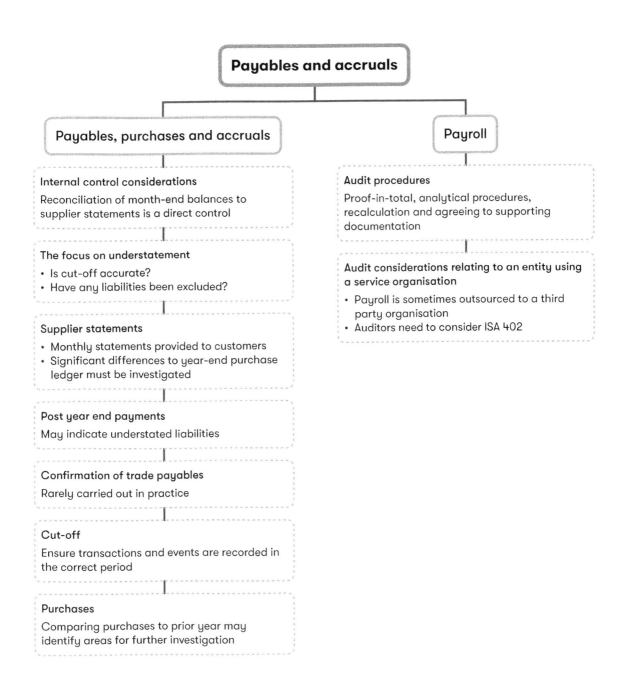

**Payables and accruals**

**Payables, purchases and accruals**

**Internal control considerations**
Reconciliation of month-end balances to supplier statements is a direct control

**The focus on understatement**
- Is cut-off accurate?
- Have any liabilities been excluded?

**Supplier statements**
- Monthly statements provided to customers
- Significant differences to year-end purchase ledger must be investigated

**Post year end payments**
May indicate understated liabilities

**Confirmation of trade payables**
Rarely carried out in practice

**Cut-off**
Ensure transactions and events are recorded in the correct period

**Purchases**
Comparing purchases to prior year may identify areas for further investigation

**Payroll**

**Audit procedures**
Proof-in-total, analytical procedures, recalculation and agreeing to supporting documentation

**Audit considerations relating to an entity using a service organisation**
- Payroll is sometimes outsourced to a third party organisation
- Auditors need to consider ISA 402

# Knowledge diagnostic

### 1. Key assertion

Substantive tests on liabilities will cover all the financial statement assertions for payables and accruals but with an emphasis on testing for **understatement,** ie completeness.

### 2. Supplier statement reconciliations

The largest figure in **current liabilities** will normally be **trade accounts payable** which is generally audited by comparison of **suppliers' statements** with **purchase ledger accounts**.

### 3. Payables confirmation

A trade payables confirmation may be carried out but is often not necessary as **supplier statements** will provide documentary evidence from third parties.

### 4. Auditing payroll

Key payroll audit procedures include analytical review, a proof-in-total, recalculation and agreement of key figures to supporting documentation.

### 5. Use of a service organisation

A **service organisation** provides services to user entities, such as processing payroll. There may be special considerations for the auditor of a user entity when that entity makes use of a service organisation.

# Further study guidance

## Question practice

Now try the following from the Further question practice bank [available in the digital edition of the Workbook]:

Section A Q46 on cut-off

Section B Q72b(i) 'Fenton Distributors' on audit procedures to verify the accuracy of purchases

Section B Q83 'Understatement' on payables and accruals

## Further reading

There are technical articles on the ACCA website written by members of the AA examining team which are relevant to some of the topics covered in this chapter that you should read:

*   *The audit of assertions:* https://www.accaglobal.com/gb/en/student/exam-support-resources/fundamentals-exams-study-resources/f8/technical-articles/assertions.html
*   *The audit of wages:* https://www.accaglobal.com/gb/en/student/exam-support-resources/fundamentals-exams-study-resources/f8/technical-articles/the-audit-of-wages.html

## Own research

Obtain a recent set of financial statements for an organisation and look for the trade payables, accruals and payroll balances.

Consider the business where you are employed. Does the business make use of a service organisation for payroll? Or any other areas?

# Activity answers

## Activity 1: Supplier statements

1   The purchase ledger balances for Freda's Fabrics, Fabricated, Three Linens Co and Penelope Prints Shop are higher than the balances in the supplier statements and should all be investigated. The difference totals $248k which is 12% of the total purchase ledger balance. The reason for each difference should be investigated as they could be indicative of an understatement of trade payables.

2   For a sample of suppliers, reconcile the year-end balance on the purchase ledger to the relevant supplier statement and investigate any differences. This will ensure completeness, existence and valuation of trade payables.

## Activity 2: Post year end payments

1   The payments to Freda's Fabrics and Three Linens Co both relate to invoices that were dated before the year end but have not been included in the year-end purchase ledger. This means the purchase ledger is understated by $71,000 and purchases are understated by the same amount. An adjustment should be proposed to include the $71,000 in payables and purchases. The payment to Fabricated is correctly excluded from the purchases ledger at year-end since it relates to an invoice received after the year-end. The $8,000 payment for internet has not been included in the accruals listing. Since it relates to the provision of internet during the year ending 30 September 20X6, this indicates an understatement of accruals. An adjustment to include the $8,000 in accruals and expenses should be proposed.

2   For a sample of post year end payments in the cash book, determine whether these relate to the year ending 30 September 20X6. If they do, vouch that these amounts have been included in the purchases ledger or accruals listing to ensure completeness of payables and accruals. This test looks for unrecorded liabilities.

## Activity 3: Payroll Expense

1   The payroll expense for November and December is significantly higher than the other months in both periods and will need investigation to ensure there is not a misstatement of the expense in these months. The increase could have a legitimate explanation such as the payment of bonuses, overtime or hiring of temporary staff for a busy period. The payroll expense for December 20X5 is $1,508,000 and seems particularly high, being 28% higher than the expense in December 20X4. This will need investigation to determine whether the increase is genuine or a potential material misstatement. Excluding November and December, the total payroll expense has increased by 6%. The reason for this needs to be investigated to ensure it is for a genuine reason (eg annual salary increases, increased number of staff) rather than a material misstatement.

2   Perform analytical procedures on the monthly payroll expense, comparing to the prior year and investigate any significant differences.

3   **Further audit procedures**

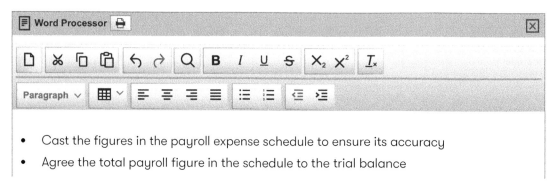

- Agree the 20X4-20X5 payroll figure to the prior year financial statements and audit documentation
- Agree the total payroll expense for all months in the schedule to the computerised wages system at Dress You Like Co
- Agree the total payroll expense for all months in the schedule to the bank statements and cash book of Dress You Like Co
- Compare the 20X5-20X6 monthly payroll expense to budgeted figures and enquire of management the reason for any significant differences

## Activity 4: Payroll

The correct answer is: Occurrence

Testing occurrence provides evidence that the transactions and events that have been recorded or disclosed have occurred and pertain to the entity. Note that existence is an assertion relating to account balances and related disclosures at the period end.

# 17

# Non-current liabilities, capital and directors' emoluments

## Learning objectives

On completion of this chapter, you should be able to:

| Syllabus learning outcomes | Syllabus reference no. |
|---|---|
| Explain the audit objectives and the audit procedures to obtain sufficient, appropriate evidence in relation to: | |
| Non-current liabilities, provisions and contingencies <br><br> (a) Evidence in relation to non-current liabilities, and <br><br> (b) Provisions and contingencies. | D4 (f) |
| Share capital, reserves and directors' emoluments: <br><br> (a) Evidence in relation to share capital, reserves and directors' emoluments. | D4 (g) |

## Business and Exam context

Many candidates who sit the ACCA Audit and Assurance (AA) exam do not work in audit practice. This can make it harder to see the practical nature of the subject and to learn to apply the knowledge learned. Consequently, we have tried to make this chapter relating to substantive procedures as practical as possible, so that you can apply your knowledge to exam scenarios.

In this chapter, we begin with the audit of non-current liabilities and provisions. Questions on long-term liabilities such as long-term loans may be linked to other areas you have studied in the AA syllabus. For example, as part of a question on going concern you may be required to list procedures to audit the ability of the company to repay a long-term loan. Procedures detailed in this chapter will be relevant, for instance, confirming the terms of the loan to a loan agreement or evidence of whether any covenants exist.

The audit of provisions is notoriously complex because of the degree of judgement used and the availability of sufficient audit evidence. This is likely to be tested in a mini scenario question so you must be able to apply your knowledge to the question's circumstances. For example, you may be asked for the substantive audit procedures in respect of a provision for legal claims.

The chapter ends looking at the audit of share capital, reserves and directors' emoluments. Every type of liability covered in this chapter can form the basis of a constructed response question in the exam, in full or in part. The audit procedures and financial statement assertions can also be tested in the form of OT questions in Section A or a longer Section B question.

# Chapter overview

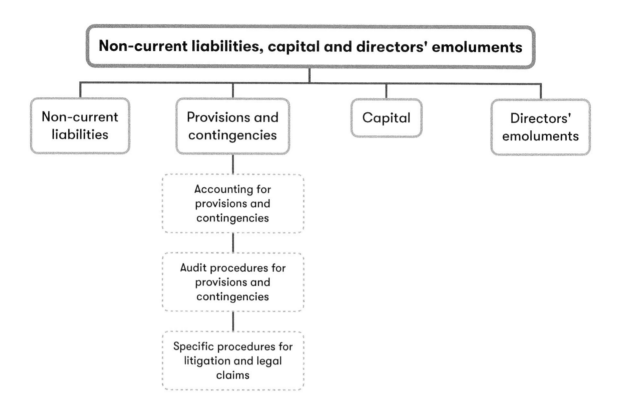

BPP

# 1 Non-current liabilities

Non-current liabilities include bank loans, debentures, and other loans repayable **more than one year after the year-end date.**

Auditors will primarily try to determine:

- **Completeness**: whether all non-current liabilities have been disclosed
- **Accuracy**: whether interest payable has been calculated correctly and included in the correct accounting period
- **Classification**: whether long-term loans and interest have been correctly disclosed in the financial statements

Audit procedures for non-current liabilities are as follows:

| Objective | Example tests |
|---|---|
| Existence | • Obtain direct confirmation from banks and other lenders of the amounts outstanding, accrued interest and what security they hold. |
| Rights and obligations | • Review direct confirmation letters from lenders. |
| Completeness | • Obtain breakdown of liabilities, compare to prior year audit working papers and for any items no longer included agree to:<br>  - Repayment amount in cash book<br>  - Inclusion as current liability if reclassified<br>• Review board minutes for evidence of any new borrowings which might not be recorded.<br>• Review cash book to ensure all new loans have been recorded. |
| Accuracy, valuation and allocation | • Perform proof in total of finance charges.<br>• Agree capital and interest amounts to confirmation letters.<br>• Recalculate finance charges agreeing interest rates to loan agreements. |
| Classification and presentation | • Review draft accounts and agree that liabilities are correctly classified as current/non-current by reference to the repayment dates in the loan agreements.<br>• Ensure disclosures are correct and in line with accounting standards by comparing disclosure to required disclosure per an accounting disclosure checklist. |

## Activity 1: Non-current liabilities

Dress You Like Co has provided Check & Co with the following schedule of non-current liabilities for the year ending 30 September 20X6:

**Non-current liabilities**

|  | Draft 20X6 | Actual 20X5 |
| --- | --- | --- |
|  | $'000 | $'000 |
| Loan with CR Bank | 2,597 | 2,896 |
|  | 2,597 | 2,896 |

**Required**

Which TWO of the following audit procedures would provide sufficient and appropriate audit evidence over the COMPLETENESS of this schedule?

☐ Review board minutes for discussions regarding long term borrowings

☐ Agree the loan interest rate to the loan agreement with CR Bank

☐ Review prior year audit working papers for any non-current liabilities no longer included

☐ Trace loan repayments to entries in the cash book

## Essential reading

See Chapter 17 of the Essential reading for additional considerations that should be made when auditing non-current liabilities.

The Essential reading is available as an Appendix of the digital edition of the Workbook.

# 2 Provisions and contingencies

## 2.1 Accounting for provisions and contingencies

## Essential reading

See Chapter 18 of the Essential reading for a summary of the accounting knowledge relevant to IAS 37: *Provisions, Contingent Liabilities and Contingent Assets* which is brought forward to this paper from your earlier Financial Accounting studies.

The Essential reading is available as an Appendix of the digital edition of the Workbook.

Accounting for provisions and contingencies is dictated by IAS 37 *Provisions, Contingent Liabilities and Contingent Assets* which provides the following definitions.

**KEY TERM**

**Provision:** a liability of uncertain timing or amount.

**Liability:** a present obligation of the entity arising from past events, the settlement of which is expected to result in an outflow from the entity of resources embodying economic benefits.

**Obligating event:** an event that creates a legal or constructive obligation that results in an entity having no realistic alternative to settling that obligation.

**Legal obligation:** an obligation that derives from:

(a) A contract (through its explicit or implicit terms);

(b) Legislation; or

(c) Other operation of law.

**Constructive obligation:** an obligation that derives from an entity's actions where:

(a) By an established pattern of past practice, published policies or a sufficiently specific current statement, the entity has indicated to other parties that it will accept certain responsibilities.

(b) As a result, the entity has created a valid expectation on the part of those other parties that it will discharge those responsibilities.

**Contingent liability:**

(a) A possible obligation that arises from past events and whose existence will be confirmed only by the occurrence or non-occurrence of one or more uncertain future events not wholly within the control of the entity; or

(b) A present obligation that arises from past events but is not recognised because:

  (i) It is not probable that an outflow of resources embodying economic benefits will be required to settle the obligation; or

  (ii) The amount of the obligation cannot be measured with sufficient reliability.

**Contingent asset:** a possible asset that arises from past events and whose existence will be confirmed only by the occurrence or non-occurrence of one or more uncertain future events not wholly within the control of the entity (*IAS 37: para. 10*).

## 2.2 Audit procedures for provisions and contingencies

Provisions and contingencies are examples of accounting estimates. They are particularly difficult to audit due to the degree of judgment required and the risk of manipulation. The audit of accounting estimates was covered in Chapter 12 Non-current Assets.

### Activity 2: Warranty provision

Check & Co have been provided with the following extracts of the draft accounts of Dress You Like Co for the year ending 30 September 20X6. Dress You Like Co make a warranty provision for faulty goods every year.

**Extract from the draft statement of profit and loss for the year ended 30 September 20X6**

|  | Draft 20X6 | Actual 20X5 |
| --- | --- | --- |
|  | $'000 | $'000 |
| Revenue (supermarket) | 53,500 | 49,000 |
| Revenue (other) | 8,200 | 6,700 |
| Total revenue | 61,700 | 55,700 |

**Extract from the draft statement of financial position as on 30 September 20X6**

|  | Draft 20X6 | Actual 20X5 |
| --- | --- | --- |
|  | $'000 | $'000 |
| Warranty provision | 263 | 279 |

**Required**

1 Which TWO of the following statements are MOST LIKELY to be true?

  ☐ There is a potential understatement of the warranty provision in the draft statement of financial position.

  ☐ There is a potential overstatement of the warranty provision in the draft statement of financial position.

☐ There is a potential understatement of the expense in the draft statement of profit and loss.

☐ There is a potential overstatement of the expense in the draft statement of profit and loss.

2   Which of the following audit procedures provides evidence over the completeness of the warranty provision?

    O   Enquiring of management as to why the warranty provision has fallen since the prior year

    O   Reviewing customer correspondence after year end for discussions relating to warranty claims

    O   Recalculation of the warranty provision

    O   Obtaining a copy of the warranty policy at Dress You Like Co and discussing this with management to gain a thorough understanding

## Essential reading

See Chapter 17 of the Essential reading for detailed audit procedures for provisions and contingencies.

The Essential reading is available as an Appendix of the digital edition of the Workbook.

## 2.3 Specific procedures for litigation and legal claims

Part of ISA 501 *Audit Evidence – Specific Considerations for Selected Items* covers contingencies relating to litigation and legal claims, which will represent the major part of audit work on contingencies. Litigation and claims involving the entity may have a material effect on the financial statements, and so will require adjustment to or disclosure in those financial statements.

## Essential reading

See Chapter 17 of the Essential reading for details of the audit procedures given in ISA 501 with regards to litigation and claims.

The Essential reading is available as an Appendix of the digital edition of the Workbook.

## Activity 3: Litigation

As part of a cost-cutting exercise at Dress You Like Co, the company froze the finance director's salary in 20X6 despite giving other directors a 5% salary increase. This decision was made based on the fact that the finance role was no more demanding than in previous years. Vinay Patel, the finance director, was not happy about this decision and left the company in March 20X6. He is now suing the company for constructive dismissal. Dress You Like Co has not made any provision or disclosure of this as they do not believe the ongoing claim has any merit.

**Required**

Describe the substantive procedures Check & Co should perform to obtain sufficient and appropriate evidence in relation to this litigation. Ensure you document the reason for each procedure.

Solution

# 3 Capital

Capital includes share capital, distributions and reserves the issued share capital as stated in the accounts must be **agreed** in total with the **share register**. An examination of transfers on a test basis should be made in those cases where a company handles its own registration work. Where the registration work is dealt with by independent registrars, auditors will normally examine the reports submitted by them to the company and obtain from them at the year-end a certificate of the share capital in issue.

The main concern with share capital and reserves is that the company has complied with the law. Auditors should check carefully whether clients have complied with local legislation about share issues or purchase of own shares. Auditors should take particular care if there are any movements in reserves that cannot be distributed and should confirm that these movements are **valid**.

Audit procedures for share capital, distributions and reserves are as follows:

| Share equity capital | • **Agree** the **authorised share capital** with the statutory documents governing the company's constitution. <br><br> • **Agree changes** to **authorised share capital** with **properly authorised resolutions**. |
|---|---|
| Issue of shares | • **Verify any issue** of share capital or other changes during the year with general and **board minutes**. <br><br> • **Ensure issue or change** is within the **terms** of the **constitution**, and directors possess appropriate **authority** to issue shares. <br><br> • **Confirm** that **cash** or **other consideration** has been **received** or **receivable(s) is included** as called-up share capital not paid. |
| Transfer of shares | • **Verify transfers of shares** by reference to: <br> - Correspondence <br> - Completed and stamped transfer forms <br> - Cancelled share certificates <br> - Minutes of directors' meeting |

| | |
|---|---|
| | • **Review the balances** on **shareholders' accounts** in the register of members and the total list with the amount of issued share capital in the general ledger. |
| Dividends | • **Agree dividends** paid and declared pre-year-end to **authority** in minute books and **reperform calculation** with **total share capital** issued to ascertain whether there are any outstanding or unclaimed dividends |
| | • **Agree dividend payments** to **documentary evidence** (say, the returned dividend warrants). |
| | • Test that **dividends do not contravene** distribution provisions by reviewing the legislation. |
| Reserves | • Agree **movements on reserves** to supporting authority. |
| | • **Ensure that movements on reserves do not contravene** the **legislation** and the company's constitution by reviewing the legislation. |
| | • **Confirm** that the **company** can **distinguish distributable** reserves from those that are **non-distributable**. |
| | • **Ensure that appropriate disclosures** of movements on reserves are made in the company's accounts by **inspection** of the financial statements. |

# 4 Directors' emoluments

Directors' emoluments are a sensitive area and would therefore be deemed to be material by their **nature**. It is important therefore that the disclosure of directors' emoluments is made accurately.

The table below lists some valid audit procedures when auditing directors' emoluments:

| Assertion | Example audit procedures |
|---|---|
| Existence | • Agree the directors' emoluments disclosed in the financial statements to a schedule of directors' emoluments for the year for each director. The schedule should show separately the individual components of emoluments: salary, bonuses, benefits, pension contributions and any other amounts such as 'golden hellos'. |
| | • Vouch salary and pension contribution amounts to monthly payroll records and bank statements. |
| | • Vouch bonuses and any 'one-off' payments to board meeting minutes and payroll records and bank statements. |
| Rights and obligations | • Verify the emoluments paid to directors during the year to their contracts of employment to ensure the directors' entitlements to these amounts. |
| Completeness | • Review board meeting/remuneration committee minutes to verify the amounts of any directors' bonuses and any other amounts and also to check that these payments have been appropriately authorised. |
| | • Review the cash book during the year and in the post year end period and ensure any significant sums have been appropriately accounted for. |
| | • |

| Assertion | Example audit procedures |
|---|---|
|  | • Ask directors to confirm in writing that the emoluments disclosed in the financial statements are complete and accurately recorded. |
|  | • Analytically review the directors' emoluments for each director in comparison to both the prior year emoluments and expected emoluments given the business's activities during the year. |
| Accuracy, valuation and allocation | • Re-cast the addition of the schedule of directors' emoluments. |
|  | • Verify that the amounts disclosed in the financial statements agree to this schedule. |
| Classification and presentation | • Obtain a copy of the returns made to the tax authorities in respect of each director and verify that all benefits have been properly disclosed in the financial statements. |
|  | • Review the adequacy of the disclosure in the directors' emoluments note to ensure it is in accordance with applicable accounting standards and local law. |

## Essential reading

See Chapter 17 of the Essential reading for additional considerations relating to director's emoluments.

The Essential reading is available as an Appendix of the digital edition of the Workbook.

## Activity 4: Director's emoluments

You are responsible for auditing the directors' emoluments of Dress You Like Co for the year ending 30 September 20X6 and have been provided with the information below:

|  | Fixed remuneration | | Variable remuneration | | |
|---|---|---|---|---|---|
|  | Salary | Pension | Bonuses | Incentive payments | Total |
|  | $ | $ | $ | $ | $ |
| G Lewis (Chair) | 120,000 | 40,000 | 90,000 | – | 250,000 |
| K Escombe (Chief Finance Officer) | 80,000 | 32,000 | 50,000 | – | 162,000 |
| M Batter (CEO) | 20,000 | 6,500 | 5,000 | 10,000 | 41,500 |
|  | 220,000 | 78,500 | 145,000 | 10,000 | 453,500 |

## Required

List the substantive procedures Check & Co should perform to obtain sufficient and appropriate evidence in relation to director's emoluments. Ensure you document the reason for each procedure.

**Solution**

---

# Chapter summary

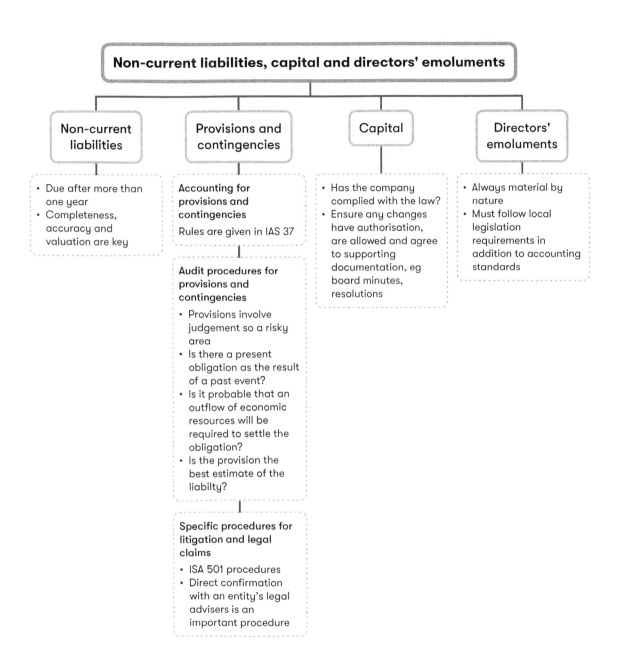

**Non-current liabilities, capital and directors' emoluments**

**Non-current liabilities**

- Due after more than one year
- Completeness, accuracy and valuation are key

**Provisions and contingencies**

**Accounting for provisions and contingencies**

Rules are given in IAS 37

**Audit procedures for provisions and contingencies**

- Provisions involve judgement so a risky area
- Is there a present obligation as the result of a past event?
- Is it probable that an outflow of economic resources will be required to settle the obligation?
- Is the provision the best estimate of the liabilty?

**Specific procedures for litigation and legal claims**

- ISA 501 procedures
- Direct confirmation with an entity's legal advisers is an important procedure

**Capital**

- Has the company complied with the law?
- Ensure any changes have authorisation, are allowed and agree to supporting documentation, eg board minutes, resolutions

**Directors' emoluments**

- Always material by nature
- Must follow local legislation requirements in addition to accounting standards

# Knowledge diagnostic

### 1. Non-current liabilities

Non-current liabilities are usually authorised by the board and should be well documented.

### 2. Key documentation relating to non-current liabilities

**Bank letters** and **loan agreements** will be key evidence in respect of loans.

### 3. Auditing provisions and contingencies

The accounting treatments for provisions and contingencies are complex and involve judgement and this can make them difficult to audit.

### 4. IAS 37 criteria

Procedures on provisions and contingencies will focus on the criteria established in accounting standards for their recognition, ie:

- Is there a **present obligation** as a result of past events?
- Is an outflow of benefits **probable**?
- Has the amount been **estimated reasonably**?

### 5. Share capital and reserves

The main concern with share capital and reserves is that the company has complied with the law.

### 6. Director's emoluments

Directors' emoluments are **material by their nature**.

### 7. Disclosure of directors' emoluments

The auditor will need to make sure the **disclosure** of directors' emoluments is complete, accurate and compliant with both applicable accounting standards and local legislation.

 BPP

# Further study guidance

## Question practice

Now try the following from the Further question practice bank [available in the digital edition of the Workbook]:

- Section A Q8 'Food Poisoning' looks at litigation and claims
- Section B Q67(e) 'Heels' covers audit procedures for a provision

## Further reading

There is a technical article on the ACCA website written by a member of the AA examining team which is relevant to some of the topics covered in this chapter that you should read:

- *The audit of assertions: https://www.accaglobal.com/gb/en/student/exam-support-resources/fundamentals-exams-study-resources/f8/technical-articles/assertions*.html

## Own research

- Think of a listed company you know. Look on their website for a copy of the report on their directors' remuneration.
- For the same company, find a copy of their most recent financial statements on their website. Does the company have any provisions or contingencies? Think about the audit procedures that might have been used to audit these. Are the provisions mentioned in the key audit matters section of the audit report?

 **BPP**

# Activity answers

### Activity 1: Non-current liabilities

The correct answers are:

- Review board minutes for discussions regarding long term borrowings
- Review prior year audit working papers for any non-current liabilities no longer included

### Activity 2: Warranty provision

1   The correct answers are:

- There is a potential understatement of the warranty provision in the draft statement of financial position.
- There is a potential understatement of the expense in the draft statement of profit and loss.

In 20X5 the warranty provision was 0.005% of total revenue. In 20X6 the revenue was higher than the previous year, however the warranty provision fell and is only 0.004% of total revenue. We would expect the warranty provision to increase in line with revenue unless there is a valid reason, eg an improvement in the quality of goods due to using higher quality fabrics.

2   The correct answer is: Reviewing customer correspondence after year end for discussions relating to warranty claims

This procedure would enable Check & Co to consider the level of claims made against Dress You Like Co after the end of the reporting period and therefore assess whether the level of warranty provision made is sufficient, namely is it complete.

### Activity 3: Litigation

#### Substantive procedures – litigation

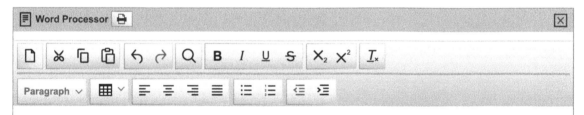

- With management's permission, send a letter of enquiry to Dress You Like Co's external legal advisers requesting their opinion of the likely outcome of the case and an estimation of the financial implications. Note that most third parties, such as legal advisers, will not meet with the external auditor and so an enquiry letter is usually sent.

- Review correspondence after year end between Dress You Like Co and their external legal advisers to see if there is any indication of the outcome of the litigation.

- Read the board minutes after year end looking for discussion of the litigation which may provide evidence about its likely outcome.

- Review correspondence with Vinay Patel relating to the litigation in order to establish the likely outcome of the claim.

- Discuss the appropriate accounting treatment for the litigation with the current directors of Dress You Like Co.

### Activity 4: Director's emoluments

#### Salary:

- Vouch salary amounts to monthly payroll records and bank statements to ensure the amounts are accurate.

- For Mary Batter, obtain her start date from the HR department and vouch this to board meeting minutes. Recalculate her salary on a pro-rata basis to ensure it is accurately recorded.

**Pension:**

- Vouch the pension amounts to monthly payroll records and bank statements to ensure the amounts are accurate.

**Bonuses:**

- Vouch the level of bonuses awarded to board meeting minutes, payroll records and bank statements to ensure they have been authorised and are accurately recorded.

**Incentive payments:**

- Review the employment contract for Mary Batter to verify that there is a clause outlining that this payment is applicable.
- Vouch the level of this payment to board meeting minutes, payroll records and bank statements.

**General:**

- Recast the schedule to ensure the note is accurate.
- Review the disclosure to ensure that it is in accordance with applicable law and accounting standards.

# Skills checkpoint 4

# How to approach audit evidence questions

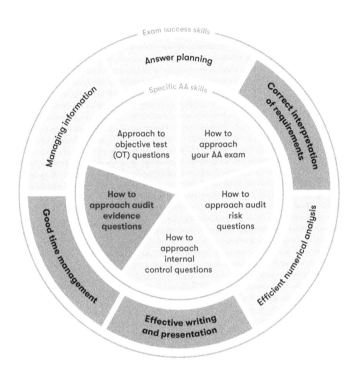

## Introduction

The external auditor must obtain sufficient appropriate audit evidence to support their auditor's opinion, they do this by conducting audit procedures.

Audit procedures can feature in both sections of the exam. In Section A, you may be required to choose the most appropriate audit procedure from a list of options or to explain the specific assertion that evidence may be gathered over by conducting a particular audit procedure. In Section B, you will need to draft audit procedures which are relevant to the requirement which may or may not specify an audit assertion.

There are two types of audit procedures: tests of controls and substantive procedures.

You must read the question requirement very carefully because if the requirement states 'describe audit procedures' then you can answer with either tests of controls OR substantive procedures. However, if you include tests of controls in a solution to a requirement that asks for substantive procedures, those tests will not score any marks.

Candidates' biggest weakness in audit evidence questions is that they fail to describe the audit procedure in sufficient detail. A well-explained procedure will score one mark but very often candidates only score ½ mark because their procedure is not fully explained.

We recommend that you use a **'verb-document-reason'** approach to describing audit procedures in order to be assured of gaining one mark per point.

This skills checkpoint will therefore focus on how you can achieve this.

# Skills Checkpoint 4: How to approach audit evidence questions

### AA Skill: How to approach audit evidence questions

A step-by-step technique for ensuring that your approach to audit evidence questions the 'verb-document-reason' technique is outlined below. Each step will be explained in more detail in the following sections and illustrated using requirements from a selection of past exam questions.

> **STEP 1:**
>
> Identify exactly what is being asked in the requirement: audit procedures, tests of controls or substantive procedures?
> Are specific assertions being tested?

> **STEP 2:**
>
> Consider how you might generate your answer.
> Is there a scenario you should use?
> Can you remember the accounting treatment for the item? Would that give you a starting point?
> What audit procedures have you learnt/used at work?
> Can you use the mnemonic AEIOU to help you to generate audit procedures?

> **STEP 3:**
>
> Write out your audit procedure using the '**verb-document-reason**' approach.
> What do you want to be done (eg recalculate, agree, vouch)?
> To which document (eg invoice, physical asset, board minutes)?
> Why (eg to ensure that receivables are recoverable (valuation))? You might choose to link this to an assertion

# Exam success skills

The following illustration provides examples from a series of past exam questions.

For this question, we will also focus on the following exam success skills:

- **Correct interpretation of requirements.** Here you need to identify whether you are being asked for audit procedures (tests of controls or substantive procedures) or just one of them. You should also identify whether you need to describe audit procedures which are relevant to a specific financial statement assertion.
- **Effective writing and presentation.** A well-explained audit procedure will earn you one mark. Use the 'verb-document-reason' approach to maximise your marks.
- **Good time management.** When answering audit evidence questions, spend some time thinking and constructing a detailed audit procedure rather than writing out any and every test you can think of.

# Skill Activity

**STEP 1** Identify exactly what you are being asked for in the requirement: audit procedures, tests of controls or substantive procedures.

Also identify whether the requirement is testing audit procedures that relate to a particular assertion.

**Required**

(a) Describe substantive procedures you should perform to obtain sufficient appropriate evidence in relation to:

    (i) Inventory held at the third-party warehouses; and

    (ii) Use of standard costs for inventory valuation.
    **(4 marks)**

(b) Describe substantive procedures the auditor should perform in relation to the **COMPLETENESS** of the year-end trade payables of ABC Co. **(5 marks)**

(c) List **THREE** substantive analytical procedures you should perform on the shift managers' salary system. **(3 marks)**

(d) Describe the audit procedures you should perform to ensure that jewellery inventory is valued correctly. **(4 marks)**

(e) **Intangible assets**

During the year, DEF Co obtained a patent from a competitor. The directors have discussed the accounting treatment with your firm and you are satisfied that it is appropriate to treat this as an intangible asset. As they purchased the patent at what they believe to be below market value, the directors wish to carry it at its fair value which they estimate to be substantially above the cost price. They have estimated that the useful life of the patent is 20 years.

Describe substantive procedures you would perform to obtain sufficient and appropriate audit evidence in relation to the above matter. **(4 marks)**

Whilst each of the separate requirements is testing audit evidence, they are each worded slightly differently and you should therefore analyse the requirement before writing your answer.

| Requirement | Analysis |
|---|---|
| (1) | **Substantive procedures:**<br>• Tests of detail and/or<br>• Analytical procedures<br>**Relating to:**<br>• Inventory held by third parties<br>• The use of standard costs to value inventory |
| (2) | **Substantive procedures** relating to:<br>• **COMPLETENESS** of trade payables |
| (3) | Substantive **analytical procedures** |
| (4) | **Audit procedures:** |

| Requirement | Analysis |
|---|---|
| | • Tests of control and/or<br>• Substantive procedures<br>Relating to:<br>• **Valuation** |
| (5) | **Substantive procedures** relating to:<br>• **Information in the scenario** |

**STEP 2** Now that you have understood what the requirement demands, you are much better placed to answer it. Consider the following:

- Is there a scenario you should use?
- Can you remember the accounting treatment for the item? Would that give you a starting point?
- What audit procedures have you learnt/used at work?
- Can you use the mnemonic AEIOU to help you to generate audit procedures?

Completed answer plan

**Required**

Let's consider two of the requirements:

(2) Describe substantive procedures[40] the auditor should perform in relation to the **COMPLETENESS** of the year-end trade payables of ABC Co. **(5 marks)**

(5) **Intangible assets**

During the year, DEF Co obtained a patent from a competitor. The directors have discussed the accounting treatment with your firm and you are satisfied that it is appropriate[41] to treat this as an intangible asset. As they purchased the patent at what they believe to be below market value, the directors wish to carry it at its fair value which they estimate to be substantially above the cost price. They have estimated that the useful life of the patent is 20 years.

Describe substantive procedures you would perform to obtain sufficient and appropriate audit evidence in relation to the above matter. **(4 marks)**

[40] Tests of detail/analytical procedures. No scenario. No particular accounting treatment to be aware of. AEIOU: Analytical procedures: Review balances owed to each supplier year on year to identify any that look unusually low. Compare payables payment period year on year to identify any unexpected change. Inspection: Inspect cash book payments post y/e to identify large payments where the liability did not exist at the y/e. Inspect invoices received post y/e and agree to GRN for evidence of any unrecorded liabilities. Recalculation: Reconcile a sample of trade payable balances to supplier statements to identify any unrecorded liabilities

[41] Use scenario: Accounting treatment as an intangible agreed so no marks for audit procedures re IAS 38 criteria. Accounting treatment: Initially recognise at cost (vouch purchase price to invoice and cash book payments to determine whether capitalised cost is appropriate). Plans to revalue patent (vouch to external valuer's report/use of an expert/trace accounting entries). Amortisation (company to industry benchmarks to determine if useful life is reasonable)/recalculate amortisation.

**STEP 3** Write out your audit procedure using the 'verb-document-reason' approach.

- What do you want to be done (eg recalculate, agree, vouch)?
- To which document (eg invoice, physical asset, board minutes)?
- Why (eg to ensure that receivables are recoverable (valuation))? You might choose to link this to an assertion.

Start each audit procedure on a new line.

**Suggested solution**

(2)  Substantive procedures relating to COMPLETENESS of year-end trade payables

- Compare[42] the list of trade payables balances[43] with the previous year to identify any potentially significant omissions.[44]

    [42] verb
    [43] document
    [44] reason

- Compare[45] the payables payment period[46] with the previous year to identify any unexpected change.[47]

    [45] verb
    [46] document
    [47] reason

- Review[48] the cash book payments/bank statements after the end of the year[49] for payments which could indicate the existence of unrecorded trade payables.[50]

    [48] verb
    [49] document
    [50] reason

- Inspect[51]invoices received post year-end[52] and agree to goods received notes for evidence of unrecorded liabilities.[53]

    [51] verb
    [52] document
    [53] reason

- Reconcile[54] a sample of payables balances to supplier statements[55] and investigate differences which could indicate significant unrecorded liabilities.[56]

    [54] verb
    [55] document
    [56] reason

(5)  Intangible assets

- Obtain[57]purchase documents[58] to verify the cost[59] of the intangible asset

    [57] verb
    [58] document
    [59] reason

- Review[60] the directors' estimate of fair value[61] of the patent and consider the assumptions made[62] for reasonableness/ Obtain third-party evidence concerning valuation to assess the fair value for reasonableness

    [60] verb
    [61] document
    [62] reason

- Consider[63] whether the length of useful life[64] is reasonable[65] in relation to the legal terms of the patent.

    [63] verb
    [64] document
    [65] reason

- Recalculate[66]amortisation charge[67] for the period to ensure it is calculated according to the entity's policy[68].

    [66] verb
    [67] document
    [68] reason

# Exam success skills diagnostic

Every time you complete a question, use the diagnostic below to assess how effectively you demonstrated the exam success skills in answering the question. The table has been completed below for the examples used above to give you an idea of how to complete the diagnostic.

| Exam success skills | Your reflections/observations |
|---|---|
| Correct interpretation of requirements | Did you identify the type of audit procedures you were required to describe? |
| Effective writing and presentation | Did you fully explain your procedure using the 'verb-document-reason' approach in order to secure one mark per procedure? |
| Good time management | Did you spend enough time thinking about what was required in order to produce your best answer in the time available? |

**Most important action points to apply to your next question**

## Summary

You are likely to see audit evidence questions in both Section A and Section B of the exam. You must know the difference between tests of controls and substantive procedures and be confident as to which audit procedures provide evidence over which financial statement assertions.

As you move into practising questions as part of your final revision, you will need to practise taking in information from a scenario quickly (using active reading), accurately understanding the requirements, and creating an answer plan and a final answer that addresses the requirements in the context of the scenario.

 BPP

# Not-for-profit organisations

## Learning objectives

On completion of this chapter, you should be able to:

| Syllabus learning outcomes | Syllabus reference no. |
|---|---|
| Apply audit techniques to not-for-profit organisations. | D7 (a) |

## Business and Exam context

This chapter looks at the audit of not-for-profit organisations. Such entities may or may not be required to have a statutory audit under legislation. They may choose to have a non-statutory audit under the terms of a charitable deed or as part of good practice.

The points made in this chapter about the issues inherent in these entities are relevant for any kind of assurance work in not-for-profit organisations. These entities will have particular features, the most obvious being the difference in objectives of the entity, which will affect the way the work is carried out.

In this chapter, we look specifically at the aspects of audit planning, evidence and reporting in not-for-profit organisations and how these differ from for-profit organisations.

An exam question on not-for-profit organisations may come up as a scenario-based question on audit planning or evidence. In this case, use your knowledge of not-for-profit organisations as well as the clues given in the scenario to generate ideas for your answer.

Previous exams have included written requirements relating to audit planning and the system of internal control (such as the control environment) relating specifically to not-for-profit organisations. This topic can equally be examined in the form of OT questions in Section A.

Remember, the issues relating to small companies that we have discussed in this book may also apply to small not-for-profit organisations as well.

# Chapter overview

# 1 Introduction

## 1.1 Objectives of not-for-profit organisations

Before considering what a not-for-profit organisation's audit will entail, it will be helpful to consider the types of entities that might exist with objectives other than to make a profit and their objectives, as these will impact on the way that they report and the audit that is carried out.

For example, a hospital could operate at a profit by not spending all the money it receives in its budget. However, the key objective of a hospital is to provide health services to the public, not to make a profit. As its income is fixed, it is more likely to focus on **cost saving** so that it can operate within its budget.

### Example - Not-for-profit organisations

| Type of organisation | Objective | Focus |
|---|---|---|
| Charities and friendly societies | To carry out the charitable purpose | May involve fundraising, receiving donations, managing invested funds, controlling costs |
| Schools | To provide education | Likely to involve managing a tight budget (either from fees or government funds) |
| Clubs, associations, societies, unions | To further the aims of the club, provide a service for members | May include managing subscriptions paid and keeping costs of running the club down |
| Housing associations | Managing the related houses and providing facilities for residents | May involve rent collection and maintenance costs or even building costs of future developments. |
| Local councils, public services | To provide local services to a budget based on public money | Likely to be focused on value for money, as they are in the public eye. |

This section can be linked back to the performance measures we covered in Chapter 5 when we looked at value for money (VFM) audits in the context of internal audit. The performance measures were **economy**, **effectiveness** and **efficiency**.

## 1.2 Audit of not-for-profit organisations

Organisations may fall within the scope of statutory audit if the entities concerned are limited liability companies. Organisations not incorporated may require an assurance engagement due to the requirements of regulatory or governing bodies, eg the Charity Commission.

When carrying out an audit of a not-for-profit organisation, it is vital that the auditor establishes:

- Whether a statutory audit is required
- If a statutory audit is not required, what the objectives of the engagement are
- What the engagement is to report on
- To whom the report should be addressed
- What form the report should take

# 2 Planning the audit

The planning procedures undertaken for not-for-profit organisations will **differ very little** from those for profit-making organisations. However, the auditor should have specific regard to any laws, regulations or guidelines imposed on the entity by any regulatory body.

The scope of the auditor's work will be detailed in the engagement letter.

## 2.1 Risk assessment

The auditor should, during the planning stage, fully assess the risks associated with the not-for-profit organisation. There are certain risks applicable to not-for-profit organisations that might not necessarily be applicable to other small companies.

Small not-for-profit organisations will generally suffer from **internal control deficiencies** common to small enterprises, such as **lack of segregation of duties** and the use of **unqualified staff**. Shortcomings may arise from the staff's lack of training and also, if they are volunteers, from their attitude, in that they may resent formal procedures.

The auditors will have to consider particularly carefully whether they will be able to obtain adequate assurance that the accounting records do reflect all the transactions of the enterprise and bear in mind whether there are any related **statutory reporting requirements**.

**Activity 1: Audit risks**

Midvale League is a small association. It runs several local football leagues for various ages and stages. It employs a general administrator and some casual staff to run the bar. Any player who appears in more than 30% of a team's games for the season is required to pay a subscription to the association. The subscriptions pay for the administrator's wages, the referee's fees, team coaches' expenses and a lease on a sports club comprising a clubhouse, changing facilities and three football pitches. The administrator also acts as grounds person. There is a bar in the clubhouse which is run for the benefit of members at a profit which covers bar staff wages and contributes to other expenses of the club. The association pays a local firm of accountants to prepare management accounts every quarter and to produce annual financial statements which it then audits for the benefit of members of the club.

**Required**

Identify any audit risks arising from The Midvale League.

Solution

# 3 Audit evidence

Obtaining audit evidence from not-for-profit organisations may be a problem, particularly where organisations have informal arrangements and this may impact on the auditor's report.

 **Activity 2: Charity audit**

You have recently been appointed auditor of Links Famine Relief, a registered charity which receives donations from individuals to provide food in famine areas around the world.

The charity is run by a voluntary management committee, which has monthly meetings and employs the following full-time staff:

(1) A director, Mrs Roberts, who suggests fundraising activities and payments for relief of famine, and implements the policies adopted by the management committee

(2) A secretary and bookkeeper, Mr Beech, who deals with correspondence and keeps the accounting records

You are planning the audit of income of the charity for the year ended 5 April 20X7 and are considering the controls which should be exercised over this area.

The previous year's financial statements to 5 April 20X6 (which have been audited by another firm) show the following income:

|  | $ | $ |
|---|---|---|
| Gifts under non-taxing arrangements | 14,745 | |
| Tax reclaimed on gifts under non-taxing arrangements | 4,915 | |
|  | | 19,660 |
| Donations through the post | | 63,452 |
| Autumn Fair | | 2,671 |
| Other income | | |
| Legacies | 7,538 | |

|  | $ | $ |
|---|---|---|
| Bank deposit account interest | 2,774 | |
| | | 10,312 |
| | | 96,095 |

## Notes.

1   Income from gifts under non-taxing arrangements is stated net. Each person who pays by deed of covenant has filled in a special tax form, which is kept by the full-time secretary, Mr Beech.

2   All gifts under non-taxing arrangements are paid by banker's order; they are credited directly to the charity's bank account from the donor's bank. Donors make their payments by deed of covenant either monthly or annually.

3   The tax reclaimed on these gifts is one-third of the net value of the gifts and relates to income received during the year; as the tax is received after the year-end, an appropriate amount recoverable is included in the statement of financial position. The treasurer, who is a voluntary (unpaid) member of the management committee, completes the form for reclaiming the income tax, using the special tax forms (in Note (a) above) and checks to the secretary's records that each donor has made the full payment in the year required by the arrangement.

4   Donations received through the post are dealt with by Mr Beech. These donations are either cheques or cash (bank notes and coins). Mr Beech prepares a daily list of donations received, which lists the cheques received and total cash (divided between the different denominations of bank notes and coins). The total on this form is recorded in the cash book. He then prepares a paying-in slip and banks these donations daily. When there is a special fundraising campaign, Mr Beech receives help in dealing with these donations from voluntary members of the management committee.

5   The Autumn Fair takes place every year on a Saturday in October; members of the management committee and other supporters of the charity give items to sell (for example food, garden plants, clothing). A charge is made for entrance to the fair and coffee and biscuits are available at a small charge. At the end of the fair, Mr Beech collects the takings from each of the stalls and he banks them the following Monday.

6   Legacies are received irregularly and are usually sent direct to the director of the charity, who gives them to Mr Beech for banking – they are stated separately on the daily bankings form (in Note (d) above).

7   Bank deposit account interest is paid gross of income tax by the bank, as the Links Famine Relief is a charity.

**Required**

List and briefly describe the work you would carry out on the audit of income of the charity, the controls you would expect to see in operation and the problems you may experience for the following sources of income, as detailed in the statement above.

(1)   Gifts under non-taxing arrangements

(2)   Tax reclaimed on gifts made under non-taxing arrangements

(3)   Donations received through the post

(4)   Autumn Fair

Solution

---

## Activity 3: Save the Accountants

'Save the Accountants' is a charitable foundation set up to provide financial assistance to accountants who have fallen on hard times. Its principal sources of income are:

- Cash donations collected on the high streets of major towns
- Regular donations by a number of the largest accountancy firms
- Annual donations by wealthy individuals

**Required**

What audit procedures would you do to test the completeness of income?

**Solution**

---

## Essential reading

See Chapter 18 of the Essential reading for a more detailed discussion on audit evidence considerations for not-for-profit organisations.

The Essential reading is available as an Appendix of the digital edition of the Workbook.

# 4 Audit reporting

For incorporated not-for-profit organisations, the reporting requirements of ISA 700 *Forming an Opinion and Reporting on Financial Statements* apply. Additionally, the reporting requirements of the governing body will need to be encompassed in the auditor's report.

Where an association or charity is having an audit for the benefit of its members or trustees, or if the entity is government funded and highly regulated, the standard auditor's report may not be required or appropriate. The auditor should bear in mind the objectives of the audit and make suitable references in the auditor's report. However, the ISA 700 format will still be relevant.

The auditor should ensure that they make the following matters clear:

- The addressees of the report
- What the report relates to
- The scope of the engagement
- The respective responsibilities of auditors and management/trustees/directors
- The work done
- The opinion drawn

# Chapter summary

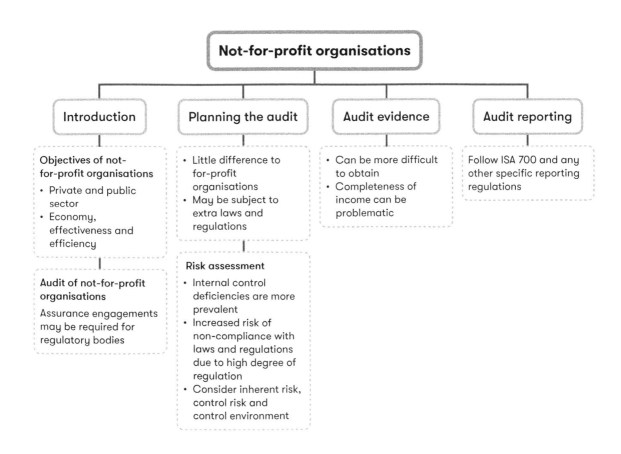

# Knowledge diagnostic

### 1. Not-for-profit organisations

There are various types of not-for-profit organisations which do not exist for the purpose of maximising shareholder wealth but which may still require an audit. Not-for-profit organisations include **charities, clubs and societies**.

### 2. Planning

When planning the audit, all relevant regulations must be understood.

### 3. Audit risk

The audit risks associated with not-for-profit organisations may well be different from other entities.

### 4. Risk areas

Particular **risk** areas for the auditor of not-for-profit entities are:

- Complexity of regulation
- High level of cash receipts
- Competence of staff and volunteers
- Segregation of duties

### 5. Audit approach

The audit approach is likely to be mainly **substantive.**

### 6. Audit evidence

Obtaining audit evidence may be a problem, particularly where organisations have informal arrangements.

### 7. Auditor's report

The auditor must consider the requirements of ISA 700 as well as any specific reporting regulations.

# Further study guidance

## Question practice

Now try the following from the Further question practice bank [available in the digital edition of the Workbook]:

- Section B Q84 'Tap'
- Section B Q86 'Ajio'

## Further reading

There are no technical articles on the ACCA website which are relevant to the topics covered in this chapter.

## Own research

(a) Consider a non-for-profit organisation you are familiar with. What is the objective and focus of this organisation? Does the organisation require an audit?

(b) Can you find the audited financial statements for a large charity on that charity's website? Look through the different income streams. How would you go about auditing these?

# Activity answers

## Activity 1: Audit risks

### Audit risks

The **valuation of Midvale League's club lease** may be problematic, it is certainly likely to be their biggest financial commitment. The auditor will need to determine whether a lease contract exists and if so the premises will need to be included **at cost as a right-of-use asset** on the statement of financial position. The cost of the right-of-use asset is likely to be the initial measurement of the lease liability (ie, the present value of future lease payments) plus any initial direct costs incurred by Midvale League. Midvale League will also need to recognise a **lease liability** and this is initially measured at the **present value of lease payments not paid at the commencement date of the lease**. The discount factor used in the calculation of the present value is the interest rate implicit in the lease (or Midvale League's incremental borrowing rate if the interest rate implicit in the lease is not readily determinable). Midvale League may well not have this information which increases audit risk. Over the lease term, the lease liability is increased by the interest on the lease liability and recognised as a finance cost in the statement of profit or loss. The lease liability is reduced by the lease payments (instalments made).

If Midvale League does not have the cash flow to meet the lease payments, this may affect **going concern** as it could lose the facilities and have nowhere from which it can operate its activities in the foreseeable future, in which case the purpose of the association is gone.

Note that the lease is **unlikely** to satisfy the optional recognition exemption criteria from IFRS 16 *Leases* unless the lease is a short-term lease (lease term less than 12 months) which seems unlikely from the scenario.

The auditors will also have to consider the **role of the general administrator**, who fulfils a number of roles. General administrators are clearly key to the association, and it might have difficulties if they were incapacitated, not least perhaps in affording a replacement and any sickness benefit it was required to pay by law.

It is unclear what degree of financial record-keeping the administrator takes on. The audit firm is hired to produce quarterly management accounts. The association will gain some assurance from the fact that it prepares the accounts, but there is also a risk that **day-to-day transactions are not properly recorded**, as there appears to be **nobody with financial expertise** at Midvale League. Given that the administrator will record or maintain the relevant records to be passed on to the accountancy firm, there is also an issue of **segregation of duties** here.

The auditors should be aware of any legal issues relating to the bearing of a licence for the bar, particularly perhaps the danger that the licence might be jeopardised by the sale of liquor to underage drinkers. The **loss of the licence** to serve alcohol could severely diminish the income of the club to the point where it could no longer function.

The auditors will also need to pay attention to the membership of the association from the point of view of **completeness of income**.

## Activity 2: Charity audit

The audit consideration in relation to the various sources of income of the Links Famine Relief charity would be as follows:

 BPP

(1) **Gifts made under non-taxing arrangements**

This type of income should not present any particular audit problem, as the donations are made by banker's order direct to the charity's bank account and so it would be difficult for such income to be 'intercepted' and misappropriated.

Specific tests required would be as follows:

(i) Agree a sample of receipts from the bank statements to the cash book to ensure that the income has been properly recorded.

(ii) Agree a sample of the receipts to the special tax forms to ensure that the full amount due has been received.

Any discrepancies revealed by either of the above tests should be followed up with Mr Beech.

(2) **Tax reclaimed on gifts made under non-taxing arrangements**

Once again, this income should not pose any particular audit problems. The auditors should inspect the claim form submitted to the tax authorities and calculate whether the amount of the claim represents one third of the net value of the covenants recorded as having been received.

(3) **Donations received through the post**

There is a serious problem here, as the nature of this income is not predictable and also because of the lack of internal checks, with Mr Beech being almost entirely responsible for the receipt of these monies, the recording of the income and the banking of the cash and cheques received. The auditors may ultimately have to express a qualified opinion in this area.

Notwithstanding the above reservations, specific audit tests required would be as follows:

(i) Agree the details on the daily listings of donations received to the cash book, bank statements and paying-in slips, observing whether the details agree in all respects and confirming that there is no evidence of any delay in the banking of this income.

(ii) Agree the donations received by reference to any correspondence which may have been received with the cheques or cash.

(iii) Consider whether the level of income appears reasonable by performing analytical procedures to make comparison with previous years and in light of any special appeals that the charity is known to have made during the course of the year.

(iv) Carry out, with permission from the management committee, surprise checks to vouch the completeness and accuracy of the procedures relating to this source of income.

(4) **Autumn Fair**

Once again, there is a potential problem here because of the level of responsibility vested in one person, namely Mr Beech.

Specific work required would be as follows:

(i) Attend the event to observe the proper application of procedures laid down and count the cash at the end of the day.

(ii) Agree any records maintained by individual stallholders to the summary prepared by Mr Beech.

(iii) Inspect the vouchers supporting any expenditure deducted from the proceeds in order to arrive at the net bankings.

(iv) Agree the summary prepared by Mr Beech to the entry in the cash book and on the bank statement.

### Activity 3: Save the Accountants

#### Cash collections

- Discuss procedures for cash collection with management and assess risk of fraud, loss, robbery or error.

- Discuss selection criteria for collectors and collection procedures with management.
- Observe the cash collection, recording and banking process.
- Trace a sample of cash received control lists to cash records and bank statements.
- Reperform a reconciliation of total cash received to income.
- Perform an analytical review of cash donations per month vs previous year taking into account factors such as number of collectors and weather.

**Regular donations by a number of the largest accountancy firms and wealthy individuals**

- Obtain and compare analysis of major/regular contributions with previous year.
- Send circularisation letters to confirm material amounts donated by the large accountancy firms and wealthy individuals.
- Circularise tax authorities to confirm contributions made where tax deductions have been claimed.

# 19

# Audit review and finalisation

## Learning objectives

On completion of this chapter, you should be able to:

| Syllabus learning outcomes | Syllabus reference no. |
| --- | --- |
| Explain the purpose of a subsequent events review. | E1 (a) |
| Explain the responsibilities of auditors regarding subsequent events. | E1 (b) |
| Discuss the procedures to be undertaken in performing a subsequent events review. | E1 (c) |
| Define and discuss the significance of the concept of going concern. | E2 (a) |
| Explain the importance of and the need for going concern reviews. | E2 (b) |
| Explain the respective responsibilities of auditors and management regarding going concern. | E2 (c) |
| Identify and explain potential indicators that an entity is not a going concern. | E2 (d) |
| Discuss the procedures to be applied in performing going concern reviews. | E2 (e) |
| Discuss the disclosure requirements in relation to going concern issues. | E2 (f) |
| Explain the purpose of and procedure for obtaining written representations. | E3 (a) |
| Discuss the quality and reliability of written representations as audit evidence. | E3 (b) |
| Discuss the circumstances where written representations are necessary and the matters on which representations are commonly obtained. | E3 (c) |
| Discuss the importance of the overall review in ensuring that sufficient, appropriate evidence has been obtained. | E4 (a) |
| Discuss the procedures an auditor should perform in conducting their overall review of financial statements. | E4 (b) |

| Syllabus learning outcomes | Syllabus reference no. |
|---|---|
| Explain the significance of uncorrected misstatements. | E4 (c) |
| Evaluate the effect of dealing with uncorrected misstatements. | E4 (d) |

# Business and Exam context

This chapter will consider the reviews that take place during the completion stage of the audit, which include subsequent events and going concern. These are both important disclosure issues in the financial statements because, if the disclosures are not correct, this will impact on the auditor's report.

In this chapter, we also consider the use and reliability of written representations from management as audit evidence.

Financial reporting knowledge is particularly important at the review stage of the audit. Auditors need to be able to interpret accounts and understand the requirements of specific accounting standards. Analytical procedures must be used when undertaking the final review of the financial statements.

Immaterial misstatements may not be corrected by the audit client. The final part of this chapter looks at how the auditor should respond to uncorrected but immaterial misstatements.

The review stage of the audit is very important and likely to come up in the exam, both in Section A and in Section B. For example, in the exam, you could be asked to describe audit procedures which should be performed in relation to a subsequent event. It is very important that you understand the difference between the review stage of the audit and the earlier testing stage and are able to describe the auditor's responsibility in respect of misstatements.

Other topics likely to be examined include:

- Matters requiring written representations
- Going concern indicators, and audit procedures to test the going concern basis of accounting
- The effect of subsequent events on the auditor's report

# Chapter overview

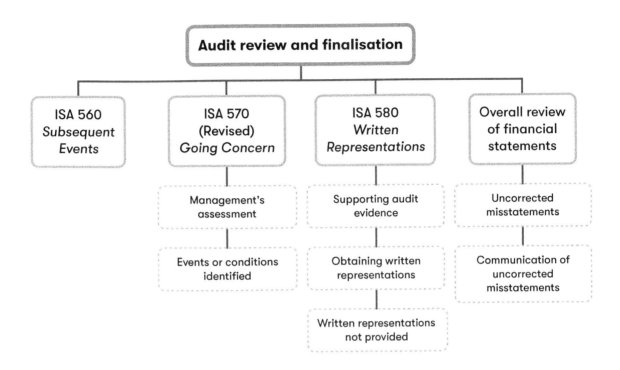

# 1 ISA 560 *Subsequent Events*

**KEY TERM**

> **Subsequent events:** 'Events occurring between the date of the financial statements and the date of the auditor's report, and facts that become known to the auditor after the date of the auditor's report' (ISA 560: para. 5(e)).

Financial statements may be affected by events that occur after the date of the financial statements. IAS 10 *Events after the Reporting Period* deals with the treatment in the financial statements of events occurring after the period end. For financial reporting purposes, these events are categorised in one of two ways:

Those that provide evidence of conditions that existed **at** the date of the financial statements (**adjusting** events)

Examples:

- Settlement of a court case
- Sale of inventory after year end providing evidence of its net realisable value at year end
- Fraud or error showing the accounts are incorrect

Those that provide evidence of conditions that arose **after** the date of the financial statements (**non-adjusting events**).

Examples:

- Dividends declared after the year end
- Fire causing destruction of major plant
- Announcement of a major restructuring

The auditor should consider the effect of subsequent events on the financial statements and on the auditor's report.

| Active duty | | Passive duty | |
| Year end | Auditor's report signed | F/S issued | AGM |

**Audit procedures undertaken to identify material subsequent events (adjusting and non-adjusting)**

(a) Review the procedures management has established to ensure that subsequent events are identified.

(b) Read board minutes held after the date of the financial statements up to the date of signing the auditor's report.

(c) Read the entity's latest available interim financial statements, budgets and cash flow forecasts.

(d) Enquire, or extend previous oral or written enquiries, of the entity's legal counsel concerning litigation and claims.

(e) Enquire of management as to whether any subsequent events have occurred which might affect the financial statements.

(f) Obtain a written representation as to the completeness of subsequent events identified by management.

**Auditor becomes aware of a material subsequent event:**

(a) Discuss matter with management to determine whether the FS need amendment.

(b) If management amends FS the auditor should extend audit procedures to the items that require adjustment or disclosure and issue a new, unmodified auditor's report.

(c) If management refuses to make amendment in FS then auditor should either:

  (i) (If not yet released auditor's report) reissue a report with a modified opinion; or

  (ii) (If have released auditor's report) seek legal advice.

**Auditor becomes aware of a material subsequent event:**

(a) Discuss matter with management

(b) If management amends FS auditor should issue a new auditor's report including an emphasis of matter or other matter paragraph to explain the revision to the previously issued FS.

(c) If management refuses to make amendment in FS then auditor should seek legal advice.

### Activity 1: Subsequent event

You are an audit senior in Check and Co and you are finalising the audit of Dress You Like Co for the year ending 30 September 20X6. Revenue is $51,895,000 and profit before tax is $1,025,000.

During the audit, you learnt that the finance director left the company in March 20X6 and was suing the company for constructive dismissal. After much discussion between the audit partner and directors of Dress You Like Co, the company agreed to make a provision of $100,000 in relation to this claim.

It is now 18 November 20X6 and the auditor's report has not yet been signed. As part of your finalisation procedures, you have spoken to Dress You Like Co's legal counsel and they have informed you that the finance director has won the case. Dress You Like has been ordered to pay damages of $500,000 by the court.

**Required**

Explain whether the financial statements of Dress You Like Co for the year ending 30 September 20X6 will need amending in relation to the result of the court case with the legal director.

Solution

**Essential reading**

See Chapter 19 of the Essential reading for further detail on subsequent events.

The Essential reading is available as an Appendix of the digital edition of the Workbook.

# 2 ISA 570 (Revised) *Going Concern*

**Going concern basis of accounting:** Under the **going concern basis of accounting**, the financial statements are prepared on the assumption that the entity is a going concern and will continue its operations for the foreseeable future. General purpose financial statements are prepared using the going concern basis of accounting, unless management either intends to liquidate the entity or to cease operations, or has no realistic alternative but to do so.  (ISA 570 (Revised): para 2)

If the going concern basis is not appropriate, the financial statements are prepared on a **break-up basis**.

ISA 570 (Revised): para 9 states that the objectives of the auditor are:

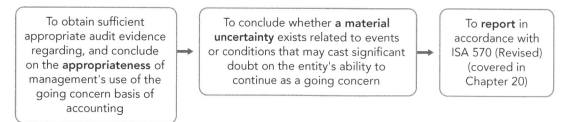

To obtain sufficient appropriate audit evidence regarding, and conclude on the **appropriateness** of management's use of the going concern basis of accounting → To conclude whether **a material uncertainty** exists related to events or conditions that may cast significant doubt on the entity's ability to continue as a going concern → To **report** in accordance with ISA 570 (Revised) (covered in Chapter 20)

The auditor must remain **alert** throughout the audit for evidence of events or conditions that may cast significant doubt on the entity's ability to continue as a going concern.

Examples of events or conditions, which may cast doubt on whether the going concern basis of accounting is appropriate are shown below. These are sometimes referred to as **going concern indicators**.

---
**Financial**

- Net liability or net current liability position
- Fixed-term borrowings approaching maturity without realistic prospects of renewal or repayment; or excessive reliance on short-term borrowings to finance non-current assets
- Indications of withdrawal of financial support by creditors
- Negative operating cash flows
- Adverse key financial ratios, eg high gearing, low current ratio, poor profit margins
- Substantial operating losses or significant deterioration in the value of assets used to generate cash flows
- Arrears or discontinuance of dividends
- Inability to pay creditors on due dates
- Inability to comply with the terms of loan agreements
- Change from credit to cash-on-delivery terms with suppliers
- Inability to obtain new financing

---
**Operational**

- Management intention to liquidate the entity or to cease operations
- Loss of key management without replacement
- Loss of a major market, key customer, licence, or principal supplier
- Labour difficulties
- Shortages of important supplies
- Emergence of a highly successful competitor

---
**Other**

- Non-compliance with capital or other statutory requirements
- Pending legal or regulatory proceedings against the entity that may, if successful, result in claims that are unlikely to be satisfied
- Changes in legislation or government policy expected to adversely affect the entity
- Uninsured or underinsured catastrophes when they occur

## 2.1 Management's assessment

IAS 1 *Presentation of Financial Statements* contains a specific requirement that management makes an assessment of an entity's ability to continue as a going concern.

The auditor shall **evaluate management's assessment** of the entity's ability to continue as a going concern. However, if this assessment covers less than 12 months from the date of the financial statements, the auditor shall ask management to extend its assessment period to **at least 12 months** from that date. The auditor shall also enquire of management its knowledge of events or conditions beyond the period of the assessment that may cast significant doubt on the entity's ability to continue as a going concern.

Based on the audit evidence obtained, the auditor should determine if, in their judgement, a material uncertainty exists related to events or conditions that, alone or in aggregate, may cast significant doubt on the entity's ability to continue as a going concern.

## 2.2 Events or conditions identified

If events or conditions are identified that may cast significant doubt on the entity's ability to continue as a going concern, the auditor shall obtain sufficient appropriate audit evidence to determine whether a material uncertainty exists by performing additional audit procedures which shall include the following:

 **BPP**

| Requesting management to make its assessment where this has not been done |
| --- |
| Evaluating management's plans for future action |
| Evaluating the reliability of underlying data used to prepare a cash flow forecast and considering the assumptions used to make the forecast |
| Considering whether any additional facts or information have become available since the date management made its assessment |
| Requesting written representations from management and those charged with governance about plans for future action and the feasibility of these plans |

Specific **audit procedures** relevant to the above that the auditor could perform include:

| Analysing and discussing cash flow, profit and other relevant forecasts with management |
| --- |
| Analysing and discussing the entity's latest available interim financial statements |
| Reading the terms of debentures and loan agreements and determining whether any have been breached |
| Reading minutes of the meetings of shareholders, those charged with governance and relevant committees for reference to financing difficulties |
| Enquiring of the entity's lawyer about the existence of litigation and claims, and the reasonableness of management's assessments of their outcome and the estimate of their financial implications |
| Confirming the existence, legality and enforceability of arrangements to provide or maintain financial support with related and third parties and assessing the financial ability of such parties to provide additional funds |
| Considering the entity's plans to deal with unfilled customer orders |
| Reviewing events after period end to identify those that either mitigate or otherwise affect the entity's ability to continue as a going concern |
| Obtaining and reviewing reports or regulatory actions |

The auditor shall consider whether a material uncertainty exists related to events or conditions which may cast doubt on the entity's ability to continue as a going concern, as this will have an impact on the opinion issued in the auditor's report. You will learn about how going concern impacts the auditor's report in Chapter 20.

## Activity 2: Truckers

You are planning the audit of another client of Check & Co, Truckers Co. The company's principal activities are road transport and warehousing services, and the repair of commercial vehicles. You have been provided with the draft accounts for the year ended 31 October 20X6.

| | Draft 20X6 | Actual 20X5 |
| --- | --- | --- |
| SUMMARY STATEMENT OF PROFIT OR LOSS | $'000 | $'000 |
| Revenue | 10,971 | 11,560 |
| Cost of sales | (10,203) | (10,474) |
| Gross profit | 768 | 1,086 |
| Administrative expenses | (782) | (779) |
| Finance costs | | |

|  | (235) | (185) |
|---|---|---|
| Profit/(loss) for the period | (249) | 122 |
| SUMMARY STATEMENT OF FINANCIAL POSITION | $'000 | $'000 |
| Non-current assets | 5,178 | 4,670 |
| Current assets | | |
| Inventories of parts and consumables | 95 | 61 |
| Receivables | 2,975 | 2,369 |
| Total current assets | 3,070 | 2,430 |
| | 8,248 | 7,100 |
| Share capital and reserves | 3,544 | 3,793 |
| Non-current liabilities | | |
| Bank loan | 750 | 1,000 |
| Finance lease liabilities | 473 | – |
| | 1,223 | 1,000 |
| Current liabilities | | |
| Bank loan | 250 | – |
| Overdraft | 1,245 | 913 |
| Trade payables | 1,513 | 1,245 |
| Finance lease liabilities | 207 | – |
| Other payables | 203 | 149 |
| Total current liabilities | 3,481 | 2,307 |
| | 8,248 | 7,100 |

You have been informed by the managing director that the fall in revenue is due to:

- The loss in July 20X6 of a long-standing customer to a competitor; and

- A decline in trade in the repair of commercial vehicles.

Due to the reduction in the repairs business, the company has decided to close the workshop and sell the equipment and spares inventories. No entries resulting from this decision are reflected in the draft accounts.

During the year, the company replaced a number of vehicles, funding them by a combination of leasing and an increased overdraft facility. The facility is to be reviewed in January 20X7 after the audited accounts are available.

The draft accounts show a loss for 20X6 but the forecasts indicate a return to profitability in 20X7 as the managing director is optimistic about generating additional revenue from new contracts.

**Required**

From the scenario above identify features which might cause you to have doubts about Truckers' going concern status.

Solution

### Essential reading

See Chapter 19 of the Essential reading for further detail on going concern including the responsibilities of management.

The Essential reading is available as an Appendix of the digital edition of the Workbook.

# 3 ISA 580 *Written Representations*

> **Written representations:** Written statements by management provided to the auditor to confirm certain matters or to support other audit evidence. They do not include the financial statements, assertions or supporting books and records.

There are three main areas where written representations are necessary:

> To **confirm that management has fulfilled its responsibilities** for the preparation of the financial statements, that all transactions have been recorded and reflected therein and that all relevant information and access has been provided to the auditor as agreed in the terms of engagement

> A number of **ISAs require written representations** (such as fraud, laws and regulations, estimates, going concern, related parties and subsequent events)

> To **support other audit evidence** relevant to the financial statements if determined by the auditor

## 3.1 Supporting audit evidence

Although written representations are a form of audit evidence, they are from an internal source and **on their own they do not provide sufficient appropriate audit evidence** about the issues they relate to.

The representations should relate to matters where they are necessary to **support** audit evidence. For example:

- Where knowledge of facts is confined to management, eg management's future plans or intentions that may affect the classification of assets or liabilities
- Where the matter is principally one of judgement, eg whether a receivable is a doubtful debt or not

## 3.2 Obtaining written representations

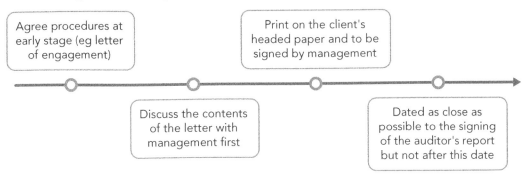

Agree procedures at early stage (eg letter of engagement)

Discuss the contents of the letter with management first

Print on the client's headed paper and to be signed by management

Dated as close as possible to the signing of the auditor's report but not after this date

## 3.3 Written representations not provided

If management does not provide one or more requested written representations, the auditor shall:

- Discuss the matter with management
- Re-evaluate the integrity of management and evaluate the effect this may have on the reliability of representations and audit evidence in general
- Take appropriate actions, including determining the impact on the auditor's report

(ISA 580: para. 19)

### Activity 3: Written representations

In which of these situations would a written representation from the management of Dress You Like Co be required?

(1) To confirm that management has adjusted or disclosed all events subsequent to the date of the financial statements where adjustment or disclosure is required

(2) To confirm that management has disclosed any fraud affecting Dress You Like Co

(3) To confirm the disposal of delivery vans with a material value

○ (1) only

○ (1) and (3) only

○ (1) and (2) only

○ (2) and (3) only

### Essential reading

See Chapter 19 of the Essential reading for further detail on written representations including an example of a written representation letter.

The Essential reading is available as an Appendix of the digital edition of the Workbook.

# 4 Overall review of financial statements

At the finalisation stage, the financial statements are reviewed to determine whether they are consistent with the auditor's understanding of the entity. ISA 520 *Analytical Procedures* states the auditor shall design and perform analytical procedures to assist in forming that overall conclusion (ISA 520: para. 6).

The review will determine whether:

| |
|---|
| Financial statements are prepared using **acceptable accounting policies, consistently applied and appropriate** to the entity. |
| Information included in financial statements is **compatible** with audit findings. |
| There is adequate **disclosure** and proper classification and presentation of information |
| Financial statements comply with **statutory requirements** and **other regulations.** |

When considering whether the accounting policies are appropriate, auditors should consider:

- Policies commonly adopted in particular industries
- Policies for which there is substantial authoritative support
- Whether any departures from applicable accounting standards are necessary for the financial statements to give a true and fair view
- Whether the financial statements reflect the substance of the underlying transactions and not merely their form

## 4.1 Uncorrected misstatements

> **Misstatement:** 'A difference between the reported amount, classification, presentation, or disclosure of a financial statement item and the amount, classification, presentation, or disclosure that is required for the item to be in accordance with the applicable financial reporting framework. Misstatements can arise from error or fraud' (ISA 450: para. 4(a)).

An **uncorrected misstatement** is a misstatement that the auditor has accumulated during the audit and that has not been corrected (ISA 450: para. 4(b)).

During the audit, a schedule will have been maintained of misstatements identified that have not been corrected by the client.

Some of these may have been individually immaterial but the schedule must be reviewed at this stage before the audit opinion is finalised. The effect of the uncorrected misstatements must be considered in aggregate as their combined effect may be material and thus could affect the audit opinion.

## 4.2 Communication of uncorrected misstatements

ISA 450 *Evaluation of Misstatements Identified during the Audit* requires the auditor to communicate uncorrected misstatements and their effect to those charged with governance, with material uncorrected misstatements being identified individually. The auditor shall request uncorrected misstatements to be corrected. The auditor shall also communicate the effect of uncorrected misstatements relating to prior periods.

The auditor shall request a written representation from management and those charged with governance as to whether they believe the effects of uncorrected misstatements are immaterial (individually and in aggregate) to the financial statements as a whole. A summary of these items shall be included in or attached to the representation.

ISA 450 requires the auditor to document the following information:

(a) The amount below which misstatements would be regarded as clearly trivial

(b) All misstatements accumulated during the audit and whether they have been corrected

(c) The auditor's conclusion as to whether uncorrected misstatements are material and the basis for that conclusion (ISA 450: para. 15)

# Example - Uncorrected misstatements

The following schedule illustrates the summary of uncorrected misstatements following the audit of Dress You Like Co for the year ending 30 September 20X6. Revenue is $51,895,000 and profit before tax is $1,025,000.

| Description | Statement of profit or loss | | Statement of financial position | |
|---|---|---|---|---|
| | DR | CR | DR | CR |
| Damaged white shirts to be written down | 2,500 | | | 2,500 |
| Inventory item DYL120008P to be written down to NRV | 1,200 | | | 1,200 |
| Correction of item DYL120008P cost allocation | 6,000 | | | 6,000 |
| Write off of aged receivables | 5,000 | | | 5,000 |
| Invoice #103965 under recorded | | 1,000 | 1,000 | |
| Outstanding cheque 2411 | 10,250 | | | 10,250 |
| Accrued internet cost | 8,000 | | | 8,000 |
| Loan interest miscalculation | 7,000 | | | 7,000 |
| Transposition error | 5,000 | | | 5,000 |
| Depreciation correction | 8,000 | | | 8,000 |
| **Total** | **52,950** | **1,000** | **1,000** | **52,950** |
| **Overall total** | **51,950** | | | **51,950** |

Materiality has been calculated at 5% of profit before tax which is $51,250 ($1,025,000 × 0.05) and 0.5% of revenue which is $259,475 ($51,895,000 × 0.005).

Individually, none of the uncorrected misstatements in the schedule are material to profit before tax or revenue. However, we can see that overall the impact to the statement of profit and loss is a debit of $51,950. This is material to profit before tax.

Check & Co must ask the management of Dress You Like Co to correct the misstatements. If the management refuse to do this, the financial statements will be materially misstated and Check & Co will have to modify the opinion in their auditor's report. You will learn more about the different types of modification in the next chapter.

# Essential reading

See Chapter 19 of the Essential reading for further detail on the overall review of financial statements.

The Essential reading is available as an Appendix of the digital edition of the Workbook.

# Chapter summary

**Audit review and finalisation**

## ISA 560 *Subsequent Events*

- **Adjusting events:** provide evidence of events/conditions that existed at the date of the FS
- **Non-adjusting events:** provide evidence of events/conditions arising after the date of the FS
- Auditor has an **active** duty up to the date the auditor's report is signed, then a **passive** duty

## ISA 570 (Revised) *Going Concern*

- If GC basis not appropriate – **break up basis** used
- Auditor to remain **alert** for GC **indicators** throughout audit

**Management's assessment**

- Must be for at least **12 months**
- Auditors must **evaluate**
- Does a **material uncertainty** exist?

**Events or conditions identified**

Perform additional audit procedures

## ISA 580 *Written Representations*

- To confirm management has **fulfilled its** responsibilities in preparing FS and all transactions included
- Required by **other ISAs**
- To **support** other audit evidence

**Supporting audit evidence**

Not sufficient audit evidence on their **own**

**Obtaining written representations**

**Date** as close as possible to the date of the auditor's report

**Written representations not provided**

May impact auditor's report

## Overall review of financial statements

Perform **analytical procedures**

**Uncorrected misstatements**

- **Schedule of uncorrected misstatements** maintained by auditors
- Uncorrected misstatements may be material in **aggregate**

**Communication of uncorrected misstatements**

- To those charged with governance
- Ask client to **correct**

# Knowledge diagnostic

**1. Subsequent events**

**Subsequent events** are events occurring between the period end and the date of the auditor's report and also include facts discovered after the auditor's report has been issued.

**2. Subsequent events review**

The auditor has a duty to perform procedures to identify **subsequent events** up to the date of the auditor's report.

**3. Impact of subsequent events**

If further events are discovered after the date of the report, the auditor should discuss with client management and take appropriate action.

**4. Going concern**

The auditor must consider the appropriateness of the **going concern** basis of accounting.

**5. Impact of going concern**

If the entity has inappropriately used the going concern basis of accounting or a material uncertainty exists, this may impact on the auditor's report.

**6. Written representations**

The auditor obtains **written representations** from management concerning its responsibilities and to support other audit evidence where necessary.

**7. Overall review of financial statements**

Before issuing the audit opinion, the auditor should carry out an **overall review** of the financial statements.

**8. Uncorrected misstatements**

The auditor must keep a schedule of uncorrected misstatements as these may be material in aggregate.

# Further study guidance

## Question practice

Now try the following from the Further question practice bank [available in the digital edition of the Workbook]:

- Section A Q11-Q13, Q26, Q47-50
- Section B Q66 (c) 'Parker' on going concern
- Section B Q87 'Going concern'
- Section B Q88 'Audit review and finalisation'

## Further reading

There are some technical articles on the ACCA website written by members of the AA examining team which are relevant to some of the topics covered in this chapter that you should read:

- *Subsequent events:* https://www.accaglobal.com/gb/en/student/exam-support-resources/fundamentals-exams-study-resources/f8/technical-articles/subsequent-events.html
- *Going concern:* https://www.accaglobal.com/gb/en/student/exam-support-resources/fundamentals-exams-study-resources/f8/technical-articles/going-concern.html

## Own research

Look for financial statements of well-known companies online. Can you find an example of a subsequent event? How has this been dealt with by the auditors?

# Activity answers

## Activity 1: Subsequent event

### Financial statements – Dress You Like Co

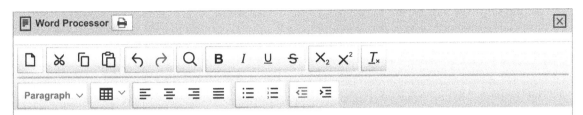

Dress You Like Co have made a provision of $100,000 for a court case but the settlement was for $500,000 and so the provision is understated by $400,000 on the statement of financial position. Correspondingly, profit in the statement of profit and loss is overstated by the same amount and expenses are understated by $400,000. The amount of the misstatement is 0.8% ($400,000/$51,895,000) of revenue and 39% ($400,000/$1,025,000) of profit before tax. It is therefore borderline material to revenue but material to profit before tax.

The settlement of a court case between the year-end date and the date the financial statements are signed is an adjusting event. The financial statements of Dress You Like Co for the year ending 30 September 20X6 will need to be adjusted before the auditor's report is signed.

## Activity 2: Truckers

### Trucker's going concern status

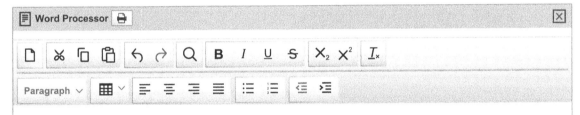

The following factors might cause doubt about Trucker's going concern status:

- Fall in gross profit margin (20X6: 7%; 20X5: 9.4%). This will make a return to profitability difficult.

- Truckers is making losses. This will make negotiations with the bank difficult.

- Receivables are taking longer to pay (20X6: 99 days; 20X5: 75 days). This will squeeze cash flow coming into the business. Irrecoverable debts will increase the existing loss.

- A worsening liquidity ratio (0.88 in 20X6; 1.05 in 20X5). Loan and lease commitments may not be met.

- An increasing reliance on short-term finance. The overdraft can be recalled by the bank at any time. It should not be used to finance long-term investment.

- Increased gearing (20X6: 63% [750 + 250 + 1,245/3,544]; 20X5: 50% [1,000 + 913/3,793]). Interest on debt must be paid from a decreasing cash position.

- Loss of major customer. Other customers may follow, worsening the company's prospects.

- Loss of commercial customers. This represents loss of regular income which means damage to company's reputation.

- Overdraft facility to be reviewed three months after the year-end. This short period is probably not long enough to see any improvement in the company's future prospects and therefore may not be renewed.

- Despite the managing director's optimism, there is no evidence to support the forecasts of additional revenue from new contracts.

## Activity 3: Written representations

The correct answer is: (1) and (2) only

Confirming that management has adjusted or disclosed all events subsequent to the date of the financial statements where adjustment or disclosure is required is a requirement of ISA 560 *Subsequent Events*.

ISA 240 *The Auditors' Responsibilities Relating to Fraud in an Audit of Financial Statements* requires a written representation from management which, amongst other things, requires management to confirm that they disclosed any fraud or suspected fraud affecting the entity.

No management representation is required for the disposal of a non-current asset. Sufficient appropriate audit evidence should be available via other means (eg observing contracts, cash received in bank statements etc) and would not need to be supported by a written representation.

# Reports

## Learning objectives

On competition of this chapter, you should be able to:

| Syllabus learning outcomes | Syllabus reference no. |
| --- | --- |
| Identify and describe the basic elements contained in the independent auditor's report. | E5 (a) |
| Explain unmodified audit opinions in the auditor's report. | E5 (b) |
| Explain the circumstances in which a modified audit opinion may be included in the auditor's report. | E5 (c) |
| Explain the impact on the auditor's report when a modified opinion is issued. | E5 (d) |
| Describe the format and content of key audit matters, emphasis of matter and other matter paragraphs | E5 (e) |
| Discuss the reporting implications of the findings of going concern reviews. | E2 (g) |

## Exam context

The auditor's report is the means by which the external auditors express their opinion on the truth and fairness of a company's financial statements. It is for the benefit of the shareholders principally, but also for other users, as the auditor's report is usually kept on public record with the filed financial statements.

Auditor's reports are covered by the following ISAs:

- ISA 700 (Revised) *Forming an Opinion and Reporting on Financial Statements*
- ISA 701 *Communicating Key Audit Matters in the Independent Auditor's Report*
- ISA 705 (Revised) *Modifications to the Opinion in the Independent Auditor's Report*
- ISA 706 (Revised) *Emphasis of Matter Paragraphs and Other Matter Paragraphs in the Independent Auditor's Report*
- ISA 720 (Revised) *The Auditor's Responsibilities Relating to Other Information*

These ISAs were revised in 2015. The IAASB believes that the revisions are essential to the continued relevance of the audit profession globally. The aims of the revisions were to respond to users, who said that:

- The audit opinion is valued, but could be more informative
- More relevant information is needed about the entity and the audit

(IAASB, 2016)

You will not be expected to reproduce a full auditor's report in the exam; however, you need to know and understand the elements that make up a standard auditor's report. You might also be required to explain the appropriate modification to the audit opinion for a scenario in a Section A or a Section B question.

If you are given a scenario in a Section B question and asked whether the auditor's report should be modified and why, you should apply the following four steps:

(a) Discuss the accounting issue

(b) Assess whether the issue is material (include a calculation)

(c) Consider the type of modification (ie qualified opinion, adverse opinion or disclaimer of opinion)

(d) Discuss the impact on the auditor's report

Remember that some issues will only impact the auditor's report (emphasis of matter, other matter) but not the auditor's opinion.

You should also be able to identify the issues which need to be reported in the Key Audit Matters paragraph of the auditor's report.

It is very important that you are aware of the reporting implications detailed in ISA 570 (Revised) *Going Concern* when faced with scenarios in which a company has going concern problems. This is an area where students have struggled in the past and this has been highlighted in recent examining team's reports. Do not forget to take into account any information you are given in the scenario. For example, if you know a material uncertainty exists and management has provided disclosures, the auditor's report issued will depend on the adequacy of those disclosures.

# Chapter overview

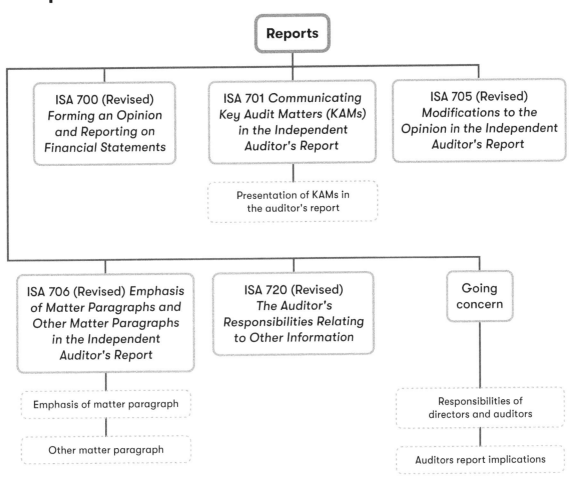

# 1 ISA 700 (Revised) *Forming an Opinion and Reporting on Financial Statements*

> **PER alert**
>
> Objective 20 of the PER performance objectives is to evaluate and report on audit. The knowledge you gain in this key chapter will assist you in demonstrating the achievement of this objective in practice.

ISA 700 (Revised) *Forming an Opinion and Reporting on Financial Statements* establishes standards and provides guidance on the form and content of the auditor's report issued as a result of an audit performed by an independent auditor on the financial statements of an entity. It requires the auditor to give an opinion on whether the financial statements are prepared, in all material respects, **in accordance with the applicable financial reporting framework**.

To do this, the auditor needs to consider the following key points:

> Whether sufficient appropriate audit evidence has been obtained (ISA 330)

> Whether uncorrected misstatements are material (ISA 450)

## 1.1 Basic elements of the auditor's report

The auditor's report should include the following basic elements, normally in this order:

(a) Title

(b) Addressee

(c) Auditor's opinion

(d) Basis for opinion

(e) Going concern (if relevant)

(f) Emphasis of matter paragraph (if relevant, can also be placed after key audit matters (KAM) paragraph)

(g) Key audit matters (KAM) (for audits of **listed** entities only)

(h) Other matter paragraph (if relevant)

(i) Responsibilities for the financial statements

(j) Auditor's responsibilities for the audit of the financial statements

(k) Report on other legal and regulatory requirements (if relevant)

(l) Name of audit engagement partner

(m) Signature of the auditor

(n) Auditor's address

(o) Date of the auditor's report

## 1.2 Unmodified opinion

> **Unmodified opinion:** An unmodified opinion is the opinion expressed by the auditor when the auditor concludes that the financial statements **are** prepared, in all material respects, in accordance with the applicable financial reporting framework (ISA 700: para. 16).

If the auditor concludes that the financial statements as a whole are not free from material misstatement or cannot obtain sufficient appropriate audit evidence to make this conclusion, the auditor must **modify** the opinion in accordance with ISA 705 (Revised) *Modifications to the Opinion in the Independent Auditor's Report*. We discuss modifications to the opinion in Section 3 of this chapter.

## Example 1 - Unmodified auditor's report with unmodified opinion (listed entity)

The standard report as laid down by ISA 700 (Revised) looks like the following (in overview):

**INDEPENDENT AUDITOR'S REPORT**

To the shareholders of the company [or other appropriate addressee.]

### Opinion

[Includes the individual statements and the reporting period under review for the company being audited. It can use either 'give a true and fair view' or 'presents fairly, in all material respects' and states the relevant GAAP adopted.]

### Basis for opinion

[This is always presented after the opinion and explains how the audit was conducted: the role of ISAs and the IESBA *Code of Ethics* as well as the audit evidence being sufficient and appropriate to provide a basis for the auditor's opinion.]

### Key audit matters

[As per ISA 701, matters of most significance from the audit; required for all listed entities.]

### Other information

[As per ISA 720, communicates that there is nothing to report regarding other information.]

### Responsibilities of management and those charged with governance for the financial statements

[Preparation and fair presentation of the financial statements, including internal controls, and the assessment of the company's ability to continue as a going concern.]

### Auditor's responsibilities for the audit of the financial statements

[A detailed summary of the auditor's objectives, starting with obtaining reasonable assurance about the financial statements being free from material misstatements due to fraud or error. Stresses the role of professional judgment and scepticism over accounting policies and estimates, judgments, internal controls, presentation, disclosure and communicating key audit matters and other issues with those charged with governance.]

### Report on other legal and regulatory requirements

[Form and content of this section of the auditor's report will vary depending on the nature of the auditor's other reporting responsibilities.]

Signed

[Auditor's name and/or signature, address and date of the auditor's report.]

## Essential reading

See Chapter 20 of the Essential reading for more on the auditor's report including a full reproduction of the auditor's report.

The Essential reading is available as an Appendix of the digital edition of the Workbook.

# 2 ISA 701 *Communicating Key Audit Matters (KAMs) in the Independent Auditor's Report*

The communication of KAMs is only relevant to the audit of **listed** entities.

> **Key audit matters:** those matters that, in the auditor's professional judgment, were of most significance in the audit of the financial statements of the current period. Key audit matters are selected from matters communicated with those charged with governance.
>
> (ISA 701: para. 8)

Examples include:

| |
|---|
| Areas where the risk of material misstatement has been assessed as high at the planning stage, for example complex accounting transactions |
| Areas of the financial statements where management have had to exercise significant judgement, for example asset valuations or accounting estimates where there is a high level of uncertainty |
| The effect on the audit of significant events or transactions that occurred during the period, for example the acquisition of a subsidiary |

KAMs relate to matters which are already included in the financial statements.

**KAMs do not constitute a modification of the report** or of the opinion. No separate audit opinion is issued in relation to each KAM.

## 2.1 Presentation of KAMs in the auditor's report

Each KAM detailed in the auditor's report should refer to the related disclosure in the financial statements and will explain:

(a) Why the matter was considered to be significant and therefore a KAM

(b) How the matter was addressed in the audit

KAMs will be communicated in the auditor's report of a listed entity where there are matters that required significant auditor attention.

Whether the auditor's opinion is unmodified or modified is unrelated to the KAM. The auditor's opinion for a listed entity can be unmodified and a KAM still need to be communicated because of the fact that matters have required significant auditor attention. If the auditor's opinion is modified, KAMs will still be communicated if there are matters that have required significant auditor attention.

Where the auditor's opinion is modified (see Section 3) in relation to a KAM, the issue would **not** be disclosed in the KAM, paragraph but in the 'Basis for modified opinion' paragraph.

Any concerns relating to an entity's ability to continue as a going concern would **not** be disclosed in the KAM, paragraph but in the 'Material uncertainty relating to going concern' paragraph (see Section 6).

### Essential reading

See Chapter 20 of the Essential reading for more on KAMs including an example of how they could appear in the auditor's report taken from ISA 701.

The Essential reading is available as an Appendix of the digital edition of the Workbook.

## 3 ISA 705 (Revised) *Modifications to the Opinion in the Independent Auditor's Report*

The auditor will give a modified audit opinion when:

(a) The auditor concludes, based on the evidence obtained, that the financial statements as a whole are not free from material misstatement; or

(b) The auditor is unable to obtain sufficient appropriate audit evidence to conclude that the financial statements as a whole are free from material misstatement.

In both circumstances there can be two 'levels' of modified opinion:

(a) **Material but not pervasive**, where the circumstances prompting the misstatement are material

(b) **Material and pervasive**, where the financial statements could be misleading

**Pervasiveness:** a term used to describe the effects or possible effects on the financial statements of misstatements or undetected misstatements (due to an inability to obtain sufficient appropriate audit evidence). There are three types of pervasive effect:

(a) Those that are not confined to specific elements, accounts or items in the financial statements

(b) Those that are confined to specific elements, accounts or items in the financial statements and represent or could represent a substantial portion of the financial statements

(c) Those that relate to disclosures which are fundamental to users' understanding of the financial statements (ISA 705 (Revised): para. 5(a))

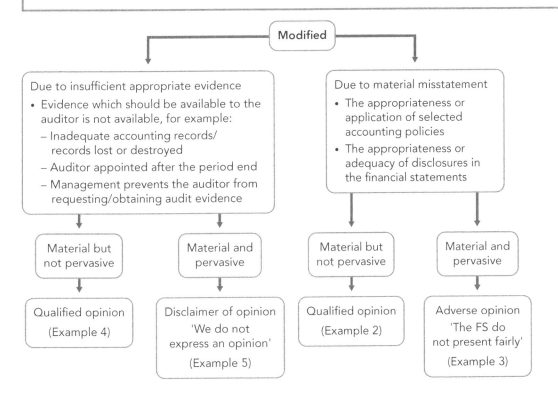

### Example 2 - Qualified opinion due to material misstatement of inventories (extract from auditor's report)

**Qualified Opinion**

We have audited the financial statements of ABC Company (the Company), which comprise the statement of financial position as at 31 December 20X1, and the statement of comprehensive income, statement of changes in equity and statement of cash flows for the year then ended, and notes to the financial statements, including a summary of significant accounting policies.

In our opinion, except for the effects of the matter described in the Basis for Qualified Opinion section of our report, the accompanying financial statements present fairly, in all material respects, (or *give a true and fair view of*) the financial position of the Company as at 31 December 20X1, and (*of*) its financial performance and its cash flows for the year then ended in accordance with International Financial Reporting Standards (IFRSs).

**Basis for Qualified Opinion**

The company's inventories are carried in the statement of financial position at xxx. Management has not stated inventories at the lower of cost and net realisable value but has stated them solely at cost, which constitutes a departure from IFRSs. The company's records indicate that had management stated the inventories at the lower of cost and net realisable value, an amount of xxx would have been required to write the inventories down to their net realisable value. Accordingly, cost of sales would have been increased by xxx, and income tax, net income and shareholders' equity would have been reduced by xxx, xxx and xxx, respectively.

## Example 3 - Adverse opinion due to material misstatement with a pervasive effect (extract from auditor's report)

**Adverse Opinion**

We have audited the financial statements of ABC Company (the Company), which compromise the statement of financial position as at 31 December 20X1, and the statement of comprehensive income, statement of changes in equity and statement of cash flows for the year then ended, and notes to the financial statements, including a summary of significant accounting policies.

In our opinion, because of the significance of the matter discussed in the Basis for Adverse Opinion section of our report, the accompanying financial statements do not present fairly (or *do not give a true and fair view of*) the financial position of ABC Company as at 31 December 20X1, and (*of*) its financial performance and its cash flows for the year then ended in accordance with IFRSs.

**Basis for Adverse Opinion**

As explained in Note X, the company has included houses built for re-sale (including related land) at a cost of $X as non-current assets and depreciated them at a rate of X%, resulting in depreciation of $X. Under International Financial Reporting Standards, these should have been included as inventory in the financial statements and no depreciation should have been provided in respect of these. The carrying value of the houses represent 90% of the company's total assets and the company's records indicate that ... [explanation of the effect on amounts presented in the financial statements].

## Example 4 - Qualified opinion due to inability to obtain sufficient appropriate audit evidence about the carrying amount of inventory (material but not pervasive) (extract from auditor's report)

**Qualified Opinion**

We have audited the financial statements of ABC Company (the Company), which comprise the statement of financial position as at 31 December 20X1, and the statement of comprehensive income, statement of changes in equity and statement of cash flows for the year then ended, and notes to the financial statements, including a summary of significant accounting policies.

In our opinion, except for the possible effects of the matter described in the Basis for Qualified Opinion section of our report, the accompanying financial statements present fairly, in all material respects, (or *give a true and fair view of*) the financial position of ABC Company as at 31 December 20X1, and (*of*) its financial performance and its cash flows for the year then ended in accordance with IFRSs.

### Basis for Qualified Opinion

With respect to inventory having a carrying amount of $X the audit evidence available to us was limited because we did not observe the counting of the physical inventory as at 31 December 20X1, since that date was prior to our appointment as auditor of the company. Owing to the nature of the company's records, we were unable to obtain sufficient appropriate audit evidence regarding the inventories quantities by using other audit procedures.

## Example 5 - Disclaimer of opinion due to inability to obtain sufficient appropriate audit evidence about multiple elements of the financial statements (inventories and accounts receivable – material and pervasive) (extract from auditor's report)

### Disclaimer of Opinion

We were engaged to audit the financial statements of ABC Company (the Company), which comprise the statement of financial position as at 31 December 20X1, and the statement of comprehensive income, statement of changes in equity and statement of cash flows for the year then ended, and notes to the financial statements, including a summary of significant accounting policies.

We do not express an opinion on the accompanying financial statements. Because of the significance of the matters described in the Basis for Disclaimer of Opinion section of our report, we have not been able to obtain sufficient appropriate audit evidence to provide a basis for an audit opinion on these financial statements.

### Basis for Disclaimer of Opinion

We were not appointed as auditors of the company until after 31 December 20X1 and thus did not observe the counting of physical inventories at the beginning and end of the year. We were unable to satisfy ourselves by alternative means concerning the inventory quantities held at 31 December 20X0 and 20X1 which are stated in the statement of financial position at XXX and XXX, respectively. In addition, the introduction of a new computerised accounts receivable system in September 20X1 resulted in numerous errors in accounts receivable. As of the date of our auditor's report, management was still in the process of rectifying the system deficiencies and correcting the errors. We were unable to confirm or verify by alternative means accounts receivable included in the statement of financial position at a total amount of XXX as at 31 December 20X1. As a result of these matters, we were unable to determine whether any adjustments might have been found necessary in respect of recorded or unrecorded inventories and accounts receivable, and the elements making up the income statement, statement of changes in equity and statement of cash flows.

## Essential reading

See Chapter 20 of the Essential reading for further details on each type of modification.

The Essential reading is available as an Appendix of the digital edition of the Workbook.

## Activity 1: The auditor's report

Check & Co is also the auditor of Research Co and is currently finalising the audit of its financial statements for the year ending 31 December 20X6. Research Co designs, develops and produces medical scanning equipment to be used in hospitals and doctors' surgeries. The financial statements of Research Co show revenue of $98 million, profit before tax of $20 million and net assets of $78 million for the year ending 31 December 20X6.

During the audit, the team learnt that Research Co capitalised $2.5 million of development costs in the year, relating to a new portable scanning machine for ambulances. However, the audit team also found evidence that Research Co have been unable to sell any of the portable scanning machines since they are too large to fit in a standard ambulance. Further audit procedures discovered there was no market for the machines elsewhere.

The directors of Research Co have refused to remove the development costs from their statement of financial position as they believe that ambulances will probably get bigger in the next few years and they will be able to sell the machines then.

**Required**

1   Explain why the inclusion of the development costs on Research Co's statement of financial position for the year ending 31 December 20X6 is an issue for the auditors.

2   Provide a calculation to show whether the matter in part (1) is material.

3   Assume management refuses to correct the financial statements for the matter in part (1). What modification to the auditor's opinion would Check & Co need to make and why?

4   Explain how the modification will impact the structure and form of the auditor's report.

**Solution**

# 4   ISA 706 (Revised) *Emphasis of Matter Paragraphs and Other Matter Paragraphs in the Independent Auditor's Report*

## 4.1   Emphasis of matter paragraph

> **Emphasis of matter:** An emphasis of matter paragraph is a paragraph included in the auditor's report that refers to a matter appropriately presented or disclosed in the financial statements that, in the auditor's judgement, is of such importance that it is fundamental to users' understanding of the financial statements *(ISA 706 (Revised): para. 7(a))*.

**Examples** of circumstances where the auditor may include an emphasis of matter paragraph are:

| An uncertainty relating to the future outcome of exceptional litigation or regulatory action |
|---|

| A significant subsequent event that occurs between the date of the financial statements and |
|---|

| the date of the auditor's report, for example a fire at the entity's production facilities |
| --- |
| Early application (where permitted) of a new accounting standard that has a material effect on the financial statements |
| A major catastrophe that has had, or continues to have, a significant effect on the entity's financial position |

An emphasis of matter paragraph is **not** used to highlight any going concern issues. Such issues would be disclosed in a 'material uncertainty related to going concern' paragraph (Section 6).

For **listed** entity audits, the same issue would **not** be included within the emphasis of matter paragraph and the KAM paragraph.

(a) If the issue is fundamental to users' understanding and has required significant audit attention than it should be disclosed as a key audit matter.

(b) However, if the issue is fundamental to users' understanding but has not required significant audit attention, for example a subsequent event, then it should be disclosed within the emphasis of matter paragraph.

Where an emphasis of matter paragraph is used:

| It can come immediately **before or after** the key audit matters, depending on the significance of the information |
| --- |
| It is entitled 'Emphasis of matter' |
| The paragraph makes a clear reference to the matter being emphasised and to where the relevant disclosures that fully describe the matter can be found in the financial statements |
| The paragraph must state that the auditor's **opinion is not modified** in respect of the matter emphasised |

## Example 6 - Emphasis of matter paragraph (extract from auditor's report)

**Emphasis of Matter**

We draw attention to Note X of the financial statements, which describes the effects of a fire in the company's production facilities. **Our opinion is not modified in respect of this matter.**

## 4.2 Other matter paragraph

> **Other matter paragraph:** a paragraph included in the auditor's report that refers to a matter other than those presented or disclosed in the financial statements that, in the auditor's judgement, is relevant to users' understanding of the audit, the auditor's responsibilities or the auditor's report (ISA 706 (Revised): para. 7(b)).

**Examples** of circumstances where the auditor may include another matter paragraph are where the prior year financial statements:

| Have not been audited |
| --- |
| Have been audited by another auditor |

For listed entity audits, the same issue would not be included within the other matter paragraph and the KAM paragraph.

Where another matter paragraph is used:

| |
|---|
| It usually comes immediately after the key audit matters |
| It is entitled 'Other matter' |

## Example 7 - Other matter paragraph (extract from auditor's report)

**Other Matter**

The financial statements of ABC Company for the year ended 31 December 20X0 were audited by another auditor who expressed an unmodified opinion on those statements on 31 March 20X1.

## Essential reading

See Chapter 20 of the Essential reading for further details on emphasis of matter and other matter paragraphs.

The Essential reading is available as an Appendix of the digital edition of the Workbook.

## Activity 2: Modified opinions and modified auditor's reports

You are the audit manager of Check & Co and are reviewing the key issues identified in the files of several audit clients, each of which has a year end of 30 September 20X6.

1   The first audit client is Little Bees Co (LB). The fieldwork stage for this audit has been completed and the draft financial statements show a profit before tax of $175,000.

    LB has valued a certain inventory line at its total cost price of $17,000. These inventory items have not been sold for a number of years and it is unlikely that they can be sold in the future unless the price is reduced to $3,000. The finance director is confident that the issue will be resolved and no write down was made with regards to this balance.

    **Required**

    Which of the following options correctly summarises the impact on the auditor's report if the issue remains unresolved?

    O   Adverse opinion

    O   Disclaimer of opinion

    O   Qualified opinion

    O   Unmodified opinion

2   The second audit client is Hayden Co (Hayden).

    On 1 January 20X6, Hayden implemented a new accounting system; this was generally a success, with the exception of February 20X6 when one month of Hayden's inventory records were lost. Despite several attempts, the audit team was unable to perform alternative audit procedures to verify material inventory transactions in February 20X6, although the year-end inventory count went smoothly.

    **Required**

Which of the following options correctly summarises the impact on the auditor's report of the above issue?

○ Disclaimer of opinion

○ Qualified opinion

○ Unmodified opinion

○ Unmodified opinion with emphasis of matter paragraph

3 The third audit client is Maker Co (Maker), a listed construction company which specialises in residential housebuilding. One of Maker's construction workers, Edward Shift, was dismissed in August 20X6 after turning up for work under the influence of alcohol. In September 20X6, Mr Shift began a case against Maker for unfair dismissal.

**Required**

Which TWO of the following audit procedures should be performed in order to form a conclusion as to the appropriate accounting treatment of the above claim in the year end year-end financial statements?

☐ Recalculate Mr Shift's wages and salaries for the year to verify that he was only paid up to the date of dismissal

☐ Review the construction work performed by Mr Shift in August 20X6 to determine whether there are any concerns over the quality of his work and whether Maker's health and safety procedures were followed

☐ Review legal correspondence relating to the claim in order to determine Maker's lawyers' opinion as to the likely outcome of the claim

☐ Review the post year end cash book in order to determine whether any payments were made to Mr Shift

4 Mr Shift has sent such a huge amount of paperwork to Maker detailing the extent of his claim along with supporting medical documentation and character references that the audit team has had to devote a significant amount of audit attention to this area of the audit. The directors have not made any reference to the claim in the financial statements and you agree with Maker's lawyers' indication that it is highly unlikely that Mr Shift will be successful in his claim.

**Required**

Based on the above information indicate whether the audit opinion should be modified or unmodified and the appropriate disclosure which should be made in the auditor's report:

| Audit opinion | Disclosure in the auditor's report |
|---|---|
| Audit opinion: | Modified |
| | Unmodified |
| Disclosure in the auditor's report: | Emphasis of matter paragraph |
| | Key audit matter paragraph |
| | Material uncertainty related to going concern paragraph |
| | No disclosure required |
| | Other matter paragraph |

# 5 ISA 720 (Revised) *The Auditor's Responsibilities Relating to Other Information*

> **Other information:** financial or non-financial information (other than the financial statements and the auditor's report thereon) included in an entity's annual report *(ISA 720 (Revised): para. 12(c))*.
>
> **Annual report:** a document, or combination of documents, prepared typically on an annual basis by management or those charged with governance in accordance with law, regulation or custom. Its purpose is to provide owners (or similar stakeholders) with information on the entity's operations and the entity's financial results and financial position as set out in the financial statements *(ISA 720 (Revised): para. 12(a))*.
>
> **A misstatement of the other information:** exists when the other information is incorrectly stated or otherwise misleading (including because it omits or obscures information necessary for a proper understanding of a matter disclosed in the other information) *(ISA 720 (Revised): para. 12(b))*.

The objective of the auditor is to respond appropriately when documents containing audited financial statements include other information that could **undermine the credibility** of the financial statements and the auditor's report.

Examples of other amounts or other items that may be included as other information are as follows:

- Overview of strategy
- Financial summaries or highlights
- Planned capital expenditures
- Financial ratios
- Explanations of critical accounting estimates and related assumptions

(ISA 720 (Revised): Appendix 1)

## 5.1 Material inconsistencies

ISA 720 (Revised) (para. 14) states that the auditor shall read the other information to identity **material inconsistencies** with the audited financial statements. In reading and considering the other information, the auditor should also consider whether the auditor's understanding of the entity and its environment needs to be updated. The process is as follows:

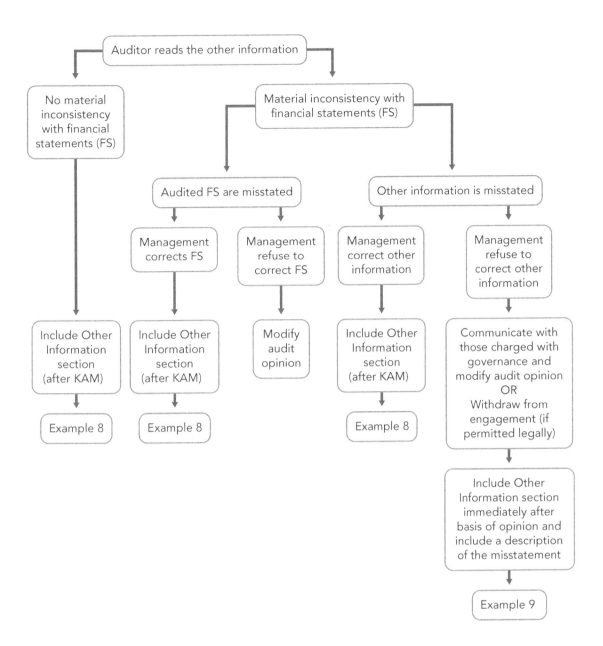

## 5.2 Reporting

The auditor's report will always include a separate 'Other Information' section when the auditor has obtained some or all of the other information as of the date of the auditor's report. For listed entities, the section is also included if other information is expected to be received after the date of the auditor's report.

### Example 8 - Other information section

The Other Information section is placed after the Key Audit Matters section and where the other information is not materially misstated it would be worded as follows:

---

**Other Information**

Management is responsible for the other information. The other information comprises the [information included in the X report, but does not include the financial statements and our auditor's report thereon.]

Our opinion on the financial statements does not cover the other information and we do not express any form of assurance conclusion thereon.

In connection with our audit of the financial statements, our responsibility is to read the other information and, in doing so, consider whether the other information is materially inconsistent with the financial statements or our knowledge obtained in the audit or otherwise appears to be materially misstated. If based on the work we have performed, we conclude that there is a material misstatement of this other information, we are required to report that fact. We have nothing to report in this regard.

*(ISA 720 (Revised): Appendix 2)*

### Example 9 - Material misstatement of other information

If the auditor concludes that there is a material misstatement of the other information, the 'Other Information' section is placed immediately after the basis of opinion section. It will state:

As described below, we have concluded that such a material misstatement of the other information exists.

This statement is followed by a description of the misstatement (ISA 720 (Revised): Appendix 2).

# 6 Going concern

## 6.1 Responsibilities of directors and auditors

It is the **directors' responsibility** to determine whether or not an entity is a going concern.

According to ISA 570 (Revised), it is the **auditor's responsibility** to make an assessment as to whether the directors' conclusion is appropriate. This should be based on the results of the going concern review performed by the auditor. The auditor must consider:

(a)  Whether the use of the **going concern basis is appropriate**;

(b)  Whether **adequate disclosure** has been made of any **material uncertainties** affecting going concern; and

(c)  Whether management's assessment was **adequate**.

If there is concern about any of the items above, then the auditor should consider the implications for their auditor's report.

## 6.2 Auditor's report implications

There are three main scenarios:

### 6.2.1 Scenario 1: Going concern basis is appropriate but a material uncertainty exists

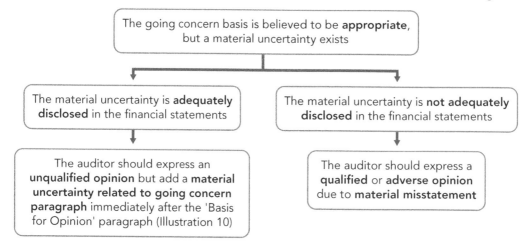

## Example 10 - Material uncertainty related to going concern (extract from auditor's report)

We draw attention to Note X in the financial statements, which indicates that the company incurred a net loss of $Z during the year ended 31 December 20X1, and as of that date, the company's current liabilities exceeded its total assets by $Y. As stated in Note X, these events or conditions, along with other matters as described in Note X, indicate that a material uncertainty exists that may cast significant doubt on the company's ability to continue as a going concern. **Our opinion is not modified in respect of this matter.**

### Key Audit Matters

Key audit matters are those matters that, in our professional judgment, were of most significance in our audit of the financial statements of the current period. These matters were addressed in the context of our audit of the financial statements as a whole, and in forming our opinion thereon, and we do not provide a separate opinion on these matters. In addition to the matter described in the 'material uncertainty related to going concern' section, we have determined the matters described below to be the key audit matters to be communicated in our report.

[Description of each key audit matter in accordance with ISA 701. Note that where a matter is the subject of a 'material uncertainty related to going concern' paragraph, the **same** matter would **not** also be a KAM.]

### 6.2.2 Scenario 2: Going concern basis inappropriate

> The going concern basis is believed to be **inappropriate**

⬇

> The auditor should express an **adverse opinion** due to **material and pervasive misstatement**

### 6.2.3 Scenario 3: Management unable or unwilling to make assessment

> The directors are unwilling/unable to make an assessment as to whether or not the going concern basis is appropriate

⬇

> The auditor should express a **qualified** or **disclaimer of opinion** due to **insufficient appropriate audit evidence**

The auditor shall communicate with those charged with governance events or conditions that may cast doubt on the entity's ability to continue as a going concern. This will include:

- Whether the events or conditions constitute a material uncertainty
- Whether the use of the going concern assumption is appropriate in the preparation and presentation of the financial statements
- The adequacy of related disclosures
- Where applicable, the implications for the auditor's report

(ISA 570 (Revised): para. 25)

## Activity 3: Going concern

Check & Co is the auditor of TH Co (TH). The audit fieldwork is complete; however, your audit senior has raised an outstanding issue.

The directors of TH have made appropriate disclosures relating to worries over going concern in the financial statements. Your audit senior has a significant level of concern regarding the use of the going concern basis but feels the disclosure is appropriate and agrees with the use of the going concern basis. You concur with the audit senior's conclusions.

**Required**

Based on the above information indicate whether the audit opinion should be modified or unmodified and the appropriate disclosure which should be made in the auditor's report:

| Audit opinion | Qualified | Disclaimer of opinion | Adverse | Unmodified |
|---|---|---|---|---|
| Disclosure in the auditor's report | Emphasis of matter paragraph | Material uncertainty relating to going concern | No disclosure required | |

| Audit opinion | Disclosure in the auditor's report |
|---|---|
| | |

**Solution**

# Chapter summary

**Reports**

## ISA 700 (Revised) *Forming an Opinion and Reporting on Financial Statements*

- Has sufficient appropriate audit evidence been obtained?
- Are there any material misstatements?

## ISA 701 *Communicating Key Audit Matters (KAMs) in the Independent Auditor's Report*

- Selected from matters communicated to those charged with governance
- Matters the auditors judged to be most significance in the current audit period
- Not a modification

Presentation of KAMs in the auditor's report
Why and how?

## ISA 705 (Revised) *Modifications to the Opinion in the Independent Auditor's Report*

- Modification due to insufficient audit evidence: Material and not pervasive = qualified
- Modification due to insufficient audit evidence: Material and pervasive = disclaimer
- Modification due to material misstatement: Material but not pervasive = qualified
- Modification due to material misstatement: Material and pervasive = adverse

## ISA 706 (Revised) *Emphasis of Matter Paragraphs and Other Matter Paragraphs in the Independent Auditor's Report*

Emphasis of matter paragraph
- Matter appropriately presented in FS and fundamental to user's understanding
- Opinion not modified

Other matter paragraph
Refer to a matter not presented in FS that is fundamental to user's understanding

## ISA 720 (Revised) *The Auditor's Responsibilities Relating to Other Information*

- Financial or non-financial information included in the FS
- Auditors must review for material inconsistencies

## Going concern

Responsibilities of directors and auditors

Management's responsibilities:
- Use of the going concern basis appropriate?
- Adequate disclosure made of any material uncertainties?
- Management's assessment adequate?

Auditors report implications
Include a material uncertainty related to going concern para where there is uncertainty over GC that has been adequately disclosed

# Knowledge diagnostic

### 1. Purpose of auditor's report

The auditor is required to produce an auditor's report at the end of the audit which sets out their opinion on the **truth** and **fairness** of the financial statements. The report contains a number of consistent **elements** so that users know the audit has been conducted according to recognised standards.

### 2. Elements of the auditor's report

The elements of the auditor's report are specified by ISA 700 (Revised).

### 3. Unmodified/modified opinions

The opinion in the auditor's report may be **unmodified** or **modified**.

### 4. Key audit matters

For listed entity audits the auditor should report areas of the audit which have required significant audit attention as **key audit matters**. These should also be reported to those charged with governance.

### 5. Modified opinions

Auditors will modify their opinions when the financial statements are not free from **material misstatement** or when they have been **unable to obtain sufficient appropriate evidence**.

### 6. Types of modified opinion

There are three types of modified opinion: a **qualified** opinion, an **adverse** opinion and a **disclaimer** of opinion.

### 7. Modified reports

A report may be modified by an **emphasis of matter** or **other matter** paragraph. These do **not** affect the opinion.

### 8. Other information

Auditors shall review the **other information** to determine whether there are any material **inconsistencies** or whether other information is materially misstated.

### 9. Going concern

It is the directors' responsibility to determine whether an entity is a going concern and the auditor's responsibility to assess whether this is appropriate.

### 10. Material uncertainty relating to going concern paragraph

Uncertainty over going concern will lead to the inclusion of a **'Material uncertainty related to going concern'** paragraph being included in the auditor's report (provided that the issue is adequately disclosed).

### 11. Adverse opinion

Material misstatement in relation to going concern is likely to be one of the rare circumstances where an adverse opinion is issued.

 BPP

# Further study guidance

## Question practice

Now try the following from the Further question practice bank (available in the digital edition of the Workbook):

- Section A Q14-Q15 and Q51-Q55
- Section B Q58(b) 'Audit and assurance engagements' on reporting by exception
- Section B Q89 'Wiseguys National Bakeries'
- Section B Q90 'Homes 'r' Us'
- Section B Q91 'Builders Merchants'

## Further reading

There are a number of technical articles on the ACCA website written by members of the AA examining team which are relevant to some of the topics covered in this chapter that you should read:

- *The auditor's report* (https://www.accaglobal.com/gb/en/student/exam-support-resources/fundamentals-exams-study-resources/f8/technical-articles/auditor-report.html)
- *Going concern* (https://www.accaglobal.com/gb/en/student/exam-support-resources/fundamentals-exams-study-resources/f8/technical-articles/going-concern.html)

## Own research

The IAASB has a section on its website devoted to auditor reporting which contains guidance on areas such as key audit matters and details on the development of the current auditing standards. You can view this at https://www.iaasb.org/focus-areas/new-auditors-report

# Activity answers

## Activity 1: The auditor's report

1 Research Co have included $2.5 million of development costs on their statement of financial position which do not meet the criteria of IAS 38 *Intangible Assets*. IAS 38 includes a number of criteria which must be satisfied before development costs can be capitalised including commercial feasibility of the asset for sale. Since the machines are currently too large to fit in the ambulances and there is no other market, Research Co have not met this criteria and the development costs should not have been capitalised. The $2.5 million should be expensed to the statement of profit and loss. Otherwise, intangible assets and profits will both be overstated, and expenses will be understated.

2 The development costs are 3.2% of net assets, 2.6% of revenue and 12.5% of profit before tax. Therefore, they are material to both the statement of financial position and the statement of profit and loss.

3 **Modification due to management refusal**

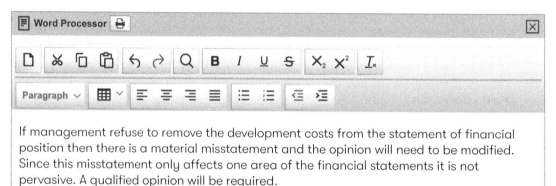

If management refuse to remove the development costs from the statement of financial position then there is a material misstatement and the opinion will need to be modified. Since this misstatement only affects one area of the financial statements it is not pervasive. A qualified opinion will be required.

4 **Impact on audit report**

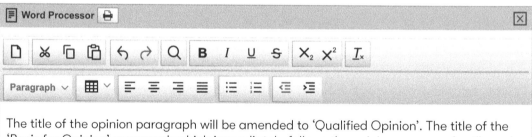

The title of the opinion paragraph will be amended to 'Qualified Opinion'. The title of the 'Basis for Opinion' paragraph which immediately follows the opinion paragraph will need to be amended to 'Basis for Qualified Opinion'. This paragraph states the reason for the qualification and quantifies its effect on the financial statements. Its positioning will not change due to the qualification.

## Activity 2: Modified opinions and modified auditor's reports

1 The correct answer is: Qualified opinion

LB has not valued inventory at the lower of cost and net realisable value on a line by line basis, which is contrary to the accounting standard IAS 2 *Inventories*.

If it had, then the inventory line would have been written down by $14,000 ($17,000 cost less $3,000 NRV). Inventory is therefore overstated in the statement of financial position.

The misstatement is material as it represents 8% of profit before tax ($14,000/$175,000), so management should correct this misstatement in the financial statements.

 BPP

As the Finance Director has refused to amend this misstatement then the auditor's opinion will need to be modified. As management has not complied with IAS 2 and the misstatement is material but not pervasive, a qualified opinion would be necessary.

The auditor's report would include a qualified opinion section, together with a basis for qualified opinion section explaining both the material misstatement in relation to the inappropriate valuation of inventory and quantifying its effect on the financial statements.

2    The correct answer is: Qualified opinion

Check & Co has been unable to gather sufficient appropriate audit evidence over the inventory transactions which occurred in February 20X6, and these are considered to be material.

It has, however, been able to gather sufficient appropriate audit evidence over the year-end inventory balance and so this issue is considered to be material but not pervasive.

As such a qualified opinion would be expressed, and a basis for qualified opinion section would be included to explain the potential impact of the loss of inventory records.

An emphasis of matter paragraph would not be issued as the issue is not believed to be fundamental to the financial statements.

3    The correct answers are:

- Review legal correspondence relating to the claim in order to determine Maker's lawyers' opinion as to the likely outcome of the claim
- Review the post year end cash book in order to determine whether any payments were made to Mr Shift

Recalculating Mr Shift's wages and salaries for the year to verify that he was only paid up to the date of dismissal and reviewing the construction work performed by Mr Shift in August 20X6 to determine whether there are any concerns over the quality of his work and whether Maker's health and safety procedures were followed are audit procedures relating to wages and salaries and inventory rather than to the accounting treatment of the claim itself.

4    Unmodified audit opinion with a key audit matter paragraph

The directors have not made any reference to the claim in the financial statements. This seems appropriate as you agree with the lawyer's indication that the claim will not be successful. Therefore, an unmodified audit opinion would be issued.

However, Maker is a listed entity and the claim has taken up a significant amount of audit time and so this would be included within the key audit matters section.

The issue would not be included as an emphasis of matter (since it has been dealt with as a key audit matter) and there is no indication that it impacts Maker's ability to continue as a going concern.

## Activity 3: Going concern

Unmodified audit opinion with material uncertainty relating to going concern section

TH's directors have made appropriate disclosures of worries over going concern in the financial statements, and the auditor feels that the disclosure is appropriate. The audit opinion will therefore be unmodified.

However, significant concern over going concern still exists and so the auditor will include a 'material uncertainty relating to going concern' section in their report.

Note. The emphasis of matter paragraph is used to highlight matters which are fundamental to users' understanding of the financial statements, with the exception of matters relating to going concern.

# Skills checkpoint 5

## Approach to objective test (OT) questions

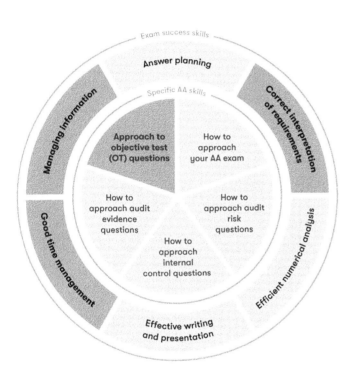

## Introduction

Section A of the Audit and Assurance (AA) exam consists of objective test (OT) case questions.

Section A questions will focus more on syllabus areas A and E but can come from any area of the syllabus. This means that candidates need to study the whole syllabus. Section A will include three OT case questions.

Each OT case question is worth 10 marks and contains a group of five single OT questions (each worth two marks) and based on a single scenario. The questions can be any combination of the OT question types detailed below. OT questions are auto-marked; you must answer the whole question correctly to earn the two marks. There are no partial marks.

OT cases are written so that there are no dependencies between the individual questions. So, if you did get the first question wrong, this does not affect your ability to get the other four correct. The OT case scenario remains on screen so you can see it while answering the questions.

The following types of OT question commonly appear in the AA exam:

| Question type | Explanation |
| --- | --- |
| Multiple choice (MCQ) | You need to choose one correct answer from four given response options. |

| Question type | Explanation |
|---|---|
| Multiple response (MRQ) | These are a kind of multiple choice question, except you need to select more than one answer from a number of given options. The question will specify how many answers need to be selected, but the system won't stop you from selecting more answers than this. It is important to read the requirement carefully. |
| Fill in the blank (FIB) | This question type requires you<br><br>to type a numerical answer into a box. The unit of measurement (eg $) will sit outside the box, and if there are specific rounding requirements these will be displayed. |
| Drag and drop | Drag and drop questions involve you dragging an answer and dropping it into place. Some questions could involve matching more than one answer to a response area and some questions may have more answer choices than response areas, which means not all available answer choices need to be used. |
| Drop down list | This question type requires you to select one answer from a drop down list. Some of these questions may contain more than one drop down list and an answer has to be selected from each one. This requires the same skills as a multiple choice question. |

# Skills Checkpoint 5: Approach to OT questions

## AA Skill: Approach to OT questions

A step-by-step technique for approaching OT questions is outlined below. Each step will be explained in more detail in the following sections as the OT case question 'Minnie Co' is answered in stages.

**General guidance for approaching OT questions**

**STEP 2: Answer all questions.**

There is no penalty for an incorrect answer in ACCA exams; there is nothing to be gained by leaving an OT question unanswered. If you are stuck on a question, as a last resort, it is worth selecting the option you consider most likely to be correct and moving on. Make a note of the question, so if you have time after you have answered the rest of the questions, you can revisit it.

**Guidance for answering specific OT questions**

**STEP 3: Read the requirement first!**

The requirement will be stated in bold text in the exam. Identify what you are being asked to do, any technical knowledge required and what type of OT question you are dealing with. Look for key words in the requirement such as "which **TWO** of the following," or "which of the following is **NOT**".

**Guidance for answering specific OT questions**

**STEP 4: Apply your technical knowledge to the data presented in the question.**

Take your time working throug the narrative in each distractor as well any calculations and read through each answer option with care. **OT questions are designed so that each answer option is plausible.** Work through each response option and eliminate those you know are incorrect

# Exam success skills

The following question is a Section A OT case question from a past exam worth 10 marks.

For this question, we will also focus on the following exam success skills:

- **Managing information.** It is easy for the amount of information contained in an OT case questions in Section A to feel a little overwhelming. **Active reading** is a useful technique to avoid this. This involves focusing on each of the five requirements first, on the basis that until you have done this the detail in the question will have little meaning and will seem more intimidating as a result.

- Focus on the requirements, highlighting key verbs to ensure you understand the requirement properly, and correctly identify what type of OT question you are dealing with. Then read the rest of the scenario, underlining and annotating important and relevant information, and making notes of any relevant technical information you think you will need.

- **Correct interpretation of requirements.** Identify from the requirement the different types of OT question. This is especially important with multiple response questions to ensure you select the correct number of response options.

- **Good time management.** Complete all OT's in the time available. Each OT is worth two marks and should be allocated 3.6 minutes which means you have 18 minutes for each OT case question.

# Skill activity

The following scenario relates to Questions 1 to 5.

You are the audit manager of Daffy & Co and you are briefing your team on the approach to adopt in undertaking the review and finalisation stage of the audit of the financial statements for the year ended 31 December 20X7.

During the audit of Minnie Co, an uncorrected misstatement was identified with regards to a property balance which was revalued during the year. The revaluation was carried out by an independent expert valuer and incorrect assumptions were provided to the valuer. The audit team's audit procedures have determined that the property is overvalued by $600,000.

The following additional issues have also arisen during the course of the audit of Minnie Co.

(a) Depreciation has been calculated on the total of land and buildings. In previous years, it has only been charged on buildings. Total depreciation is $2.5m and the element charged to land only is $0.7m.

(b) Minnie Co's main competitor has filed a lawsuit for $1m against them alleging a breach of copyright; this case is ongoing and will not be resolved prior to the auditor's report being signed. You have concluded that the outcome of the lawsuit is uncertain. The matter is disclosed as a contingent liability.

Profit before tax for the year ended 31 December 20X7 is $10m.

**1. Which TWO[69] of the following statements correctly describe the auditor's responsibility in relation to misstatements?**

[69] This is a MRQ where you are required to select TWO options. This is a knowledge based requirement so firstly consider what you know about the auditor's responsibilities in relation to misstatements and then select TWO options which are closest to your initial thoughts.

- The auditor must accumulate misstatements over the course of the audit unless they are immaterial.

- As part of their completion procedures, auditors shall consider whether the aggregate of uncorrected misstatements in the financial statements is material.

- In deciding whether the uncorrected misstatements are material, the auditor shall consider the size and nature of the misstatements.

- The auditor is required to consider misstatements relating to transactions and account balances, but not misstatements related to qualitative disclosures.

**2. Which of the following steps should you take first in relation to the uncorrected misstatement in respect of the revalued property[70]?**

[70] This is an MCQ requiring one correct answer to be selected. The property has been overvalued by $600,000 which is 6% of PBT so this is clearly a material issue. The question asks what is the first step you would take. Modifying the audit opinion would be a last resort after you have exhausted all other avenues.

- Accumulate the misstatement along with other uncorrected misstatements in a schedule of unadjusted audit differences. If the aggregate is material, ask the directors to correct the misstatements.

- Ask the directors to correct the specific misstatement, explaining that it is material to the financial statements.

- Speak to the expert valuer to assess the methodology used in performing the valuation.

- Modify the audit opinion, because the misstatement is material.

**3. Select the correct option from the drop down list to summarise the effect of the depreciation charged on land and buildings on the financial statements?**[71]

[71] This is a drop down list question. Here you need to select the appropriate option for each drop down list. Firstly, you must decide whether the issue with the depreciation is material to the financial statements or not. Then you must decide whether this will lead to assets being overstated or profit being understated. Note that there is no partial marking – you must get both drop downs correct in order to score the 2 marks.

| Material<br>Drop down list | No | Yes |
| --- | --- | --- |

| Financial statement impact<br>Drop down list | Assets are overstated | Profit is understated |
| --- | --- | --- |

| Material | Financial statement impact |
| --- | --- |
|  |  |

**4. You have concluded that knowledge of the litigation is not fundamental to understanding the financial statements.**

In light of this, drag the appropriate description in to the relevant box to indicate the audit opinion which would be given and how the matter would be disclosed in the auditor's report.

| Audit opinion | Adverse | Disclaimer | Qualified | Unmodified |
| --- | --- | --- | --- | --- |
| Disclosure in the auditor's report | Basis for adverse opinion | Basis for qualified opinion | No related disclosure | Material uncertainty related to going concern |

| Audit opinion | Disclosure in the auditor's report |
| --- | --- |
|  |  |

**5. Having commenced audit fieldwork on Minnie Co on 1 February 20X8, the audit was completed on 20 February 20X8. The auditor's report is due to be signed on 5 March 20X8. Minnie Co's board plans to issue the financial statements on 30 April 20X8.**

| 1 February 20X8 | 20 February 20X8 | 5 March 20X8 | 30 April 20X8 |
|---|---|---|---|
| | | | |

# Skill activity

**STEP 1**  Answer the questions you know first.

If you are having difficulty answering a question, move on and come back to tackle it once you have answered all the questions you know. It is often quicker to answer discursive style OT questions first, leaving more time for calculations. The AA exam does not have many calculations but you may be asked to calculate financial statement ratios.

All of the questions in Minnie are discursive style questions. However, Questions 2 and 3 require you to calculate materiality and consider the financial amount of the error and so it may make sense to answer Questions 1, 4 and 5 first as it is likely that you will be able to complete them comfortably within the 10.8 minutes allocated to them.  Any time saved could then be spent on the calculations required to answer Questions 2 and 3.

**STEP 2**  Answer all questions.

There is no penalty for an incorrect answer in ACCA exams, there is nothing to be gained by leaving an OT question unanswered. If you are stuck on a question, as a last resort, it is worth selecting the option you consider most likely to be correct, and moving on. Make a note of the question, so if you have time after you have answered the rest of the questions, you can revisit it.

Two of the five questions in the OT case are MCQ's. With an MCQ, you have a 25% chance of getting the question correct so do not leave any unanswered. It is obviously more difficult to get a drop down list or drag and drop question (like Questions 3 and 4) correct by guessing.

**STEP 3**  Read the requirement first!

The requirement will be stated in bold text in the exam. Identify what you are being asked to do, any technical knowledge required and what type of OT question you are dealing with. Look for key words in the requirement such as "which TWO of the following," or "which of the following is NOT"

Question 1 is a MRQ, you need to follow the instructions carefully and only select two **correct** responsibilities. Read through each statement carefully knowing that you are looking to identify the responsibilities that are **correct**.

**STEP 4**  Apply your technical knowledge to the data presented in the question.

Work through calculations, taking your time, and read through each answer option carefully. OT questions are designed so that each answer option is plausible. Work through each response option and eliminate those you know are incorrect

To answer Questions 2 and 3, you need to determine whether the error in the property valuation and the depreciation misstatement are material. We would usually use 5% of profit before tax as an estimate to determine whether or not a misstatement is material.

# Exam success skills diagnostic

Every time you complete a question, use the diagnostic below to assess how effectively you demonstrated the exam success skills in answering the question. The table has been completed below for the Minnie Co activity to give you an idea of how to complete the diagnostic.

| Exam success skills | |
|---|---|
| Managing information | Did you read each of the five requirements first? |
| | Did you actively read the scenario highlighting relevant data required such as the year end date, the property overvaluation, the depreciation amounts, the value of the lawsuit and the profit before tax? |

| Correct interpretation of requirements | Did you identify the correct technical knowledge needed to answer each requirement? For example, using your knowledge of the auditor's responsibilities in relation to misstatements in question 1 and types of modifications to the audit report in question 5. |
| --- | --- |
| | Did you identify what type of OT question you were dealing with? For example, knowing that only one correct answer is required for a multiple choice question. |
| Good time management | Did you manage to answer all five questions within 18 mins? |
| | Did you manage your time well by answering questions one, four and five first? |
| Most important action points to apply to your next question | |

## Summary

30% of the AA exam consist of OT questions. Key skills to focus on throughout your studies will therefore include:

- Always read the requirements first to identify what you are being asked to do and what type of OT question you are dealing with.
- Actively read the scenario highlighting key data needed to answer each requirement.
- Answer OT questions in a sensible order dealing with any easier discursive style questions first.

# Index

## A

Annual report, 426

Anomaly, 249

Assertions, 160

Assurance engagement, 7

Audit committees, 39

Audit documentation, 150

Audit evidence, 160

Audit plan, 148

Audit risk, 108

Audit sampling, 245

Audit software, 252

Audit strategy, 147

Auditor rights, 20

Auditor's expert, 300

Automated tools and techniques, 112, 252

## B

Big data, 254

## C

Cold review/ Post-issuance review, 91

Confidentiality, 73

Constructive obligation, 362

Contingent asset, 362

Contingent liability, 362

Control risk, 108

Corporate governance, 33

Cost, 295

## D

Data analytics, 254

Detection risk, 109

Development, 273

Direct assistance , 301

## E

Embedded test facility, 253

Emphasis of matter, 422

Engagement letters, 89

Exception, 318

External confirmations, 315

## F

Fair, 3

Final audit, 149

## Fraud, 123

Fraud risk factors, 123

## G

General IT controls, 183

Going concern basis of accounting, 400

## H

Hot review/ Pre-issuance review, 91

## I

Information processing controls, 184

Inherent risk, 108

Intended users, 7

Interim audit, 149

Internal audit function, 300

ISA 315 Identifying and Assessing the Risks of Material Misstatement, 176

## K

Key audit matters, 418

## L

Legal obligation, 362

Liability, 362

## M

Management's expert, 161, 270

Material, 109

Materiality, 6

Misstatement, 406

## N

Net realisable value (NRV), 295

Non-compliance with laws and regulations (NOCLAR), 73

Non-response, 318

Non-sampling risk , 109

## O

Obligating event, 362

Other information, 426

Other matter paragraph, 423

## P

Peer review, 91

Performance materiality, 110

Pervasiveness, 419

Population, 245

Practitioner, 7

Present fairly, 3

Professional judgement, 107

Professional scepticism, 107

Provision, 362

**R**

Removal of auditors, 21

Remuneration, 21

Research, 273

Resignation of auditors, 22

Responsible party, 7

**S**

Sampling risk, 109, 248

Service auditor, 351

Service organisation, 351

Significant risk, 119

Subsequent events, 398

Substantive procedures, 162

System of internal control, 176

**T**

Test data, 253

Tests of controls, 162

The objective of an audit, 3

The objectives of an auditor, 3

Those charged with governance, 224

Tolerable misstatement, 249

Tolerable rate of deviation, 249

True, 3

**U**

Unmodified opinion, 416

User auditor, 351

User entity, 351

**W**

Walk-through tests, 182

Written representations, 404

# Bibliography

Charity Commission for England and Wales. (2014) Charities Sorp (FRS 102). [Online]. Available from: www.charitysorp.org/media/619101/frs102_complete.pdf [Accessed October 2022].

Charity Commission for England and Wales. (2014) Charities Sorp (FRSSE). [Online]. Available from: www.charitysorp.org/media/619092/frsse_complete.pdf [Accessed October 2022].

Companies Act 2006. [Online]. Available from: www.legislation.gov.uk/ [Accessed October 2022]. http://www.nationalarchives.gov.uk/doc/open-government-licence/version/3/

Contains Parliamentary information licensed under the Open Parliament Licence v3.0.

Department for Communities and Local Government (2011). *Best value statutory guidance.* [Online]. Available from: https://assets.publishing.service.gov.uk/government/uploads/system/uploads/attachment_data/file/5945/1976926.pdf [Accessed October 2022]. Contains Parliamentary information licensed under the Open Parliament Licence v3.0.

Financial Reporting Council. (2016) *Guidance on Audit Committees.* [Online]. Available from: https://www.frc.org.uk/getattachment/6b0ace1d-1d70-4678-9c41-0b44a62f0a0d/Guidance-on-Audit-Committees-April-2016.pdf [Accessed October 2022].

Financial Reporting Council. (2014) *Guidance on Risk Management, Internal Control and Related Financial and Business Reporting.* [Online]. Available from: https://www.frc.org.uk/getattachment/d672c107-b1fb-4051-84b0-f5b83a1b93f6/Guidance-on-Risk-Management-Internal-Control-and-Related-Reporting.pdf [Accessed October 2022].

Financial Reporting Council. (2018) *The UK Corporate Governance Code.* [Online]. Available from: https://www.frc.org.uk/getattachment/88bd8c45-50ea-4841-95b0-d2f4f48069a2/2018-UK-Corporate-Governance-Code-FINAL.pdf [Accessed October 2022].

ICAEW (2016) Data analytics for external auditors [Online]. Available at: https://www.icaew.com/international-accounting-and-auditing/international-auditing-perspectives/data- [Accessed January 2021].

IFRS Foundation. (2016) *IFRS.* [Online]. Available at: http://ifrs.org [Accessed October 2022]

International Auditing and Assurance Standards Board. (2020) *2020 Handbook of International Quality Control, Auditing, Review, Other Assurance, and Related Services Pronouncements.* [Online]. Available from https://www.iaasb.org/publications/2020-handbook-international-quality-control-auditing-review-other-assurance-and-related-services [Accessed October 2022].

International Auditing and Assurance Standards Board. (2016) *Auditor reporting.* [Online]. Available from www.iaasb.org/projects/auditor-reporting [Accessed October 2022].

International Auditing and Assurance Standards Board. (2019) *Identifying and Assessing the Risks of Material Misstatement.* [Online]. Available from https://www.iaasb.org/publications/isa-315-revised-2019-identifying-and-assessing-risks-material-misstatement [Accessed October 2022].

International Federation of Accountants. (2015) *Auditor reporting – illustrative key audit matters.* [Online]. Available from: https://www.iaasb.org/publications-resources/auditor-reporting-illustrative-key-audit-matters [Accessed October 2022].

International Federation of Accountants. (2015) *Framework for International Education Standards for Professional Accountants and Aspiring Professional Accountants.* [Online]. Available from: https://www.iaesb.org/standards-pronouncements [Accessed October 2022].

International Federation of Accountants. (2020) *Glossary of terms.* [Online]. Available from: https://www.iaasb.org/publications/2020-handbook-international-quality-control-auditing-review-other-assurance-and-related-services [Accessed October 2022].

International Federation of Accountants. (2017) International Auditing and Assurance Standards Board Fact sheet. [Online]. Available from: https://www.ifac.org/system/files/uploads/IAASB/International-Auditing-and-Assurance-Standards-Board-Fact-Sheet.pdf [Accessed October 2022].

International Federation of Accountants. (2017)) *International Education Standards.* [Online]. Available from: https://www.iaesb.org/standards-pronouncements [Accessed October 2022].

International Federation of Accountants. (2016(e)) *International Framework for Assurance Engagements.* [Online]. Available from: https://www.iaasb.org/projects/assurance-engagements-completed [Accessed October 2022].

International Federation of Accountants. (2019) *Who we are* [Online]. Available https://www.ifac.org/who-we-are/our-purpose [Accessed October 2022].

National Audit Office. (2016) *Assessing value for money.* [Online]. Available from: www.nao.org.uk/successful-commissioning/general-principles/value-for-money/assessing-value-for-money [Accessed October 2022].

Organisation for Economic Co-operation and Development. (2010) *Corporate Governance and the financial crisis: conclusions and emerging good practices to enhance implementation of the Principles.* [Online]. Available from: www.oecd.org/corporate/ca/corporategovernanceprinciples/44679170.pdf [Accessed October 2022].

Organisation for Economic Co-operation and Development. (2015) *Principles of Corporate Governance.* [Online]. Available from: http://dx.doi.org/10.1787/9789264236882-en [Accessed October 2022].

# Tell us what you think

Got comments or feedback on this book? Let us know.
Use your QR code reader:

Or, visit:
**https://bppgroup.fra1.qualtrics.com/jfe/form/SV_9TrxTtw8jSvO7Pv**

## Need to get in touch with customer service?

www.bpp.com/request-support

## Spotted an error?

www.bpp.com/learningmedia/Errata